Recreation Leadership and Supervision

Guidelines for Professional Development

This is a volume in the

SAUNDERS SERIES IN RECREATION.

GEOFFREY C. GODBEY, *Consulting Editor*

Professor
The Pennsylvania State University

Richard G. Kraus, Ed.D.

Department of Recreation and Leisure Studies
Temple University

Gay Carpenter, Ed.D.

Department of Recreation and Leisure Studies
San Jose State University

Barbara J. Bates, Ed.D.

Department of Recreation and Leisure Studies
San Francisco State University

Recreation Leadership and Supervision

Guidelines for Professional Development

Second Edition

SAUNDERS COLLEGE PUBLISHING
Philadelphia   New York   Chicago
San Francisco   Montreal   Toronto
London   Sydney   Tokyo   Mexico City
Rio de Janeiro   Madrid

Address orders to:
383 Madison Avenue
New York, NY 10017
Address editorial correspondence to:
West Washington Square
Philadelphia, PA 19105

This book was set in Caledonia by Hampton Graphics, Inc.
The editors were John Butler, Carol Field, and Lynne Gery.
The art director was Nancy E. J. Grossman.
The text designer was Arlene Putterman.
The cover designer was Larry R. Didona.
The production manager was Tom O'Connor.
The printer was Fairfield Graphics.

LIBRARY OF CONGRESS

CATALOG CARD NO.: 80-53924

   Kraus, Richard G.
     Recreation leadership.

   Philadelphia, Pa.: Saunders College
   400 p.
   8101   801010

RECREATION LEADERSHIP   ISBN   0-03-057674-1

1234 144 98765432

CBS COLLEGE PUBLISHING
Saunders College Publishing
Holt, Rinehart and Winston
The Dryden Press

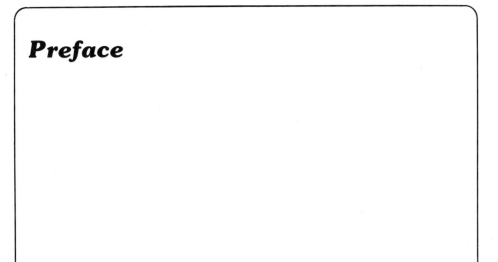

Preface

This second edition of a book first published in 1975 has been designed to provide a highly useful and up-to-date text for both undergraduate and graduate courses in recreation leadership and supervision.

The first edition has been heavily revised in order to provide a much stronger emphasis on current trends in both leadership and supervision in contemporary leisure service agencies. Unlike other books, which focus primarily on professional roles in activity leadership and program development, this text presents a more complex and realistic view of the tasks faced by recreation practitioners today.

Job performance in public recreation departments, park departments, and voluntary, therapeutic, commercial, private, industrial and armed forces programs is described. Leadership guidelines for working with numerous special populations are provided, along with supervisory techniques for the full spectrum of personnel management and staff development. The recreation field today demands that its professionals be fully accountable and that they provide a demonstrably significant form of community and social service, to justify community support at a time of fiscal austerity and competing priorities. This book seeks to promote such accountability by stressing high-caliber professional development for a maturing and growing field of governmental and social service.

In addition to providing course aids such as suggested assignments, case studies and class exercises, the Appendix includes helpful suggestions for designing course outlines. This text was designed to be practical, readable and yet scholarly, and it offers numerous illustrations and guidelines drawn from recreation agencies throughout the United States and Canada.

In preparing this edition of *Recreation Leadership and Supervision,* the original two authors were joined by Prof. Gaylene Carpenter, formerly of Temple University and now of the California State University at San José, who has had a strong background of supervisory experience in both public and voluntary agencies. The authors wish to express their appreciation to numerous recreation and park professionals who contributed materials that were used in the book and to college and university recreation educators who gave suggestions that were helpful in revising and improving it.

RICHARD KRAUS, *Philadelphia, Pennsylvania*
GAYLENE CARPENTER, *San José, California*
BARBARA BATES, *San Francisco, California*

Contents

Foundations of Recreation Leadership

Part One

Foundations of Recreation Leadership and Supervision

Chapter One

This text is concerned with the role of leadership and supervision in organized recreation programs in the United States and Canada. It explores the functions of recreation professionals and presents guidelines for effective leadership and supervision in public, voluntary, therapeutic, commercial and other types of settings for leisure involvement.

Many early recreation textbooks stressed the view that leaders worked chiefly with children and youth in municipally sponsored playgrounds or community centers. The recreation leader's task was seen as consisting chiefly of leading or organizing sports and games, music, arts and crafts, and similar activities on a face-to-face basis.

Today it is recognized that leaders work with people of all ages and with varied population groups. In addition to the traditional function of direct activity leadership, they have numerous other responsibilities keyed to the fullest possible development of group members and to specialized goals of sponsoring agencies. Often, they may be expected to direct or supervise other functions of a social-service or administrative nature. Thus, both leadership and supervision are complex areas of professional performance, requiring special training and considerable expertise. To understand more fully the roles of recreation professionals today, it is necessary to examine the place of organized recreation service in the modern community.

RECREATION SERVICE TODAY

In both the United States and Canada, recreation represents a major area of responsibility on federal, state or provincial, and local government levels. In the United States, for example, thousands of cities, towns, villages and special districts provide networks of parks, playgrounds, community centers, sports areas, arts workshops and other programs and facilities to meet the leisure needs of their residents.

A host of voluntary, non-profit agencies, such as the YMCA, YWCA, YM-YWHA, Boy Scouts, Girl Scouts, Boys' Clubs, Girls' Clubs and similar organizations, provide recreation—along with other important educational or social services—to millions of children, youth and adults. Other non-profit, special-interest organizations sponsor activities and events related to sports and fitness needs, outdoor recreation and tourism, the arts, hobbies and similar concerns.

Organizations serving such special populations as the mentally ill or mentally retarded, the physically disabled and the aging provide therapeutic recreation services designed to promote the overall process of recovery or to enrich the lives of the disabled. Colleges and universities today provide recreation to their students, faculty and staff in the form of clubs, intramural sports and other social or cultural programs. Thousands of companies sponsor extensive recreation programs for their employees, and commercial recreation enterprises have become a major focus of business investment and expansion. More and more real estate developers today incorporate recreation as a key element in their sales "package."

The list of recreation sponsors is almost endless and has led to the dramatic growth of recreation as a career field. Hundreds of thousands of men and women are employed today in leisure-related settings as playground leaders, senior center directors, youth club leaders, street gang workers, hospital recreation specialists, park managers, leisure counselors, resource planners, recreation educators, and in similar roles.

To understand fully the responsibilities of recreation leaders and to develop principles and guidelines for effective recreation leadership and supervision today, it is essential to understand both the meaning of recreation and the social factors that have encouraged its growth in recent years.

RECREATION DEFINED

Recreation has traditionally been described as activity or experience voluntarily chosen and carried on within one's leisure, either because of the satisfaction or pleasure it provides or for other important values or benefits for the participant and the sponsoring group or organization.

Recently, some authorities have suggested that recreation should not be regarded as the leisure activity or experience itself. Instead, they propose, it should be perceived as the emotional effect of participation—a sense of self-fulfillment, achievement, freedom or other forms of satisfaction.

In either case, recreation should be seen as leisure-time involvement that helps to enrich one's personality by balancing work, study and self-maintenance activities with other kinds of creative experience and self-expression.

At one time recreation was justified chiefly as a means of restoring the individual for more work. Today it is seen as fully justified in its own right, existing side-by-side with work as part of a holistic life framework, contributing both to the quality of daily living and to the physical and mental health of the participant. Constructive, creative and challenging leisure activity contributes not only to one's happiness but also to one's competence and effective functioning in a variety of spheres, including work, family and community.

GROWTH OF RECREATION

What accounts for the remarkable growth of interest in recreation that has taken place over the last two or three decades? Many key social factors have been responsible for this development, the most important being the steady growth of free time in the twentieth century.

Expansion of Leisure

Leisure—meaning free or discretionary time—has expanded dramatically in recent decades. The causes are obvious: the shortened work-week, the increased number of holidays, longer vacations and longer periods of retirement through Social Security and other pension plans. The availability of such labor-saving devices as automatic washers and power mowers has also simplified our lives by reducing the time needed to carry out many of the tasks of daily living.

U.S. News and World Report pointed out in 1978 that city and suburban residents had on the average about 11 percent more leisure time available than they had had a decade before. A statistical report compiled by the U.S. Department of Commerce gave details of the changes that had occurred:

> In the last decade, Americans have markedly changed their lifestyles—they are working fewer hours for pay, spending less time on family matters and devoting themselves much to leisure.
> Time spent on family care, which . . . includes shopping and cleaning house as well as child care, dropped from 25.4 hours a week to 20.5 hours during the decade. . . . Leisure time went up for all groups sampled, but for single men the increase was most dramatic—from 36 hours a week to nearly 45 hours.[1]

Development of Leisure Technology

Bolstered by a generally affluent economy, this expanded new leisure has given rise to a host of technological inventions that have, in turn, created new

---

[1]"Less Work and More Play Is U.S. Trend." *Washington Post*, December 28, 1977, n.p.

forms of play. Artificial snow and chair-lifts, skin- and scuba-diving, power-boating and water-skiing, artificial ice rinks and hang-gliding and sky-diving are only a few of the new kinds of equipment or technologically based forms of outdoor recreation. Indoor leisure makes extensive use of television and its electronic variants, including home videotape recorders and videodiscs, stereo systems and electronic screen games. Many other innovative forms of play reflect modern technology and add to the surge in recreational participation today.

Growth of Cultural Programs

With a steadily increasing number of young people entering college each year, more and more individuals have been exposed to a variety of learning experiences that have broadened their range of leisure interests, particularly in the area of cultural activity. This in turn has encouraged a widespread expansion of the arts throughout society. The past two decades have seen a steady growth of opera, ballet, theater and symphony orchestras, with cities of all sizes constructing cultural centers and many regional ballet and theater companies reaching huge new audiences. Attendance at art galleries, museums and libraries has also expanded markedly.

Increased Travel and Tourism

The fuller commitment of national and state governments to developing a greater number of forests, seashores, parks and other recreation resources designed to meet leisure needs has led to the promotion of travel and tourism of all kinds. In addition, the creation of diversified and appealing new amusement complexes such as Disney World and Six Flags Over Georgia has provided new incentives for vacation travel. Despite the impact of rising fuel costs and energy shortages in the mid- and late 1970's, the following statistics were reported in 1979:

> Foreign travel by Americans climbed by an estimated 6 percent in the past year, with record outlays of 12.6 billion dollars. Vacation trips within the U.S. soared, despite the rising cost of fuel for the family car. There were at least 210 million recreation visits to national parks last year, almost double the number of a decade ago. Sales of recreational vehicles soared by 25 percent. Major tourist attractions set attendance records nearly everywhere.[2]

---

[2]"Leisure: Where No Recession Is in Sight." *U.S. News and World Report,* January 15, 1979, p. 41.

Needs of Special Populations

Another important aspect of recreation's expansion in recent years has stemmed from the recognition that it represents an essential human need for all groups in society, particularly for the mentally and physically disabled. There has been a dramatic push toward providing recreation for special populations, both as a form of treatment for those in institutional and residential settings, and as a vital service for those living in the community. Increased efforts are being made to eliminate architectural barriers that exclude disabled persons from access to recreational facilities, and the overall goal of mainstreaming the handicapped in community recreation programs has become more widely accepted and practiced.

Societal Acceptance of Recreation and Leisure

Accompanying these developments has been the recognition that recreation and leisure are highly significant and desirable aspects of modern life.

Our Puritan heritage and the influence of the Protestant work ethic tended to demean recreation for earlier generations. It was often condemned or seen as worthwhile only if it contributed to work efficiency. However, with increased evidence that constructive forms of play promote healthy living and make an important contribution to community life, recreation and leisure have gained a new respect and level of support from business, religious and governmental leaders. For example, industry-sponsored sports and fitness programs have become increasingly widespread; Roland Thornhill, Minister of Development of the Province of Nova Scotia in Canada, recently commented:

> In West Germany, a cardiac conditioning program resulted in a drop of almost seventy percent in absenteeism among workers with some history of cardiovascular problems. In Sweden, an employee fitness program cut absenteeism by nearly fifty percent. Exercise breaks, similar to one started this year by the Canadian Department of Health and Welfare, have reduced errors in a textile mill in Europe by more than thirty percent. . . . The time is here for Canadians to realize that recreation within a company is a direct asset for the employer and not only a fringe benefit for the employee.[3]

On many other levels, the value of constructively spent leisure has been substantiated. Dr. Robert H. Felix, formerly Director of the National Institute of Mental Health, has pointed out that recreation is an extremely valuable therapeutic medium in the treatment of the mentally ill and serves as a "great healing force" in promoting psychological well-being.

---

[3]Roland Thornhill: "Employee Programs and Industrial Development." *Recreation Management,* January 1979, pp. 34–36.

Recreation, however, is not useful only in treating the mentally ill. It is important for all persons to have a healthy balance between work and play. Recreation offers the opportunity for relaxation, a change of pace, and time to pursue creative interests and develop meaningful and supportive social relationships with others. Particularly in an era in which so many persons lead isolated or alienated lives in an increasingly urbanized society, the value of recreation in self-discovery and as a form of creative personal release is crucial. Gray has written of recreation as a form of "exploring inner space":

> Tension, boredom, feelings of impotence, monotony, and frustration are common in contemporary society. Unsatisfactory patterns of human relationships combined with . . . isolation from a natural environment lead to emotional disorders which show up as anxiety, insecurity, depression, alienation, lack of confidence, and a poor self-image.[4]

While recreation obviously cannot provide a panacea for all such problems, for many persons it offers personal satisfactions, meaningful involvement with others and the opportunity for getting more pleasure out of life that is extremely beneficial. Thus, a powerful case can be built for the value of recreation in improving both physical and mental health in the community.

As a consequence of the factors just described, recreation has become immensely popular in a wide variety of forms. It is not unusual today to see leisure featured in the mass media. Entire sections of newspapers are devoted to leisure and recreation, as are segments of daily television programs aired locally and nationally.

TRENDS IN RECREATIONAL PARTICIPATION

Several specific trends in recreational participation may be cited to illustrate the growth of leisure activity today, in terms of both numbers of participants and amounts of money spent on recreation.

Sports and Outdoor Recreation. Outlays on admissions to spectator sports of every kind have climbed steadily to more than $2 billion a year, with thoroughbred horse racing, major league baseball and collegiate football the most popular events. It has been estimated that more than 300 million such attendances are recorded each year.

In terms of participation in specific activities, 103.5 million individuals swim each year. Bicycling is the second most popular sport with 75 million participants, while fishing and camping are enjoyed by 63 million and 58 million enthusiasts, respectively. By the late 1970's, *Time* magazine reported that a record 87.5 million Americans over the age of 18 were engaging regularly in some form of athletic activity, for both recreative and fitness purposes. A 1979 report indicated that more than 56 million Americans had enjoyed varied forms of aquatic recreation during the previous year, using an armada of 11.2 million boats and spending a total of $6.6 billion for boats,

---

[4]David E. Gray: "Exploring Inner Space." *Parks and Recreation*, December 1972, p. 18.

motors, accessories, fuel, docking and launching, insurance and similar expenses.

Cultural Activities and Hobbies.   Seventy-eight million Americans are reported to visit museums each year, and 62 million attend at least one performance of live theater. There is a growing audience for modern dance and ballet of about 15 million persons, and the disco craze at its peak has burgeoned into a $4 billion industry, including records, lighting and sound installations, admissions and equipment.

In terms of hobbies, there are 36 million gardeners, 16 million stamp collectors and 10 million bridge enthusiasts. According to economists, the overall recreation boom shows no sign of slackening, with predictions that summertime outdoor recreational participation will be four times greater in the year 2000 than it was in 1960. Indeed, *U.S. News and World Report* predicts that leisure spending will rise to a total expenditure of $300 billion per year by 1985.[5]

FUNCTIONS OF RECREATION SPONSORS

Within this total picture, each major type of recreation sponsor has a unique set of functions and program goals.

Municipal Recreation and Park Departments.   Local recreation and park departments have three major functions: (a) to provide parks, playgrounds, centers, swimming pools, golf courses, auditoriums, stadiums, nature centers and other specialized facilities that house a wide variety of leisure activities; (b) to sponsor numerous programs under direct leadership, such as sports clinics and leagues, children's day camps, art classes and festivals, senior centers and varied types of special events' and (c) to take the lead in promoting community awareness of recreational needs and coordination of varied leisure programs and services throughout the community.

In addition to recreation and park departments as such, many other local government agencies, such as school boards, housing authorities, police departments, libraries, museums and youth commissions, may also share responsibility for providing specialized recreation services.

Voluntary, Non-Profit Agencies.   A second major force in community leisure programming today stems from voluntary, non-profit agencies sponsored by private citizens, boards or federations rather than by government. These include both religious and secular youth-serving organizations, settlement houses and privately operated community centers, groups serving economically disadvantaged or disabled populations, and many other special-interest organizations that promote participation in the arts, sports or other pastimes.

It is important to recognize that such organizations do not usually recognize themselves primarily as recreation agencies. Instead, they tend to

[5]"The Boom in Leisure—Where Americans Spend 160 Billions." *U.S. News and World Report,* May 23, 1977, pp. 62–63.

refer to themselves as social agencies or multi-service community organizations. However, recreation often represents one of their key offerings, and so they must be accurately perceived as part of the spectrum of leisure opportunity within the modern community.

Private Organizations. Numerous private membership organizations, such as country clubs, yacht clubs, fraternities and sororities, service clubs and fraternal orders, provide recreation and social programs for their members. Some groups, such as the Kiwanis and Rotary Club, may also sponsor or assist varied programs serving the community, such as summer camping for disabled children and youth.

Commercial Enterprises. This represents the largest single aspect of organized recreation service, and includes many different types of profit-oriented enterprises such as commercially owned ski centers, bowling alleys, movie theaters, resorts, dance halls, skating rinks, amusement complexes and gambling casinos. In the past, commercial recreation has not been closely identified with the organized recreation movement, but a number of colleges and universities have begun to prepare professional personnel to work in this field.

Industrial Programs. Frequently referred to as "employee recreation programs," these are usually part of larger and more complex personnel services and are intended to promote good relations between workers and management, to reduce absenteeism and the accident rate, to improve the physical and mental health of employees and to contribute to the favorable image of the industrial concern.

Campus Organizations. While many elementary and secondary schools offer sports and club programs, it is on the college or university level that the fullest recreation programming is found. This may range from intramural and sports club competition to social events, dances, performing arts or film series, game rooms, outing societies and varied special-interest groups. Campus recreation programs, which are usually an integral part of the overall student-life program, are intended both to provide healthy and constructive leisure outlets and to enrich the overall college learning experience by supplementing more formal curriculum offerings.

Others. A variety of other types of sponsors may be identified, including *armed forces recreation* (which is really a specialized branch of government service), *therapeutic recreation* (which cuts across the board, as it may be offered by many different kinds of agencies), and *residence-connected recreation* (which includes recreation facilities and activities connected with apartment or condominium projects, and "leisure villages" for the retired). Each of these types of sponsors is described in fuller detail in later chapters.

The basic point is that, far from being a fun-oriented activity that is provided only for children and youth, recreation today meets the needs of many different kinds of groups in society. It may have widely diversified program emphases, goals and objectives, depending on the nature of the sponsoring organization. In addition, it may also be closely linked to other significant programs and services in which recreation is only one element.

Thus, recreation has become a complex career field with a host of different job titles and areas of special expertise, many of which will be presented and analyzed in this text. This text is primarily concerned with those aspects of professional recreation service that fall under the headings of *leadership* and *supervision*. These terms refer both to levels of employment or job function and to important processes that underlie all programming and facility management.

UNDERSTANDING LEADERSHIP

Earlier in this chapter, it was suggested that while leadership was once seen rather narrowly as the face-to-face process of directing groups involved in recreation program activities, today it must be approached in more complex ways. Leaders have a variety of functions other than simply directing activities, and the term "leadership" itself implies certain skills and abilities that are needed on all levels of professional service.

Exactly how *should* leadership be conceptualized with respect to recreation service today?

The term *leadership* is familiar to most people. One tends to think of a leader as an individual possessing certain qualities: a man or woman who is forceful and has confidence, good judgment and an aura of authority—a person whom others are willing to trust and follow.

A typical dictionary definition of the word *leader* is

> One who or that which leads; as: (1) A person or animal that goes before to guide or show the way, or one who precedes or directs in some action, opinion or movement; esp.: (a) A guide; conductor, (b) One having authority to precede and direct . . . .[6]

This definition suggests that leaders guide, direct or even command. However, the contemporary literature in the field of group dynamics and social psychology stresses the role of the leader as an enabler or catalyst rather than a director. Davis describes leadership as

> . . . the ability to persuade others to seek defined objectives enthusiastically. It is the human factor which binds a group together and motivates it toward goals.[7]

Pfiffner and Presthus assert that leadership is

> . . . the art of coordinating and motivating individuals and groups to achieve desired ends.[8]

---

[6]*Webster's New International Dictionary.* Cambridge, Massachusetts, G. and C. Merriam Co., 1954.
[7]Keith Davis: *Human Relations at Work.* New York, McGraw-Hill Book Co., 1967, pp. 96–97.
[8]John M. Pfiffner and Robert V. Presthus: *Public Administration.* New York, Ronald Press, 1968, p. 92.

Slavson described leadership as involving (a) the ability to understand and to respond to the desires and needs of a group; (b) the capacity to help the group express these desires constructively and progressively; and (c) the power to focus the attention of a group upon one's self.[9] Finally, Tannenbaum and Massarik describe leadership as:

> . . . interpersonal influence . . . directed through the communication process, toward the attainment of a specified goal or goals.[10]

Recreation leaders tend to operate in a variety of group situations. In some cases, leaders may work with highly structured and stable clubs and groups, with a considerable amount of close interaction. In others, they may supervise programs in which large numbers of individuals take part without developing significant group ties or continuing affiliations. Leaders may be responsible for organizing playground or day camp activities, sports leagues and tournaments, and classes in the performing arts, or they may supervise pool complexes or sportsman's centers and the like. Leaders may work closely with single individuals or facilitate group interactions with a small group of individuals in counseling or other one-to-one roles. In other situations, they may work with dozens or even hundreds of participants in a relatively impersonal way, with little group interaction. In some cases, they may exert leadership influences on co-workers or representatives of other community agencies, without having a direct link to their program activities.

Levels of Employment

An important factor that influences the nature of recreation leadership stems from the individual's level of employment. Four such levels are as follows:

Direct Program Leadership. The leader is directly responsible for the face-to-face leadership of individuals or groups of participants in recreation program activities.

Team Leadership. The individual is a member of a team of other recreation professionals on the same level and must cooperate with them in planning and carrying out program and other job functions.

Supervisory Leadership. The leader is in charge of a number of subordinate workers, such as seasonal or part-time leaders, and must supervise them in carrying out their job responsibilities.

Administrative Leadership. The individual must mobilize, motivate and provide direction for an entire staff, helping them achieve their full potential in terms of job performance. He or she must also work cooperatively with other agency or department administrators and within the community at large.

Realistically, it is often necessary for an individual to function on more than one level, e.g., to be part of a team of equals and at the same time

---

[9]S. R. Slavson: *Creative Group Education.* New York, Association Press, 1948, p. 24.
[10]Robert Tannenbaum and Fred Massarik: "Leadership: A Frame of Reference." *Management Science.* October 1957, p. 3.

provide direct program leadership to participants, or to supervise other, subordinate employees. Again, each such situation may necessitate somewhat different approaches to leadership.

It is essential to recognize that leadership is *not* confined to individuals who are directly identified as leaders by their job titles. In other words. a marine sergeant in a combat unit, a surgeon carrying out a delicate operation, the director of an amateur theater group and the head of a company's sales division must all show leadership if they are to be effective. Leadership is a vital part of all group operations and organizational processes.

In addition to possessing personal traits that command respect and the skills that enable one to help others move in constructive directions, leaders must also be *willing* to assume such responsibilities. Clearly, some persons enjoy assuming positions of responsibility, while others do not and withdraw from them. Finally, it should be recognized that leadership is not necessarily good; history provides many examples of ineffective or destructive leaders who have failed both themselves and those whom they sought to lead.

Recreation Leadership Defined

In this text, recreation leadership is defined as *the process of working effectively with groups of participants or co-workers, in order to encourage, mobilize and direct their fullest efforts in carrying on successful recreation programs*.

Beyond this, recreation leadership may be analyzed or understood in a number of other ways. It may be seen as (a) a formal professional role, based on job titles and agency hiring procedures; (b) a specific set of functions and tasks appropriate to a given job situation; (c) a set of interpersonal behaviors that come into play as part of group and staff relationships; and (d) a group of personal qualities that help to make for success in leadership roles. Each of these aspects of recreation leadership is examined in full detail in Chapter Three.

UNDERSTANDING SUPERVISION

A second major focus of this text is *supervision*. While this is closely linked to leadership in the sense that successful supervisors must possess leadership qualities and must work closely with leaders, it represents a distinctly separate aspect of professional involvement.

Meaning of Supervision. Essentially, supervision may be regarded in two ways: (a) as a job level, commonly described as "middle management," and usually designated by a title that conveys the status of "supervisor," and (b) as a process, involving the coordination, direction and evaluation of other workers.

In a generic sense, supervisors are individuals who are responsible for making sure that other employees perform effectively, e.g., the foreman or forewoman on the assembly line, the director of a task force, or the head of a particular branch of service. Therefore, <u>training and staff development are usually important responsibilities</u>. Two-way communication is another important responsibility; supervisors must make sure that workers understand the wishes and policies of top management and, at the same time, that management is aware of the needs of lower-level employees.

Functions of Supervisors in Recreation

In the field of recreation, as later chapters will show in detail, the tasks of supervisors vary with their specific areas of employment and their exact job assignments. In a municipal recreation and park department, for example, there are usually three different types of supervisory positions:

Area Supervisors.   These are individuals who are responsible for organizing all recreation programs and facilities within a single major area or district of a city or township.

Facility Supervisors.   These persons are in charge of a single major facility, such as a large athletic complex, community center, aquatic center or community arts workshop; usually they are responsible for coordinating the work of several other leaders or numerous program elements within the facility.

Special Service Supervisors.   These are specialists in a given area of service, such as the creative arts or programs for the elderly or the handicapped; they are responsible for planning and carrying out programs, events and special services within this area of responsibility on a citywide or systemwide basis.

In non-public settings, such as therapeutic, voluntary agency or commercial recreation programs, although the title of "supervisor" may not be used as commonly, the functions tend to be the same. They include planning, organizing, controlling and evaluating programs, along with the key tasks of helping to train, assign, assist and motivate other subordinate personnel.

RELATIONSHIP BETWEEN LEADERSHIP AND SUPERVISION

As suggested earlier, although leadership and supervision are identified by distinctly separate job titles and descriptions, in actual practice they are closely linked to each other.

First, both are part of the same professional continuum. Typically, most individuals gain their early experience in the recreation field as leaders, either through summer, volunteer or part-time employment, or through full-time, face-to-face involvement as playground leaders, therapists or activity specialists. If they remain in the field and are successful in carrying out their assigned tasks, they tend to take on challenges that involve a higher level of responsibility. In time, either through promotion within the system or by moving to another agency, they are likely to become supervisors or administrators. When this happens, their past experiences as leaders are essential in helping them function effectively in their new roles.

Even if the supervisor is no longer directly concerned with actual leadership responsibilities (in the sense of working with groups of participants as an assigned task), it is essential that he or she understand them fully. In order to plan and coordinate programs effectively, to assist face-to-face leaders who may be having difficulty, or to provide sound in-service training, counseling or meaningful evaluation and personnel recommendations, the supervisor must be skilled in leadership principles and techniques.

Beyond this, although the supervisor may no longer be working directly with participants, he or she must be concerned with their needs and interests in order to help leaders develop programs that will challenge and involve them. In many ways— in terms of planning and scheduling activities, publicizing them and developing effective community relations—the supervisor continues to function as a leader, except that it is on a higher and more complex level of responsibility.

For these reasons this text deals with both leadership and supervision within a single conceptual framework. Many of the guidelines for effective leadership represent important areas of understanding for supervisors, and many of the suggested techniques for staff development functions of supervisors are of direct concern to leaders.

CONCEPTUAL BASE FOR RECREATION LEADERSHIP AND SUPERVISION

In developing effective models for recreation leadership and supervision today in varied community settings, it is essential to understand the context within which leisure services are provided in modern society.

A philosophical framework must be established that takes into account the changes that have occurred in community life in recent years, as well as the economic realities that affect the programs of government, voluntary agencies and commercial enterprises. Changing lifestyles and social values, new perceptions of leisure as a social force and new attitudes regarding the rights of formerly deprived populations, such as the physically or mentally disabled, all affect the roles of recreation leaders and supervisors.

Fundamental to the development of a sound philosophical base for professional service in recreation is the need to understand the role of play in human life. This is essential because we have for so long trivialized play as a childish activity that is without importance. To be fully effective, the recreation professional must understand and respect the meaning of play and its role in human development and societal structures.

Meaning of Play in Human Life

Far from representing a trivial aspect of human behavior, play is regarded by anthropologists as having great symbolic value. Indeed, scientists have noted that although play is found within the entire class of mammals, only humans appear to play throughout their entire life span. The more advanced a species is on the evolutionary scale, the more diverse and frequent are its play activities. Norbeck writes:

> For all forms of life, play may be defined as voluntary, pleasurable behavior that is separated in time from other activities and that has a quality of make-believe. Play thus transcends ordinary behavior. Human play differs uniquely from that of other species, however, because it is molded by culture, consciously and unconsciously. That is, human play is conditioned by learned attitudes and values that have no counterpart among nonhuman species.[11]

From an anthropological point of view, Norbeck writes that because play is universally found human behavior, it is therefore presumably vital to human life. He urges that play not be regarded simply as a form of diversion, rest from more serious activities, or childish behavior. Instead, play should be regarded as both a biological and a sociocultural phenomenon that has significance in many ways.[12] The distinguished psychologist and authority on learning behavior, Jerome Bruner, confirms this view, pointing out that the ability to play is closely linked to creative and inventive thinking among children and to developing interesting and fulfilling lives among adults. Numerous other social scientists have attested to the value of recreative behavior as part of personal adjustment, helping youth learn appropriate social values and patterns of group involvement, pre-vocational exploration of potential career interests, and maintaining emotional well-being and positive family relationships.[13]

While it is important for recreation leaders and supervisors to have a solid understanding of the meaning and value of play to individuals as a *personal* experience—for the reasons cited above, or to meet needs for pleasure, fitness, challenge or social experience—it is also important for them to understand recreation as a *social* phenomenon.

Recreation as a Social Phenomenon

Recreation leaders should understand that recreation is a key aspect of modern community life and of today's economic structure. In addition, they

---

[11]Edward Norbeck: "Man at Play." *Play: A Natural History Magazine Special Supplement,* December 1971, p. 53.

[12]*Ibid.*

[13]Jerome S. Bruner: "Child Development: Play Is Serious Business." *Psychology Today,* January 1975, p. 83.

should perceive recreation as a movement that embraces the interests of hundreds of colleges and universities that provide professional preparation in it, thousands of different government agencies, tens of thousands of voluntary, private and commercial organizations, hundreds of thousands of professional workers, millions of participants and volunteer leaders and, finally, billions of dollars spent each year. They should also recognize that it includes an immense variety of activities, ranging from the informal, free, self-directed activities that we carry on each day, such as reading or chatting with friends, to the establishment of huge business enterprises that provide highly structured, expensive activities, such as nationwide sports or entertainment networks.

In addition, recreation professionals should have a sound understanding of the goals of community recreation as they have been presented in the literature by authorities in the field. While each public or voluntary agency is likely to have somewhat distinct emphases or objectives, their goals may readily be grouped under the following eight categories:

1. Improving the quality of life through the creative and constructive use of leisure.
2. Contributing to the physical and mental health of the population by providing a wide range of enjoyable and inexpensive recreation opportunities for people of all ages and both sexes.
3. Strengthening community life by improving and enriching democratic values and increasing participation in civic activities.
4. Providing a positive reinforcement to prevent or counteract antisocial forms of play, such as juvenile delinquency.
5. Enriching the cultural and creative life of the community and supplementing the formal process of education for all ages.
6. Improving safety standards and preventing accidents related to recreation by offering organized play programs in safe, supervised surroundings.
7. Offering special services needed by the poor or the physically, mentally or socially disabled to meet their unique needs within integrated social situations wherever possible.
8. Protecting and beautifying the natural environment by providing attractive parklands, plazas or other scenic areas, including the rehabilitation and recreative use of waterways adjoining the community.

In addition to understanding and being able to verbalize these desirable social goals and values, recreation professionals should be aware of the difficult issues and trends that face their field today. As suggested earlier, the last two decades have represented a period of great social change and shifting lifestyles, which have made the task of designing meaningful leisure programs extremely difficult.

Changing Social Values and Lifestyle Patterns

During the past two decades, our society has moved away from many of the standards and values that past generations supported. The Protestant ethic has come increasingly under fire. Although most individuals today still understand and respect the need to work, they no longer regard work as the primary thrust in their lives. Many business leaders have sought to make work itself more creative and challenging, in part by giving employees the opportunity to structure their own work patterns through shorter work-weeks or by means of flexible work scheduling. Such new approaches provide workers with solid new blocks of free time and present recreation professionals with a clear challenge to offer leisure activities that will provide participants with many of the significant values and satisfactions they no longer find in their work.

For many young people in particular, the pursuit of pleasure as an end in itself has become a keynote of modern life. There is a new emphasis on a hedonistic, thrill-seeking way of life that may include risky adventures, drugs, alcohol, gambling or even aggression and violent behavior.[14] Increasing numbers of people rank high on a "sensation-seeking" scale; subject to boredom in work and disliking routine in their lives, they seek out both jobs and high-risk leisure pastimes that offer them excitement and challenge. Some seek release through riding roller-coasters, sky-diving, hang-gliding, motorcycle hill-climbing or similar forms of "risk" recreation. Others indulge in the forms of socially disapproved pleasure-seeking mentioned earlier, as evidenced by numerous recent statistical reports.

Examples of Socially Disapproved Play. A 1979 report to Congress by the U.S. Department of Health, Education and Welfare noted that use of marijuana by teen-agers, particularly boys, had increased sharply, with half the class of 1978 admitting to having smoked marijuana during the last year, and 37 percent being identified as current users.[15] Cigarette smoking and alcohol abuse continue to represent major health problems in the United States, with the overall cost of such activities (including both direct health-care charges and losses due to lost production and wages, fires, motor accidents and violent crime attributed to them) amounting to close to $60 billion in a single year. Within an increasingly permissive society, teen-age sexual intercourse has become more and more widespread, according to a recent study by population experts at the Johns Hopkins School of Hygiene and Public Health.[16]

Gambling, both legal and illegal, has become increasingly widespread; 44 states have legalized some form of wagering, such as casinos, slot machines, racetrack betting and other games, to gain public income. Law enforcement authorities now estimate that the Mafia takes in a $25 billion profit

---

[14]Marvin Zuckerman: "The Search for High Sensation." *Psychology Today*, Febuary 1978, pp. 38–46, 96–99.
[15]"More Teens Reported Using Marijuana." Associated Press, April 19, 1979.
[16]Spencer Rich: "63% of Teen-Age Girls Have Had Sex, Study Shows." *The Philadelphia Inquirer*, July 8, 1979, p. 2–A.

each year from such ventures as the manufacture and sale of pornographic books, magazines and movies, narcotics and gambling—far more than the profit made by any major, legitimate industrial concern in the country today.

What does all this mean? It suggests that if we are to take advantage of leisure to enrich our lives culturally and creatively and to build a healthy, strong society, we must develop more positive and constructive attitudes toward leisure and recreation. Recreation professionals in particular must offer a range of challenging, inexpensive and accessible leisure opportunities to counter the appeal of less desirable pastimes.

New Trends in Sport. Another example of changing social values that must be considered in developing a conceptual base for recreation leadership and supervision lies in the area of sports competition. In recent years, many have criticized our national mania for highly competitive, violent team sports like hockey and football, and the prevailing emphasis on "winning at all costs." The rapid growth of the New Games movement, which stresses participation by all in informal, cooperative and creative forms of play, illustrates this trend. Similarly, many physical education programs now stress individual and dual forms of sport that have lifelong leisure potential, as well as challenging outdoor recreation activities and coeducational games and contests. This does not mean that competitive sports are being totally de-emphasized:

> Although the new physical education de-emphasizes competition, traditional team sports are still part of programs in secondary schools. But now schools offer options, with more intramural and individualized sports that children of both sexes can play regardless of their ability or handicaps.[17]

Spurred on by the feminist movement and Title IX of the Educational Amendments Act passed by Congress in 1972, schools and colleges have given increasing emphasis to sports for girls and women. In the early 1970's, 284,000 high school girls participated in interscholastic sport; several years later the number was 1.6 million, nearly a sixfold increase. Similar growth in participation has taken place on the collegiate level. This trend has had a marked influence on recreation program planners, who can no longer limit participation by girls and women to traditionally conceived "feminine" activities, but must provide full opportunity and encouragement for them through a wide range of athletic and other offerings.

Similar changes have occurred with respect to providing fuller program services for special population groups that have been poorly served in the past, for example, the aging, the physically and mentally handicapped, the economically disadvantaged and racial and ethnic minorities. Examples of innovative programs and leadership approaches in these areas appear throughout this text.

Environmental and Energy-Related Concerns. For a number of years, outdoor recreation authorities have been concerned about the need to guard

---

[17]Sally Reed: "The New Physical Education Benefits Everyone." *The New York Times*, April 22, 1979, Education Section p. 24.

against pollution and overuse of the natural environment, as well as the widespread effort to reclaim waterways and other resources that have been ruined by industrial wastes. Increasing efforts have been made to plan outdoor recreation areas and programs that respect the needs of primitive environments. With the advent of energy shortages, this issue has become increasingly important. There is fuller recognition that we have reached an "era of limits." We can no longer expend fuel recklessly or despoil the natural environment with impunity.

More and more, recreation leaders and supervisors are promoting vigorous, close-to-home activities in which people are able to participate with their friends and neighbors, building physical health and positive social values, rather than relying on "machine-made" or spectator-oriented forms of play. As environmental concerns and energy shortages continue in our society, this will be the trend of the future.

Educating for Leisure.   In developing a conceptual framework for recreation leadership and supervision in the 1980's and beyond, it is important to recognize some of the key problems that face people living in modern, urban society. Our lives are marked by a variety of pressures and tensions. They are often contradictory, in that our living circumstances are frequently overcrowded, yet we tend to be isolated or alienated from others. We feel that job demands are excessive, yet we suffer from boredom that compels many of us to seek out artificial and self-destructive forms of stimulation. The incidence of marital breakup has increased markedly, with family living patterns undergoing rapid change. Young people strike out against traditional constraints, while older individuals today often resist compulsory retirement.

To meet many of these challenges, we need to improve the quality of life and to provide a sense of pleasure, reward, significant involvement and challenge through constructive recreational opportunities. Yet, for many, it is difficult to overcome the lingering sense of guilt about play. A major challenge to recreation professionals today is the need to contribute to education for leisure—to help people of all ages understand the important role of leisure in their lives, and to build varied, enriching forms of recreational participation.

Meeting the Fiscal Challenge.   A key problem facing many public and voluntary agency administrators today is the need to develop more adequate means of financial support. Because of steadily increasing operational costs in recent years, many local governments have been forced to freeze or even cut their expenditures for recreation and parks, as well as for other community services. A national study of large cities, carried out in 1979, showed that 60 percent of the municipal recreation and park departments surveyed had suffered severe fiscal cutbacks in recent years.[18]

As a consequence, many public agencies in both the United States and Canada have come to rely increasingly on fees and charges to provide bud-

[18]Richard Kraus: *New Directions in Urban Parks and Recreation: A Trends-Analysis Report.* Philadelphia, Pennsylvania, Temple University and Heritage Conservation and Recreation Service, Spring 1980.

getary support. However, when recreation and park departments shift their program emphasis from directed activities to managing facilities for which admission fees can be charged, it becomes more and more difficult to meet the leisure needs of the poor, the disabled and the dependent aging individuals in our society.

The real challenge is to create fuller public understanding of the value of recreation and to mobilize a strong base of citizen support so that recreation facilities and programs are more adequately financed. Beyond this, it is necessary to build a stronger linkage of public, voluntary, private and commercial agencies to cooperate in meeting total community needs for leisure programs. It is no longer possible, if it ever was, to think of recreation as the primary or sole responsibility of the public recreation and park department.

The recreation professional cannot be seen simply as a "play leader" in a narrow sense. Instead, he or she must become a promoter of recreation programs and opportunities on a broad basis throughout the community. In a sense, the role has become one of catalyst, or "animateur," a term used in a number of European countries and eastern Canada to describe the task of stimulating and organizing community recreation programs. In therapeutic recreation service, for example, it is not enough for the specialist who works with the mentally retarded to provide programs within special schools or residential institutions alone. Instead, he or she must work closely with other community agencies and sponsors, such as Y's, service clubs, camps or youth organizations, for cooperative programming and referral opportunities. In so doing, the therapeutic recreation worker becomes an advocate for varied social services that benefit the handicapped person and his or her family.

Beyond this, leaders must also be able to seek out other forms of financial support from government or foundations, community chest funds, businesses and individual donors. In the process, they will help to increase total community awareness of the vital function played by recreation agencies in meeting community needs, and will strengthen the role of leisure services as part of the total spectrum of community life.

FUTURE OF ORGANIZED RECREATION SERVICE

Because of the fiscal cutbacks that have taken place in many government agencies and voluntary organizations, concern has been expressed about the future of organized recreation service. With the limited pool of job openings in such programs, there is a serious risk that our colleges and universities are turning out an excessive number of graduates in recreation and leisure services.

However, it seems abundantly clear that the field of recreation itself will continue to thrive in years ahead. Leisure itself will become increasingly available to all segments of the population. Although a portion of the workweek will remain committed to the eight-hour day, for millions of others

... the work week will shrink. The U.S. Chamber of Commerce believes that employers should expect a four-day, 32-hour work week for most workers by 2000. Increases in vacation and holiday time will also sustain the growth in leisure time.[19]

Assuming a reasonably healthy national economy, it is projected that recreational participation will continue to expand and that spending on leisure opportunities will grow steadily. Furthermore, government on all levels has recognized the need to improve recreation services; we are far from providing adequate opportunities for great masses of people. With respect to overall community needs, for example, a recent federal urban recreation study concluded that

> ... most public recreation programs are under-financed and understaffed. These programs are often limited in scope, poorly-distributed, seasonal, and serve only small segments of the population. They usually fail to meet the diversified recreation needs of present urban residents. . . . While a wide variety of program opportunities exist in most cities, many problems reduce their effectiveness and success.[20]

This problem is even more severe with respect to programs meeting the needs of special populations. To illustrate, the same study concluded that

> Recreation and leisure time opportunities are most limited for handicapped persons, senior citizens, and the economically and socially-disadvantaged. . . . The recreation needs of handicapped individuals are gaining more recognition from park and recreation agencies; however, wide disparities exist in the quality of recreation services provided. Few municipal park and recreation agencies provide adequate, accessible, professionally-staffed therapeutic recreation programs for the handicapped.[21]

Thus, the need is great, and the federal government is gradually moving toward a recognition that it must assist local government agencies in meeting these needs through more comprehensive and effective program services. However, it is also obvious that government must form a fuller partnership with other recreation agencies and sponsors to meet these important social needs. This has important implications for the recreation movement as a whole. In the past, the recreation profession generally was thought of as including only public and voluntary organizations and workers. Our programs of higher education in recreation and parks tended for the most part to ignore commercial recreation, religious organizations, industrial or employee recreation programs, and similar aspects of the field. However, it has been apparent that when government agencies could not, for financial reasons, pro-

---

[19]Jonathan Wolman: "The Future of Working: Less of It for More of Us." *The Philadelphia Inquirer*, September 3, 1978, pp. 1-E, 5-E.

[20]*National Urban Recreation Study*, Executive Report. Washington, D.C., U.S. Dept. of Interior, 1978, p. 50.

[21]*Ibid.*, p. 59

vide adequate services, voluntary and other private organizations have tended to take over responsibility for them.

Diana Dunn, in a recent analysis of the impact of Proposition 13 and other fiscal constraints on the recreation and park field, concluded that one or more of the leisure service delivery system components would continue to grow in the future. Whether these components are public, voluntary, private or commercial,

> . . . employees will be needed and creative, aggressive people with skills and vision will be hired for a wide range of leisure-related careers. If the traditional "recreation movement" will reach out, the time is right for it to have a more significant impact on leisure and recreation in America than it ever has had before. . . .
>
> Demands for leisure services and recreation opportunities will accelerate in this country, and there will be an ever-increasing need for good people to commit their careers to fulfilling this demand. In this context, leisure careers have an incredibly bright future.[22]

It is essential that those entering this field have a clear understanding of the types of positions and job opportunities that exist now and that will continue to grow in our society. Chapter Two presents a thorough analysis of recreation as a career field, outlining the types of positions on leadership and supervisory levels that are found in various types of agencies, as well as their specific job functions and responsibilities and the standards or requirements used in selecting candidates to fill them. Following this, the text provides detailed examples of both the kinds of leadership principles that apply to *all* positions in the field and specific guidelines that are useful in specialized types of agencies.

SUGGESTED EXAMINATION QUESTIONS OR TOPICS FOR STUDENT REPORTS

1. Define recreation, both as it is presented in the text and in terms of your own understanding of it.
2. What evidence is cited in this chapter to show the growth and acceptance of recreation as an important public concern and an area of government responsibility? Outline a number of specific, important goals for the provision of community recreation programs.
3. Define both leadership and supervision, and show their relationship in terms of professional development and with respect to working relationships within agencies.

---

[22]Diana Dunn: "Leisure Careers in an Era of Limits." *Journal of Physical Education and Recreation*, April 1979, p. 38.

SUGGESTED ACTION ASSIGNMENTS OR GROUP PROCESS ACTIVITIES

1. Using interviews or questionnaires, survey a group of participants in a recreation program to learn their understanding of the term "recreation" and their motives for participating.
2. Do a study of leadership in action—either of yourself or of another leader—and identify and tally the functions and behaviors observed.
3. Do a simple analysis of recreation programs or opportunities in your community or neighborhood, illustrating as many of the different types of sponsors described in this chapter as possible.
4. In groups of three or four persons, "brainstorm" (see Chapter 14) to identify new tasks that will become necessary for recreation leaders and supervisors to accomplish in order to keep pace with social change.

Career Opportunities in Recreation Service

Chapter Two

As Chapter One has pointed out, the field of recreation service has expanded remarkably in the United States and Canada during the past several decades. This chapter outlines the background of recreation as a career field and describes the specific areas of employment in which individuals may specialize. Both students of the field and those who are presently employed in it can benefit from understanding the full breadth of career opportunity in recreation.

The chapter goes on to describe the process of job selection and the standards used to screen individuals for employment in leisure programs. Following this, it presents a number of steps that colleges and universities, practitioners working in the field and their professional societies are taking to upgrade and strengthen recreation as a career field. Finally, the chapter concludes with a set of guidelines or suggestions to individuals who are studying in this field in college or university recreation and park departments.

BACKGROUND OF RECREATION AS A CAREER FIELD

There have been specialists in recreation for many centuries, in the sense that recorded history gives many examples of professional entertainers and athletes, and entrepreneurs who operated places of amusement for profit. However, recognition of recreation as a career field did not come until the latter part of the nineteenth century, when the park and playground movements were initiated in American cities and when voluntary organizations like the Young Men's Christian Association were established.

For the first time, leisure was recognized as a significant social concern. Courses in play leadership were developed by the Playground Association of America and were included in the curricula of teacher-training programs in a number of colleges. As the National Recreation Association sponsored graduate training programs in recreation administration, people began to be more aware of recreation as a distinct career field. For a time, individuals received training in a number of varied fields, such as physical education, social group work or, for those who were planning to become park managers, horticulture and civil engineering. However, it was not until the development of separate curricula in a handful of colleges in the late 1930's that distinct programs of professional preparation in recreation came into being.

At the end of World War II, only a dozen or so colleges had separate curricula in this field. By 1960, the number had climbed slowly to 64. Then during the mid- and late 1960's, professional preparation in recreation and parks expanded at an accelerated rate. There were several reasons for this development:

1. During the 1960's, it was apparent that professional employment in recreation had expanded rapidly in recent years. A nationwide study of work-force requirements in recreation concluded that there would be a need for hundreds of thousands of new recreation and park professionals in the years ahead. The U.S. Department of Labor reported that employment opportunities were excellent in this field because of widespread shortages of leisure-service personnel in local government, hospitals and youth-serving organizations:

> Opportunities for recreation workers are expected to increase rapidly at least through the mid-1970's. Thousands of recreation workers will be needed annually to allow for growth and to replace personnel who leave the field because of retirements, death, and transfers to other occupations. . . . Increased leisure time and rising levels of per capita income should foster growth in almost all recreational fields during the next ten years.[1]

2. The federal government made a major contribution to the field when it published the findings of the Outdoor Recreation Resources Review Commission in 1962. Based on an extensive inventory of the nation's park and outdoor recreation systems, the Commission's report resulted in the establishment of the Bureau of Outdoor Recreation (later to become the Heritage Conservation and Recreation Service) within the Department of the Interior, the passage of the Land and Water Conservation Fund Act and extensive new programs of outdoor recreation.

3. A third significant factor in both the United States and Canada was the merging of recreation and park agencies on the local level and the growth

---

[1]*Employment Outlooks for Recreation Workers.* Occupational Outlook Report Series (Bulletin No. 1450–69). Washington, D.C., U.S. Department of Labor, 1966–1967, pp. 2–3.

of professional organizations. The National Recreation and Park Association in the United States and the Canadian Parks/Recreation Association in Canada lent considerable strength to professional development in recreation and parks.

4. The changing role of recreation in many communities also increased interest in the field. Particularly in suburban communities, new departments were established that rapidly developed extensive networks of sports facilities, swimming pools, golf courses, nature centers, arts programs and similar areas and activities. In the larger cities, recreation received impressive financial support through such federally funded operations as the Community Action Programs of the Office of Economic Opportunity.

5. Recreation and parks gained increased acceptance as a degree field in higher education. Many new community colleges, designed to meet the needs of students who might otherwise not attend college and to provide qualified personnel to carry out vitally needed human services, established two-year recreation and park curricula. Many senior colleges shifted their focus away from strictly academic, liberal arts orientation to emphasis on career-directed degree programs, and numerous college physical education departments established new recreation programs in order to assure their students of more diversified job opportunities.

Thus, there was a dramatic growth in professional preparation programs in parks and recreation, with more than 330 separate two- and four-year curricula (many with graduate programs as well) and 37,500 student majors by the late 1970's.[2]

TYPES OF JOB OPPORTUNITIES IN RECREATION TODAY

A listing of the types of sponsoring agencies and positions open to graduates of recreation and park curricula today includes the following:

Municipal Recreation and Park Agencies. Jobs are available for administrators; supervisors; center directors; sports, arts or special population specialists; playground leaders; planners and researchers; public relations officers; senior center managers; and parks managers.

Commercial Recreation. Positions in this field include resort managers; retirement community, condominium or other real-estate development recreation directors; golf course, ski center, or tennis center managers; amusement complex managers and planners; bowling center operators; family-oriented multi-recreation complex directors; travel and tourism specialists.

State and Federal Agencies. Rangers; naturalists and outdoor education specialists; park directors; planners and researchers; extension agents; conservation workers and foresters; wildlife managers; nature center or museum directors; grants and technical assistance coordinators.

---

[2]Thomas A. Stein and Donald Henkel: "Recreation and Park Education in the United States and Canada—1978." *Parks and Recreation*, January 1979, pp. 29–36.

Industrial Recreation.   Employee recreation program directors; company facility managers; resort, camp or center directors for unions; pre-retirement counselors; physical fitness program specialists.

Armed Forces.   Service club directors; special activities supervisors; youth activities directors; sports specialists; entertainment coordinators; Red Cross area directors and Veterans Administration rehabilitation personnel.

Outdoor Recreation.   Outdoor educators and interpreters; researchers and planners; camp counselors and managers; trail developers; nature center managers.

Colleges and Universities.   Faculty members in parks, recreation or leisure services or studies departments; campus recreation directors; intramural and sports clubs directors; recreation extension specialists; research and grants personnel; college union managers.

Therapeutic Recreation.   Recreation or activity therapy specialists and supervisors; camp directors for the disabled; program directors in national organizations serving the ill and handicapped; personnel in state hospitals, developmental centers for the retarded, nursing homes, physical rehabilitation centers, drug and alcohol abuse treatment centers, youth centers, youth correctional centers and prisons; researchers and planners.

Youth-Serving Agencies.   Positions are available for activity specialists, program supervisors, facility managers and administrators in YMCA's, YWCA's, Girl Scouts, Boy Scouts, Boys' Clubs, Girls' Clubs, settlement houses and community centers, Children's Aid Societies, Police Athletic Leagues and religiously affiliated youth organizations.[3]

In another listing of the types of positions found today in recreation service, a special issue of *Leisure Today* identified the following professional job opportunities:

Resort Manager	Community Center Director
Recreation Therapist	Golf Pro
Museum Guide	Senior Citizen Programmer
Leisure Counselor	Church Recreation Director
Tour Guide	Municipal Recreator
Theme Park Manager	Outdoor and Waterway Guide
Travel Agency Consultant	Voluntary Agency Supervisor
Condominium Social Director	Concessionaire
Fitness Specialist	Activity Outfitter
Travel Planner	Camping Director
Naturalist	Environmental Interpreter
Dance Instructor	Ski Instructor
Playground Leader	Tennis Pro
Armed Forces Recreation	Youth Director
Administrator	Aquatics Specialist

---

[3]Reynold E. Carlson, Janet R. MacLean, Theodore R. Deppe and James A. Peterson: *Recreation and Leisure: The Changing Scene.* Belmont, Cal., Wadsworth Co., 1979, pp. 315–316.

Park Ranger
Handicapped Program Planner
Forester
Circus Performer
Hotel Manager
Community Education Worker
Stadium Manager
Prison Recreation Specialist
Ski Patroller
Youth Sports Coach
Industrial Recreation Specialist
Sightseeing Guide
Concert Promoter
Leisure Education Specialist
Cruise Ship Activity Director

Community Development
   Programs Specialist
Activity Director
Camp Counselor
Park Superintendent
Carnival Game Operator
Campground Attendant
Youth Agency Worker
Recreation Aide
Administrator
Animal Handler
Recreation Facility Manager
High-Risk Recreation Facilitator
Professor[4]

It has been estimated that several million individuals are employed within the full range of leisure-related programs and businesses, including the fields of travel and tourism, the manufacture and sale of recreational equipment and supplies, professional entertainment and similar services. However, the bulk of these positions should not be considered part of the recreation movement, because they do not demand professional training in recreation as such for employment. Typically, many positions either do not require any degree at all or may require a degree in some other specialized area. For example, a golf pro must know a great deal about golf, but need not necessarily have training in recreation. A circus performer must be highly skilled on the trapeze or with snarling lions, but need not understand the theory of leisure in modern society.

Those who need to have specialized training in recreation as a career field tend to be leaders, supervisors, administrators, planners and researchers within such major areas of employment as public and voluntary agencies, therapeutic programs, the armed forces, campus recreation and industrial programs.

STANDARDS FOR SCREENING APPLICANTS FOR RECREATION POSITIONS

Because the recreation field is so diversified, there has been no single standard or mechanism for selection of those who seek employment in it. Essentially, the following types of screening procedures are used today throughout the field: (a) registration; (b) certification; (c) Civil Service position requirements; and (d) other job specifications or qualification systems.

---

[4]"Careers in Recreation and Leisure: A Look at the Potential." *Journal of Physical Education and Recreation (Leisure Today)*, April 1979, p. 1.

Registration

Registration is the process by which professional societies screen and identify qualified practitioners in their respective fields. Hines points out that early registration programs came about chiefly because of the desire of professionals to upgrade qualifications and professional practices in recreation and parks. A report issued by the North Carolina Society in 1953 pointed out that ". . . in most of the United States, any barber can be a recreation leader, but no recreation leader can be a barber without a licence."[5] North Carolina in 1954 became the first state to initiate a registration plan for recreation administrators on a statewide basis. Societies in other states, such as California, New York, Wisconsin, Washington, Colorado and Texas, also initiated registration plans during the 1950's. Essentially, the process was one in which the society established a set of educational or experiential requirements (for example, a degree in recreation or a related field, and a certain number of years of professional experience) that applicants had to meet to become registered at a particular level. Usually, several types of positions, such as leader, supervisor and superintendent or administrator, were identified.

Because registration is a voluntary process and individuals need not be registered *by law* in order to qualify for positions, it has tended to lack force in application. However, in some cases, registration plans have involved the cooperation of state governmental agencies. For example, in 1966 the Indiana General Assembly granted the Indiana Outdoor Recreation Council the power to set standards, establish leadership criteria and formulate guidelines for local departments. The New York State Recreation and Park Society has a voluntary registration plan that was developed with the help of consultants from the New York State Division for Youth, the state Education Department, and the state Department of Civil Service. Thus, its recommended standards have had an impact on the qualifications established by these agencies.

On the national level in the United States, the National Recreation and Park Association (NRPA) has implemented a process of national registration, based on guidelines in a model registration plan approved by the NRPA Board of Trustees in 1973, through which it has reviewed and approved the plans of a number of state societies. Enforcement of this process has been carried out through NRPA's Personnel Referral Service, in which candidates registered through one of the approved state society plans are favored in the job placement process.

Since 1970, the National Therapeutic Recreation Society (NTRS), a branch of NRPA, has had a separate voluntary registration plan for individuals employed in the field of therapeutic recreation. Its standards were revised in 1977 to include the following elements:

---

[5]For a full discussion of professionalism in parks and recreation, see Richard Kraus: *Recreation and Leisure in Modern Society*. Santa Monica, California, Goodyear, 1978, Chapter 12.

Revised Registration Standards of National Therapeutic Recreation Society[6]

1. **Therapeutic Recreation Assistant**

    a. Two years of successful full-time paid experience in the therapeutic recreation field.
    OR
    b. Two hundred clock hours in-service training in the therapeutic recreation field.
    OR
    c. A combination of "a" and "b" may be substituted.

2. **Therapeutic Recreation Technician I**

    a. Successful completion of NTRS-approved, 750-hour training program for Therapeutic Recreation Technician I.

3. **Therapeutic Recreation Technician II**

    a. Associate of arts degree from an accredited college or university with an emphasis in therapeutic recreation.
    OR
    b. Certification or other proof of satisfactory completion of two academic years of study in recreation with an emphasis or option in therapeutic recreation and current employment in therapeutic recreation.
    OR
    c. Certification or other proof of satisfactory completion of two academic years of study in a skills area (Physical Education, Drama, Arts and Crafts, Art, Dance, Music) and two years of professional work experience in therapeutic recreation.

4. **Therapeutic Recreation Leader**

    a. (Provisional and nonrenewable) Baccalaureate degree from an accredited college or university with a major in recreation.
    OR
    b. (Registered) Baccalaureate degree from an accredited college or university with a major in therapeutic recreation or a major in recreation and an option or emphasis in therapeutic recreation.
    OR
    c. (Registered) Baccalaureate degree from an accredited college or university with a major in recreation and one year of professional work experience in therapeutic recreation.

---

[6]See *Therapeutic Recreation Journal*, First Quarter 1978, pp. 59–60.

5. Therapeutic Recreation Specialist

a. Master's degree from an accredited college or university with a major in therapeutic recreation, or a major in recreation *and* an option or emphasis in therapeutic recreation.

OR

b. Master's degree from an accredited college or university with a major in recreation and one year of professional work experience in therapeutic recreation.

OR

c. Baccalaureate degree from an accredited college or university with a major in therapeutic recreation, or a major in recreation *and* an option or emphasis in therapeutic recreation and three years of professional work experience in therapeutic recreation.

OR

d. Baccalaureate degree from an accredited college or university with a major in recreation and four years of professional work experience in therapeutic recreation.

6. Master Therapeutic Recreation Specialist

a. Master's degree from an accredited college or university with a major in therapeutic recreation, or a major in recreation *and* an option or emphasis in therapeutic recreation, plus two years of professional work experience in therapeutic recreation.

OR

b. Master's degree from an accredited college or university with a major in recreation and three years of professional work experience in therapeutic recreation.

OR

c. Baccalaureate degree from an accredited college or university with a major in therapeutic recreation or a major in recreation *and* an option or emphasis in therapeutic recreation and six graduate credits in therapeutic recreation, plus five years of professional work experience in therapeutic recreation.

OR

d. Baccalaureate degree from an accredited college or university with a major in recreation and 12 graduate credits in therapeutic recreation, plus six years of professional work experience in therapeutic recreation.

By the late 1970's, about 3,000 individuals had become registered in one of the NTRS categories. A number of state departments of mental health and other agencies that supervise nursing homes or other long-term care facilities have stipulated that individuals working at given job levels must possess qualifications similar to the NTRS standards, or must actually be registered with NTRS, to be employed in patient-care programs.

However, registration plans provide effective means of screening personnel only for those public or voluntary agencies that are willing to adopt or respect the plans.

Certification

Certification consists of a formal process by which an application for entry into a profession is reviewed and approved. In such fields as medicine, law, accounting and occupational therapy, it is customary for state certifying boards to attest to the certification of candidates within the field. [Certification ✗ may be based on the candidates' having completed a required course of study in an accredited institution, or on their passing an examination developed with the assistance of the major professional organization in the state, or both.] It is usually based on such criteria as the candidate's education, experience, performance on written and oral tests, and personal recommendations.

Once an individual is certified in a given field, he or she is normally "licensed" to practice anywhere within the certifying state or in other states that have reciprocal arrangements with that state. In the field of recreation and parks, only a few states, such as New Jersey and Georgia, have established by legislation formal certification procedures used to identify qualified community recreation and park professionals on a statewide basis. Such plans are extremely flexible in that they permit the substitution of years of experience in the field for college training. This is done through "grandfather clauses," which allows persons already working in the field to become certified on the basis of their experience. During the first few years after Georgia enacted a recreation certification law in 1968, 136 professionals were certified as Administrators, with 128 of these qualifying under the "grandfather clause."

In Canada, a somewhat similar situation prevails. In the province of Ontario, for example, the State Department of Education issued a regulation in 1971 that clearly defined the requirements for Muncipal Recreation Directors' Certificates. This regulation outlined five tracks through which individuals might qualify for an Interim Municipal Recreation Certificate, based on various combinations of degree programs, in-service training courses, and professional experience. However, advertisements of job openings in professional recreation and park journals in Canada suggest the "preference will be given" to those holding the Permanent Municipal Recreation Directors' Certificate, not that this certificate is required of all candidates.

Within the field of therapeutic recreation service, only one state, Utah, has been successful in passing a law restricting the practice of "recreation therapy" to professionally certified personnel. Efforts have been made to pass a similar law in California, thus far without success.

Civil Service

Within a wide range of government departments—including not only municipal recreation and park departments but also federal, state and local outdoor recreation and therapeutic or social service agencies—the most common means of screening individuals for employment is through Civil Service requirements. Civil Service refers to the governmental personnel structure that attempts to provide a politically neutral system of employment under which individuals are hired because of their formal qualifications rather than because of political patronage or favoritism. Operating on all levels of government, Civil Service involves a complicated job classification system and a detailed procedure for appointments, probation, promotions, separation and personnel benefits and rights.

On the federal level, full-time professional employees in such agencies as the National Park Service or the Veterans Administration are normally part of the federal Civil Service system. Similarly, all state employees (with the exception of upper-echelon administrators and part-time or seasonal workers) in hospitals, penal institutions, recreation and park departments, and other agencies are Civil Service employees.

On the local level, Civil Service Boards (often operating under the supervision of State Civil Service Commissions) control most government hiring in counties, towns, cities and villages through what is commonly known as the "career service" or "competitive service." Those not subject to merit system regulations include elected officials, persons appointed to special commissions or boards, the heads of departments and, sometimes, individuals working under special contracts. Essentially three forms of classified service are found in most cities and towns:

Competitive Class.   All positions filled through competitive examination fall into this class, which covers the majority of full-time recreation and park employees.

Noncompetitive Class.   Positions with definite requirements, but for which competitive written examinations would not be practical, are placed in this class. Such factors as the candidate's education, work history or armed forces record may be evaluated, and specific skills may be tested.

Labor Class.   This includes unskilled labor positions for which there may be no educational or competency requirements other than sound health or good physical condition.

Examinations

Examinations, which are used in competitive class position selection, are usually of two types: *open* examinations, which any qualified candidate may take, and *closed* examinations, which are usually for promotional purposes for candidates already employed in the department. They may involve assessment of written, oral or skills competencies.

Written Examinations. These measure the individual's general knowledge of the field and his or her ability to perform in a specific area of service, and include questions having to do with recreation philosophy, program development, community and public relations, administrative methods, leadership, safety and first aid, current issues and trends, and similar concerns. They may include both objective (short-answer) and subjective (essay) questions. Often, they are prepared on a state wide level, although they may be actually given by a county Civil Service Commission; some large cities may make up their own written examinations.

Oral Examinations. These tend to be used for promotional appointments to higher levels of responsibility. Candidates are assessed through interviews with panels of interviewers or judges who are given several criteria on which to rate each candidate. Such examinations (which usually involve questions measuring knowledge of the field or problem-solving ability) are not the same as job interviews, which tend to be used chiefly as get-acquainted sessions that allow hiring officials or key administrators to make personal judgments about applicants.

Skills Tests. In some departments, emphasis may also be given to performance tests in such skills areas as arts and crafts, sports, dance or music to determine the leadership ability of program specialists in these areas.

Position Classification System

The entire personnel selection process in government agencies is based on the establishment of a *position classification system.* This involves organizing positions into groups or classes on the basis of the specific duties or responsibilities of each position and on the qualifications or requirements that must be met by those applying for it. A position classification system includes the following basic elements: position, class and series.

Position refers to a specific job "slot" that normally would have a descriptive title and place in the personnel structure of an organization. It must be differentiated from the person who holds it in that the person may leave or change, while the position normally remains.

Class refers to a group of positions, which may be found in different departments, that have roughly comparable responsibilities and qualifications and are subject to the same policies with respect to selection, pay, promotion and similar personnel matters.

Series describes a vertical classification of employees within a common specialization who have a gradation of skills, education or seniority, so that they have different salary ranges and status levels. Thus, a Recreation Therapist Series might run from Recreation Therapist Trainee to Senior Recreation Therapist.

Usually a position classification defines and names each position, places it within a class or series, assigns it a salary range, and outlines its responsibilities and required qualifications or credentials in a written job description. The essential purposes of position classification systems are to (a) help determine what the functions of workers throughout an organization are and to organize work assignments effectively; (b) provide a logical basis for developing appropriate pay levels by developing whole classes of comparable positions; (c) reduce a wide variety of occupations or specializations to manageable proportions, so recruitment, testing, hiring and promotion of personnel can be done efficiently and on the basis of specific criteria; and (d) provide a basis for determining orientation and job-training needs.

In developing a Civil Service system, career entrance and promotion must be considered. Typically, lower-level positions are regarded as "entry-level" jobs. In many large municipal departments, a candidate may enter only at the lowest level of the "leader" series and must then move up through the various grades by seniority, favorable personnel evaluations or promotional examinations. In many cases, advancement through the ranks of a single series is fairly automatic, but advancement to a new series requires a more involved process of application and review.

Examples of Job Descriptions in Government Agencies

To illustrate the types of positions that are offered in state, local and other specialized government agencies operating within a Civil Service framework, the following examples of job descriptions are offered.

Example I

Agency.   State of Idaho, Department of Parks and Recreation

Title of Position.   Park Manager

Definition

Under direction, to be responsible for the operation of an individual park within the state park system, to plan, organize, and supervise park employees in maintenance and construction work, and to do related work as required.

Examples of Work Performed

Plans, directs, and participates in the maintenance of park and recreation structures, facilities and areas including public kitchens, bath houses, public docks, campgrounds and trailer camps; plans and schedules the placing of men and machinery to perform a definite program of work; orders materials necessary; recommends the transferring or hiring of workers; recommends improvements in operating procedures; supervises the construction and maintenance of roads, boat ramps, recreational facilities and picnic areas; supervises the maintenance of the park lighting and water systems for building and recreational facilities; supervises the mowing of large areas in the park; assigns, supervises and trains staff in department policies and procedures; provides information for the public on the park and its uses, and assists visitors as necessary; maintains records and prepares reports.

Minimum Qualifications

EDUCATION AND EXPERIENCE

Graduation from an accredited four-year college in park management, forestry, recreation or closely related field, and one year's full-time paid experience in park management or general construction work.

KNOWLEDGES AND ABILITIES

1. Knowledge of the layout and construction of parks and their facilities.
2. Knowledge of the standards and desirable methods of providing parks and park facilities.
3. Knowledge of the principles, practices and equipment used in parks and parks facilities construction and maintenance.
4. Knowledge of the proper seasonal timing of the activities for which he is responsible.
5. Ability to lay out, direct and supervise the work of crews performing semi-skilled and unskilled work, and to obtain efficient results.
6. Ability to get along well with the general public, park visitors, and recreation participants.

Example II

Agency.   Macon-Bibb County Recreation Department, Macon, Georgia

Title of Position.   Recreation Superintendent

Duties

Assist and advise the governing authority on formulation of policies and basic procedures.

Execute policies, rules and regulations of the governing authority.

Plan, promote, organize, supervise, develop and direct through executive, administrative and supervisory staff, program, services and operations.

Instigate surveys and studies of recreation and park needs, and interpret them to the governing authority and to the people.

Formulate (with cooperation of governing authority and staff) long-range plans for acquiring, designing, developing and constructing parks, areas and facilities to meet the needs and demands of the people.

Administer total services assigned to the park and recreation department.

Develop and organize department in such a manner that the working relationships between its personnel, and those of other departments are maintained at a high level of mutual understanding.

Interpret to all other department heads the needs and responsibilities of his department.

Encourage and lead staff in full cooperation with all community agencies.

Work closely with all administrative and supervisory staff in directing and guiding them to a cooperative realization of department goals and objectives.

Hold membership with and participate in the programs offered by national, state, regional and local professional recreation and park organizations, encouraging staff to do the same.

Select, supervise and direct training of staff, encouraging and leading them in the acquisition of new knowledge and the development of new skills for an efficient performance of responsibilities by a program of in-service training and participation in workshops and institutes.

Prepare budgets, supervise expenditure of funds and be responsible for accurate accounting of funds.

Qualifications

A degree from an accredited college or university in Recreation Leadership or Park Management, or a master's degree in Recreation and Park Administration.

A minimum of five years' experience as an executive in a recreation and park department with previous experience and/or training in related fields such as landscape architecture, physical education, horticulture, engineering, political science, finance, land and personnel management.

A good character, with acceptable personal qualities and the ability to command respect and cooperation from a staff of specialists, members of the governing authority and the public at large.

A thorough knowledge of the philosophy of recreation; appreciation of the activities which make up the community recreation program; ability to administer efficiently the areas and facilities constituting a recreation system; capacity for cooperating with and interpreting recreation to city authorities, civic clubs, private agencies and the public; understanding of the problems of the community with respect to recreation; ability to enlist the best efforts of a staff of employees; and other qualities that characterize the promoter, organizer and executive.

Minimum age should be 30 years.

Example III

Agency.   Flint, Michigan, Recreation and Park Board

Title of Position.   Senior Recreation Leader

General Statement of Duties

Position title covers the following functional assignments; Supervisor of Boys' and Men's Activities; Supervisor of Girls' and Women's Activities; Supervisor of Senior Citizens' Activities; Recreation Activity Specialist; Swimming Pool Manager; Playground Area Supervisor.

Supervises and participates in planning, scheduling, organizing and directing recreational and social activities in the various municipal recreation centers; instructs assistants in phase of recreation work; performs related work as required.

Supervision Received

Works under the supervision of a Park Board recreation employee of higher grade who suggests programs and reviews work for effectiveness.

Supervision Exercised

Exercises working supervision over a few employees engaged in conducting recreational activities.

Examples of Duties

1. Supervises and coordinates a group of subordinates engaged in conducting individual and team sports and athletic activities of all types.
2. Demonstrates and explains techniques, procedures, materials, equipment and supplies used in dramatics, nature and outing, dancing, arts and crafts, music and social recreation.
3. Organizes, promotes, leads, teaches and conducts a comprehensive program of games, athletics, bowling, aquatics and sport activities for all appropriate ages and for both sexes.
4. Consults with individuals and community groups to determine their recreational interests, needs and desires.
5. Leads a well-rounded program of diversified activities suited to the needs and interests of people who attend the center.
6. Organizes, leads and acts as an advisor to clubs and other community groups.
7. Assists in organizing, promoting and directing tournaments, shows, pageants, socials, exhibits and special events.
8. Visits various playgrounds or community centers to inspect grounds and equipment; reviews work of subordinates and makes suggestions for improvements.
9. Maintains discipline and safety; administers simple first aid.
10. Instructs new recreation assistants in work or various phases of specialized activities.
11. Participates in staff conferences concerning the recreation program; makes oral and written reports; acts as liaison officer for superior.

Minimum Entrance Requirements

Graduation from a college with a bachelor's degree in Recreation or related field of education, *or* equivalent to two years of college, majoring in Recreation or related educational fields, and two years of experience in a recreational position.

Thorough knowledge of the more common physical and social activities, or one of the more specialized activities such as dramatics, manual arts or crafts, folk dancing, music or rhythm.

Knowledge of the purposes and aims of organized recreational work.

Ability to follow written and oral instructions.

Ability to maintain cooperative working relationships with children and the general public.

Ability to meet the physical, mental and visual standards of the job.

Ability and willingness to work in a manner that will not needlessly endanger the safety of one's self, other persons and equipment.

Example IV

Agency.   State of Indiana, Department of Mental Health

Title of Position: Recreational Director XII

General Statement of Duties

Responsible administrative work directing the recreation program in a state institution. Employee is responsible for planning, organizing and co-ordinating program activities, and for the supervision of lower-level employees working in the program. Work is performed independently to secure desired results, but matters of policy are discussed with the Coordinator of Activity Therapy or an adminstrative official.

Examples of Work (Illustrative Only)

Plans, directs, coordinates and integrates recreational activities to meet specific needs, interests and abilities of patients or inmates.

Supervises preparation of budget estimates for the recreation program, personnel, equipment, supplies and facilities.

Plans, assigns and supervises the work of recreation personnel in specific program areas and activities to insure a well-rounded, effective recreation program.

Directs the maintenance and compilation of records and statistics of the recreation program and reviews data.

Conducts studies and experiments for developing new recreation techniques.

In the Department of Mental Health, maintains contact with appropriate medical authorities in order to develop and conduct medically approved plans and policies which will meet the needs, capabilities and interest of the patients.

Assists in the general rehabilitation of patients or inmates; performs related work as assigned.

Requirements for Work

Extensive knowledge of the principles and practices of institutional recreation programs.

Extensive knowledge of the rules and regulations of a variety of sports, games and other recreation activities.

Working knowledge of the principles and practices of recreation administration.

Ability to plan, assign and supervise the work of others engaged in a recreation program.

Ability to adapt recreation policies, procedures, plans, methods, tools and techniques to specific situations.

Ability to establish and maintain harmonious relationships with patients or inmates of a state institution.

Minimum Experience and Educational Requirements

A master's degree in hospital recreation, recreation in rehabilitation or recreational therapy, and one year of full-time paid experience in recreation; or a master's degree in recreation, and two years of full-time paid experience in recreation. In non-mental institutions, physical education is an acceptable field of education and experience.

It is obvious that these recreation and park positions in public agencies vary considerably. The functions are extremely diverse and reflect the wide range of specializations in this field. Typically, a medium-sized city would have leadership and supervisory personnel assigned to such specialties as (a) program areas, such as arts and crafts, music, aquatics, social and cultural activities, the aging or the physically or mentally disabled; (b) various types of facilities, such as parks and playgrounds, nature centers, sports complexes or community centers; (c) maintenance, such as tree crew foremen, maintenance engineers, construction foremen, custodians or security supervisors; (d) administrative functions related to personnel direction, fiscal management and a variety of other functions.

Again, in terms of education and experience requirements, no single system prevails. Some departments—particularly in the field of therapeutic recreation—maintain a strict requirement for specialized college degrees in the field. Others, including many municipal and county park departments, are prepared to accept a high school diploma and appropriate experience as adequate preparation for a position of considerable responsibility. A typical pattern is to balance the educational requirement with appropriate amounts of full-time, paid experience in recreation. In some cases, such experience is equated, year for year, with study.

Effectiveness of Civil Service Procedures

Since Civil Service represents the most common mechanism for screening personnel who seek to enter the field of governmental service in recreation and parks, it is appropriate to question its effectiveness. While it has the potential for developing a true merit system of well-qualified recreation and park personnel, it tends to have the following weaknesses:

1. Within geographical regions, there is often a lack of uniform job titles, descriptions, qualifications and pay scales for comparable positions. Counties, cities and townships frequently employ individuals doing essentially the same job under widely varying titles, position descriptions and salaries. In addition, the existing Civil Service personnel standards are frequently below the standards recommended by professional recreation and park societies.

2. Educational requirements for specific positions are often so flexible

or poorly enforced that a large proportion of Civil Service positions in recreation and parks continue to be filled by candidates who have not had specialized training in this field. Many agencies require that candidates have a degree in recreation, parks or a "closely allied field," which may be as remote from leisure services as history, physics or a foreign language.

3. The examination process tends to be ineffective when it includes questions that are not relevant to the field of recreation and parks. In some cases, examinations concentrate too narrowly on specific skills or knowledge of activities, or on knowledge of English or other areas of general information, rather than on the important professional abilities that recreation and park professionals should possess.

4. One of the most vexing problems related to Civil Service personnel selection in recreation and parks stems from the fact that although this system was intended to do away with patronage, political favoritism continues to influence many local government jurisdictions. When competitive examinations are not required, it is common practice for seasonal, part-time or specialist jobs to be awarded to "party faithful" or to persons with appropriate contacts. High-level administrative jobs tend too often to be assigned to individuals with limited background in the field.

It should be noted that these criticisms do not apply to *all* Civil Service systems. In some, the government merit system operates as an excellent means of attracting, screening and holding well-qualified professionals.

Job Specifications in Other Settings

In other settings, such as voluntary agencies or private or commercial organizations that employ recreation personnel, the hiring procedure tends to be somewhat simpler and more flexible than in government. However, many organizations, particularly those that are part of nationwide federations that are concerned with maintaining a high level of staff competence, do prepare specific job descriptions on various levels or in different specializations. Customarily, they may either recommend or require that local agencies hire individuals for specific positions according to certain criteria.

In those organizations that are influenced strongly by policies of their national headquarters, a centralized national staff develops guidelines for professional positions, as well as personnel training procedures and materials.

Personnel Policies of YMCA

To illustrate, approximately 6,000 registered professional staff persons are employed by the 1,800 Young Men's Christian Associations in the United States. Each year, about 500 persons enter YMCA service as professional workers. They enter as "staff associates" or "directors" for a two-year period during which they and the employing agency test their aptitude for YMCA work. Positions are usually classified according to such titles as General Director, Youth Director, Physical Education Director, Program Director, Executive Director, Youth Outreach Director, Membership Director, and Business Director.

In addition to general responsibilities that are outlined for all professional workers in the YMCA, each specific title has a set of assigned functions. For example, the Y Youth Director has the following responsibilities:

> Assists boys and girls through organized groups and informal education to develop attitudes and social habits consistent with Christian principles.
>
> Integrates programs and activities with efforts of parents, school, church and community leaders.
>
> Guides the Youth Program Committee of the Board of Directors in formulating policies for youth program.
>
> Identifies youth needs and organizes group programs to meet these.
>
> Enlists, trains and supervises volunteer group leaders.
>
> Interprets YMCA to youth members, parents and public.
>
> Manages business aspects of youth department.
>
> Generally responsible for day camp and sometimes for resident camp programs.
>
> Maintains adequate records and makes reports.

The National Council of the YMCA recommends that YMCA staff members have the following qualifications: (a) commitment to YMCA purpose and goals; (b) integrity of character and interest in working with young people for their personal and social growth; (c) sound health; and (d) an undergraduate degree or equivalent, preferably in one of the social or behavioral sciences, such as psychology, economics, sociology, government or education, or in liberal arts generally. In addition, professional training of YMCA staff directors should include such areas as leadership of informal groups; counseling and guidance; administration of social and religious agencies; leadership supervision and training; and an understanding of the history, objectives, programs and methods of the YMCA.

Personnel Policies of Boys' Clubs of America

Similarly, the Boys' Clubs of America has an extremely flexible personnel hiring policy for professional staff workers. To be certified as a full-time administrator in a Boys' Club, one must meet the following criteria: (a) education, with a degree from an accredited four-year college; (b) satisfactory performance in two years of program leadership or administrative work in a Boys' Club or as a member of the National Staff; and (c) a total of ten training credits in conferences and training sessions sponsored by the Regional or National Manpower Development Committees of the Boys' Clubs of America or other authorized training institutions.

Hiring policies in many voluntary community organizations that serve special populations are equally flexible. Many such agencies employ specialists in therapeutic recreation. For example, the Association for the Help of Retarded Children in New York City has a Group Work, Recreation and Camping Program in which individuals are employed on such levels as Director, Supervisor, Group Leader, Assistant Group Leader, Children's Program Leader, or Trip Leader. Responsibilities of the Supervisor are stated as follows:

General Statement

Under the direction of the Director of Group Work, Recreation and Camping Services, assist with the planning and conduct of recreation and camping services for mentally retarded persons primarily by working directly with groups of mentally retarded persons on a long-term and short-term demonstration basis.

Examples of Work

1. Assist with the work involved in planning, organizing and carrying out the department's total recreation services.
2. When so assigned, provide direct recreation leadership for groups of children and adults.
3. Teach recreation and leisure-time skills on both a group and an individual basis.
4. Supervise volunteers and other part-time personnel assigned to program.
5. Assist with supervision and in-service training of total staff.
6. Maintain required records and reports.

In such organizations, although there is a trend toward employing new workers who have studied in specialized college degree programs in therapeutic recreation service, it is still often possible for individuals without such backgrounds to find leadership positions. In general, private and commercial recreation agencies are even less likely to have fixed educational or experience requirements for positions or to have rigid hiring expectations or procedures. They are usually not as concerned with formal credentials as they are with demonstrated ability to do the job, as determined through past experience or references.

OVERVIEW OF PRESENT STANDARDS IN RECREATION AND PARK SERVICE

The illustrations of job responsibilities and qualifications that have just been cited present an extremely diverse picture, in which some organizations maintain a standard of requiring employees to have appropriate educational background in recreation and parks, while others have almost no formal expectation. This picture was borne out by a survey of public recreation and park personnel in the United States carried out in the late 1970's.[7] Henkel and Godbey found that only a limited proportion of full-time staff members held degrees in the field. In an editorial written for *Parks and Recreation,* Henkel described the challenge facing the field:

> Park, recreation, and leisure service practitioners seek professionalism, but appear reluctant to make the necessary commitments for it . . . .
>
> We have a "hodge-podge" of state registration and certification plans that, until recently, have had little commonality. We have a field in which anyone can, and does, practice. . . . Even when positions not requiring higher education are eliminated, only 40 percent of the personnel employed in remaining positions have training in parks and recreation.
>
> It is rare to see a job specification requiring or even suggesting registration and certification, except in therapeutic recreation. Most park and recreation personnel employed in the armed forces, correctional institutions, hospitals, and college unions, to name a few, are strangers in paradise and often a frill. Commercial recreation entrepreneurs, with rare exception [do not consider] the employment of a park and recreation graduate. . . .[8]

Part of the problem, Henkel suggests, is that employers shy away from national standards in order to protect their own local interests, and that they are unwilling to support stronger efforts to upgrade the quality of recreation and park personnel. He concludes, "We have few standards we are willing to recognize and stick by. So, why worry about standards and professionalism?"

The question is a very real one for the college student who is majoring in recreation, parks or leisure studies. As in many other areas of human service today, where budget constraints are in effect, the job market is extremely competitive. It is made more so by the fact that many hiring agencies do not require that applicants have special training in recreation or be registered by appropriate professional societies. It should be a prime obligation of all practitioners in the field to promote and support higher standards for recreation personnel and to support such criteria in their own hiring efforts.

Employment Opportunities as a Concern. In the mid-1970's, many college recreation and park educators began to take a serious look at the job market in their field. It was apparent that the supply–demand balance in leisure services had shifted, and there was a potential oversupply of recreation and park graduates for a limited number of job openings.

It should be made clear that well-qualified graduates are still able to obtain promising positions. A number of colleges and universities have carried out surveys of their recent graduates and have found that most have

---

[7]Donald Henkel and Geoffrey Godbey: *Parks, Recreation and Leisure Services Employment in the Public Sector: Status.* Arlington, Virginia, National Recreation and Park Association, 1977.
[8]Donald Henkel: "Standards: Who Needs Them?" Editorial. *Parks and Recreation,* November 1978, p. 17.

continued to find work in the field.[9] In a regional survey of future job opportunities in northern California, Weiskopf and Negley found a generally optimistic picture, with a wide variety of full-time, seasonal and part-time positions available in recreation and park agencies of all types, including voluntary, private, commercial and therapeutic departments.[10]

However, the northern California survey also recommended that college and university curricula be strengthened and keyed more directly to changing patterns of career opportunity, and that fuller efforts be made to expand the job market for recreation and leisure service graduates.

Any examination of recreation leadership and supervision should include a realistic presentation of potential career directions and what students should do to equip themselves most effectively for work in the field upon graduation. The concluding section of this chapter therefore deals with the responsibilities of colleges and universities, practitioners and professional organizations, and students themselves. Each of these groups has a distinct stake in the process of interaction between the educational institution and professional work in the field; ultimately, all benefit when strong programs of pre-professional and ongoing professional development are established.

RESPONSIBILITIES OF COLLEGES AND UNIVERSITIES

Colleges and universities with recreation and park majors must develop or revise their curricula so that they are closely linked to societal needs, and must enhance their programs so that they have solid academic strength as well as practical content. Smith and Williams have outlined a set of excellent guidelines for educational institutions in this field. It is their responsibility to

1. Create viable courses, curricula, and learning experiences for students, based on current employment needs and developing trends in leisure service.
2. Be involved in the community and with practitioners, to insure that their courses and curricula are geared to existing practices in the field.
3. Act as an effective screening agent for the leisure services profession by counseling and advising students in career orientation, professional growth, and personal development.
4. Establish, when appropriate, certificate and other short-term programs in specialized areas of the field to meet local employment needs.
5. Work actively within local areas to create non-traditional em-

---

[9]Karen Loupassakis, John Scott and Cathy Ward: "A Study of Recreation Graduates." Upper Montclair, New Jersey, Montclair State College, 1979.
[10]Donald C. Weiskopf and James P. Negley: *1978 Manpower Study of the Sacramento Area and Northern California Region.* Sacramento, California, American River College, 1978.

ployment opportunities for graduates. Be visible, articulate and politically astute advocates for professional development in recreation and parks at all times.

6. Carry out follow-up surveys of graduates in order to measure the college's success in the placement process.

7. Actively assist students in job development skills and placement; advise them as to possible limitations in job advancement and remuneration, discrimination and job satisfaction in relation to their educational background.

8. Develop at the institution a comprehensive system of leisure resources on employment and career opportunities, including the NRPA *Employ* publication, job interview techniques, résumé writing, and other needed skills.

9. Expose students to non-traditional employment opportunities, such as travel agencies, recreation land and equipment sales, industrial recreation, recreation/park maintenance, and private facility management, through course work and practical experience.

10. Infuse leisure education into curricular experiences to enable students to strengthen their personal philosophies of leisure.[11]

It is essential that each institution develop its own special expertise and curriculum emphasis based on its unique resources, tradition, faculty strengths and regional factors. Similarly, it should strive to meet appropriate professional standards, as outlined in national accreditation criteria, and should be sure that the level of preparation and academic content it is providing is consistent with the degrees it offers.

It is extremely important, as Smith and Williams point out, for recreation educators to maintain close and positive professional relationships with practitioners in the field. They should serve them in a variety of ways, by assisting with planning and research studies and program evaluations, and in other consultant and training roles. However, this should also be a two-way process, with practitioners serving colleges as speakers, part-time instructors, field-work supervisors or members of curriculum advisory committees. Only if there is close communication between the two groups, with practitioners both respecting and contributing to the educational process, will it be possible to establish and enforce higher educational standards and requirements for hiring in the field.

Similarly, it will not be enough for college recreation departments to establish new curricula in such non-traditional fields as commercial recreation, and expect that their graduates will then automatically be hired within this growing and diverse field. They will have to develop close ties with commercial recreation organizations by having representatives from such groups serve on advisory councils and as guest speakers, doing research and planning for and with them, and placing field-work students in such settings.

---

[11]Larry Smith and Larry R. Williams: Presentation at 1977 SPRE Institute on Community College Curricula, Las Vegas, Nevada.

This will encourage the commercial organizations to identify with the organized recreation movement and to employ individuals specially trained in this field.

Finally, college and university recreation, park and leisure studies must continue to upgrade themselves in two ways: (a) by enriching their own academic status and gaining the respect of other disciplines through full participation in the scholarly life of the institution, and (b) by improving the quality of their performance as far as the special needs of recreation education are concerned. Success in this area can best be measured by the evaluation criteria that have been developed through the NRPA accreditation process that is being used to review degree programs throughout the United States and identify those that meet professionally established standards.

All these efforts, taken together, will be extremely helpful to colleges that wish to strengthen their curricula and professional ties. This in turn will assist students in obtaining full-time positions after graduation and help those already employed to further their career potential within a diversified field of leisure service.

RESPONSIBILITIES OF PRACTITIONERS AND PROFESSIONAL ORGANIZATIONS

A second important responsibility for strengthening recreation and parks as a career field belongs to the practitioners who work in the field and to their major professional organizations. As Henkel has indicated, professionals themselves are too often reluctant to support strong professional standards. Increasingly, however, leading recreation and park practitioners are recognizing that the field is undercut by the lack of adequate employment standards, and they are working closely with leading educational institutions to remedy this situation.

Smith and Williams present a number of recommendations in this area. In their view, professionals must

1. Actively seek qualified leisure service graduates for entry-level positions. They must also develop clear job descriptions and expectations for agency personnel, and recruit effectively through professional media and conferences for qualified staff members.
2. Cooperate closely with local colleges in establishing meaningful on-the-job work experiences through internships, field work, field trips and part-time and full-time employment opportunities.
3. Support the concepts of registration and certification for recreation and park workers through legislative action at the state level. Support and assist in the accreditation process nationally.
4. Work with local department administrators and Civil Service departments to upgrade personnel standards for entry-level or pro-

motional appointments and to limit the use of "allied field" degree options as educational requirements.

5. Encourage present employees who lack formal educational background in recreation and parks to enroll in college course work on a continuing education basis. Encourage all employees to take part in professionally sponsored or in-house in-service education activities, including regional workshops and conferences.

6. Expand the concept of part-time roles and flexible work schedules for agency personnel in a variety of employment sectors.

7. Promote interagency cooperation, i.e., school, youth-serving agencies and the private sector, to strengthen the concept of professionalism and promote employment of trained recreation and park personnel.

8. Serve as successful role models, e.g., as advisory committee members, instructors, speakers, field-work supervisors and advisors, for recreation and park curricula.[12]

In addition to such efforts, practitioners must work closely with their professional organizations to strengthen and expand employment opportunities and standards. Typically, they may serve on accreditation visiting teams or as speakers at legislative hearings, and they may publicize their job openings through NRPA's *Employ* or at conference "job marts." In addition, they should participate actively in continuing education programs sponsored by professional organizations and educational institutions, which serve those who are already at work in the field.

Continuing Education Programs. As part of its general program of field service, the National Recreation and Park Association has organized many special workshops for recreation and park personnel, most frequently on the administrative level. Typically, such workshops and institutes are carried out in cooperation with leading colleges or universities, using their staff resources and facilities. Among the leading programs presented in the past have been the *Indiana University Executive Development Program*, a series of two one-week sessions held a year apart, jointly sponsored by the University's Department of Recreation and Park Administration and its Graduate School of Business; the *North Carolina State University Revenue Sources Management School,* also consisting of two one-week sessions held a year apart at Oglebay Park, West Virginia; and the *Michigan State University Park and Recreation Law Enforcement Institute*, co-sponsored by the American Park and Recreation Society (a branch of NRPA), the University's Department of Park and Recreation Resources, and the University's School of Criminal Justice. In the field of therapeutic recreation, the *Therapeutic Recreation Management School,* co-sponsored by the University of Maryland's recreation department and Oglebay Park, West Virginia, has been outstanding in providing formal continuing education opportunities for persons already employed in the field.

---

[12]*Ibid.*

Such workshops, designed to promote both general executive development and expertise within specific areas of professional concern, are based on the following conviction, as expressed by Henkel, manager of the NRPA Office of Education and Professional Services:

> It is said that education should be a continuous and lifelong process—a process that requires not only the acquisition of basic skills and knowledge gained in the classroom, but practical application as well. Increasingly, the concept of formal education for youth and practical application for adults is blurring into a continuum of alternating experiences, especially for professionals.[13]

Apart from their value in helping to improve professional practices, such workshops are extremely important in that they help to persuade many leading practitioners—who may not have had earlier academic training in the field—of the value of such specialized training. As an example of cooperation between colleges and universities and professional organizations, they help to unite the field in the promotion of a higher level of service delivery and hiring standards.

In recent years, the National Recreation and Park Association has expanded the number and variety of its professional activities and in-service or continuing education programs. In 1980, for example, its professional development program included five regional conferences, two national forums on Innovative Recreation Programming, a national workshop on Computers in Recreation and Parks, two Revenue Sources Management Schools, three Park Planning and Maintenance Schools, two Executive Development Programs, and one Arts Management School.[14]

RESPONSIBILITIES OF STUDENTS

Finally, recognizing that the job market in recreation and parks is much more competitive today than it was a decade ago, majors in this field should assume a large level of responsibility for insuring their own success. First, they should recognize that the fact that the field exists and a college is willing to accept them as major students in leisure services does not mean that the field is right for them. Thus, at the very outset, they should ask themselves whether they really understand the field and its demands, and whether they have had enough background in the field to have a reasonable degree of assurance that they are suited to it in terms of personal qualities, skills and attitudes.

Next, they should study the job market intensively at an early point and throughout their college careers in order to prepare and develop themselves as fully as possible for later full-time placement and job advancement. Smith and Williams list the following guidelines that should be helpful to all student majors in recreation and parks:

1. Establish short- and long-range career objectives based on per-

---

[13]Donald Henkel: "NRPA Continuing Education." *Parks and Recreation*, August 1972, pp. 26–31.
[14]Events listed in *Parks and Recreation*, December 1979, p. 22.

sonal needs, skills and objectives. Work closely with faculty members, counselors and career development centers in doing this.

2. Expect a competitive job market, in which quality and quantity of applicants are the norms, for full-time, year-round employment in the field.

3. Be willing to work part-time or seasonally to gain as much valuable practical experience as possible to complement the formal educational experience. Recognize that such involvements often lead to full-time positions by providing both useful contacts and the specific amounts of paid experience that some positions require in the candidate's background.

4. Expect and be willing to work odd hours, weekends, evenings, and holidays, when recreation programs are often carried on.

5. Investigate all avenues (both traditional and non-traditional) of the recreation field at an early point in the college program.

6. While in college, enhance employability by developing and practicing those skills (communication, leadership, good work habits) that are needed for success on the job. If possible, develop specialized skills, such as public relations techniques, that might be of special interest to potential employers.

7. Attain meaningful volunteer experiences in the community, business world or on campus to develop personal strengths.

8. Become involved in local, state and national professional recreation and park activities, and attend professional development workshops or conferences.

9. Study specific requirements that may exist for positions within the federal or state Civil Service system or within major national federations that employ recreation personnel, and take preliminary steps to insure eligibility for entry-level positions.[15]

It is particularly important for students to recognize the value of the eighth guideline cited above. By joining relevant professional organizations, students receive professional publications, have the opportunity to attend conferences and special meetings, and become more fully involved in the field. They begin to have a sense of themselves as professionals and become aware of the full range of recreation programs and services that exist today. Holding offices or serving as committee members of student sections gives valuable interpersonal experience and frequently helps students get to know older professionals and work with them as part of a team.

RECREATION AS A CAREER FIELD: CONCLUDING STATEMENT

This chapter has described the development of recreation, parks and leisure services as an area of public service and professional education today. It has

---

[15]Smith and Williams, *op. cit.*

pointed out some of the real problems that leaders and supervisors face with respect to opportunities existing within a competitive market. It should be stressed that *many* fields of employment face similar problems today. The same financial factors that limit expansion of recreation and park programs also affect social work agencies, libraries, the public schools and many other human-service fields. Some educators have suggested that it would be advisable for colleges to limit the number of recreation and park majors they will admit, or for a moratorium to be placed on new curricula in the field. Apart from the difficulty that would be involved in carrying out such measures, most educators take the position that there should be no arbitrary restriction of programs.

It is generally accepted that the market for preparing recreation majors should be open, competitive and subject to students' making intelligent choices for themselves. Under such circumstances, the colleges that have the most effective programs and turn out the most highly qualified graduates who are successful in obtaining good positions in the field will prosper. Colleges with weaker programs probably will find their enrollments declining, and some will phase out their curricula in this field, as they have done in other pre-professional academic fields.

The implications of this problem are twofold: (a) colleges and universities should initiate or continue courses in recreation and parks only if they are thoroughly convinced, on the basis of careful documentation, that there is a real need for such programs in their regions; and (b) they must then make every effort, as outlined in this chapter, to equip their students with the needed skills and resources, to counsel them wisely and to assist them through the entire process of professional development and job placement.

Within this framework, one important developmental experience involves learning the nature and principles of recreational leadership and supervision. In addition to being important professional functions within the broad field of leisure service, these two areas of responsibility provide an exciting and challenging opportunity for personal involvement. Although this chapter has sought to give readers a rounded—and perhaps overly cautious—view of the field, students should also be assured that the area of human service they are preparing to enter will offer them many rich and rewarding experiences.

SUGGESTED EXAMINATION QUESTIONS OR TOPICS FOR STUDENT REPORTS

1. On the basis of information provided in this chapter and your own observation and experience, what were the key factors promoting the rapid growth in professional education in recreation and parks in the United States and Canada?
2. Select one of the three levels of higher education (two-year, four-year, or graduate curricula). Develop several guidelines (objectives and

course listing) for recreation and park curricula on this level, including the types of program options that you believe should be offered.

3. What actions should professional organizations take to upgrade and strengthen career preparation in recreation and parks?

4. Identify the level of job opportunities and hiring requirements in two or more specialized areas of recreation service, such as industrial, commercial, therapeutic or voluntary agencies, as described in the current literature.

SUGGESTED ACTION ASSIGNMENTS OR GROUP PROCESS ACTIVITIES

1. Carry out a survey of recreation and park curricula in your region that might be used for guidance to high school students seeking to enter the field.

2. Discuss and compare *registration* and *certification*. Do you believe that the profession should be moving toward either? Would you be willing to become either registered or certified, if either became a condition of employment?

3. How well do you believe your college or university's recreation curriculum measures up to the guidelines suggested by Smith and Williams? After a discussion, share your perceptions with your faculty.

4. Discuss with one or two other classmates how well you believe that you personally meet the suggested responsibilities that students have for equipping themselves for employment in the recreation field.

Principles of Recreation Leadership

Chapter Three

The previous two chapters have described the social context in which recreation leadership and supervision have developed in recent years in the United States and Canada. In addition, they have presented some of the key trends in the development of recreation and leisure services as a career field today.

This chapter examines recreation leadership in greater detail, providing a set of useful principles for its successful operation. As defined in Chapter One, leadership refers to the process of inspiring others to work together effectively in a common effort. The leader is perceived primarily as an enabler and catalyst, rather than a director or teacher. It should be stressed that leadership exists on a variety of levels, within any field of human or social service. In recreation, administrators, supervisors and face-to-face leaders all exert leadership in different ways—with participants or representatives of the public, with co-workers and with community officials, volunteers, personnel from other agencies and numerous other individuals.

EMPHASIS ON FACE-TO-FACE LEADERS

This chapter is most directly concerned with the full-time professional leader who works directly with groups in community centers, hospitals, senior centers, industrial recreation programs, playgrounds and a host of other types of settings.

Within many municipal recreation and park departments, there has been a trend away from having full-time professional leaders assigned to playgrounds or centers on a regular basis. Instead, direct leadership responsibilities tend to be carried out by part-time, seasonal or volunteer workers, while full-time professional workers operate on a higher level of supervisory or administrative responsibility. This is particularly true in recreation and park departments in smaller communities, where the relatively few regular staff members must play a managerial role, while actual programs are run by seasonal employees or part-time specialists.

However, in many other situations, such as senior centers, hospitals or voluntary youth agencies, direct program leadership continues to be a function of regular full-time employees. In this chapter, leadership is examined from four different perspectives: (a) as a professional title or role; (b) as a set of functions or tasks; (c) as a set of interpersonal behaviors; and (d) as a set of personal qualities.

Recreation Leadership as a Professional Title or Role

Just as those who work in the field of education in a direct, face-to-face service role are called "teachers," and those who provide direct medical care are known as "doctors" or "nurses," those who lead and direct recreation activities are usually called "leaders."

Typically, the title of "leader" is applied to individuals who are responsible for conducting activities in playgrounds, parks, community centers or similar leisure settings. Many Civil Service classification systems refer to the responsibility of providing direct recreation programs as the "leadership" level. Positions are given titles such as *Recreation Leader, Assistant Recreation Leader* and *Senior Recreation Leader.* Sometimes, degrees of seniority or rank are shown by titles such as *Leader I, Leader II* and *Leader III.* In some departments, leaders may be designated as *Recreation Group Worker* or *Recreation Director,* but such titles are in the minority. In other settings devoted to serving special populations, the titles *Therapeutic Recreation Worker* and *Activities Therapist* are likely to be used.

The recreation leader is commonly seen as holding an entry-level position, although in large Civil Service departments, some employees are likely to spend their entire careers at this level. Such positions should require college training in the field of recreation if they are to be regarded as fully professional. They should have clearly defined responsibilities and job-eligibility requirements, and should be part of a career ladder that provides reasonable opportunities for transfer.

Recreation Leadership as a Set of Functions or Tasks

A second way of perceiving recreation leadership is as a set of specific job-related tasks. For example, a playground leader might have such functions as

(a) planning a daily and weekly program schedule; (b) directing games of low organization, sports, arts and crafts, or music activity; (c) ordering and maintaining needed equipment and supplies; and (d) controlling the behavior of children on the playground and maintaining effective safety standards.

Similarly, a recreation therapist in a psychiatric hospital might be expected to (a) develop program activities for patients; (b) work closely with doctors, nurses and other adjunctive therapists; (c) counsel patients on their leisure needs and interests; (d) supervise volunteer workers in the department; (e) keep clinical notes on the progress of patients; and (f) take part in regular team evaluation meetings during which individual patients are reviewed.

Such functions and tasks constitute the act of leadership within any specific area of recreation service. Technical competence in carrying out these functions is essential for the effective leader. In some situations, leaders may be called upon to contribute to department budget planning, public and community relations, facilities planning, arranging transportation or lunch programs, or planning and carrying out clinics, festivals or other special events. The recreation leader's job tends to be more significant and challenging if he or she holds such auxiliary responsibilities in addition to direct activity leadership. It is important to recognize, however, that although administrative tasks of this type are essential, the leader's most important responsibility is working with people creatively. Helping people grow and find rewarding leisure satisfactions, thereby improving the quality of their lives, must be the leader's key task.

Recreation Leadership as a Set of Interpersonal Behaviors

The leader's behavioral style may contribute to or detract from his or her effectiveness in carrying out the functions that have just been described. How *do* recreation professionals behave in order to achieve successful programs? It is possible to identify certain behavioral approaches that may be clearly linked to successful performance with participants or co-workers.

For example, a recreation supervisor, in addition to such *technical* acts as filling out reports, preparing schedules or assigning personnel to job stations, must also engage in a set of *interpersonal* behaviors. These will involve such interactions as communicating, assisting, rebuking, clarifying, giving support, praising, criticizing, guiding, inspiring or motivating group members. Such behaviors should be as positive, constructive and consistent as possible.

In general, "democratic" leadership behavior is believed to be more effective than "autocratic" or "laissez-faire" (permissive) behavior, according to the findings of research studies described in Chapter Four. Similarly, "participative" supervisors, who display consideration for the attitudes, feelings and needs of those working under their direction, and who strive to involve them in meaningful decision-making and problem-solving roles, are believed to be more successful than other types of supervisors in developing worker responsibility and positive motivation.

In another analysis of group leadership styles, Ball and Cipriano identify two contrasting options: "content-oriented" or "leader-oriented" and "group-oriented" approaches.[1] The first style is generally characterized as somewhat formal, impersonal and distant, the major emphasis being placed on getting work accomplished. In contrast, the group-oriented leader is more flexible, permissive and concerned with close, warm and personal group involvements and an informal, sharing group process, rather than with material accomplishment.

A leading psychologist and authority on organizational behavior, Fred Fiedler, sees leadership primarily in terms of relationships, and makes a distinction between two types of leaders—"task-motivated" leaders, who are oriented primarily toward work and accomplishment, and "relationship-motivated" leaders, who are concerned with people and with group processes. In Fiedler's view, successful leadership depends very heavily on specific situations, and there is no such thing as the perfect leader for every situation:

> Task-motivated leaders tend to be very pleasant and very considerate when everything is under control. They tend to get uptight and more punitive and controlling when the situation is less under their control.
>
> Relationship-motivated people tend to be a little more businesslike when everything is under control and more concerned with personal relationships when things are a little less controlled and more touchy.[2]

A fuller analysis of group leadership styles and behaviors is found in Chapter Four.

Recreation Leadership as a Set of Personal Qualities

Finally, successful recreation leadership may be conceived of in terms of the specific personal qualities of the leader. The professional literature and leadership manuals published by municipal departments and voluntary agencies identify numerous personal qualities or abilities as essential to high-level leadership performance. For example, Carlson, Deppe, MacLean and Peterson cite as important leadership qualities such characteristics as knowledge of self and others, knowledge of the organization and its purposes, and the ability to plan and organize, encourage initiative, work democratically, make decisions and communicate effectively.[3]

---

[1] Edith L. Ball and Robert E. Cipriano: *Leisure Services Preparation: A Competency-Based Approach.* Englewood Cliffs. New Jersey, Prentice-Hall, 1978, pp. 177–178.

[2] Fred Fiedler: "How to Be a Successful Leader: Match your Leadership Situation to Your Personality." *Leadership*, November 1979, p. 28.

[3] Reynold E. Carlson, Janet R. MacLean, Theodore R. Deppe and James A. Peterson: *Recreation and Leisure: The Changing Scene.* Belmont, California, Wadsworth Co., 1979, pp. 303–304.

In a number of such sources, there is general agreement that the successful recreation leader should have the following qualities:

1. A basic conviction that all human beings have worth and dignity, and a determination to help them improve the quality of their lives.
2. A strong belief in the importance of leisure in modern life and in the contribution to be made by recreation both as a personal experience and as a form of social service.
3. The ability to work effectively with others, drawing forth their best efforts as a catalyst or enabler, rather than as an authoritarian director.
4. The ability to think clearly and logically, to understand and analyze problem situations, and to arrive at intelligent conclusions.
5. Skill in communicating effectively with others, both verbally and in writing.
6. Such personal qualities as warmth, patience, empathy for the needs and feelings of others, and a sense of humor—all of which contribute to the ability to get along well with others.
7. A sound knowledge of human nature, both in an abstract sense (understanding individual or group psychology as described in the theoretical literature) and in terms of having a practical understanding of human behavior.
8. Good judgment, a strong sense of personal responsibility and high moral standards in all areas of human relationships.
9. Specific knowledge of an interest in the field of recreation, including personal enthusiasm for varied forms of personal participation, as well as having leadership skills in some areas of activity.
10. Awareness of the community and the varied factions that constitute it, as well as awareness of the interplay of different organizations, agencies and social groups in community life.
11. Emotional and psychological maturity. Successful leaders should understand themselves and others, should be as free from irrational prejudice as possible, and should be able to manage disagreement or opposition constructively.
12. A high level of motivation, and the ability to work hard; personal ambition, initiative, energy, confidence and "stick-to-it-iveness."
13. The quality of being a "self-starter"—being able to identify goals clearly and move toward them forcefully and directly.
14. The ability to learn from defeats or mistakes, not rationalizing them, but facing them squarely and turning them into positive assets.
15. Integrity, honesty and loyalty to the organization one works for, and to its goals and philosophy.
16. The capacity for making difficult decisions and then standing by them, without stalling or equivocating.

17. The ability to be both visionary and practical; having high ideals and visions of what might be possible in the future, and at the same time maintaining a realistic sense of practical problems that must be overcome in the present.
18. Flexibility, in the sense that the individual is ready to grow and change over time, rather than cling to outmoded views or professional attitudes.
19. A point of view that sees cooperation rather than competition and jealousy as a way of life.
20. The ability to trust others and to delegate power and responsibility to them.

These qualities would obviously be important in any professional field that involves working closely with other human beings. For the professional recreation leader or supervisor they are essential. The qualities must be coupled, however, with a sound overall philosophy of recreation service and the ability to define and work toward appropriate professional and personal goals.

PHILOSOPHY OF RECREATION SERVICE

Any attempt to develop a meaningful set of principles of recreation leadership must be based on a full understanding of the background of the recreation movement in society, both past and present, and of the specific philosophy and goals of recreation professionals in modern communities.

The organized recreation movement had many roots in the nineteenth century, including the development of national, state and municipal parks, the establishment of settlement houses and other youth-serving organizations and, most important, the development of playgrounds for children in crowded city slums. Their purpose was to provide safe, healthy, supervised settings in which children of poor families might play. Too often, in teeming city streets, children were tempted into gambling, drinking, theft, vice or other delinquent pastimes that led to a life of crime. Thus, recreation was thought of primarily as a social service geared to protect both children and the community around them.

Playground leaders stressed the positive values of constructive play. Carefully organized and directed programs were seen not only as a means of preventing juvenile delinquency but also as a way of exposing young children—many from newly arrived immigrant families—to desirable social values by supplementing their education, providing cultural opportunities and teaching skills that would be useful throughout their lives. In addition, recreation was seen by such pioneers of the early play movement as Joseph Lee and Luther Gulick as a way of strengthening community life by giving citizens an opportunity to work together purposefully to meet common social needs.

This, then, was the traditional heritage of the recreation movement. However, during the early and middle decades of the twentieth century, its scope broadened markedly in both the United States and Canada. Instead of being primarily for the children of the poor, recreational programs were extended to meet the needs of all age groups and social classes. The merger of recreation and park departments, and their establishment in many smaller and suburban communities, marked the beginning of growing networks of athletic facilities, including golf courses, tennis courts, skating rinks, swimming pools, marinas and arts centers. These were elaborate and attractive facilities, which appealed to the middle and upper classes and which often were at least partially supported by fees imposed on their users.

So, in many communities, recreation and park agencies today have two distinct kinds of emphases.

First, there are goals that are based on the view of recreation as a form of social service geared specifically to meeting the needs of the socially or economically disadvantaged, or to providing rehabilitation for the physically and mentally disabled. The goals of recreation, when seen in this light, would clearly be to overcome social pathology, to provide cultural and educational enrichment, to serve as a vehicle for counseling and employment of youth or to help integrate discharged mental patients or physically handicapped persons into community life.

Second, there are goals that emphasize the value of recreation in meeting general personal and community needs for healthy and constructive leisure activities that provide enjoyment, without other social purpose or outcomes. As an extension of this view, there is the philosophical position that public recreation is clearly an amenity for which users should pay, just as if it were a business selling a product rather than a vital form of community service to which all citizens are entitled.

During the past several years, there has been disagreement among many recreation professionals whether the essential purpose of this field is to provide pleasure and personal enrichment or significant social services. Some have warned that to give recreation the task of attempting to overcome social disabilities existing in our society makes it a "welfare" operation, and that this is a burden it should not attempt to take on. Others argue that the problems of modern urban life are such that recreation cannot possibly function effectively—and indeed justify its existence as a tax-supported institution—unless it deals with social issues and attempts to meet head-on the critical problems of our communities.

The authors of this text believe that recreation and park professionals must work toward goals that encompass *both* viewpoints. This can best be done if they are buttressed by a sound philosophy of government responsibility for recreation and park services, and by a full awareness of the meaning of play in human life, as described in Chapter One.

Specifically, they should be fully aware of the goals of the agency in which they are employed—whether public department, voluntary organization, hospital or industry—and be prepared to work toward the attainment of those goals. This may pose a problem if a conflict in values exists. The leader should recognize that there may be three sets of values or expectations in any group situation: those of the sponsoring department or agency, those of the group members and the leader's own values and needs.

Goals of Sponsors. As suggested earlier, the goals of sponsoring agencies may vary widely. For example, recreation programs for the mentally retarded are likely to place heavy emphasis on the goals of helping individuals learn to live independently in the community and of reducing inappropriate behavior or appearance. Recreation in a correctional institution is geared to promoting favorable morale in the penal setting and to developing constructive social values, as well as to introducing leisure interests and attitudes that will be helpful to residents after their return to the community. Recreation programs sponsored by religious organizations are likely to give emphasis to promoting special moral or spiritual values, to strengthening family-centered recreation activities and to reinforcing the tie between young people and the religion itself. However, in all situations, the sponsoring agency is likely to have a distinct set of goals and purposes for recreation and social programs carried out under its name.

Goals of Group Members. It is essential that the leader be able to accept and work constructively with the agency's goals if he or she is to be an effective staff member. At the same time, the leader must be able to understand and respond to the needs and wishes of the participants who are being served. Group members often may be trying to satisfy personal needs that are somewhat in conflict with the overall values of the sponsor. In some cases, participants may resent or resist the regulations and expectations of the organization.

Although the leader seeks to understand these needs or drives, this does not mean that he or she accepts them completely. Instead, the leader must interpose his or her own views and judgment and strive to balance the desires of group members, when they are not desirable or constructive, with more mature and justifiable purposes. This often may require that the leader act as a strong spokesperson for the viewpoint of the agency and enforce its regulations or expectations, even though this may not be popular with group members.

Goals of the Leader. Finally, the recreation leader must recognize that he or she has a distinct philosophy of recreation service and values system related to program goals and priorities, and that these are also influenced by his or her own personal needs—for respect or affection from others, for a sense of accomplishment or social purpose, or to exert influence or even power within a group. It is important that these needs be in reasonable harmony with the values and goals of the sponsoring organization. For example, the leader cannot function effectively in the service of an organization if there is serious disagreement with its basic philosophy.

In such situations, it is important to recognize that just as one's philosophy of recreation may be verbalized and discussed, so one's approach to leadership, like the behavior of group members, may be analyzed and interpreted. The truly effective leader must be sensitive both to his or her own attitudes and motivations and to the reasons that group members behave as they do.

For this reason, the study of group dynamics and the process of group leadership has become an extremely important element in the various disciplines of social service, including recreation. It underlies basic approaches to leadership training, staff development, program-planning and problem-solving, and is dealt with in Chapter Four. The leader who is skilled in group dynamics will be much more capable of helping participants understand and define their own goals and of developing creative conflict-resolution processes with agency directors or board members.

If a sponsoring agency has an extremely limited philosophy and is concerned primarily with having large numbers of participants, the leader should be in a position to help the agency understand the more significant values and outcomes that it is capable of achieving. Similarly, if group members see their purposes narrowly—to win games or to sponsor a successful dance or carnival—the leader should help them realize the broader possibilities of the group recreational experience in their lives.

PRINCIPLES OF RECREATION LEADERSHIP

In summing up, certain key guidelines or principles may be used to describe both the make-up and the day-by-day functioning of the successful recreation leader.

1. The leader must operate on the basis of a sound philosophy of recreation and leisure. He or she must regard recreation as a significant aspect of human life, with a high potential for enhancing human growth and development, and improving the total quality of community life.

2. The leader should have a sound knowledge of the basic theories of play and its value within the developmental process of human beings on different age levels. He or she should also be familiar with psychological principles that will be helpful in working constructively with various individuals in improving motivation, dealing with individual or group behavior problems, and promoting healthy social values.

3. The leader should be extremely sensitive to the process of group dynamics and should make use of whatever approach is likely to be most effective within a given situation or with a particular group in order to achieve desired outcomes. At the same time, he or she should attempt to move in the direction of democratic involvement, exposing participants as fully as possible to the processes of shared group decision-making, program-planning and overall self-management.

4. The leader should respect the needs of individuals within the groups he or she serves, and must clearly recognize the differences *among* individuals in these groups. At the same time, it is necessary to balance these concerns with an awareness of the needs or rights of the groups themselves, of the agencies that sponsor them and of the larger community.

5. The leader must regard recreation not as an end in itself, but rather as a means to an end. Thus, a successful carnival, a tournament victory, an art exhibit or a high level of playground attendance is worthwhile only if it has helped to achieve the important purposes of community recreation, in terms of the constructive and creative use of leisure, or significant outcomes for participants.

6. The leader should strive for a reasonable balance between competition and cooperation, recognizing both as important forms of group activity.

7. The leader should attempt to create an effective organization for planning and carrying out programs in order to realize as large a return as possible on all facilities, activities and staff services.

8. The concerned leader should constantly evaluate the effectiveness and the specific outcomes of his or her programs, as well as the quality of his or her own functioning. In so doing, it is necessary to measure outcomes against the stated goals of the agency or department, the expressed or evident wishes of participants and the leader's own personal and professional goals.

9. Leaders must constantly seek to promote desirable social values, consistently making their own views or moral positions known and setting a constructive example for participants. At the same time, the leader should *accept* group members as they are and *seek* to help them change in more desirable or positive directions.

10. Leaders should be alert to changing professional policies and national trends in the field of recreation service, and should apply these, when appropriate, to their own situations. This involves being active *as* professionals, in state, regional or national societies, or through continuing education workshops and courses.

11. Leaders should strive to achieve fuller community awareness and support of desirable programs in such areas as mainstreaming the handicapped, preventing environmental pollution and achieving ecological benefits, or developing leisure education or leisure counseling projects. This often may be done through alliances or cooperative action with other community groups concerned with such priorities or needs.

12. Successful leaders must be prepared to accept responsibilities and risks, to experiment and explore, to initiate, to pioneer. They cannot be satisfied with programs that just "get by," or with repeating the status quo. "Tired blood" is bad enough in an individual, but in a program concerned with promoting exciting and creative human involvement, it is fatal. Therefore, the effective leader must constantly seek to innovate, to build his or her program and to promote more meaningful services.

SUGGESTED EXAMINATION QUESTIONS OR TOPICS FOR STUDENT REPORTS

1. Two basic views of recreation service are presented in this chapter: one with a primary emphasis on its role as an amenity or pleasure-oriented

activity, and the other regarding it as an important social service. How would the particular setting in which recreation is provided, or the population that is served, affect the emphasis stressed in recreation programs?

2. Examine the role of leaders within a particular type of recreation agency or program, and identify their major responsibilities and the personal qualities they must possess.

3. Summarize and discuss several of the key principles of recreation leadership that are presented at the conclusion of this chapter.

SUGGESTED ACTION ASSIGNMENTS OR GROUP PROCESS ACTIVITIES

1. Select a public, voluntary or other agency that does *not* have an explicit set of goals or statement of its philosophy. On the basis of the literature and interviews with the staff of this agency, develop such a written statement for it.

2. Select a public, voluntary or other agency that *has* such a statement. On the basis of careful observation of its structure and program, evaluate its effectiveness in achieving its goals or living up to its philosophy.

3. Prepare a list of the skills, abilities and personal qualities of leaders that you feel you presently possess. Identify a number of areas in which you need to strengthen yourself.

Group dynamics represents an important theoretical area of study in the field of social psychology. At the same time, it has been the subject of much applied research in such areas as business management, public administration, armed forces leadership and social group work. It is also an important area of understanding for those concerned with recreation leadership and supervision.

UNDERSTANDING GROUP DYNAMICS

Group dynamics is essentially concerned with achieving an understanding of the nature and role of groups in modern life. It examines the way groups are formed, the status and interrelationship of members, how different types of group structures affect the attitudes and productivity of members, how groups influence larger social institutions and, finally, how different types of leadership approaches affect group processes. Such knowledge is directly useful to those working on any level of leadership, supervision or administration. Reeves writes:

> Group dynamics is the study of the forces exerted by the group on the individual or by the individual on the group. We are thus concerned with group dynamics literally in almost every moment of our lives. . . .
> In striving to be a more effective member of the groups to which we belong, our first objective is to increase our sensitivity to the impact of our own personality on others. . . . The person who has a clear understanding of what makes him tick can, if he wishes, adjust more positively and more quickly to changes in a group situation. . . . Self-knowledge is closely related to intellectual and emotional maturity. The more a person studies

group dynamics, the more easily he will increase his own self-knowledge. And this in turn will make quicker and easier the necessary decisions about groups in which he wants to seek or maintain membership.[1]

Through a study of group dynamics one is able to understand such forms of behavior within groups as the aggression of some members toward others, the withdrawal of group members or the particular psychological mechanisms or relationships that are developed. The different aspects of interaction among group members—their cohesiveness, their attitudes toward their leaders or the organization itself, the existence of cliques or factions, their ways of attacking problems or difficulties—all are part of the study and practical uses of group dynamics.

Beal, Bohlen and Rudabaugh point out that many individuals are active within such organizations as the Red Cross, the PTA, the Boy Scouts, Community Chest, League of Women Voters, or in groups that operate within any of a hundred areas: religious, political, civic, educational, trade, business, patriotic, fraternal, recreational or social. Within such groups, those who are leaders or those who would like to become leaders often have difficulty understanding just how the group process operates:

> Many of us feel insecure within our groups. Perhaps we have had problems working with other group members. . . . We may have difficulty communicating with others; when we speak we seem to "rub people the wrong way." We wonder what others really think of us and the job we are doing.
>
> Often we have difficulty figuring out what makes other group members "tick." Why don't certain members take more interest?[2]

Even persons who have developed the skill of effective leadership with considerable success often have done so instinctively, or with a subconscious awareness of group processes and appropriate techniques. Often, they find it difficult to explain their own approaches or to help others become successful leaders. Thus, it is extremely important for all who are preparing to work with other people in groups to become as aware as possible of the findings of research in this field and to learn the basic principles that underlie effective group leadership.

IMPORTANCE OF GROUP DYNAMICS TO RECREATION PROFESSIONALS

Knowledge of group dynamics is extremely useful in increasing personal awareness and sensitivity to the needs and behavior of others, and in helping

---

[1]Elton T. Reeves: *The Dynamics of Group Behavior.* New York, American Management Association, 1970, pp. 12, 17.
[2]George M. Beal, Joe M. Bohlen and J. Neil Rudabaugh: *Leadership and Dynamic Group Action.* Ames, Iowa, University of Iowa Press, 1962, p. 13.

one function more effectively with people in a variety of group relationships. Specifically, such knowledge and expertise may be applicable in the following kinds of situations.

Socially Oriented Groups of Participants. In working with groups in which the primary emphasis is on social involvement and in which the group process can contribute to the enjoyment or personal growth of the participants, a knowledge of group dynamics obviously can be valuable for the recreation leader. Such groups might include social clubs for children and youth, membership groups in senior centers, therapeutic groups of patients in hospitals, after-care centers, or sheltered workshops, or leisure counseling groups.

Activity-Oriented Groups of Participants. In many recreation groups, the primary focus is on taking part in activities. Examples might be highly structured team situations, as in sports, or groups that have a much looser social framework, such as an arts and crafts workshop. In such settings, the activity itself determines much of what happens in the group, and individuals tend to gain status or influence on the basis of their skill or degree of success in the activity, rather than through interpersonal skills. However, even here there are many opportunities for meaningful social interaction and for the behavior of group members or leaders to have a significant effect on group outcomes and processes.

Working with Volunteers or Advisory Groups. Recreation leaders and supervisors are frequently called upon to work with groups of volunteers, committees of members, parents' groups, community center or neighborhood councils, or similar groups. In such situations, an understanding of the factors promoting successful group process is essential.

Professional Team Relationships. In all situations in which a leader or supervisor must work with other members of professional teams, a knowledge of human relationships is helpful in promoting constructive teamwork. Particularly in staff development processes, which may involve in-service education, attempts to improve motivation or productivity, or problem-solving sessions, there are a number of useful group dynamics techniques.

Administrative Interaction. Within all public and voluntary agencies, high-level supervisors or administrators must work closely with other civic officials, officers of other departments or organizations, and municipal boards and commissions. While one might expect that by the time individuals had reached this level of authority they would be consistently effective in working with others, this is not necessarily the case. The same basic principles of group dynamics that are helpful in working with groups of participants or co-workers are likely to apply also in such high-level situations.

In addition to the typical group situations that have just been described, recreation leaders today are likely to find themselves in many other different and unique kinds of groups. For example, O'Connor describes a variety of "leisure clinics," "stress workshops," "women's worry clinics," and other mental-health-oriented programs sponsored by community agencies in Colorado.[3] Pape and Walsh give similar examples of varied programs dealing with life enrichment, parenting, women's issues, health care and family needs that have been co-sponsored by Illinois park districts and mental health departments.[4] The scope of recreation and park programs has increased so widely that group dynamics has become an extremely important concern of leisure professionals.

In all such situations, groups of human beings have the capability of working or playing with each other in highly constructive, positive and rewarding ways or, conversely, in ways that involve conflict, tension and destructive behavior. In part, this may be an inevitable effect of the psychological make-up of individual group members. However, it may also be heavily influenced by the nature of the group process and the leadership that is being exerted. As one approaches the study of group dynamics, it is necessary first to understand the meaning of groups as such.

A BASIC UNDERSTANDING OF GROUPS

There is no single, universally accepted definition of the term "group." Obviously, it is more than just a number of people. Reeves states

> . . . a group consists of two or more people with common objectives. These objectives may be religious, philosophical, economic, recreational, or intellectual, or they may include all these areas.[5]

Muzafer and Carolyn Sherif emphasize the structure and influence of the group upon its members:

> A group is a social unit which consists of a number of individuals who stand in more or less status and role relationships to one another, and which possesses a set of values or norms of its own regulating the behavior of individual members, at least in matters of consequence to the group.[6]

Hartford defines group in the following terms:

> . . . at least two people—but usually more, gather with common purposes or like interests in a cognitive, affective and social interchange in single or repeated encounters sufficient for the participants to form impressions of each other, creating a set of norms . . . developing goals . . . evolving a sense of cohesion.[7]

---

[3]Constance O'Connor: "Self-Awareness Programs: A New Frontier in Recreation." *Parks and Recreation*, October 1979, pp. 43–45.

[4]Carolyn Pape and Joseph A. Walsh: "Prevention in the Park: Recreation and Mental Health." *Parks and Recreation*, October 1979, pp. 40–41, 68.

[5]Reeves, *op. cit.*, p. 11.

[6]Muzafer Sherif and Carolyn Sherif: *Groups in Harmony and Tension.* New York, Harper Bros., 1953, p. 2.

[7]Margaret E. Hartford: *Groups in Social Work.* New York and London, Columbia University Press, 1972, p. 26.

Hinton and Reitz describe the term "group" in the following ways: (a) a group must consist of at least two or more people but with no upper limit on number, although realistically most functioning groups involve 20 members or less (if a group becomes larger, sub-groups are likely to appear); (b) groups are not merely random collections of individuals but involve behavioral interdependence in that members influence each others' behavior and perceive themselves psychologically as a group; (c) groups show memory for their past experience, although membership may change, and are capable of learning and responding as an entity; and (d) groups may meet the psychological and physical needs of members, such as the need for affiliation, security, social contact or emotional support.[8]

Summing up this discussion, groups should be regarded as units of two or more people who have a meaningful relationship with each other in terms of sharing common goals, purposes or needs. To the extent that their contact is a close and enduring one, they are likely to have common values and attitudes, and membership in the group will influence both the behavior of the group members and the overall setting in which the group exists.

In recent years, belonging to groups has become something of a vogue in many urban centers. The sociologist Amitai Etzioni points out that unlike many traditional kinds of groups—such as village, family or ethnic units—these modern groups are deliberately composed, usually for one specific purpose:

> There are groups to help bewildered widows to cope and groups to teach homemakers to arrange flowers; groups to increase consciousness and groups to reduce weight; groups for sex therapy and groups for block patrols, and groups for—you name it. All replace, in part, past reliance on family, church, community and professionals. They thus fill a void left by institutions that are crumbling and professionals who are less trusted than in earlier decades.[9]

Types of Groups

Social scientists have identified a number of different types of groups in society. These might include family groups, youthful cliques or gangs, clubs, religious groups, neighborhood associations, political groups, union locals, service clubs or societies, groups of workers in an industrial plant and many others. There are a number of ways of classifying groups. Some sociologists have divided them into two broad categories: *primary groups,* which are important groups to which we have a deep and enduring affiliation and which affect our lives strongly, and *secondary groups,* which are more transitory, or less important and influential.

[8]Bernard L. Hinton and H. Joseph Reitz: *Groups and Organizations.* Belmont, California, Wadsworth Co., 1971, pp. 31–32.
[9]Amitai Etzioni: "Groups: The Sense of Belonging." *The New York Times,* March 28, 1978, p. C–1.

Slavson divided groups into three categories: (a) *compulsory groups,* in which membership is automatic or in which there is little choice about belonging, such as one's family, work team or armed forces unit; (b) *motivated groups,* in which membership is voluntary but influenced by such motivations as the need for recognition, social acceptance or approval, such as fraternal orders or clubs, church membership, honor societies or service clubs; and (c) *voluntary groups,* in which one's chief reasons for joining are the need for social activity, friendship or interest in a given type of activity, such as socially or culturally homogenous groups, activity-oriented groups or hobby clubs.[10]

Other authorities have classified groups on the basis of their structure and degree of official status: *formal,* in which membership is enforced in some way and has prescribed rules or obligations; *semi-formal,* in which there is a choice about membership but in which there are clear membership expectations and criteria; and *informal,* which represent fluid or casual associations or social contacts.

Approaches to the Study of Groups

Early studies in the field of group behavior dealt with observations of groups in social welfare, discussion groups in the adult education movement and work groups in industry. Schools of social work gradually emphasized the knowledge of "small group process" as part of the basic competence of social workers.

During the 1930's, experimental research in group dynamics dealt with the effects of different types of leadership on group members in the armed forces, business and religious organizations, and education. At that time, Moreno and Jennings developed an approach to the study of groups called "sociometry," which scientifically examined the nature of interaction patterns among group members.

During the 1940's and 1950's, emphasis was given to the use of small groups as the basis for theory building in social psychology and for the improvement of training and administrative practices in a variety of institutions. In one study of the combat record of the American soldier in World War II, for example, it was found that small squads of soldiers who had developed a high degree of cohesion and friendship had higher levels of combat effectiveness and morale than other units, and that this process was more effective than Army indoctrination efforts in creating effective fighting units. Other studies, such as the famous Roethlisburger research at the Western Electric Company in Ohio, showed that small work groups had more effect on employee production than company policies or other corporate incentives.

Throughout this period of systematic analysis of groups, certain elements of group behavior or structure were identified. These represent the charac-

---

[10]S. R. Slavson: *Creative Group Education.* New York, Association Press, 1948, pp. 17–23.

teristics that the group worker, leader or supervisor must seek to understand if he or she is to work more effectively with groups. Examples of such characteristics, as identified and described by Hemphill and Westie, follow:

1. *Autonomy.*   The degree to which a group functions independently of other groups.
2. *Control.*   The degree to which a group controls or regulates the behavior of group members.
3. *Flexibility.*   The degree to which a group's activities are marked by informal procedures rather than by rigidly structured procedures.
4. *Hedonic Tone.*   The degree to which group participation is accompanied by a general feeling of pleasantness or agreeableness.
5. *Homogeneity.*   The degree to which members of a group possess similar characteristics.
6. *Intimacy.*   The degree to which members of a group are familiar with the personal details of one another's lives.
7. *Participation.*   The degree to which members of a group apply time and effort to group activities.
8. *Permeability.*   The degree to which a group permits ready access to membership.
9. *Polarization.*   The degree to which a group is oriented toward a single goal which is recognized and accepted by all members.
10. *Potency.*   The degree to which a group has significance for its members.
11. *Stability.*   The degree to which a group persists over a period of time with essentially the same characteristics.
12. *Stratification.*   The degree to which a group orders its members into clearly defined status hierarchies.[11]

In addition to these characteristics of groups, researchers identified certain important group properties that became the focus of considerable study.

Essential Properties of Groups

These include the following: group cohesiveness, group morale, group norms, group structure and group productivity.

Group Cohesiveness.   This may briefly be described as the force that tends to hold a group together. It varies widely since it is the result of many factors, such as the type and strength of the leadership, the nature of group objectives and the degree of group homogeneity. It has been found that cohesiveness is directly proportional to the group's identification with its major objectives. Reeves writes

> If the central objective of the group seems to its membership to be worthy of a considerable sacrifice in order to attain it, group solidarity will be high. . . .

[11]John K. Hemphill and Charles M. Westie. In Hinton and Reitz, *op. cit.*, pp. 5–6.

It is possible for a group's leaders to choose their actions with the express purpose of directly raising its cohesiveness. Group tasks can be assigned to teams made up of members who have interacted less frequently or less effectively than others. As these teams succeed in their tasks, new and stronger interpersonal relationships will be formed and cohesiveness will therefore increase.[12]

In general, it has been found that cooperation creates a higher degree of cohesiveness than competition does. If some members of a group are too dominating, cohesiveness will decrease. Highly cohesive groups are usually able to accept hostility from external sources and return it, without fighting internally. Such groups tend to be highly productive and able to work efficiently on assigned tasks.

Group Morale. Group morale may be described as a positive and optimistic feeling about the group, and a conviction that it is a successful or important body worthy of support. It is heavily influenced by the nature of the group's goals; for example, the following factors tend to strengthen group morale:

1. Having positive, easily recognized and understood objectives which the group members themselves support fully.
2. Achievement of satisfactions, such as self-expression, recognition or a sense of prestige, from group involvement.
3. A shared feeling of progress being made toward group goals.
4. Realistic levels of aspiration and achievement that are set beyond past accomplishments of the group, but not unrealistically so. There should be both immediate and long-range objectives.
5. Equality of sacrifice or gain within the group. No one member should either be called upon to give too much or receive excessive rewards from the group's activities.
6. A high degree of self-identification with the group that may be achieved through such devices as special rituals, slogans or uniforms.

Group Norms. These represent the values, traditions and standards of behavior that are characteristic of a group. Most individuals tend to base their personal values on the views of those around them—originally from family contacts, then from play groups or other peers, and ultimately from the enduring group associations, or reference groups, that persist throughout life. It seems to be a normal mode of behavior to act or react in ways that people one respects consider to be socially acceptable. Hare says,

> Some individuals are . . . relatively insensitive to pressures, but a person cannot remain a social being . . . and stand wholly apart from social pressure.[13]

Group sanctions is the term used to describe the way in which groups enforce their norms. Sanctions may range from mild censure to actual expul-

---

[12]Reeves, *op. cit.,* p. 108.
[13]A. Paul Hare: *Handbook of Small Group Research.* New York, Free Press, 1962, p. 169.

sion from a group. While some sanctions may involve a formal punishment by authority or an outside force, most group sanctions are imposed by the group members themselves, and thus have considerable weight and influence.

However, many groups are able to enforce their norms without having to rely on sanctions. The success of organizations such as Weight Watchers seems to stem from the emotional identification of members with the total group, their desire to be approved by other members and a sense of responsibility for the group that prevents them from letting down group expectations and standards.

Group Structure. Instead of being simply collections of individuals who share uniform roles and levels of status, most groups tend to develop differentiated functions, identities and degrees of prestige in their membership. Typically, some members are perceived as influential leaders, while others are followers. Some are identified with the "in-group" or power structure, while others are peripheral to group decisions and influence. There are also likely to be cliques or sub-groups of friends who relate closely to each other. This pattern of relationships and expected behaviors and roles is normally referred to as *group structure.* Shaw writes,

> Each group member is more or less aware of this group structure and often can verbalize it quite clearly; yet there is no explicit statement concerning the organization of the group. Group structure may therefore be either formal or informal; it may be explicitly recognized and stated or merely implicit in the functioning of the group. In either case, the group structure exerts a pervasive influence upon the behavior of the members of the group.[14]

Group Productivity. Group productivity refers to the overall effectiveness of group members in working together to achieve their goals. In general, it depends on three elements: task demands, resources and process.

Task demands consist of the job to be done, and whether or not it is within an appropriate range of activities or responsibilities for the group. If task demands are excessively difficult, or are so simple that they do not represent a challenge, group productivity is likely to be low. Similarly, if goals are unclear, or if assigned tasks are not attractive, group members may not accept them fully, and this too will limit productivity.

The *resources* available to a group, in terms of accomplishing a given task, also limit potential productivity. Resources include all of the relevant knowledge, abilities, skills and tools possessed by the members of the group. It is best that important capabilities be well distributed among group members, rather than concentrated in a few individuals.

Process refers to the way in which people use their resources: the actual steps and individual or collective actions taken by group members in carrying out a task. It may include ways of communicating, sharing responsibilities and resolving disagreements.

---

[14]Marvin E. Shaw: *Group Dynamics: The Psychology of Small Group Behavior.* New York, McGraw-Hill Book Co., 1971, p. 236.

A great deal of research has been done in the area of group productivity. Much of it has concentrated on the effectiveness of groups in carrying out assigned tasks in comparison with the effectiveness of individuals. On the basis of a considerable bulk of experimental findings, Shaw reports that a number of plausible generalizations have been developed regarding the productivity of groups. These follow:

1. The mere presence of others increases the motivation level of a performing individual; individuals perform better in the presence of others than they do alone.
2. Group judgments are superior to individual judgments on tasks that involve random error.
3. Groups usually produce more and better solutions to problems than do individuals working alone.
4. Groups usually require more time to complete a task than do individuals working alone.
5. Groups learn faster than individuals.
6. More new and radical ideas are produced by both individuals and groups when critical evaluation of ideas is suspended during the production period.[15]

These findings suggest the extreme importance of groups throughout our lives. Hartford points out that

> . . . not only do one's values, beliefs and behaviors seem to stem from his interactions with others, but one's very impression of himself or herself—one's identity, one's assessment of his own worth, also develop from associations with others.[16]

Etzioni points out that most people need the warmth of continuous positive support from others, and suggests that part of the power of groups to influence—or control—their members stems from the "social-psychic" hold they have on them. Part of the "hidden agenda" of groups, he says, is based on the emotional involvement that results from continued, repeated togetherness, which serves as an antidote to the loneliness and isolation that affects many people in modern life. He writes,

> Groups work most effectively when their bonds are rather strong, when their members are deeply invested in one another. Alcoholics Anonymous often does for alcoholics what psychiatrists often cannot do, precisely because the emotional bonds in A.A. are stronger and much more encompassing than in therapy, and help is available not just a few hours a week, but whenever needed, and for as long as needed. Some of the most effective drug-withdrawal groups are live-in, around-the-clock groups.[17]

In all investigations of group dynamics, it is appropriate to ask, "What is the effect of group leadership? Under what kinds of leadership are groups

---

[15]*Ibid.*, pp. 79–83.
[16]Hartford, *op. cit.*, p. 34.
[17]Etzioni, *op. cit.*, p. C-16.

most likely to function effectively, to develop and maintain constructive interrelationships, and to be highly productive?"

THE STUDY OF GROUP LEADERSHIP

Within the field of group dynamics, leaders are described as individuals who have a strong influence on group decisions, lead groups toward their goals and affect the level of group performance, and help groups define their character. Steiner writes,

> Leaders are persons assigned to the leader role by an experimenter, either with or without the enumeration of special duties and functions.
> Leaders are persons identified as such by observers or by group members.
> Leaders are persons whose presence and/or behavior in the group strongly influence the group's activities or products.
> Leaders are persons who are highly chosen by other members as friends, confidants or co-workers.
> Leaders are persons whose suggestions, commands, or example are regularly accepted and followed by other group members.
> Leaders are persons who occupy certain positions within an institutionalized role structure—foremen, lieutenants, company presidents.
> Leaders are persons with whom others identify, and who therefore inspire and channel the activities of group members.
> Leaders are persons who are observed to perform certain specified functions.[18]

It is apparent that these descriptions refer chiefly to leaders of an informal nature, that is, individuals who assume leadership roles within groups but who do not have an official or appointive status. It is possible to achieve leadership status in a variety of ways.

Elected Leaders. In political life and in large membership organizations, it is customary for leaders to be selected by choice of the majority through formal voting procedures. Presumably, leadership candidates are widely known to their constituency and are chosen by virtue of their capability and past performance, although too often such choices may be determined by clever political manipulation or adroit marketing of the candidate's image.

Appointed Leaders. In business firms and many other types of organizations, it is customary for high-level administrators to appoint individuals to leadership positions. This is done customarily because the administrator is familiar with the personality and skills of his or her subordinates and is able to judge their capability for assuming leadership responsibilities.

Career-Process Leaders. This describes the type of leader who assumes a post of responsibility after having come up through the career ranks of an

---

[18]Ivan D. Steiner: *Group Process and Productivity.* New York and London, Academic Press, 1972, p. 174.

organization. The most obvious example is the individual who rises through the "merit system" of Civil Service advancement procedures.

Inherited Leaders.   This is most obvious in those nations with royal families, where the post of ruler is passed from parent to child. It operates less formally in political life, when wives, brothers or other close relatives may inherit the "mantle" of leadership and replace a key political figure who becomes ill or dies. It may also operate in other areas of public life, for example, when close associates of a key official may, with popular consent, take over a post when the official retires or dies.

Emergent Leaders.   This describes the type of leader who emerges as the choice of a group because, in a given situation or over a sustained period, he or she displays the qualities necessary to assume leadership responsibilities and help the group achieve its goals. Instead of being formally elected or appointed, the emergent leader takes on this role without official recognition or approval.

Within the field of recreation and parks, examples may be given of each category of leader. The *elected leader* is found in any recreation club or organization that elects its own officers, such as a senior citizens club or a neighborhood council. The *appointed leader* may be illustrated by the commissioner or superintendent of recreation and parks, who is appointed to his post by the mayor or city council. The *career-process leader* includes the majority of professionals who attain supervisory or administrative positions by rising through the hierarchy of an organization and meeting formal requirements along the way. The *inherited leader* is less widely found, but an example might be a husband who succeeds his wife as chairman of a community recreation board or commission, or a commercial recreation company in which ownership passes from one generation to the next. Finally, the *emergent leader* is to be found in any kind of work team or group of recreation participants in which one individual emerges with leadership responsibilities because of his or her contributions to the group and overall personality.

FUNCTIONS OF GROUP LEADERSHIP

In situations in which members are encouraged to participate in the overall process of planning and carrying out activities, the leader has two basic types of functions. These are *task functions*, which relate to the business or project the group is working on, and *group-relations functions*, which are concerned with maintaining a positive and constructive set of relationships among the members. Skill in carrying out these functions is not innate, and can be learned by leaders.

Typically, task functions include such actions as (a) *initiating*, or proposing group goals, procedures or other ideas; (b) *opinion or information seeking*, which asks for information, suggestions or ideas; (c) *opinion or information giving*, which involves providing information, ideas or opinions; (d) *clarifying*, by interpreting what has been said, giving examples or suggesting alternatives; (e) *summarizing* or restating what has been said, and then offering possible conclusions or decisions for the group's consideration; and (f) *agreement-seeking,* which involves helping the group determine whether a consensus has been reached.

Group-relations functions are less concerned with practical accomplishment than with the feelings of the group members toward themselves and toward others. These leadership tasks include: (a) *encouraging* others and establishing an attitude of warm acceptance; (b) *expressing group feelings* by drawing out the apparent moods and attitudes of group members; (c) *harmonizing* disagreements by reducing tension and encouraging members to explore their differing views; (d) *modifying* the leader's own position or admitting to a mistake or inappropriate position, in order to draw group members together; (e) *keeping communication channels open,* and facilitating a maximum amount of participation and discussion by all; and (f) *evaluating,* by suggesting ways of measuring the group's effectiveness or giving a direct estimate of its success.

James McGregor Burns suggests that there are different levels or degrees of leadership. At a lower level, he identifies *transactional leadership,* which is essentially "brokerage leadership": helping participants carry out rather practical but superficial actions, which do not have a lasting or significant effect.

At a higher level, Burns suggests, is *transforming leadership.* This is a dynamic process in which fundamental change is brought about, and in which the participants or followers are actually transformed in important ways. Burns writes that in the political arena, for example, the relationship goes "from fulfilling wants to needs, to aspirations, to expectations, and finally to political demands."[19]

THEORIES OF GROUP LEADERSHIP

Over the past several decades, several basic theories of group leadership have been presented. Four of these, the *trait, situational, functional,* and *contingency* theories, are described here.

Trait Theory of Leadership

One of the earliest theories of leadership, this suggested that there were certain specific traits or qualities shared by all successful leaders. It stemmed from the philosophical orientation of the western world, which held that human beings could become whatever they wished, provided that they worked hard and persevered in their efforts. Thus, individuals became leaders because of their personal drive and attributes, and individual character-

---

[19]James McGregor Burns: "What Makes You a Leader?" *Leadership,* May 1979, p. 34.

istics were seen as the major determinants of leadership. In public life, industrial, political or military figures were widely adulated, and the view became accepted that there were one or more unique and innate traits that were shared by all great leaders.

However, scientific research on leadership revealed that no single set of traits or identifiable qualities characterized all leaders. Certain qualities tended to appear frequently enough to permit some generalizations. Research by Stogdill and others showed that group leaders tended to have traits related to ability, sociability and motivation to a higher degree than did other group members. Group leaders rated high with respect to *ability* in such categories as intelligence, insight, verbal facility and adaptability. Leaders exceeded group members in *sociability* factors, such as responsibility, social participation, cooperativeness and popularity. With respect to *motivation,* group leaders had a higher level of initiative and persistence than did group members.

Other important factors may include the willingness to make decisions when needed, and to risk making incorrect decisions; charisma, defined as personal magnetism and appeal; the ability to project a "parent image" to members of the group; the quality of being fair and impartial; and the drive for power or influence over others.

Situational Theory of Leadership

This view suggests that leaders arise or emerge in situations in which their personal qualities or capabilities will best serve group members.

In some situations, a group may require a leader who will be a forceful morale-builder, and external representative or negotiator, or an expert in human relations. The qualities called for in the leader of a military squad in battle are likely to be bravery, a cool head, a knowledge of military tactics, sound judgment and the ability to inspire. On the other hand, a group of educators selecting a chairman to head a team to carry out a study and issue a report might require an individual with knowledge of the subject, experience in the field, the ability to communicate in both written and verbal forms, and a high level of scholarly ability. Thus, the situational theory has held that leadership selection is most likely to be affected by the demands and needs of a given situation rather than by possession of a particular leadership trait or a set of traits.

Functional Theory of Leadership

This theory suggests that leadership arises from the complex needs of the group for specific kinds of tasks to be performed. Many of these responsibilities may be undertaken by different members of the group, and so it is assumed that leadership is a shared process in which the functions to be performed determine who the leaders are at any given time.

For example, a work team in a large organization that has been assigned responsibility for a major project will require different kinds of leaders. It will need some individuals who are highly creative and who can generate exciting ideas. Others must be practical, to sift through these proposals and follow through with careful planning. The team may need resource persons with specialized knowledge or skills (how to select equipment, how to set up a marketing plan, how to solve personnel problems), persons with public relations skills, evaluators and others to fill a variety of different functions. It may also require one individual who has the special ability to coordinate others and get them to work together effectively, and who may serve as "program manager" or the nominal leader of the group.

Contingency Theory of Leadership

Fiedler determined that the relationship of one's leadership style to his effectiveness with a particular group could be measured only if three situational variables were considered: (a) the leader's *position power*, meaning the degree of legitimate authority and the ability to give rewards or punishment; (b) the *structure of the task*, meaning how clearly its goals and solutions are outlined in advance and made known to group members, the implication being that the more structured the task is, the more favorable the situation is for the leader; and (c) the *personal relationship* between the leader and other group members, with emphasis on their mutual feeling tone, and the support and loyalty the leader is able to elicit.

The contingency model of leadership is significant in that it demonstrates that the type of leadership behavior that is most likely to be effective depends on the situation and the task to be performed; in addition, it specifies ways of examining tasks to determine what leadership behaviors are likely to be most successful in carrying them out.

More recently, Fiedler has identified two primary kinds of leadership styles: *task-motivated* and *relationship-motivated.* As the contingency theory would suggest, the effectiveness of each of these types of leaders in a given situation depends on the difficulty of the job to be performed and the degree of control in the situation.[20]

Shaw summarizes the conclusions reached by Fiedler:

> These patterns of behavior determine the relative effectiveness of leaders in various situations. The task-oriented leader tends to be more effective when the situation is either highly favorable or highly unfavorable for the leader, whereas the relationship-oriented leader tends to be more effective in situations that are only moderately favorable or moderately unfavorable.[21]

---

[20]Fred Fiedler and Martin M. Chemers: "What's Your Leadership Style?" *Leadership,* November 1979, p. 29.
[21]Shaw, *op. cit.,* p. 278.

RESEARCH IN GROUP LEADERSHIP STYLES

There have been numerous studies of group behavior and the effects of different styles of leadership. At a comparatively early point it was determined that the same group will behave in markedly different ways when operating under different leaders. Several studies of group leadership styles showed that:

> Leaders of more effective groups tended to play a more differentiated role than leaders of less effective groups; they spent more time in planning, providing materials and assistance, and discussing action to be taken.
> More effective leaders delegated authority to others more frequently than less effective leaders.
> More effective leaders checked up on subordinates less often, and were more supportive in manner than less effective ones.
> More effective leaders were able to develop cohesiveness among their group members to a fuller degree than less effective ones.
> In general, it was found that effective leaders placed stress on developing good working teams, with a friendly, cooperative group climate, high internal loyalty and broad involvement in decision-making and policy formulation.[22]

Other studies of small problem-solving groups found that different members assumed different leadership roles. Typically, one member in a group assumed the role of social–emotional needs satisfier," while another became a "task-accomplishment specialist." It was commented that this seemed to parallel many family structures, in which mothers tended to assume the role of meeting social and emotional needs, while fathers emphasized task accomplishment.

Lewin Studies of Group Leadership

Probably the best known series of studies of different leadership styles and their effects on participants was carried out by Kurt Lewin and a number of associates.[23] Four comparable groups of ten-year-old boys were observed as they successively experienced *autocratic, democratic,* and *permissive* (laissez-faire) adult leadership. Each group met after school and engaged in varied hobby activities, such as arts and crafts, for three six-week periods. In each period they had a different adult leader who employed a different leadership style.

The <u>autocratic</u> leader assigned all responsibilities and made all decisions, without discussing his plans with group members or seeking their views. He dispensed rewards and punishments in an authoritarian fashion,

---

[22]Dorwin Cartwright and Alvin Zander: *Group Dynamics: Research and Theory.* New York, Harper and Row, 1960, pp. 487–489.
[23]See Ralph K. White and Ronald Lippitt: *Autocracy and Democracy.* New York, Harper Bros., 1960.

remaining aloof from active participation with the group except when demonstrating activities. The *democratic* leader shared policy-making and decisions about group activities with the participants. He helped them clarify the goals of the group and made his own standards and expectations known to the group. Rather than rigidly assign them to sub-groups, he gave group members the choice of working with their close friends. The *permissive* leader gave help when needed but otherwise remained aloof from the group. He permitted them to make all decisions and made no attempt to guide or evaluate the group's activities.

Using movies and observational records, extensive records were kept of each group's participation day to day. It was found that in autocratically run groups, members tended to depend heavily on the adult leader and did not develop the capacity for taking independent action. When the autocratic leader absented himself, group members had difficulty carrying on. By contrast, in democratic and permissive leadership groups there was considerably more friendly interaction and interdependence. When there were difficulties or sudden emergencies, members of the democratically led groups were best able to work together, express individual views, and come to group decisions. The expression of hostility was 30 times as great in the autocratic as in the democratic groups, and there was considerably more scapegoating in the autocratic groups than in the other two.

In general, group members tended to prefer the democratic and permissive leaders to those who were autocratic. While the studies did not prove that democratic leadership was the only effective form of leadership, they did demonstrate its value under the experimental conditions described. Realistically, many individuals are so accustomed to autocratic direction that they feel secure with it, and it takes time for them to handle themselves in a mature way in a democratically led group. In fact, a number of studies in industrial and problem-solving situations that followed the Lewin experiments showed that autocratically directed groups tended to have a higher level of productivity, although personal satisfaction was generally greater in groups that were democratically led.

One might conclude that in recreation situations, in which the satisfaction of group members, their development in terms of personal growth and maturity, and their ability to function well as members of society are key goals, democratic leadership is the most appropriate.

Sherif Studies of Group Manipulation

Another series of studies, carried out by Muzafer and Carolyn Sherif during the 1950's, dealt with the experimental production of group structures, norms and hostile intergroup relationships. These studies involved camping programs for boys in Connecticut and Oklahoma.[24]

------

[24]Muzafer Sherif and Carolyn Sherif: *An Outline of Social Psychology*. New York, Harper Bros., 1956, pp. 192–202, 293–300.

In the first experiment, 24 boys who were about 12 years old were divided into two evenly matched groups called the "Red Devils" and the "Blue Dogs." Each group developed a hierarchical structure, with status roles and power relations based on the members' size, their ability in games, intelligence and personality characteristics. The group developed its own set of norms, methods of praise and punishment, secret hideouts and the like. The "Red Devils" and "Blue Dogs" were exposed to a period of friction, which was deliberately caused through the use of competitive games and other devices intended to cause frustration. The experimenters succeeded in bringing about strongly hostile attitudes and behavior, with each group holding negative stereotypes and expressing considerable antagonism toward the members of the opposite group.

In the second series of experiments, known as the Robber's Cave Experiment, the experimenters again induced a series of mutually frustrating and competitive activities that resulted in highly negative behavior between the groups, including physical violence, name-calling, sneak raids, insulting posters, and considerable bitterness and accusations.

Although staff members were instructed, after the period of intergroup friction, to do away with the hostility as much as possible, they found it extremely difficult to do this. The Sherifs write,

> Perhaps the most remarkable observation of this period was that, in spite of their efforts to break up the in-groups by bringing the boys all together in camp duties and activities, campfires, birthday parties, and athletic events emphasizing individual rather than group competition, the preferences of the boys tended, on the whole, to follow the in-group lines. The old songs, names, and sterotypes derogatory to the out-group continued to crop up. Such observations indicate a strong tendency for attitudes toward in-group and out-group to persist even though the conditions which gave rise to them no longer exist.[25]

Various devices, such as involving members of both factions in a camp-wide softball team against a team of outsiders or calling on all the boys to cooperate in a major camp emergency, were used in trying to reduce the hostility and re-establish a state of cooperation and mutual acceptance. Ultimately, this was accomplished.

Implications of Sherif Studies. These experiments provided an excellent demonstration of the tendency of groups to coalesce and rapidly develop their own norms, loyalties and internal group structure. They showed how ready the group members were to engage in hostile, aggressive behavior against those whom they had recently regarded as their friends, but whom they now saw as enemies. The effect of aggression—as exemplified in competitive camp activities—was worthy of notice. Although it is generally assumed that by giving vent to aggression one can reduce one's level of hostility, these experiments showed that the more competition the campers engaged in, the greater their antagonism grew.

---

[25]*Ibid.*, p. 299.

The Sherif studies provide a graphic example of the *power* of group leadership to influence the attitude and behavior of group members, for both positive and negative goals. It is worth comment that the experimenters found it easier to promote negative and hostile values and behavior than to build constructive and desirable intergroup relationships.

There have been few recent research studies with direct relevance for recreation situations. Chapter Eleven, however, describes the principles involved in the development of "T-groups," "encounter" or "sensitivity" groups. This movement represented the major thrust in group dynamics during the 1960's and early 1970's. It has much potential for developing improved human relationships in both leader-participant and work-team group situations.

RELATIONSHIP OF RECREATION WITH SOCIAL GROUP WORK

As indicated earlier, the human service field most active in using group dynamics approaches in the preparation of professionals and in daily practice has been social group work. Those active in this field have made sustained attempts to relate theoretical understandings of group process to actual programs of social service. It is important for recreation professionals to understand the basic concepts of this field for two reasons:

1. Recreation leaders often work with problem groups, in which they must provide direct counseling, organize "rap" sessions or work in other meaningful ways to assist group members. In such situations their function is closely related to the goals of social group work, and it is helpful for them to understand this field.

2. Recreation personnel often work side-by-side with social group workers in hospitals, rehabilitation centers, youth homes or correctional institutions. It is important for them to be able to communicate and cooperate effectively with each other in such settings, as well as in other agencies where recreation leaders may be employed by, or may themselves employ, a social worker. This is particularly true given the expansion of recreation agency functions into many social-service areas in recent years.

Social Group Work Defined

Konopka has defined this field in the following terms:

> Social group work is a method of social work which helps individuals enhance their social functioning through purposeful group experiences and to cope more effectively with their personal, group, or community problems.[26]

---

[26]Gisela Konopka: *Social Group Work: A Helping Process.* Englewood Cliffs, New Jersey, Prentice-Hall, 1963, p. 20.

Although group workers may be employed in a variety of situations, their goal generally is to enhance the personal and social growth of participants through the group process, in such areas as (a) individualization, through which participants gain positive self-concepts and become better able to interact with other members; (b) sense of belonging, which derives from healthy, group experiences and acceptance by others; (c) capacity to participate, learning to take responsibility and share in group activities and decision-making, thus becoming more effective as a citizen in the overall community; (d) gaining increased respect for differences among people, particularly those of other races, creeds or personal background, and so gaining a fuller sense of self-worth; and (e) experiencing a warm and accepting social climate, which promotes a free interplay of human personalities without excessive defensiveness or hostility.[27]

Social Group Work Principles

While it is difficult to outline a single set of working principles, the following guidelines apply generally to the approach of social group workers.

1. Social group workers have a helping and enabling function rather than a directive one; it is their task to help group members move toward greater independence and autonomy.

2. Workers should form meaningful relationships with various group members and should seek to understand both their overtly stated needs and their concealed needs and drives, which may be revealed only as the group process continues over time.

3. Workers should strive to accept all group members, although they may not approve of all their behavior. They should then attempt to guide members in positive directions that will bring about constructive changes in their lives.

4. Workers should recognize each group member as an individual, but should also see him or her as a participant within the total group structure, subject to its influence and having unique roles, status levels, and affiliations with others.

5. Workers recognize that group members learn best from the results of their own decisions and efforts, and therefore give members latitude to plan and carry out their own activities and projects.

7. In order to understand their groups better, workers study them consciously and analyze individual and group behavior, systematically keeping records, such as narratives, anecdotes and other reports.

Distinction Between Recreation and Social Group Work

As indicated earlier, recreation leaders and social group workers have a degree of similarity of purpose, and often work together in agency or institu-

---

[27]*Ibid.*, pp. 44–46.

tional programs. However, there are certain clear differences between them. Recreation leaders tend to work with larger numbers of participants, and usually do not become involved deeply with single individuals or small groups. Although many recreation leaders do develop intense bonds with participants, more commonly their role is primarily concerned with organizing, planning, scheduling and directing activities.

In contrast, social group workers usually do not regard provision of activities as a primary focus on their work. Instead, recreation becomes an important medium through which to work. The group worker's primary goal is in the area of human relationships. Activities are a way of reaching and involving members of youth groups, gangs, groups in treatment or adult groups, in order to deal with problems, strengthen the members' participation in community life or bring about other constructive individual and social change.

In general, it is the emphasis on the use of recreation (in institutions or child-care agencies, for example) as a psychodynamic medium that distinguishes social group workers from recreation leaders. Recreation personnel must not confuse themselves with social workers, or attempt to play the role of specialist in group dynamics. They are not usually trained to do this sort of job, and while they may have a high degree of intuitive understanding and the ability to relate well to groups, this is not enough.

Instead, recreation leaders and supervisors should be knowledgeable enough about the group process to be able to use it effectively in working with varied groups of participants, community advisory groups and co-workers. Those who have worked with groups over a period of time know that the development of democratic, self-governing group capabilities is often time-consuming and frustrating. Most members of clubs and other groups often are not willing to assume regular responsibilities, attend meetings and work consistently on committees. In such a situation the leader must be ready to work with the loyal few who can be counted on, to help them take responsibility to the greatest degree possible and to play a directive role when necessary.

APPLICATION OF GROUP DYNAMICS PRINCIPLES

With these limitations, the final message of this chapter is that recreation leaders and supervisors must be as aware as possible of the significance of group dynamics. They should understand how groups function, what their values are and how they may be worked with to enrich program outcomes for all participants. In many cases recreation leaders and supervisors themselves can improve group processes by bringing this kind of knowledge and awareness to bear. In other cases specialists in group dynamics may be brought in to diagnose and work with the situation. For example, in some recreation and park departments, sensitivity training programs have been established to improve interpersonal relationships among staff members.

Thus, in both day-by-day program leadership and in more complicated problems involving participant or staff relations, the use of group dynamics principles and expertise is an important element in the broad field of recreation leadership and supervision. A number of specific approaches involving skilled group leadership, dealing with processes such as communication, participation, developing group standards and commitment, are presented in the remainder of this chapter. Other group dynamics approaches in such specialized areas as values clarification are presented in Chapter Eleven, which deals with staff-development processes.

Communication Process. Communication is generally thought of as the process by which information, ideas, needs and attitudes are expressed, usually in verbal or written form, although other methods may be employed. Too often, in autocratically run organizations, communication tends to be one-way, from the top of the hierarchy to the bottom. An effective system of two-way communication, in which information is freely shared and discussed and all group members or agency employees have the opportunity to express their views, is essential to the health of any organization.

To achieve this, group leaders must establish definite means of communication that provide the opportunity for group members to share their views and participate actively in goal-setting and decision-making processes.

Both formal and informal means of communication should be developed for sharing information, ideas, plans and administrative decisions and policies; these should include both verbal and written channels. Efforts should be made to insure two-way communication processes or truly "open-door" policies and other opportunities for feedback and a full discussion of views.

Group Participation. Research indicates that group productivity is related to members' having the opportunity to participate in goal-setting and policy development. The more members are able to participate in meaningful group processes, the more positive their attitudes toward the group are likely to be. Members who participate most fully are those who understand and are in agreement with the group's purposes, feel secure in it and are confident that their contribution is important to the overall effectiveness of the group. They are most likely to agree with and support the group's goals and decisions.

It is therefore desirable to maximize the percentage of members who participate actively—attending meetings and special events, speaking up in discussions and holding offices or committee memberships.

Leaders must recognize that while it may sometimes appear to be easier and more efficient to do a job themselves, rather than share responsibility, in the long run this attitude hampers the group's progress. Leaders should therefore permit and encourage members to take part in policy decisions and other opportunities for meaningful group interaction.

Those members who tend to dominate group affairs should be helped to understand that, while meaning well, they probably are inhibiting the participation of other members.

Developing Group Standards. Successful groups have high standards or expectations of member behavior, participation in group programs, responsible performance in assigned tasks and successful work completion. In contrast, unsuccessful groups tend to have weak or inconsistent attendance, sloppy discussion and programs and other projects that are poorly carried out. Group members should examine their expectations of each other and of the overall group performance, and should define what is needed to achieve success and satisfaction of all members.

There should be full participation in setting group expectations and standards, and these should be well understood by all members.

Group standards should be realistic, and should be reviewed or evaluated from time to time.

Groups should consider the goals and expectations of the sponsoring organization or community in setting their own standards, and should strive to have them in harmony.

Both formal leaders and group members with high status (informal leaders) should exemplify group standards in their personal behavior, thereby acting as models for other members.

A healthy and strong group does not just happen, nor is it the automatic outcome of a leader's good will or effort. Instead, it comes about gradually, as a result of intelligent and perceptive leadership that encourages group members to take responsibility and to recognize the group as an important force in their lives.

Johnson and Johnson deal with this essential principle in a discussion of group cohesion, which they define as

> . . . the sum of all the factors influencing members to stay in the group; it is the result of the positive forces of attraction toward the group outweighing the negative forces of repulsion away from the group.[28]

They stress that members' attraction to a group will be affected by their assessment of the desirable and undesirable outcomes of group membership. The outcomes expected from membership in any group will depend heavily on such factors as the nature of the group and its goals, its success in achieving goals, how well the group suits the individual member's needs and personal values, and the quality of group interpersonal experiences. Obviously, each person's attraction to the group will vary over a period of time, and the cohesive power of the group will also vary from member to member. To achieve the highest level of consistent member involvement and loyalty, it is essential that leaders strive to build an atmosphere of cooperation, trust and acceptance.

---

[28]David W. Johnson and Frank P. Johnson: *Joining Together: Group Theory and Group Skills.* Englewood Cliffs, New Jersey, Prentice-Hall, Inc., 1975, p. 233.

SUGGESTED EXAMINATION QUESTIONS OR TOPICS FOR STUDENT REPORTS

1. Define group dynamics and show why, in your view, it is essential that recreation leaders and supervisors be knowledgeable in this area.
2. Identify and discuss several of the key aspects of groups (such as their types, their properties or characteristics, or their effects on participants) that you believe can be illustrated in recreational groups.
3. What are the major implications for recreational leaders of the Lewin-Lippitt-White or Sherif studies in group leadership styles and methods? Go to original reports of these studies to document your response.
4. Present and summarize several of the basic principles of social group work that are presented in this chapter. To what extent would these apply to recreation leadership?

SUGGESTED ACTION ASSIGNMENTS OR GROUP PROCESS ACTIVITIES

1. Carefully examine a recreation club or other fairly stable group of participants. Analyze its structure, the roles played by various members of the group, and their allegiances, cliques or friendships.
2. Examine an agency or institution in which social group work is practiced as the primary discipline. Determine the role of recreation in this setting.
3. Hemphill and Westie identified several characteristics of groups that the leader or supervisor must seek to understand in order to work effectively with groups. Evaluate a group with which you have an ongoing relationship (with respect to these characteristics) in order to determine the effectiveness of the leader in working with this group.
4. Examine a group that you are involved with (including possibly a group that has been organized to carry out assignments in your class), and record the number of times that individuals perform any of the task or group-relations functions described in this chapter. Share your observations with individual group members.

Recreation Leadership Applied

Part Two

Activity Leadership Methods

Chapter Five

One of the keys to the success of every recreation leader is the ability to lead groups productively in varied forms of play activity. Obviously, the leader's role includes many other tasks and responsibilities. However, unless he or she is able to select appropriate activities and present them to groups of participants so effectively that they will become deeply involved in satisfying and rewarding play, the overall recreation program cannot be fully successful.

This chapter provides a thorough analysis of the process of activity leadership, including (a) the selection of appropriate activities; (b) an analysis of effective leadership personality; (c) basic concepts of teaching and learning; and (d) leadership techniques in several areas, including games, music, creative dramatics, arts and crafts, dance, nature activities and sports.

SELECTION OF APPROPRIATE ACTIVITY

Three important factors should be considered when selecting recreation activities for inclusion in a public or voluntary-agency program. These are (a) whether the activity has appeal, that is, whether people *want* to take part in it and *enjoy* it; (b) whether it is socially acceptable and promotes positive or constructive values; and (c) whether the activity is administratively appropriate, in terms of the kinds of leadership, equipment or facilities it might require for participation. In addition to these general factors, the choice of appropriate recreational activities for any group depends on the following elements:

1. The *age* of the group, since one's tastes and interests with respect to leisure activity are affected by one's chronological age.

2. The *physical health* and general *fitness* level of the participants, which influence the choice of activity or require that it be modified.
3. The *psychological* or *mental status* of the participants. Obviously, if one or all of the members of a group were emotionally disturbed or mentally retarded, it would affect their ability to participate satisfactorily in certain activities.
4. The *size* of the group. A very large group cannot receive the same degree of personal attention and instruction for each member that a much smaller group might.
5. The *amount of time* to be given to the activity. Certain activities require two or three hours or more to be carried out successfully, while others can be enjoyed in just a few moments.
6. The *facility* available to the group, and its potential for different types of program activities.
7. The *previous recreational experience* of the group, which provides a base for new learning and affects the group's attitude toward different forms of recreational activities.

When selecting activities for a group, the leader should be aware of all these factors and should choose experiences that will meet the needs and interests of group members as completely as possible. Beyond this, he or she should make sure that the activity is in harmony with the goals of the sponsoring organization as well as with his or her own philosophy of recreation service.

The leader should be fully aware of the kinds of social interaction encouraged by the activity. What sorts of group relationships are promoted? Is it a game in which players compete vigorously against each other? Is it an arts and crafts activity in which each participant works on his or her own project? Is it a dramatic presentation with close, cooperative small-group interaction? Depending on the needs of group members, any one of these outcomes might be highly desirable.

Recognizing all these factors, the leader should encourage group members themselves to select and plan activities and, when possible, take on much of the direct responsibility for organizing and carrying them out.

EFFECTIVE LEADERSHIP PERSONALITY

There is obviously no single effective leadership personality. It is not possible to say that a leader must be highly gregarious or extroverted to be effective with groups, or that he or she should be extremely dynamic, humorous or sensitive, have a loud or soft voice, or possess any other specific attribute.

However, it is obvious that the leader's personality and manner of relating to group members will have a considerable effect on his or her ability to involve them successfully in recreational activities. If the leader is enthusiastic and lively when presenting activities, group members are likely to share his or her interest. The leader should be well organized and able to "get things rolling" with a minimum of delay or confusion. He or she should be able to present activities so they are easily understood, and should be well prepared with the materials or equipment needed for participation.

Beyond this, the leader should be able to view the activity not just as a single event or experience, but as part of a continuing series of involvements in leisure pursuits for participants. In this sense, he or she must regard each activity as providing an opportunity for pleasure, satisfaction and personal growth through healthy social involvement and the exercise of individual, creative expression.

Ability to Teach.   Finally, the leader must be able to *teach* effectively.

It is true that much recreation leadership does not involve teaching as such; supervising children on a playground and taking them on a trip are not essentially instructional acts. However, a major portion of the leader's responsibility *does* involve teaching. He or she introduces activities such as games, dances, arts and crafts, or sports. And, just as a schoolteacher does, the leader must teach the participants the *skills* involved in the activity if they are to carry it out successfully and enjoy it to its fullest.

Obviously, then, leaders should know how to teach activities, because teaching is an important part of their work. Supervisors should also be familiar with this process, because it is their responsibility to help leaders become *better* teachers. Thus, on both levels, effective teaching is a key concern of recreation professionals.

While many persons are instinctively good teachers, others have difficulty in breaking down activities into their component parts and in communicating them to participants. And even those who are strong natural teachers can improve, if they become more fully aware of the principles of skilled teaching.

BASIC CONCEPTS OF TEACHING AND LEARNING

There has been a tremendous amount of research into the psychology of learning during the past several decades, resulting in the wide acceptance of certain concepts that should be of value to any individual concerned with the teaching process.

Awareness of Individual Differences

It is essential to recognize that each learner is an individual and must learn in his or her own way. Different people benefit from different kinds of teaching methods or stimuli, and each person's retention of what has been learned also differs. Leaders must be aware of the differences among individuals, and must avoid either a standardized approach toward teaching all participants or uniform expectations of how much and what they will learn.

Realistically, this does not mean that the typical recreation leader is able to devote tremendous amounts of time to each participant and to give him or her a full measure of personally designed instruction. However, the leader should be fully aware of each group member, and individual encouragement and advice should be given whenever possible.

Learning by Doing

In general, people learn best by *doing*. It is not enough to be told about an activity; it is usually necessary to take part in it and to learn concrete skills by participation. It is not necessarily true that *all* learning requires overt responses from the learner, for it is possible for some learning to occur while one is merely sitting, observing or listening. However, the best learning occurs through involvement.

This does not always mean that a learner must be physically active. The nature of the doing depends on the activity. The best way to learn a sport, a dance skill or a craft activity is to take part in it directly. However, listening and reading are effective ways of learning essentially verbal materials, and learning about music may be based on listening to a lecture and then to music—both physically passive acts. In any case, the leader must be aware of the need to get people involved in *doing*, as rapidly and as meaningfully as possible, if they are to learn skills successfully.

Analyzing the Learning Task

It is necessary to analyze and understand the nature of the learning task when presenting any activity to participants. Exactly what are the key elements that they must learn? What actions or skills are not relevant or important? If the leader is able to identify these components and make them clear to participants, the learning process becomes immensely easier. On the other hand, if he or she is wasting energy and time in drilling participants on skills that are not crucial or that keep them from learning the important techniques, the entire process of teaching and learning is frustrated.

For example, in presenting an active group game, the primary task is to clarify the basic purpose of the game (i.e., whether it is a "tag" game, in which the purpose is to catch other players, or a "guessing" game, in which the purpose is to identify a title or object) and the sequence of play. If at the outset a leader gives major emphasis to teaching minor rules or playing strategies of a game, and not to teaching its fundamental purpose and structure, the learning task has not been properly analyzed and presented.

Selecting Appropriate Teaching Devices

When the basic skills or components of the activity have been identified, the teacher must then determine how best to communicate them to learners. Most recreation activities should be taught through demonstration—by having the leader or a selected group of participants *show* the dance, the sports skills or the arts and crafts technique. However, a variety of other inputs can and should be used. Verbal description or commentary, cues that prompt accurate response, or audiovisual aids such as diagrams, slides, loop-films or regular films may all be useful in teaching skills. It is important to experiment and determine *which* teaching devices are most effective, since it is possible to "overload the channel" by providing too many kinds of teaching inputs.

⑤ "Whole" Versus "Part" Instruction

For years there has been a controversy about the best approach to organizing skills for instruction—whether to present the entire activity as a "whole," so that individuals may learn it all at once, or to present it by "parts," in step-by-step units of instruction.

Those supporting the "part" method were influenced by the early behaviorist psychologists, who held that it is best not to teach for generalized responses but for specific behaviors in clearly defined situations. It was believed that all tasks must be divided into parts that must be learned and practiced separately. Then, as in a dance involving several parts, they are learned as a total sequence and performed as a whole. Or, in the case of an activity like swimming, which involves a number of separate skills (stroking, kicking, breathing), each skill must be identified and learned separately before the entire activity is performed simultaneously.

In contrast, those proposing the "whole" method argue that the most effective learning takes place when the task is perceived and approached in its entirety. Clearly, both approaches have merit, and both should be employed. An activity that involves several distinctly separate skills and sequences of action, such as a complicated craft activity, simply cannot be learned as a "whole" but must be taken by stages. On the other hand, many sports skills or other play activities can certainly be learned best in a single, continuous learning experience.

⑥ Motivation and Learning Readiness

Unless individuals are motivated and ready to learn, the teaching process cannot be completely successful. Motivation refers to a general level of arousal and interest, a state of willingness or eagerness for activity. There must be a physiological or psychological need in the individual that makes him or her ready to learn. Furthermore, the learner must be old enough, strong enough or experienced enough in other underlying skills to be ready to take on this new challenge. Finally, the preparedness, or "set," of the learner is important; he or she must be attentive and ready to learn.

Most of the literature concerning principles of learning deals with the ways in which children learn. However, it is generally accepted that adults learn in a different way than do children—and it is essential that recreation leaders be aware of these differences.

For example, as a person matures, his or her self-concept becomes increasingly independent and self-directed. Individuals accumulate a growing reservoir of knowledge and experience that facilitates new learning. Learning itself focuses increasingly on developmental tasks required by new social roles, and a person's time perspective changes from one of postponed application of knowledge to one of immediate application.

Because of these differences, the adult's orientation toward learning shifts from "subject" or "skill-centeredness" to "problem-centeredness." Guidelines for meaningful learning for adults include the following: (a) learning should be based on the real experience of the learner; (b) learning should give the adult as much insight into relationships as possible; and (c) learning should be consciously aimed at achieving the learner's identified goals.

Reinforcement of Learning

This important concept holds that when individuals perform correctly, their action should be immediately reinforced, so that it will be repeated correctly and ultimately fixed as a behavioral response to a stimulus. This theory was developed through the "stimulus-and-response" work of Pavlov, who developed reflex behaviors of involuntary action in response to certain stimuli in laboratory animals. An American educational psychologist, Thorndike, extended the "pleasure-pain" principle (we do what brings pleasure and avoid what brings pain) to a so-called *law of effect*. This held that when a connection between stimulus and response is made, and the subject discovers that carrying out a certain action will bring a reward, constructive learning takes place.

The use of punishment to modify behavior or discourage incorrect or inappropriate responses is the subject of considerable disagreement. Some psychologists hold that it is not a desirable means of behavior modification, because it only tends to suppress undesired responses temporarily and may bring about undesirable complications. The essential point is that positive reinforcement is believed to be more effective than punishment, resulting in faster and more efficient learning. Skinner points out that in the early phases of training, it is important to reinforce every desired response. Once learning is well under way, reinforcement should become more and more intermittent, and may be discontinued as long as the desired learning behavior is maintained.

Transfer of Learning

Once a basic skill or understanding has been achieved, learning related tasks becomes easier. "Transfer" is defined as the effect that practice of one task has upon the learning of another task. In essence, a skill that has been learned in one activity can be readily transferred to another, provided that the tasks have strongly comparable elements and that the learner both has sufficient recall of the original skill and is able to recognize its place in the new task.

(9) Practice of Skills

This is particularly applicable to the learning of physical skills in areas such as sports or dance. The "law of exercise" holds that connections between stimuli and desired responses are strengthened with use. However, practice must be distinguished from mere repetition and ideally should include both rewards and new learnings. Practice may be "massed" (provided in longer but fewer sessions) or "distributed" (provided in a greater number of briefer sessions). Generally, massed practice is more effective when the learner is highly motivated, distributed practice when the learner is less motivated. Practice that is too extended in a single session may pass the point of effective learning when it keeps repeating what has already been learned, or when participants become fatigued or inattentive.

Other Principles of Learning

A number of other concepts of effective teaching and learning may be summarized briefly.

Both "drill" and "problem-solving" approaches to learning may be used. In general, most learning psychologists today encourage the latter approach, in which the learner is encouraged to see the meaning of facts, the effect of different ways of accomplishing a task and the insights that underlie successful performance.

There is no single, optimum schedule for the learning of all skills. Instead, each skill or task must be analyzed and periods of instruction and practice scheduled according to the capacity, motivation and stage of learning of participants.

The setting of goals is an important factor in successful learning. They should be high enough to challenge learners and provide them with an incentive for working hard. On the other hand, they should not be so high that they are unrealistic or excessively difficult to accomplish. The successful achievement of a given task brings satisfaction and the willingness to attempt new tasks. Failure and frustration may result in the learner's unwillingness to continue the process or move on to other activities.

Ability grouping is a useful tool for learning activities in which it is necessary to direct the teaching method at the precise level of the group's ability, and where participants learn from each other as they pursue a common learning experience. However, placing participants in clearly defined and identifiable groups of "high ability" and "low ability" may have undesirable effects on their social attitudes and self-concepts, and so should be used with caution by leaders.

Finally, effective leaders make use of the "teachable moment." Rather than try to impose their view of when and how people should learn, they focus on a person's readiness and state of motivation. They also make use of what happens in a teaching situation to implant key concepts or insights creatively, and at the point when they will have the greatest impact on learners.

LEADERSHIP METHODS IN SPECIFIC ACTIVITIES

Obviously, there is more to effective teaching than being aware of learning theories. Each type of activity, and each learning situation, imposes its own set of appropriate leadership methods. This section offers a number of guidelines useful for recreation leaders in several major areas of program activity, including games, arts and crafts, sports, music, dance, dramatics and nature activities.

The approaches presented here are drawn from the direct professional experience of the authors and from manuals published by a number of municipal recreation and park agencies throughout the United States and Canada. The activities chosen are found primarily in playground and community center programs. Specific *examples* of activities are not presented, since this is not a program text. However, the Appendix includes a useful listing of books that may be used as resources by students and leaders seeking to practice the guidelines presented here or to enrich their programs.

Games Leadership

Many different types of games may be used in community recreation settings such as playgrounds, day camps or community centers. These include active group games, social games and mixers, dramatic games, mental games and puzzles, and a host of others. They may be used with all ages and in many settings. However, this section deals with only one type—games of low organization, such as tag, relay or simple ball games, which are often referred to as "playground games" and are used primarily with children.

Goals of Playground Games

It is important for the leader to know why a particular activity is being presented. The goals and purposes of low-organization games are as follows:
1. Games provide a useful means of organizing small-group or team activities; children enjoy playing together in such groups.
2. Games provide an opportunity for competition, and for the test of agility, strength, skill and intelligence, under controlled circumstances.

3. Supervised games may be used to help develop such character traits as cooperation, self-control, willingness to obey rules, obedience to officials and habits of fair play and sportsmanship.
4. Games provide an enjoyable form of physical exercise and help to teach skills that will later be useful in playing sports.
5. Games represent an economical use of space and equipment and a means of working with a large group of participants at one time.

Selection of Appropriate Games

The success of playground games will depend on whether you have chosen games that are suitable to the participants and the situation. The following factors should be considered.

Games should be selected primarily on the basis of the participants' age level rather than their sex. It is possible for boys and girls to play a wide variety of low-organization games together. Generally, games for children up to the age of eight years should (a) be fairly vigorous, involving fundamental skills of running, jumping, hopping, starting, stopping, throwing and catching; (b) be in simple formations and have fairly simple rules; and (c) involve individual achievement, rather than place a heavy stress on complicated team play or strategy.

Games for children over the age of eight may be more complicated, be of longer duration, and involve team play to a greater degree.

Games should be selected on the basis of adequate space and numbers of participants. If you have a large area and many players, you should attempt to involve them all in mass games. With limited numbers and space the reverse would be true. Game selection should take the weather into account; active games are suitable for a cold day, quiet games for a hot day. There should be variety in the choice of games, with the leader providing some new games, for learning and challenge, as well as some old favorites in any single games session. It is also advisable to mix active and quiet games and games with different types of social structures.

Preparation for Leading Games

Make sure you are ready, *before* any game session, in the following ways:
1. Select a number of games appropriate to the age, ability and interest of the group. Have more games ready than you will need. List them on a card so they will be readily available.
2. Review the game in your own mind. Make sure you are thoroughly familiar with its rules and playing strategy. If necessary, practice it in advance with a group of players.
3. Make sure that any needed equipment is available and that boundary lines, if necessary, are marked.
4. Arouse the interest of the boys and girls in the games session by announcing it in advance, "talking it up" or displaying posters advertising playground games at a regular time.

Organizing Teams or Groups

Most playground games involve breaking up the overall group into smaller groups or teams. This is done in one of the following ways:

1. Generally, it is best to have the leader pick the teams, alternately choosing players for Teams A and B, and keeping in mind the size and ability of each player.
2. A second approach is to have players form a line or a large circle, and then to count them off into groups or teams.

Although children tend to want to form their own teams, this may not be a good idea, because (a) the better players are often chosen first and the weaker ones last, giving the latter a feeling of rejection; (b) bigger children tend to want to be on the same team, making the sides uneven; and (c) there is a risk that you will wind up with one-sex groups, i.e., boys playing against girls, which creates unnecessary antagonism.

Before starting the game, make sure that all teams have an equal number of players. If players of two or more teams "mingle" during the game (as opposed to staying on opposite sides of a line), make sure that they are marked in some way so they can be readily identified.

Teaching the Game

There are many approaches to the actual presentation of games. Here are several useful guidelines:

1. After you have gotten the group into the proper teams or formation, make sure you have their attention. If you have a whistle, blow it as a signal for quiet. Do not overuse it. Make sure that you have everyone's attention; do not talk over crowd noise.
2. When presenting the game, stand where the maximum number of players can see you and hear you, and where you will be facing them, rather than with your back to them.
3. Create an air of expectancy by your own enthusiasm. Quickly announce the game with a brief introduction, and then begin to teach it.
4. Make your explanations clear, brief and correct. If necessary, use one or more players to demonstrate the activity. If it is at all complicated, repeat this.
5. Ask for questions if any of the players seem confused. Then start the game without further delay.
6. Minor errors or faults in play may be corrected by blowing the whistle, stopping the game briefly, showing the correct action and continuing play.
7. If an activity is going badly, with much confusion, stop it. Demonstrate it again, explain the rules, ask for questions and answer them—and then begin the activity again.
8. Make sure that rules are obeyed. If necessary, stop the game to enforce them, and then continue.

9. Keep interest high, and encourage the players enthusiastically.
10. If the game involves keeping score, let the players know the team scores from time to time.
11. End the game while interest is still relatively high rather than let it drag on and become boring.

Controlling Behavior of Participants

One of the great values of games is that they provide an opportunity for children to play vigorously and to express their energy in constructive ways. However, if the players become overexcited and wild, the leader will need to control this.

Some noise and shouting should be allowed; these are natural expressions of enjoyment and show that the game is successful. However, the leader should not permit uncontrolled "bedlam." When a whistle is blown to signify the end of play or the selection of new players, make sure that all players understand that they must be quiet.

Safety factors should be kept in mind, with all equipment used correctly and physical contact kept under control. Excessive "horseplay" or fighting should be stopped at once. The leader should insist on fair play and enforce the rules strictly. Children sometimes misbehave because they are losing and are dispirited. Give encouragement to losing teams, and rotate the make-up of teams between games to avoid this problem.

General Leadership Style

The leader's overall style or manner with the group can help to determine his or her success in leading games. The following suggestions are useful in improving one's effectiveness:

1. Always try to be at ease, optimistic, and positive in manner. Do not get overexcited or "flustered," no matter how excited children may become.
2. Throughout your leading, emphasize the positive, not the negative. Use "do's" rather than "don'ts."
3. Project your voice at all times. Speak clearly and distinctly in a pleasing but firm voice. Give one command at a time.
4. Let your interest and enthusiasm be contagious. As a leader, have fun yourself. Stress the fun and play element of games, and do not be afraid to appreciate humorous situations.
5. Depending on the game situation, you may play in the game with the children. This may be done particularly to even up the sides but not if it means displacing one child player.
6. Do not overpraise gifted individual players or permit them to dominate play.
7. Try to have every child participate successfully. Help shy or hesitant children join in. If children are physically disabled, have

them play if possible; if not, let them participate in some way, perhaps as scorer, timekeeper or judge.

Evaluating the Game Session

When the game session is over, the conscientious leader should review it thoroughly, asking questions such as the following:

Did the children enjoy the games and take part wholeheartedly? Were some of them left out, and if so, why? Were the games successful? Which ones did not work out? Why not? Should these games be played again?

Did you maintain effective discipline, or was there a behavior problem? How could you handle this more effectively? Did the children show respect for your leadership?

How could your teaching of the individual games have been improved? Were children given a voice in the selection of games? Did you keep a record of the games that were played to be used when planning future activities?

Using New Games

A final important suggestion for the games leader is that he or she investigate the use of New Games. These are games, some entirely new and others based on traditional game forms, that emphasize the fun of playing, rather than high-level skill or winning as a goal. They represent a form of joyful, creative play among people of all ages and backgrounds, in which players are encouraged to use their imaginations in devising new play experiences. The New Games movement has published a useful collection of activities and sponsors many workshops for leadership training. Its basic slogan is "Play Hard, Play Fair, Nobody Hurt."[1] It is important to recognize that New Games are not just a collection of games; instead, they stem from a philosophy of play that is immensely appealing in modern society.

Music Leadership: Community Singing

Music is one of the most popular forms of recreational activity. It may include instrumental music instruction, bands and orchestras, barbershop quartets and choral groups, rhythm bands and many other activities. Community singing is probably the most useful and widely practiced musical activity in general recreation programs; it consists of informal group singing of traditional, folk, "fun" and action songs, and has many values.

Community singing can be enjoyed by people of all ages and by those who have limited physical capability. It offers a constructive outlet for excess energy and can be a useful way of quieting a group after activity.

Community singing has the unique gift of fellowship. For many centu-

[1]See "No Victor, So No Spoils," *Time*, September 11, 1978, p. 54, and Edward R. Walsh: "New Games—In Pursuit of Creative Play," *Parks and Recreation*, May 1979, pp. 49–51.

ries, people have sung together to affirm their fellowship, and singing still has this unusual power. Singing offers an opportunity for creative expression, and it can give participants a sense of personal accomplishment and satisfaction.

Singing may be approached as an informal, impromptu experience or, with sufficient practice and training, may be used for performances and entertainment of others. Finally, it may be enjoyed in almost any setting and does not require special facilities or equipment or a high degree of leadership ability.

Preparing to Lead Songs

Although the leader need not be a skilled musician or have an outstanding voice, it helps to be able to carry a tune and sing with a fairly pleasing quality. The other important attributes of successful song leaders are enthusiasm, the ability to create a sense of good fellowship and enjoyment of music, and the ability to teach a variety of appealing songs.

When selecting songs, the leader should pick several that are familiar to the group and others that will be new to them and should be taught. He or she should practice these songs and know them thoroughly so that it will not be necessary to refer to a book or songsheet while leading.

In a small group, no musical accompaniment is usually necessary. In a larger group, it helps if the leader or a friend can play an instrument, such as a guitar or accordion. In a very large group, the most useful accompaniment is provided by a skilled pianist. In a songfest with a new group or one unaccustomed to community singing, the leader might wish to prepare songsheets or to show slides with verses on them to help people learn the words quickly.

Steps of Leading a Song

There is no one, cut-and-dried method of leading a song. However, most successful song leaders follow this sequence:

1. Get the group's attention, and announce the song clearly. Give it a brief introduction to arouse interest.
2. Sing the first verse through to give the participants a sense of what the song is like.
3. If the words are difficult, you might teach them first without the melody, one line at a time, having the participants repeat them after you. Otherwise, teach both words and music together, a line or two at a time. When an entire verse has been learned in this way, have the group learn the chorus or the next verse.
4. Sing the entire song. If the participants are doing it correctly and enjoying it, continue it until the end. If not, stop them and correct the singing.
5. Go on to a new song. Continue singing as long as interest is high.

Guides for Improving Singing

The steps of actually leading a song are rather simple. It is somewhat more difficult, however, to get people to sing *well* and to enjoy it to the fullest.

1. It is necessary to pitch the song correctly for them. An accompanist may know the proper pitch. If you do not have an accompanist, select a key that is in a comfortable range for you and see if the group members find it suits their voices.
2. When beginning a song, get the group "set," or ready, and then start with an introduction from the accompanist or a sharp, clear movement that will bring all singers in together. "Attack" and "release" each section of the song clearly.
3. Begin singing with a familiar and well-liked song. Then move on to an appealing variety, including folk songs, patriotic songs, action and novelty songs, songs with repeated choruses, songs from other lands, old show tunes and others that will have broad appeal.
4. If the group is singing well, divide it into sections for rounds and part songs. Encourage harmony and changes in volume (moving from loud to soft), and urge people to *listen* to each other, which always improves singing.
5. Recognize all sections of the audience, and reach out to them with your leadership rather than to just a few singers in the front of the group. Encourage all to take part, but do not force anyone.
6. Sing along with the group, but do not dominate them, particularly if you have a very strong voice or are using a microphone.
7. Praise and encourage the group for singing well. If you correct them, do it pleasantly and constructively.
8. Ask for requests, but select those that you feel will be most suitable for the group. Do *not* overteach; a community singing session is not a formal instruction period, and it should be lively and spontaneous.

Use of Hand Gestures. Many community song leaders make use of hand gestures in leading singing, although it is not absolutely necessary, particularly with smaller groups. With larger groups, or when more polished singing is desired, the leader may use the traditional gestures to indicate rhythm. When "conducting," make large gestures, particularly if you are leading a large group. Make generous strokes away from your body, using arms in one graceful extension from the shoulder to the fingers; the total up-and-down movement should not be more than 12 inches.

When using hand gestures, try to move in a natural, relaxed way, with arms raised high enough for all to see and hands cupped slightly, as if shaking hands. Use vigorous movements for lively songs and more flowing or graceful movements for quieter selections. It is often unnecessary to use gestures throughout a song; however, they should be used at the beginning and end, to emphasize the tempo or beat, to draw out the richness of sound, to control volume or in other special ways.

Dramatics Leadership

Recreation programs often sponsor different dramatic activities—both formal and informal—which may include charades, pantomimes, skits, puppetry, story-telling, pageants, informal dramatics and, finally, actual theater programs. The urge to act is universal and finds its greatest release among younger children. For this age group, play-acting is useful both as a form of enjoyable activity in playgounds and community centers and as a lead-up to more advanced forms of theater experience.

Values of Creative Dramatics. Creative dramatics may be defined simply as an informal approach to children's theater that makes use of spontaneous or improvised activity rather than formal plays or written scripts. It has several specific goals and purposes.

Dramatic activity encourages the development of poise and confidence, the improvement of speech and diction, and a more expressive, graceful and well-coordinated body. It also promotes imagination, creativity and a deeper appreciation of theater as an art form. Of special interest to therapeutic recreation specialists is the fact that children are able to express their feelings through acting and often enter deeply into the situations and roles they are portraying.

Creative dramatics are a valuable form of group experience; children learn to cooperate and work closely with others, and thus develop important social skills. Dramatic play provides an additional dimension to the community recreation program, and it appeals to participants who may not be as skilled in games, sports or other typical playground activities.

Lead-Up Activities in Creative Dramatics

The intelligent recreation leader does not attempt to begin dramatics with children by having them take part in full-fledged group presentations at once. Instead, various lead-up activities, such as improvisations, story telling, skits and dramatic stunts, and pantomimes, should be used as preparation for more formal drama projects.

1. Improvisations are simple forms of dramatic play in which children act out characters from stories, simple themes of daily life, moods or other familiar themes. They may be approached as individual stunts or as small-group activities. Typical improvisations that may be suggested to younger children include the following:
   a. Pretending to cook, iron, have a tea party, care for a baby, sweep the floor or rake leaves.
   b. Playing different sports, such as playing tennis, riding a bicycle, dribbling a basketball or throwing a baseball.
   c. Feeling different moods, such as "happy," "sad," "angry" or "frightened."
   d. Performing other household activities, such as brushing teeth, combing hair, answering the telephone or shoveling snow.

2. Storytelling is a popular activity for younger children. After a story has been told, children may act out different characters from it or take key parts of the action and pantomime these events. Such stories might include traditional folk tales, like *Rumplestiltskin, Cinderella,* the *Sleeping Beauty* or *Jack and the Beanstalk,* or well-known nursery rhymes, like *Jack and Jill, Simple Simon* or *Little Miss Muffet.*
3. Skits and dramatic stunts may be carried on in several ways:
   a. The leader may tell a story, such as the *Lion Hunt,* in which, as he or she tells the tale, children pantomime each event or happening.
   b. The leader may prepare a "bag of props," in which several familiar objects (e.g., paintbrush, flashlight, cap) are placed. Small groups of children are given these props and act out simple stories based on them.
   c. The leader may use charades as a lead-up activity by having individual children act out book, song or movie titles, proverbs, or famous characters for others to guess.
   d. Imaginary situations may be developed in which children are given a one-line "skeleton story" to act out, for example, "you are trying to study with a toothache," "you are bringing a poor report card home to your father," or "you are walking past a graveyard late at night."
4. Pantomimes may be used in any of the other types of creative dramatic activities or may be presented as a separate activity. There are dozens of good ideas for pantomime, including the following:
   a. You are at an amusement park; act out any of the things that happen there (eating spun candy, shooting at targets, riding the roller-coaster).
   b. You are Santa Claus, and you take presents out of your sack for a group of children. What are they?
   c. You take a trip to a farm; act out the different chores that farm boys and girls do each day (pitching hay, milking cows, finding eggs, feeding chickens and so on).
   d. You join a symphony orchestra; act out any of the players (drum, piano, violin, horn or conductor).

Presenting Group Dramatic Experiences

After children have enjoyed activities of this type for a time and have gained confidence and skill in presenting ideas through movement and speech, they are ready to engage in more structured group dramatic experiences. These may be based on stories, poems, songs or real life happenings. Although there is no single method for developing such presentations, the following sequence is fairly typical:

1. Select a story. This may be based on a story which the leader tells the children, or it may be one that the children develop independently.
2. The leader tells the story in a relaxed, informal manner, bringing out the humor or suspense in it and using direct dialogue whenever possible. The story should have interesting action and characters but should not have too complicated a plot.
3. The children and the leader discuss the story, analyzing its meaning, the different characters, the most important scenes and exciting moments.
4. Children should be selected to take different parts. They may volunteer for different roles themselves, or the leader may assign them. If the group is large enough, it may divide into several smaller groups, each of which undertakes to act out the play and assign roles to its members.
5. The story should be reviewed to develop the basic plot outline, which consists of the most important scenes that will be acted out. Then children begin to act it out. They should be encouraged (a) to be natural and to use gestures, movements and speech that feel comfortable to them; (b) to pace themselves and to speak slowly, clearly and with a sense of being the character; and (c) to begin to think of how they "feel" toward the other characters and how the stage action may be laid out so it is most effective.
6. After each of the scenes has been played, children should review the entire experience. They should be helped to analyze both themselves and others in constructive and supportive ways, and to make sound suggestions for improvement.
7. If the children wish to, the story may then be played out in its entirety for other children on the playground or for an audience of parents. It is never necessary, in informal dramatics, to have an audience. However, if children wish to, they may get great satisfaction from performing their work for others.

Leadership Guidelines

The creative dramatics leader should operate in an informal, unstructured way. Performance is not the group's primary goal, and the process is far more important than the product in informal dramatics. Nonetheless, the leader does play an important role.

First, children must gain the confidence to express themselves freely; the leader's encouragement, assistance and skill in establishing a comfortable, accepting group climate are essential if this is to be done. Next the leader must be able to present good stories or themes that the children can enjoy and consider for dramatic expression. If the group develops enough interest in dramatics to wish to put on more formal presentations, the leader must help them with the following tasks:

1. Selecting appropriate scripts.
2. Outlining a regular schedule of meeting days and hours, and setting up specific rehearsal hours that will be observed by all.
3. Casting the play and assigning other responsibilities (costumes, props, stagecraft, and so forth) to children who will not be acting.
4. Teaching simple rules of stage movement, the use of voice, acting, and so forth, to participants.
5. Getting help from arts and crafts leaders or other skilled persons in designing and making props and costumes, and assisting with lights and public-address systems, if necessary.
6. Involving parents, as volunteer aides in the project, in making costumes, helping with transportation and publicity or in other needed ways.
7. Maintaining the motivation and interest of the players through the entire process, including reassuring those who lose confidence and wish to withdraw.
8. Carrying out final "technical" and "dress" rehearsals, and polishing the performance.
9. Putting on the final performance or performances.

Arts and Crafts Leadership

Arts and crafts are enjoyed by all age groups, both sexes and individuals with a wide range of abilities and interests. They include many activities, from sculpture and oil painting or sketching to ceramics, weaving or extremely basic hobby-craft projects. Their values include the following: (a) they stimulate and encourage self-expression, imagination and creativity, and help develop an appreciation of design and color; (b) they provide a sense of accomplishment and satisfaction in the final product; (c) they encourage orderliness in caring for materials and work areas, working patiently toward a final product and cooperation with others; (d) they result in final products that may be shown to others in exhibitions or displays; and (e) they provide hours of self-absorbed enjoyment, for either individuals or small groups, in limited surroundings and at minimal cost.

General Guidelines for Leadership

The task of arts and crafts leadership involves both the skilled teaching of individual crafts or projects and the overall management or direction of arts and crafts as a program activity. The successful arts and crafts leader should be

1. Able to select appropriate activities that will suit the varied needs and interests of participants, and to present these in simple, clear ways that will motivate others to take part.
2. Well-organized in the planning of projects, gathering of materials and management of the overall program.

3. Enthusiastic and positive in approaching the activity. On the playground, for example, he or she should (a) encourage and praise participants for their efforts in a sincere way, as children can easily spot "phonies"; (b) encourage children to finish every job they start (if a child is not able to do this while the rest of the group completes a project, special time should be set aside to return to it); and (c) provide a wide variety of arts and crafts projects, so that every child, regardless of age or ability, can find interesting and rewarding activities in this area.
4. Aware of the creative values of arts and crafts. Instead of presenting mechanical or ready-made arts and crafts projects, in which the participant uses a hobby kit or "grinds" out a standardized product, the leader should present activities that provide the opportunity to be original and expressive.

Management of Arts and Crafts Sessions

Arts and crafts are approached on many different levels. They may be the partial responsibility of a leader or director who does not have special skill or background in this area, but who can direct a number of fairly simple projects. On playgrounds, arts and crafts are usually provided at regular times each week, as part of the recreation schedule, for all who wish to take part. In community centers, arts and crafts instruction is usually approached in more formal ways, with actual classes being set up on the basis of age levels, degree of skill or type of activity being presented. Often, a specific room or workshop with special equipment and storage areas is set aside only for arts and crafts, with a skilled specialist in charge of the program.

Although each of these situations may impose its own requirements or approaches, the following guidelines apply to the management of all arts and crafts activities in recreation settings:

1. Schedule arts and crafts activities on a regular basis. Make sure this is known to all participants through posters, fliers and announcements. Encourage participation in advance.
2. Keep a display of finished arts and crafts projects as a means of praising those who have done good work in the activity and interesting others to take part.
3. Know in advance what projects you will be presenting. Have a sample of the product to show participants at the preceding session to encourage attendance.
4. Be sure you have all the materials and equipment you will need for the project set out and ready to go.
5. Demonstrate each step of the craft activity clearly and precisely as you progress. Encourage children to ask questions, and make sure they are fully answered. As the group works, keep them closely supervised at all times, giving help as needed. Do *not* do the work for them.

6. Make your program so enjoyable that participants will want to come. Do not encourage onlookers; get them involved in activity. First get regular participants started with their projects, then pay attention to newcomers.
7. Allow enough time to complete the activity. If it cannot be done in a single session, make sure that all work in progress can be stored safely until the next time.
8. Maintain good discipline and order in the crafts session to avoid accidents and to permit all participants to work seriously on their projects in a quiet, controlled atmosphere.
9. Allow enough time for clean-up, and expect all participants to join in this as a matter of group responsibility. Keep a clean, well-organized area, and make sure that damaged equipment is repaired or replaced. Since it usually takes time for arts and crafts materials to be ordered and sent, requisition all needed materials well in advance.
10. If possible, plan for an arts and crafts exhibit, and invite parents and other community members. Although your goal is not to overemphasize competition, it is a good idea to give awards (ribbons, scrolls and so on) to the best artists or craftsmen in a number of categories.
11. In addition to exhibits, plan other special events or projects that make use of arts and crafts, or integrate them with other recreation activities, such as puppet shows, costume-making projects for drama programs, kite contests, poster displays, nature crafts exhibits and so on. A communitywide Arts and Crafts Fair, including both children's and adults' work, is a good year's end activity.

Many useful and enjoyable arts and crafts projects are described in the books listed in the Appendix of this text. As the leader works with these, it is important to stress two sets of goals: (a) personal creative development and expressiveness, and (b) the development of technique, or craft skills. Often, individuals realize for the first time in an arts and crafts program that they have unique talents and abilities, and they may be encouraged to join special classes or undertake more demanding and challenging types of craft hobbies.

Leadership in Recreational Dance

Dance in its various forms is a popular recreation activity that may be enjoyed by all ages, in a variety of settings. Younger children may take part in creative rhythmics, singing games and simple folk and square dances. Older children, teenagers and young adults are more likely to enjoy social dancing, more advanced folk and square dancing, or the creative types of dance, such as modern dance, ballet or jazz dance. Even senior citizens take part in social dancing and simple folk or square dancing in Golden Age clubs or special community programs. Thus dance is a uniquely useful recreation activity.

Depending on the type of dance that is being offered, it may have the following specific goals or benefits: (a) it is a valuable form of physical experience in terms of developing neuromuscular skill and coordination and in promoting fitness; (b) it is a highly social experience, providing companionship and confidence in group settings; (c) it promotes artistic and creative growth and awareness; (d) it is an important part of the cultural heritage, including important ethnic or folk traditions; and (e) when children learn dance at an early age, it has the potential to become a leisure activity or hobby that they can enjoy throughout their lifetimes.

Guidelines for Dance Leadership

One need not be a highly skilled dancer or dance teacher to present dance activities to children in recreation settings, or to conduct simple folk and square dance activities for teenagers or adults. With a minimum of preparation, such as a basic course or two, a departmental clinic or workshop, and use of appropriate manuals, most leaders can be reasonably successful in this activity. However, for more advanced or established groups in any area of dance activity, specially trained leadership is essential. Some municipal recreation and park departments hire dance specialists who go from playground to playground during the summer and lead special sessions for all participants, and who also conduct training clinics for other leaders. In some cases, it is the responsibility of specialists to plan exhibitions, concerts, festivals or other large-scale special perfomances.

The teaching of dance—beyond a beginning level—requires knowledge of steps, skills, techniques and basic principles. This is true whether the teacher is presenting folk or square dance (each of which can be highly complex activities) or modern dance or ballet (both of which demand years of training to become an advanced performer). On a recreational level, the following leadership guidelines apply:

1. The leader should know the subject well and should make a point of observing other programs, gathering useful materials and attending classes or workshops to improve his or her skills.
2. Dance sessions should be carefully planned, well publicized, set at a regular time and involve continuity and improvement in skills over a period of time.
3. Dance classes, clubs or special sessions should be publicized as widely as possible, and an attempt made to involve boys as participants; in the past, dance has been falsely regarded as a primarily feminine activity, and it should be recognized that boys can enjoy it and be highly successful in it.
4. The leader's approach to participants should be warm and encouraging rather than critical. Dance must be made fun as well as instructive.

5. Maintain control of the teaching situation; particularly among younger children or pre-teenagers, coeducational dance sessions can be boisterous if the leader does not expect and demand good behavior.
6. Plan special events, such as performances, festivals or other exhibits, at which participants can show what they have learned.
7. Integrate dance instruction as fully as possible with other program activities, such as music, theater or arts and crafts.

Specific Leadership Skills

Dance leadership skills are presented here in two categories of activity: (a) creative dance and rhythms for younger children, and (b) basic folk or square dance instruction for all ages.

Creative Dance Teaching Methods

The approach used in this field is very much like that used in creative dramatics; it places primary importance on the child's own exploration of movement rather than on the "rote" learning of dance techniques.

1. The leader should have specific goals in mind. Usually, these relate to the following:
   a. Helping children understand how the body moves, and giving them experiences in a total range of movement exploration.
   b. Promoting their awareness of different qualities of movement that use the body as a means of communication.
   c. Developing musical understandings related to rhythm, tempo, phrasing and form, and relating these to movement.
   d. Developing personal expressiveness and creativity, and relating creative movement to other aesthetic experiences, such as art, literature or music.
   e. Giving early experiences in making dances by exploring elements such as direction, levels and floor patterns.
2. The leader should use a variety of approaches to stimulate movement exploration. Some examples follow:
   a. Exploration of locomotor movement—walking, running, skipping, sliding, running, leaping.
   b. Exploration of axial (non-locomotor) movement—swinging, striking, bending, stretching, shaking, bouncing.
   c. Use of suggested movement sequences, in which the leader suggests combinations of actions, and children interpret individually.
   d. Use of images as basis for movement, such as moving like animals, machines, vehicles, fairy tale characters.
   e. Use of music or percussive accompaniment to stimulate movement.

     f. Use of moods to suggest movement, such as sadness, happiness, anger, loneliness.

     g. Exploration of movement possibilities of parts of the body: arms, hands, head, feet.

     h. Use of pictures, stories or poems to suggest movement sequences.

3. The teacher should move from simple, basic movement expression to more complex combinations and skills with young children:

     a. More difficult challenges may be presented, in terms of combinations of movement.

     b. Gradually, movement skills may be introduced in which children deliberately work on such elements as flexibility, strength, coordination or balance.

     c. Different types of elements may be combined, such as floor patterns, levels, directions and rhythmic sequences.

     d. From exploring movement individually, young children can gradually move to working in pairs or small groups.

     e. From sheer spontaneous expression, children may be guided into *planning* dance sequences, working them out more carefully and showing them to others.

Throughout this process, the leader should not be concerned about the child's technique, although an obvious outcome of creative movement experiences should be the steady improvement of the body as an instrument of dance. As children gain in ability and motivation, they will want to know how to *dance* (in a more literal sense), and it will be possible to provide increasing elements of actual instruction in dance techniques. However, pleasure and creative expression should be emphasized throughout, and learning routines and drills should not be the focus of instruction.

While this approach is used primarily with young children, in some situations, such as psychiatric treatment programs, it may also be used with teenagers or adults.

Folk and Square Dance Leadership Methods

Essentially, teaching folk dancing involves the presentation of basic skills of movement, along with individual dances, thus building a repertoire of performing ability. The leader therefore is teaching *set* material to participants and must do so in as enjoyable and informal a manner as possible. Initially, many young children and teenagers have a dislike for dance because of the way it may have been presented to them in their school physical education classes. Therefore, on the playground or in the community center it must be made a pleasant experience rather than a grim, forced exercise.

The leader should present a variety of dances of different ethnic or national backgrounds, including American square dances. These should be geared to the skill level of the participants and should involve sequential learning of more difficult dances. Different patterns or group formations should be used, including couple dances, lines, squares and circle dances without partners. The last are particularly useful if there is resistance on the part of boys about dancing with girls as partners.

The leader should seek to have everyone take part, but should not insist that they do so. It is wise to begin a dance session with familiar, easy dances, and then to include several new or more challenging dances that must be taught. If the program is a party or festival, it is best to perform chiefly dances that have already been learned and will require little instruction. The leader should gear his or her material to the bulk of dancers within the group, rather than to the very expert participants or those who are having considerable difficulty.

Presenting a Single Dance

In addition to such general suggestions, the leader should know the specific guidelines that are useful when presenting a single dance to a group.

1. Select an appropriate dance, in terms of the level of ability of the group and the skill progression that you have planned.
2. Prepare yourself, making sure that you understand the dance thoroughly and can demonstrate it clearly. Make sure you have the needed record (or sheet music for an accompanist), that your record player is operating properly and that any other needed materials are available.
3. Have the group take the appropriate function. Stand where all the participants can see and hear you most effectively and where the accompanist (if you have one) can observe your signals.
4. Briefly introduce the dance, giving some information regarding its source or background and playing a portion of its music, to arouse interest in it.
5. Demonstrate the dance yourself, with a partner or with a group of participants.
   a. If it has several distinct sections, show these one at a time. After each one has been demonstrated, have the entire group repeat the action as you give verbal cues or directions.
   b. If the dance is fairly simple, or has only one or two sections, it may be best to demonstrate it all at once, and then have the entire group repeat the action.
6. Repeat Step 5 with musical accompaniment, making sure that the participants understand the dance and are performing it correctly. Then have them go through the entire dance, section by section, without stopping.
7. If the dancers are having no difficulty, have them do the entire dance to the music. If they are having trouble, stop and re-teach the section that is giving trouble. Then have them do the dance again.

8. Other guides for effective folk dance teaching include the following:
   a. Use a distinct signal to start the dancers and the music (assuming that you are using an accompanist), such as, "Ready—begin!"
   b. As you demonstrate, stand at different points on the floor so all can observe or hear the directions and have you close to them at some point. In some circle dances, it may be best to have participants form a line, standing behind you, in order to learn the dance best.
   c. Change partners occasionally to promote social interaction and help dancers learn from each other.
   d. Do not overteach. Progress as rapidly as is possible for your group.
   e. Plan to have special events, such as festivals and demonstrations, as culminating activities and to improve interest and motivation.

Nature Activity Leadership

Nature activities have been an important part of public and voluntary recreation programs for many years. Today, with the increasing concern with the environment and the need to promote effective conservation practices, many agencies see this as a high-priority area. The types of services and programs provided by recreation and park agencies in the field of nature fall into the following categories: nature clubs and outing groups; operation of nature centers and museums; playground zoos or aquariums; playground activities, such as nature games, hobbies, collections or craft activities; construction or conservation projects; gardening projects; weather study; practice of such skills as knotcraft, using a compass, canoeing, snow skiing or use of snowshoes, camp cookery and fire-making; and a wide variety of other activities. In providing such programs, some departments are able to use their own resources; others must rely on outdoor areas owned by nearby county or state park systems. In addition to activities of this type, some institutions that serve special populations are using nature activities, for example, horticulture therapy, as a new form of treatment.

Goals of Nature Activity

Nature activities have the following values and purposes in community recreation programs: (a) they help put young people, especially those who live in built-up cities and towns, in touch with the natural environment; (b) they provide an opportunity for adventure, controlled risk and challenge; (c) they encourage participants to develop a respect for the environment, and they provide a laboratory for teaching the principles of science in the most meaningful way possible; (d) they permit public recreation and park departments to make an important contribution to community life by sponsoring or co-sponsoring conservation, clean-up, or anti-pollution programs; and (e) they are *fun*, and worth doing if for no other reasons than purely recreational ones.

General Leadership Guidelines

There are no hard-and-fast rules for success in the leadership of nature activities. However, there are some general guidelines. First, the leader *must* have expertise in this area. It is not possible to introduce children and youth to nature in meaningful ways without a solid background of knowledge and understanding of the natural environment. To improve his or her competence, the leader should attend workshops and courses, read, visit nature centers and learn as much as possible about the subject. In addition, use should be made of guest lecturers, films, displays or other learning resources to enrich the program.

1. The leader should recognize that participants' attitudes about nature will vary considerably because of their past experiences. They may range from enthusiasm and interest to boredom or even fear. Building positive attitudes and interests will take patience and encouragement.

2. The leader should demonstrate a positive and constructive attitude toward nature; his or her interest, enthusiasm and love for the environment will be "catching."

3. Nature cannot be experienced properly indoors; it must be learned through doing. Children should be involved in trips, outings, camping, visits to nature centers and other real experiences.

4. Much learning comes from discovery and use of "teachable moments" as the unexpected occurs. Therefore, the leader must be alert to such possibilities at all times.

5. Participants should share in planning projects, outings or other activities. They should be given real responsibilities and should be expected to live up to them if the nature experience is to be meaningful for them.

6. In all learning experiences, it is best to begin not with the scientific study of names, facts or processes, but rather with observation and exposure to natural experiences that will prompt interest in further study.

7. Teach sound nature principles from the outset. Do not destroy living things when putting together a collection. If collecting live specimens such as salamanders, snakes or squirrels, keep them only for a short time and then release them, unless you are certain that they can live in a healthy way in your collection. Even then, respect for animal life raises the question of whether you have a right to take them from their homes.

Examples of Nature Projects

The list of possible nature activities is almost endless. However, here are a number of appealing projects that children and youth will enjoy and that do not require tremendous expertise on the part of the leader.

1. *Nature Hobbies and Crafts.* These may encompass any of the following:
   a. Preparing labels for tree or plant identification.
   b. Doing spatter-printing with leaves or doing leaf-printing on wood sections.
   c. Making pine needle whisk-brooms.
   d. Making pine cone bird-feeders.
   e. Constructing and maintaining terrariums and aquariums.
   f. Making Christmas tree ornaments out of seed pods, pine cones, or other natural objects.
   g. Sketching, painting, or photographing nature subjects.
   h. Doing creative writing on nature themes for camp, center, or playground newspapers.

2. *Nature Science Experiments.* These involve more formal projects, and necessitate careful observation and recording of results over a period of time. Examples are as follows:
   a. Observing how long it takes beans or other types of seeds to germinate under different conditions (type of soil, light, warmth and so forth).
   b. Building simple weather stations and recording temperature, humidity, wind changes and similar information.
   c. Making careful observations of plant flowering, tree leafing, bird migration, correct times for planting and so on.
   d. Making careful collections of rocks, minerals, fossils, tree leaves, insects, driftwood, weeds or forms of water life, and analyzing and classifying these.

3. *Special Conservation Projects.* Older children, with adult help, can become involved in a wide variety of such projects on school grounds, campsites, or in parks or natural preserves. These might include
   a. Property improvement and beautification through relocation of walks and paths, construction of retaining walls, replanting or soil erosion measures.
   b. Stream and pond improvement through disposal of refuse, construction of small dams, planting of fish, or controlling of bank erosion.
   c. Planting new plants and shrubs that provide food and shelter for wildlife.
   d. Waste clean-up drives and community campaigns.

4. *Campcraft Activities.* These may be learned on playgrounds to

prepare children for overnight or longer camping trips. They include

   a. Basic camping skills, such as pitching a tent, lashing methods to construct camp "furniture," knotcraft, fire-making and camp cookery.

   b. Survival methods, including compass reading, locating natural foods, Morse code signal sending and so forth.

   c. Skills in fishing, boat handling or similar recreational activities (assuming that the recreation and parks department has ponds that can be used for instruction).

5. *Nature Games.* Many games are specially suited for the natural environment and promote observation and awareness of the outdoors.

   a. Nature retrieving or treasure hunt games involving races or relays in collecting natural objects.

   b. Nature sounds and smells—observing the environment and recording sights, sounds, smells, or other observable phenomena as a form of contest.

   c. Trailing games, or races to get to particular locations, using maps and compasses.

   d. Nature word games or memory contests, based on knowledge of the outdoors.

Sports Leadership in Community Recreation

Probably the most popular activity in community recreation is sports. Certainly, it has the highest level of active participation among children, youth and young adults in both public recreation and park departments and in many voluntary agencies. Public departments often operate ballfields, golf courses, tennis courts, swimming pools and similar sports facilities for activities sponsored by their own staff or by sports leagues or other community organizations. Sports represent a very important area of leadership responsibility.

At the same time, it must be recognized that often there is far too much stress on high-level competition and on winning at all costs. This attitude, which is prevalent in professional and college athletics, often seeps down into school sports and even community recreation programs:

> . . . today's youth sports often focus on winning and developing "junior professionals." Those children whose physical development is slower, those who aren't as skilled, spend hours on the benches for each minute they spend playing on the field. They are belittled for their mistakes instead of encouraged for their efforts. Consequently, they become discouraged. They drop out. Worst of all, they become embittered about sports of all kinds. As adults, they will avoid participation in sports and games, and will do even less to support anything that smacks of athletic endeavor.[2]

---

[2]"The Dangers of Competitive Youth Sports." *Keynote* (Boys' Clubs of America), May 1976, p. 6, n.a.

During the 1970's many school systems and recreation departments sought to reverse this trend by imposing stricter rules and controls on youth sports competition and by promoting sports activities geared to mass participation at a recreational level.

For example, the American Alliance for Health, Physical Education, Recreation and Dance, the leading professional association representing teachers, leaders and administrators in these fields, has come out vigorously against an effort to initiate national sports championships for secondary school students. Other professional societies, including the National Association of Girls and Women in Sport and the National Council of Secondary School Athletic Directors, have joined in resisting this proposed plan. In contrast, many public recreation and park departments have given strong support to developing interest in lifetime sports. To illustrate, the Philadelphia Recreation Department, in cooperation with the National Junior Tennis League, has initiated a Summer Youth Tennis Program with 71 sites, 200 courts and more than 6,000 young participants.[3]

Yet, it should be recognized that for many people, competition *is* important and promotes incentive, challenge and high levels of attendance. The key challenge is to provide opportunity for sports participation at varying levels of ability and competitive interest, so that no one is excluded and all can find satisfaction in activities of their choice.

Values of Community Sports Programs

For the reasons suggested in the preceding paragraph, it is essential that the objectives of community sports programs be clearly defined. A typical example may be found in the directives issued to base sports programs by the Special Services Program of the United States Army Air Force:

1. To provide a wide variety of sports activities which will provide opportunities and encourage maximum participation throughout the year.
2. To provide a program of sports which will meet the leisure-time needs and interests of Air Force personnel.
3. To give Air Force personnel the opportunity to develop skills and recreational capacities in a variety of sports and habits of participating therein.
4. To promote the development and maintenance of physical fitness and health.
5. To develop an enthusiastic appreciation of sports and of skilled performance.
6. To provide, for entertainment purposes, events of spectator interest.
7. To contribute to the development of such traits and qualities as will make for an integrated personality, capable of displaying leadership, followership, competitive and cooperative spirit, sociability, and teamwork.

[3]David Lott: "Junior Program a Citywide Affair." *The Philadelphia Inquirer*, August 7, 1979, p. 5-C.

8. To develop safety capacities enabling one to care for one's self and to aid others in sudden emergencies.
9. To add to the personal growth and social enrichment of the individual by providing a means for the participant to make new acquaintanceships and form new friendships.
10. To contribute to the development of unit solidarity, esprit de corps, and individual and group morale.

Range of Programs

Each agency or department sponsoring sports activities is likely to offer somewhat different services based on its goals and philosophy, the population it serves and its physical and staff resources. Small departments with limited facilities are likely to offer only a few activities. On the other hand, a big-city department with many specialized facilities is likely to offer a wide range of opportunities. For example, the Chicago Park District provides sports activities in the following team and individual sports: archery, baseball, basketball, football, handball, horseshoes, ice skating, softball, swimming, tennis, touch football, track and field, trampoline, volleyball and wrestling. In each of these areas, it may provide basic instruction, organized competition, testing programs or special events that promote community interest. It cooperates with community organizations by providing facilities or other forms of assistance to their programs.

In many cases, the Chicago Park District will provide several levels of involvement for a single sport. For example, in popular sports such as baseball, basketball or softball, it sponsors basic instruction and competitive leagues for boys, men, girls and women, and also school-based teams. In addition to the previously mentioned sports, instruction or competition is offered in bicycle derbies, bait casting, checkers and chess, dog training, golf, fishing, marble tournaments, pinochle, sailing, roller skating and table tennis.

General Principles of Sports Leadership

While these depend in part on specific program objectives, the following principles of sports leadership should apply to all situations:
1. The involvement of any participant in sports activity should take into consideration the following individual characteristics: age, physique, interests, ability, experience and the participant's stage of physiological, emotional and social maturity.
2. Involvement in athletics must be based on a comprehensive and reliable evaluation of the health status of the participant, with careful restriction of participation when possible risk is involved.
3. The leader should seek to develop the skill of all participants, using a wide variety of careful, effective instructional procedures. He or she should follow accepted principles of teaching and not rely on players learning skills "on their own."

4. Of equal importance is the need to promote healthy values toward competition, good sportsmanship, obedience to rules and team play. Effective leaders must incorporate these values in their own behavior and must constantly reaffirm them in their leadership practices.
5. The leader should make arrangements so that all players can participate and compete on appropriate levels of ability, so that they learn to meet challenges with a reasonable degree of opportunity for success.
6. The leader is responsible for making all physical arrangements for sports participation related to scheduling, registration, provision and maintenance of sports facilities, assignment of officials and presentation of awards or trophies.
7. The leader must formulate and enforce, either individually or in cooperation with community sports associations, appropriate policies with respect to eligibility, practice, team make-up, forfeits, protests and similar competitive concerns.
8. The leader should involve, as completely as possible, youth, parents and other interested representatives of the community in teaching, coaching, managing or officiating roles, on either a voluntary or a paid basis. Community representatives should also be involved in planning events and determining policies of the sports program.

Guides for Managing Sports Programs

Sports specialists or supervisors are often responsible for organizing major sports tournaments, league play or other large-scale events. To do so efficiently, they must make up schedules in cooperation with all concerned teams, coaches, sponsors and officials; arrange for indoor or outdoor facilities for play, including details of locker rooms, availability of equipment, marking fields and other needs; and carry out a wide variety of tasks with respect to public relations, safety, awards and trophies, reports and similar responsibilities.

Another important responsibility in community sports programs involves the instruction of basic sports skills. While much of this is done in school physical education departments, many municipal recreation and park agencies offer sports that are *not* taught in the schools. Even when they are, it is often necessary to provide basic skills instruction to participants who have not learned the rudiments of play or who wish to have advanced instruction.

Guidelines for Teaching Sports Skills

Effective teaching is based on a general knowledge of teaching principles and on the ability to organize sequences of instruction and to carry them out clearly and in a logical progression of skills. Guidelines for the effective teaching of sports skills are found in many physical education texts. However, some key principles are identified here:

1. To the extent that it is possible, learners should be grouped on appropriate skill and ability levels: beginner, intermediate and advanced.

2. Learners should be organized most effectively to permit demonstration and practice of the skill components of the sport. If at all possible, when working with large numbers of learners, they should be spaced so all of them can be active all the time. Two examples follow:

   a. When teaching baseball skills, it is common practice to assign players to groups on the basis of specific skills, such as hitting, pitching and infield and outfield practice. Working with separate instructors, each player gets instruction and practice for a maximum amount of time.

   b. In a sport like tennis, in which only two or four players would ordinarily be on a court at one time, learners should be organized in groups so they practice basic strokes and then rotate rapidly in hitting the ball.

3. Emphasis should be given to learning the correct way to perform each skill, but the instructor should be able to accept each individual's style or movement or unique way of performing. It is not possible in any sport to fit all players to a mold.

4. Periods of demonstration and practice should be followed by periods of actual play in order to keep interest high and to give learners a chance to practice what they have learned. However, the instructor should not hesitate to interrupt such periods of "practice-play," as in the case of a basketball scrimmage, to make teaching points.

5. As basic skills are mastered, the instructor should move players on to more advanced skills and to other areas of learning, such as rules, scoring and strategy.

Human Relations in Coaching

It is essential that recreation leaders and supervisors make every effort to develop healthy and constructive attitudes toward competition, including such elements as sportsmanship, cooperative play, accepting the rules of the game and learning to win *and* lose with grace.

Little League Baseball, which has often been accused of exploiting youngsters by subjecting them to excessive competitive pressure, today makes strenuous efforts to indoctrinate its volunteer coaches and managers in positive principles of working with young players. In one of its nationally distributed publications, "My Coach Says . . .," it stresses the important role of the coach in shaping the values of young players and serving as a healthy adult model for them. This pamphlet, prepared by Dr. Thomas P. Johnson, a leading psychiatrist and former Little League player, coach and umpire, deals with the following kinds of concerns:

"How does a coach earn respect from his players?"

"How does he get a boy to care, and to be strongly motivated?"

"How does he make use of praise—and how does he handle criticism?"

"How does he help boys who are unable to make the team?"

"How does he handle such chronic problems as swearing, dissension on the team, back talk, quarreling and fighting, or temper tantrums?"

"How does he deal with special cases, such as the 'I'm not any good' boy, the 'scapegoat,' the 'bragger,' the 'clown,' the 'tattletale,' or the injured youngster?"

"How does he help boys to handle winning streaks, slumps, or the 'big game'?"

"How does he work with parents who interfere, with boys who want to quit the team, or with subs, scrubs and benchwarmers?"

Under each of these headings, it is made clear that the coach's role is to deal positively and constructively with young people, to put victory and defeat in perspective and to help each player gain a sense of respect for himself or herself as well as for other team members. These are the important values that should be learned from participation in recreational sports.

Officiating Techniques. There are a number of other important leadership functions within the broad area of sports leadership. One of these is officiating. Although the professional recreation leader or supervisor is not usually expected to serve as an official as a routine responsibility, he or she may have to do so on occasion, or may have to act as a supervisor to officials. Many municipal departments develop detailed procedures and guidelines for officials who work in their programs. The Milwaukee County Recreation Department, for example, publishes a detailed Officials Guide for individuals employed in their baseball and softball program. This manual gives precise procedures and rules under more than 78 headings for umpires, scoremarkers and scoreboard officials. Some of these headings are listed here:

Agreements	Protests
Availability of Officials	Rain-Outs
Complaints	Re-Entry Rules
Condition of Field	Suspensions
Conduct of Players	Tie Games
Ejection (Player)	Time Limits
Forfeits	Trips to Mound
Game Rules	Uniforms
Injuries	Women and Girls' Rules
Light Failure	

As a single example, the following guidelines are provided to insure that officials behave correctly at all times:

Officials' Conduct and Actions. As an official, you must realize the importance of your responsibility. You are a representative of this department and must at all times uphold the dignity which your position demands. There is far more to good umpiring than mere knowledge of the rules.

1. *Alertness.* Be alert at all times; follow every play closely.
   a. Keep your eye on the ball.
   b. Be alive on the field. When changing positions, run, don't walk. Hustle!
   c. Be ready! Decisions must be made in a split second. Keep in mind you don't have time to think about the play.
   d. Be emphatic. Make your call in a decisive way that leaves no doubt as to the correctness of your judgment.
   e. Always bear down. Never take anything for granted.
2. *Fraternization.* Officials are not to *socialize* or *fraternize* with participants or spectators at any time before, during, or just after a game. *Do not hold valuables for participants.*
3. *Personal Control*
   a. Control your temper at all times. Be patient and keep your poise no matter how angry those around you appear.
   b. Never be sarcastic or antagonistic toward players, managers, spectators, or other officials.
   c. Do not follow or charge a player and above all do not point your finger and yell at a player.
   d. Every game is a new game. Do not hold a grudge.
   e. *Control the game* at all times. This means from the time you arrive at the field until the time you leave.
   f. Once a game has been completed and you have no further responsibility, *leave.* Do not stand around and discuss or argue about any decision you made earlier.
4. *Teamwork* on the part of officials is a *must.* Help each other out, whenever and wherever possible. Never make adverse statements about another official.

Other Activity Areas

This chapter has presented useful guidelines for leadership of program activities in such popular categories as games, arts and crafts, music, dance, dramatics, nature recreation and sports. Leadership approaches in relation to departmental responsibilities, special events or programming for special populations are described in later chapters of this text. It cannot be emphasized enough that leadership is best learned through actual experience in a realistic setting, working with groups of participants. However, if the reader will carefully review the principles outlined in this and later chapters, and strive to apply them in actual situations, it will help him or her become much more aware of the factors underlying successful activity leadership.

In addition to the types of activities described in this chapter, it should also be pointed out that certain kinds of facilities require special leadership approaches. For example, leaders who work in adventure playgrounds will not be expected to present traditional activities, such as structured games or sports. However, they should be able to provide subtle adult leadership for such self-directed activities as building forts from donated lumber and supplies, sliding or climbing on hills, rope and tire swings, building fires, outdoor cooking, or overnight camp-outs.

Vance found that most sponsors of adventure playgrounds agreed that leadership was a critical factor in the success or failure of this type of facility.[4] In addition to having the qualities needed by leaders in conventional playgrounds, adventure playground directors must also have imagination and creativity, and should be non-authoritarian, resourceful, mature, outgoing and friendly. It is particularly important that they really enjoy working with children. The ideal adventure playground leader should also have experience working in one or more of the following areas: woodworking, camping and outdoor adventure, and neighborhood youth work.

Similarly, other types of facilities or programs that have unique underlying philosophies or program content may impose special demands on their leaders.

SUGGESTED EXAMINATION QUESTIONS OR TOPICS FOR STUDENT REPORTS

1. Identify and discuss several key principles of teaching, drawn from this chapter, and illustrate them with your own experience in recreation situations, as either a teacher (leader) or a learner (participant).
2. Critically review one of the sets of guidelines for teaching an activity (such as a game, song, dance or dramatic activity) presented in this chapter. On the basis of your own experience, add useful hints for successful leadership.
3. On the basis of your own experience as a leader or participant, what are some of the key problems faced in working with a given age level in one of these areas of activity?

SUGGESTED ACTION ASSIGNMENTS OR GROUP PROCESS ACTIVITIES

1. As a class assignment, select a single game, song, dance or other activity, and lead other class members in this activity. Following this, have class members evaluate your performance. Have each member of the class do this in turn.
2. Select one type of recreation activity that you believe you are able to lead successfully. Analyze it, and determine how the skills you have in this area can be applied to an activity that you feel less confident about leading.
3. Develop a plan for an overall program of activities and a set of leadership guidelines within a major area of activity (such as sports, performing arts or nature) for a large playground or community center.

[4]Bill Vance: *U.S. Adventure Playground Report*, American Adventure Playground Association, San Francisco, Calif., 1979.

Special Events Leadership

Chapter Six

*Party,
Exhibition,
Competition,
Outing* (handwritten margin note)

Another important aspect of recreation leadership is the ability to plan, organize and carry out special events. Such events are useful in providing highlights for a seasonal program or in maintaining interest and attendance throughout the year. Hjelte and Shivers describe their value:

> The special events at every recreational facility are the occasions that give "spice" to the program. They attract new patrons, discover new talent, provide an incentive to practice, give an everchanging flavor or emphasis to the program, and create opportunity to secure some educational outcomes not otherwise possible. Their variety is endless and limited only by the imagination of the recreationist in charge and the participants who may assist in the planning.[1]

The commonest types of special events are the following:

Parties or Celebrations. These include festivals, carnivals and other novelty events that have special themes or celebrate particular occasions.

Exhibitions and Demonstrations. In these, the emphasis is on showing the work that has been accomplished, either as a display or through direct performance.

Competitions. These are one-day tournaments, playdays or field days, in which competing individuals or teams come together in a single location.

Trips and Outings. These include picnics, group excursions, camping trips and similar outings.

Each of these types of special events may make use of the various rec-

---

[1]George Hjelte and Jay S. Shivers: *Public Administration of Recreational Services.* Philadelphia, Lea and Febiger, 1972, p. 443.

reation activities described in the previous chapter, or may provide culminating experiences that build upon these activities. Therefore, the leader's skill in planning and carrying out special events is important to the conduct of the entire recreation program.

PARTIES AND CELEBRATIONS

These range from small-scale novelty events that may be held for a short time on a single playground to large-scale events, such as carnivals or huge community get-togethers, that may extend over a day or more. The list of possible themes of such parties and celebrations is almost endless. Some may involve a single novelty contest with prizes, while others combine a number of different events. Here are examples of such programs:

Amateur Show	Kite Contest
Barnyard Day	Mother and Daughter
Bicycle Rodeo	Afternoon
Backwards Day	Paper Airplane Sailing
Bubble Blowing Contest	Contest
Bring a Friend Day	Pet Fair
Circus Day	Picnic
Clown Day	Pioneer Party
Crazy Hat Day	Pirate Party
Caveman Day	Physical Fitness Day
Country Fair	Puppet Show
Doll Show	Sand Castle Contest
Dress Up Day	Scavenger Hunt
Family Day	Science Fiction Party
Freckle Contest	Smelling, Spelling or
Funny Relay Day	Tasting Bees
Gypsy Party	Soap Bubble Blowing
Globetrotters Day	Contest
Haunted House	Talent Show
Hat Show	Treasure Hunt
Hobby Show	Turtle Race
Hula Hoop Contest	Water Relays
Hi-Neighbor Night	

Several examples of novelty parties or contests follow:

Clown Day. Award prizes for different categories of costumes and for the best two-minute clown act show.

Decorate Anything Day. Children decorate anything—hats, baby carriages, shoes, coats. Prizes are given for the funniest, most unusual, most artistic and other types of decorations.

Gold Rush Day. Plant rocks of different sizes, painted gold, around the playground. Then children search for them. Prizes are given for the largest, smallest, lightest, heaviest and other kinds of "gold nuggets."

Grasshopper Day. Children compete in various types of jumping or hopping contests, such as hop tag, leap frog, broad jumping or folk dances involving hopping.

Photograph Contest. Children bring in their favorite photographs, mounted for display. Prizes are given for the most unusual, funniest, prettiest and so on.

In addition to such novelty events, recreation leaders may plan special parties or celebrations built around humorous or unusual themes or at holiday times. Examples of such special parties include:

Halloween	Thanksgiving
Christmas	New Year's Day
Washington's Birthday	St. Valentine's Day
Lincoln's Birthday	St. Patrick's Day
April Fool's Day	Easter
Passover	May Day
Independence Day	Labor Day
Veterans' Day	Columbus Day
Rodeo Party	Hawaiian Luau
Father and Son Party	Mother and Daughter Party
Doll Party	Deck the Tree Party
Space Party	Indian Pow Wow Party
Easter Egg Hunt Party	Take a Cruise Party
Olympics Party	Beach Party

Events in Special Settings

In some special settings, events of this kind may constitute a major portion of the overall program and may be based on the unique background of the setting. For example, in the Recreation and Naturalist Program of the Natural Bridge State Park, part of the Kentucky State Park System, the following types of special programs are offered each week:

Junior Naturalist Programs—including presentations on the geology and history of the area and its natural stone arches
Evening Campfires—with storytelling, singing and marshmallow roasts
Slide Programs—with presentations on rock-climbing, kayaking and identifying edible plants
Knot-Tying and Macramé Workshops—for all ages, at a campground shelter
Beginners' Square Dance Evenings—for the entire family; including folk tales, song sessions and a dulcimer workshop to show how this mountain instrument is constructed and played

Other activities and events at the Natural Bridge State Park are fitted into the daily schedules; they include "trimnastics," pool games, movies, swimming lessons, bird walks, story hours, nature walks, orienteering, paddleboat races, outdoor cooking workshops, wiener roasts, snake-lore lessons, turtle races and canoeing demonstrations. Obviously, all such activities are suited to the unique outdoor environment and to local traditions and leisure opportunities, and help to make the park's family camping program more appealing.

Planning Parties and Special Events

To carry out any large-scale carnival, celebration, festival, holiday party or other special event, the best procedure is to form a "planning" or "steering" committee that will put together the program, develop a schedule and make all necessary arrangements. This committee would be responsible for the following arrangements.:

Program. This includes the actual planning and scheduling of activities, games, contests, demonstrations, dancing, performances, music and the awarding of prizes.

Publicity. This involves getting out the word, in the form of press releases, posters or personal invitations to individuals or organizations that are invited to attend.

Physical Arrangements. This involves obtaining the site, such as a hall, auditorium, school gymnasium or field (assuming that special arrangements must be made), and also arranging the physical set-up (such as chairs or bleachers, public address system or other equipment).

Financial Planning. It may be necessary to plan a budget authorizing expenditures and estimating income for the event. This might also include responsibility for ticket sales and for organizing raffles, auctions, bazaars, sales of refreshments and so on.

Refreshments. For a small party, refreshments might be cider and doughnuts or frankfurters, hamburgers and hot coffee. At a large-scale celebration, there are often several food counters offering varied refreshments. In some cases, dozens of people may bring pot-luck casseroles, desserts or other refreshments.

Floor Committees. These individuals might assist in handling the crowd, taking care of emergencies, assisting with automobile parking and generally making sure that events flow smoothly.

Other responsibilities, depending on the situation, might include (a) getting permits to hold the event; (b) obtaining police coverage; (c) making arrangements for music, guest speakers or featured entertainers; (d) having a "trouble shooter" for the loudspeaker system; (e) obtaining prizes; (f) soliciting contributions from local merchants; (g) printing a program or journal for the event; (h) making travel arrangements; and (i) setting up first-aid or lost-child booths, portable toilets and other facilities. Many communities or organizations that hold large numbers of special events prepare guidelines or simple manuals to make sure the events are carried out efficiently. For example, the Joliet, Illinois, Park and Recreation Department publishes a special events manual giving many suggestions for organizing such programs. Under the heading of "Playground Carnival," it offers the following suggestions:

The Playground Carnival is one of the biggest attractions of the playground, where participants and their parents both get involved. You should allow enough time before the carnival in order to construct the booths, make assignments, and finalize all aspects of this special event.

Personnel: The more responsible children should be chosen to handle the booths where money is being exchanged (i.e., prize, food, ticket booths).

Publicity: You should devise ways of advertising on and off your playground. Flyers and posters should be made by the children and posted around the neighborhood and on the playground in the most conspicuous places. Another means of publicizing your event is to organize a minstrel group, with a barker and parade through the neighborhood thus announcing the event.

Finances: The leader should provide the petty cash needed for change-making purposes.

The proceeds derived from the carnival may be utilized as a donation to a charitable institution, for a year end picnic, etc. However, the amount taken in and the use must be reported at the staff meeting following the event.

Refreshments: For refreshments you may wish to have Kool Aid, lemonade, pop, etc. Parents may be willing to donate cake, cookies, cup cakes, or some other food item. Popcorn, candy bars and ice cream might also be good money makers. Signs should be made telling the prices for each item available.

Clean-Up: When the carnival is over your grounds should be neat and clean. If any refreshments are left, make sure they go to the individuals who helped in the clean-up process.

Booths: Your carnival booths may be constructed of cardboard boxes (the larger type, such as refrigerator boxes are best), rope tied to picnic tables, trees, etc. When ropes are used, crepe paper streamers should be attached.

Ticket Booth: Have children get tickets for all booths here.

Prize Booth: Prizes can be handled at one booth rather than at each booth. Prize tickets will be given at the game booths and are to be exchanged for prizes at the central booth.

In some facilities, such as treatment centers, it is necessary to make careful arrangements with other staff members when planning any special event. For example, the Connecticut State Department of Health, which works closely with activity directors in nursing homes and hospitals throughout the state, publishes a handbook on recreation programs in institutions and extended care facilities. It suggests the following guidelines for party planning:

1. Pre-plan with Administrator for all special events.
2. Check with Director of Nurses regarding patients' condition and activities planned.
3. Arrange with dietary department regarding refreshments.
4. Encourage patients to assist with planning, preparation and leadership.
5. Advise volunteers of specific duties for event.

6. Arrange with housekeeping staff for any special set-up of recreation area.
7. Have camera ready to take snapshots or slides to be shown at a later program.
8. Arrange well in advance of date for staff coverage of event.

EXHIBITIONS AND DEMONSTRATIONS

Many different kinds of exhibitions and demonstrations may be sponsored by recreation departments. Typical examples are the following.

Performing Arts. This category includes presentations by musical groups; concerts; choral presentations; folk, square, ballet or modern dance performances; readings; and one-act plays or other dramatic works.

Arts and Crafts Exhibits. Mount displays of paintings, drawings, ceramics, leathercraft, metalwork and other crafts products.

Performance of Sports Skills. Performances of fencing, gymnastics, figure skating, diving, water ballet or similar activities may be featured.

Animal Shows. Pet shows, dog obedience demonstrations and horse shows are popular events.

Each of these may be approached simply in a local playground or center or may be presented much more elaborately on a communitywide basis. In some cases, for example, the adult arts and crafts program in a community may hold an art show once a year, presenting high-quality work by dozens of artists and craftsmen for sale to the public. Theater festivals may be held with the assistance of local drama associations: animal shows with the assistance of organizations that set the standards and provide officials for judging such contests. Such events boost interest and participation in public recreation programs and enhance community awareness and approval of the department's services.

Community Festivals

One of the most popular and useful types of special events is the community festival that may be based on the folklore or traditions of a given region or community. These are often carried out on a huge scale; for example, the traditional nine-day Oktoberfest celebrated in Kitchener-Waterloo, Canada, attracts more than 350,000 celebrants each year. This lively event draws on the German heritage of the cities and is modeled after the famous Oktoberfest celebrated in Bavaria. Other major Canadian festivals include the Calgary Stampede, a sports and livestock festival; the Royal Winter Fair, an agricultural festival; the Stratford Shakespearean Festival, a drama event; and Quebec's big festival, the Winter Carnival.[2]

---

[2]Geoffrey Wall and Joanne Hutchinson: "Festival." *Recreation Canada*, December 1978, p. 21.

Prior points out that festivals and similar participatory events allow people to define the present by celebrating and reinterpreting their shared past. Together, they identify and explore cultural roots and experience a common history:

> The ways in which we respond to this need are as varied as they are personal, but they all involve people. It may be a West Indian American carnival in a Brooklyn park; it may be an Appalachian music and crafts festival in the West Virginia mountains; or it may be a Halloween parade through the streets of Greenwich Village. It is art for people's sake.[3]

In the United States, the federal government's National Endowment for the Arts has given considerable assistance to such events by providing funding for so-called Tour Events, through which traveling groups of performers are brought to new audiences in more spontaneous settings than traditional theaters, museums or concert halls. Producing such celebrations involves complex tasks. Prior writes

> A successful festival with visual impact, lively pacing, variety, and focus results from broad technical and logistical know-how. Dealing creatively with city officials, politicians, artists, and volunteers; handling promotion and publicity; planning the location of booths and stages; contracting with performers; and fitting the many pieces together into a coherent structure are some of the practical problems involved.[4]

Mobile Recreation Programs

Another form of community-based special event is the type of neighborhood demonstration, show, exhibit or performance that is part of a mobile recreation program. Many mobile recreation activities consist simply of participation in arts and crafts, science learnings, roller-skating or other do-it-yourself activities. However, they may also include bringing concerts, drama, art shows or other forms of leisure-enrichment activities to neighborhood streets and parks by using mobile bandshells or show-wagons as part of citywide touring programs.

A recent study of community mobile recreation programs showed that factors essential to their success were intelligent choice and planning of activities, a specialized staff, and local involvement and cooperation. Fisher writes that ". . . unless well organized and programmed, and unless staffed with personnel possessing specialized skills, mobile recreation will fail."[5]

---

[3]Katherine I. Prior: "Celebrations: Art for People's Sake." *Parks and Recreation*, July 1979, p. 31.
[4]*Ibid.*, p. 32.
[5]Carl Fisher: "Recreation's 'Big Wheels' Win a Place of Their Own in Programming." *Parks and Recreation*, September 1979, p. 73.

COMPETITIONS AND TOURNAMENTS

Another form of special event is the competition or tournament. This may be carried on over a period of days or weeks in separate locations, or it may be concentrated into a single day's play, as in a track-and-field or wrestling competition or a play involving a variety of different events. There are several different patterns of tournaments, chiefly in the area of sports, although card and chess tournaments may also be held. Several of the most common arrangements follow.

Individual Best-Score Tournament.   In a sport such as golf or riflery, a large number of players compete. After a set number of rounds, the player with the best score is the winner. In such tournaments there may be a preliminary round to determine eligibility, or eligibility may be determined by previous tournament play.

Team Competitions.   There are several types of team competitions, of which the elimination tournament is most common. In this, several teams compete through a series of rounds. When a team loses a game or match it is eliminated, and the team that wins the final round is the tournament winner. In another form of team competition, such as track-and-field meets, each team has a number of players who compete in different events as individual contests. The team that amasses the highest number of points (through individual team members' scoring) is the winner. This may be done by having players compete in different weight classes, as in wrestling, or in different events, as in swimming.

The leader who is responsible for conducting tournaments should be thoroughly familiar with the various types of competitions, such as *elimination* tournaments, *round robin* tournaments, *challenge* tournaments and others. He or she should also be familiar with the operation of each type of tournament and with specific details of tournament structures, such as "brackets," "rounds," "drawings," "byes," "seeding," and similar arrangements.

Other Types of Competitions

There are many other types of special events that involve competition, not as a formal tournament, but as a single program offering different events or varied forms of play. Such programs are usually known as field days or play days. They may be planned to offer contests in several different sports or games for different age levels, or they may include several events based on a single sport or activity.

For example, the Parks and Recreation Department of Phoenix, Arizona, sponsors field days in which the following events are provided for different age classes:

Table tennis (singles and   Softball throw for accuracy
   doubles)

Checkers and Chinese checkers	Jacks
Badminton	Home run derby
Soccer ball kick for accuracy	Hopscotch
Base running against time	Horseshoes
Mock track meet (novelty events)	

Sometimes, several different events may be developed around a single sport, such as the Baseball or Softball Field Days sponsored by the Chicago Park District. These involve competitions in the following events for both baseball and softball: (a) throw for distance, (b) fungo hit for distance, (c) circling the bases for time, and (d) throwing the ball around the bases relay, for teams of four players. Contestants are divided into two age classes (11 and under, and 12 to 14), and boys take part in both baseball and softball competitions, whereas girls play only softball.

Another type of competition is the "Bicycle Rodeo." Many communities sponsor such events. Normally, about six or eight different events would be selected, and competition would be organized on several age or grade levels. Examples of such events may be found in a games manual published by the Stockton, California, Department of Parks and Recreation:

Wheels Day—Bike Rodeo

Instruction: You may have to adapt some bike events to your individual playground areas. Keep safety factors for both participants and pedestrians in mind.

1. *Steering Test.* Have participant ride at comfortable speed for 30 feet between parallel lines four inches apart without getting onto or over lines. This will be easiest to judge if you place pairs of blocks on sidelines at six-foot intervals. Deduct 5 points from 100 for touching a line, 10 for going outside a line, and 15 for losing control of bike.
2. *Circle Riding.* Mark two concentric circles with diameters of 16 feet and 12 feet to make a circular path two feet wide. Have each participant stay within the path while riding four times around. Deduct 5 points from 100 for hitting a line, 10 for getting outside path, 15 for losing control.
3. *Balancing at Slow Speed.* Make a lane three feet wide and 50 feet long. Rider must go slowly enough to take at least 30 seconds to complete the distance without losing balance.
4. *Maneuvering.* Lay out a weaving type of course with boxes or blocks at 25-foot interval spacing in a straight line. This would rquire seven markers to set up a distance of 150 feet. Participant may ride at comfortable speed weaving to pass on alternate sides from marker to marker. Deduct 5 points from 100 for touching any marker, 10 points for losing control of bike.
5. *Bicycle Kick Ball Race.* Set up on 100 yard distance if possible with riders well spaced out across field. A kickball will be placed ten yards in front of each rider at starting line. On time signal, the riders mount

and start dribbling (must impel ball with foot only) down the field to finish line.

Aquatic Show

As another example of a specialized event built about a particular recreational theme or setting, many communities, park districts and camps sponsor aquatic shows, often at the beginning or end of the summer. Depending on the setting, which is typically a swimming pool or beach area, the activities are likely to include swimming races for different ages, diving exhibitions and water-ballet programs. Other novelty events may be included. The following might be among these:

1. Novelty contests, such as water basketball, water tag, water cage ball or water polo.
2. "Skish" contests in bait casting or fly casting, with floating targets.
3. Demonstrations or races of model speedboats or model seaplanes.
4. Novelty races, such as "Siamese twin" races, in which contestants must swim side-by-side in pairs with inner arms locked; "duck" races, in which swimmers must hold aluminum pie plates in their hands while swimming 25 yards; "inner-tube" races, in which each contestant sits in an inner tube while swimming with hands and feet; or "balloon-batting" races, in which contestants must keep batting rubber balloons ahead of themselves with their heads, while swimming the breast stroke for 25 yards.
5. Demonstrations of canoes being overturned and then righted.
6. Log-rolling contests, water-ski races.

In all such events, it is essential that careful planning be done in advance to insure that the timing is correct and that all the complicated factors making up such programs fit together efficiently at the last moment. It is useful to work these out carefully in advance, in terms of both schedules and assignment of necessary tasks.

④ TRIPS AND OUTINGS

Another category of special events consists of trips and outings. These may be very brief half-day trips to neighborhood parks, beaches or pools, or outings to nearby museums or sites of special interest. Transportation may be on foot, by volunteer automobile drivers, or by bus. Outings may also include more elaborate trips over longer distances and periods of time, using chartered transportation. Some communities schedule weekly trips for all the children on city playgrounds, visiting places of interest on a regular day each week. Organizations that serve adults, such as industrial recreation departments or Golden Age clubs, sometimes schedule charter flights and vacation tours to scenic destinations.

Trips provide a "break" from the routine, and offer novelty, excitement and the opportunity for new experience. They *must*, however, be carefully planned and supervised. A poorly organized trip or outing can be a disaster. Planning should include the following important elements:

1. Selecting a destination, and making arrangements with individuals to receive those making the trip.
2. Publicizing the outing, registering those who will go and obtaining parental permission slips (in the case of trips for children and youth).
3. Making arrangements for transportation and collecting fees, if necessary.
4. Providing those who are about to go on the trip with necessary details (time, place, schedule, appropriate clothing and other information).
5. Providing adequate supervision while on the trip, including safety practices and activities for the group to participate in while traveling.
6. Planning for supervision while at the destination, particularly if the group is a large one and is breaking up into smaller units.
7. Gathering the group together and making the return trip home.
8. Evaluating the trip, basing other recreation activities on it and sending notes of appreciation to those who have assisted or cooperated with the leaders.

Guidelines for Trips—New Haven, Connecticut

Many agencies develop detailed guidelines for the conduct of trips and outings. The following set of suggestions is drawn from the Trip Planning Manual published by the New Haven, Connecticut, Department of Parks and Recreation.

Pre-Planning. Trips should not be extemporaneous; they must be planned carefully. Planning should be done well in advance of the actual date of the trip. If making a trip to a state or national park, you should inquire about what facilities are available to you, the best dates to bring a large group, possible admission fees and the length of time the trip will take. Travel time should always be estimated conservatively, allowing for possible road construction, rush hour traffic or other slowdowns.

Prepare Group in Advance. Have all playground directors give children detailed information about the trip, including what the park or amusement center has to offer. If there are charges for special activities, let them know this. Make sure that they have appropriate clothing, swim suits or sports equipment.

Register Participants. After this has been done, set a date for the trip, publicize the event and register those who will be going. Have permission slips signed by parents, and include the following information: (a) sponsoring agency, (b) destination, (c) date, (d) time of departure, (e) time of return and (f) supervisor in charge of trip. The permission slip should have the parents' telephone numbers so they can be reached in case of an emergency.

Departure and Return.   Most trips are made by bus. The supervisor in charge should have a roster with the name of every child on the bus before departure; the roster should agree with the permission slips. Before departing, children should be told what group they will be with and what staff member will be responsible for them. The supervisor should let staff members know the exact time they must have their groups back at the designated meeting place for the trip home.

When the group is ready for the bus trip home, the supervisor should check each child's name against the roster before permitting the child to enter the bus. When all names have been accounted for, the bus may leave on the return trip. If any child is missing, the staff member responsible for that child should make a search. Never permit other children to look for lost or late children. You should delay the bus until a missing child is located, although it may be necessary to start the trip back after an hour has passed. In this case, the staff member responsible for the child remains behind. Do not hesitate to call on the police for assistance. With proper staff coverage, children should not be lost for more than a brief time.

Other Trip Guidelines

Particularly when a trip is being made to a state park or other large park area, it is necessary to make arrangements with the host agency and to observe rules they may set up. For example, the Atlanta, Georgia, Department of Parks and Recreation has established the following regulations for playground bus trips to Georgia state parks:

1. The State Park Superintendent will be notified by the central office of the Atlanta Parks and Recreation Department when a trip is scheduled to his park.
2. Trips are scheduled for ages five to 15 years. Children who do not meet the age classification will not be permitted to board the bus. Parental permission slips must be obtained for all children going on a trip.
3. There must be one leader for every ten children. The leader must stay with his group at all times during the trip. Each group should be limited to one bus load or its equivalent.
4. Leaders must have a planned program of games and activities and carry all necessary equipment with them on the bus. They will be expected to have the group under control at all times while in the park.
5. Group leaders must be easily identified, and should introduce themselves to the Park Superintendent immediately upon arrival.

6. Atlanta Parks and Recreation pays established fees (admission, parking, etc.), but does not pay individual swimming admissions fees.
7. Swimmers must wear swimming suits rather than cut-off jeans, whenever possible.
8. Groups will not be allowed in family camping or cottage areas, may not rent or otherwise use park boats, and must picnic only in designated picnic areas.
9. Groups must restrict their trips to weekdays only, and must limit their stay at parks to a maximum of four hours.
10. Parks which provide planned programs given by their Naturalists will do so only if the request is made two days in advance of group visit.

These rules, which are based in part upon policies established by the Georgia state park system, illustrate the need for careful controls and preparation in all trips and outings. This is particularly true when groups of disabled persons go on trips. More and more psychiatric hospitals, for example, have been experimenting with camping or wilderness trips for adolescent or adult groups, and have achieved considerable success. However, such outings require extremely thorough pre-planning and supervision if they are to be successful and provide a positive growth experience.

EVENTS FOR SPECIAL POPULATIONS

Along with series of this type that are intended to serve playground, community center or other general recreation participants, some communities plan special events for the handicapped or other populations with unique needs. For example, the San Diego, California, Department of Parks and Recreation has an extensive range of activities for senior citizens. During a recent year (1979–1980), it sponsored the following series of events for them:

October—Senior Citizens Photo Contest
October—Weekend Trip to Camp Cuyamaca
November—Senior Citizens Arts and Hobby Show
December—Christmas Variety Show for Seniors
February—Senior Citizens Valentine Dance
March—Senior Citizens Talent Shows
April—Talent Show Finals
May—Senior Citizens Rally Day

Another popular event is a Special Olympics for disabled persons. For example, each year since 1974, the St. Louis, Missouri, Division of Recreation and the St. Louis Easter Seal Society have co-sponsored a large-scale Special Olympics for the Physically Handicapped, using the facilities of the St. Louis Community College at Forest Park. Program activities include swimming, weight-lifting, wheelchair slalom, discus and shotput, bowling, archery and track. Hundreds of participants, mostly in their teens and twenties, compete with great interest and enthusiasm. Thousands of other young people with varied forms of disability, including many who are mentally retarded, compete in national and international Special Olympics events sponsored by the Joseph P. Kennedy Jr. Foundation.[6]

VALUE IN PROMOTING COMMUNITY SUPPORT

A unique value of all the different types of special events described in this chapter is that they help to promote cooperation by various community groups and strong support for recreation as a vital public service. As a single example of such involvement, the Portsmouth, Virginia, Parks and Recreation Department makes a strong effort to promote a "Partnership for People" concept through 13 neighborhood organizations called Recreation and Parks Forums, which establish budgets and help to raise substantial sums of money to support sports leagues and other community programs. The Portsmouth Parks and Recreation Department each year offers more than 2,000 hours of volunteer training in subjects such as fund-raising, volunteer recruitment, new program ideas and recreation management. An annual Mayor's Conference on Parks and Recreation, including workshop sessions, exhibits, displays and an awards banquet attended by 700 persons, helps to increase community interest in recreation.

Special events are an ideal way to mobilize the efforts of many citizens in meeting leisure needs. For example, the Annual Portsmouth Invitational Tournament (a competition featuring top collegiate senior basketball players), a popular series of summer concerts and numerous other programs are carried on with the assistance of varied community groups. Greiner writes

> A prime concern when initiating the program was the ability of low-income neighborhoods to raise the funds necessary to operate the program. This fear proved to be unfounded as several of the most distressed neighborhoods became leaders in organizing programs and raising funds. . . . The city also challenges community groups to raise funds for new facilities, equipment, and athletic teams by providing one-time matching funds. . . .
>
> Virtually every special event operated by the department is cosponsored by one or more outside organizations. This assures that the "partnership for people" idea extends to citywide activities, as well as community-based programs.[7]

Guidelines for Organizing Events

To illustrate the steps involved in planning and carrying out a community recreation event of this type, one might examine a community play day that

---

[6]"Special Olympics for the Physically Handicapped." Brochure of the St. Louis, Missouri, Recreation Division, and Easter Seal Society, April 1977.

[7]James Greiner: "A 'Proposition 13' That Works *for* Recreation." *Parks and Recreation*, June 1979, pp. 29–30.

brings together participants from a number of recreation centers or playgrounds. The following assignments must be carried out successfully: (a) planning the event; (b) obtaining a location, such as a large school parking area, that provides a smooth, safe surface; (c) publicizing the program; (d) signing up contestants (this is often done through specific grade levels in the public schools); (e) pre-registering contestants; (f) obtaining volunteer teenage or adult leaders to help run the events; (g) obtaining needed materials, such as measuring tape, chalk or flour, wooden blocks, cans or milk cartons for markers, loudspeaker equipment, certificates or ribbons; (h) organizing the event on the given day, with scorers and officials running the individual events so contestants can rotate from area to area; (i) arranging places for spectators that will be safe and will not interfere with the players; and (j) awarding prizes and preparing news releases for publicity coverage.

When scheduling special events, it is helpful to work out a master calendar well in advance to insure that participants are given basic instruction in appropriate activity areas and to permit coordination of a department's specialists and other resources. To illustrate, the Atlanta, Georgia, Department of Parks and Recreation has each playground district prepare an advance schedule of special events before the summer begins. Playgrounds within the district then structure their programs on the basis of this master schedule. A typical schedule for the Southwest district of Atlanta during a recent summer follows:

Week of	Tournaments and Contests	Weekly Themes
June 11	Checkers/Marbles Contests	Ecology Week
June 18	Carom Tournament	International Week
June 25	Hula Hoop/Frisbee	Bicycle Week
July 2	Table Soccer Contest	Space Week
July 9	Horseshoe Contest	Nature Week
July 16	Basketball Free Throw Contest	Hobo Week
July 23	Tennis Tournament	Hawaiian Week
July 30	Table Tennis Tournament	Down on the Farm Week
August 6	Cultural Arts Festival	Fantasy Week

The Phoenix, Arizona, Department of Parks and Recreation also outlines a week-by-week series of program ideas and playground themes. It suggests that special events be featured on Tuesday afternoons, with a postponement date on Wednesdays in case of bad weather. Tournaments and contests should be scheduled on Thursdays, with Fridays serving as postponement days. Other activities, such as ball games, drama, dance, crafts, storytelling, nature activities, hikes and quiet games, would be fitted into the schedule at regular times on other days and during the mornings and late afternoons. A sample schedule follows:

Week	Designation	Feature Special Event	Tournament or Contest
1	Organization—Get Acquainted— Safety on the Playground	Learn use of equipment; clean-up; Treasure Hunt	Checkers Rope Jumping
2	Learn to Swim Week	Instruction—swimming and water safety Bicycle Club hike	Horseshoes Bean Bag Toss
3	Games of Low Organization	Parade on Wheels Bicycle Rodeo Band Concert	Paddle Tennis Hand Tennis Jackstones
4	Independence Week	Celebrate July 4th Pet Show Hobby Show Camera and Movie Exhibits	Box Hockey Pick-Up-Sticks
5	Sports Week	Track and Field Day Progressive Game Day Tennis Instruction Water Carnival	Bull Board Scoop
6	Nature Week	Nature games-crafts Nature hike Activity with other playgrounds	Deck Tennis Hopscotch
7	Know Your Community	Trips to historical spots, state park Visit industry Radio programs	Clock Golf Bubble Blowing
8	Arts and Crafts Week	Exhibit of crafts made on playground Sidewalk Art Show Flower Show	Table Tennis Puzzles
9	Hobby Week	Hobby Show Model Train—all types Band Concert	Peteca Yo-Yo
10	All Nations Celebration	Citywide Playground Closing Event Games from other lands Songs and dances of other lands Water Show	Tetherball Mumblety-Peg

To sum up, this chapter has presented a wide variety of different types of special events, such as carnivals, parties, tournaments, exhibitions or trips, that may be sponsored by community recreation departments or voluntary organizations. Besides all the other values that have been cited, it should be stressed that special programs of this type have the unique benefit of encouraging different organizations—as well as their staff members, participants and community volunteers—to work closely together. Special events provide a unique challenge in group management, as individuals learn to cooperate with each other in planning activities, doing public relations, raising funds and carrying out the varied tasks involved in successful special events sponsorship.

SUGGESTED EXAMINATION QUESTIONS OR TOPICS FOR STUDENT REPORTS

1. Describe the major types of special events found in community recreation, and indicate their values in enriching the total program.
2. Select one major type of special event, such as a carnival, play day, festival or community celebration. Outline a set of guidelines for developing such a program, indicating the kinds of assistance you might need from volunteers and other community organizations.
3. Prepare a description of several different types of tournaments that are most commonly used in sports or other forms of competition. Describe the types of sports or games or circumstances of participation that are suited for each type of tournament.
4. Trips and outings are extremely useful recreation program elements. What are the major problems to be faced in organizing such events, and what are the solutions to these problems?

SUGGESTED ACTION ASSIGNMENTS OR GROUP PROCESS ACTIVITIES

1. Investigate a variety of possible locations to which recreation agencies in your community might plan trips and outings. Select the best of these and prepare a brochure or manual describing them and such elements as distance, travel time, activities and special features, costs, restrictions or other factors.
2. Plan and carry out an outing or other major event, as a class, for participants in a community agency, or as a special project for other students in your college. Evaluate this assignment thoroughly when it has been completed.
3. Plan and carry out one or more special events specifically suited to a disabled population, such as mentally retarded, blind, or orthopedically disabled persons. Do this in class, with class members role-playing the special population, or, if it can be arranged, in another community setting with a "real" population.

Management Functions of Leaders
Chapter Seven

Recreation leadership involves considerably more than simply leading or directing group activities or planning special events. In addition, the leader must carry out a variety of other important interpersonal or managerial tasks if his or her program is to run smoothly.

This chapter describes a number of these additional leadership functions and presents guidelines for carrying them out effectively. They include tasks such as planning and carrying out programs, developing effective public relations and community involvement, maintaining control of participants' behavior and practicing careful, thorough safety and accident procedures.

Such responsibilities are found not only in recreation and park department but in other types of social or therapeutic agencies as well. However, for purposes of simplification, this chapter deals with only two basic types of settings: *playgrounds* and *community center* programs, chiefly serving children and youth, that are sponsored by public recreation and park departments. Other settings for organized recreation, such as employee recreation programs, armed forces bases and commercial or campus recreation, are described in later chapters.

OVERALL LEADERSHIP RESPONSIBILITIES

The responsibilities of recreation leaders are outlined in many departmental manuals. For example, the Stockton, California, Recreation and Park Department Manual points out that leaders are expected to function in the following ways:

As an Organizer. Make a survey of your playground and neighborhood to find out what it has and what it needs. Organize and develop such activities as will . . . produce the best physical, mental and moral results.

As a Leader. Teach games, both old and new; direct club organizations and promote indoor and outdoor activities as outlined by the supervisors and in accordance with the policies of the Department.

As a Host. Encourage all persons attending the playground or center to enter into the various activities. . .

As a Coach. Develop teams and competitive events of all kinds, giving instructions when necessary. . .

As a Teacher. Promote literature and study clubs, dramatics, hand work, and nature lore. . .

As an Advertiser. Provide a bulletin board. Plan a program at least one day ahead. See that all announcements are attractively displayed. . .

As a Clerk. See that all reports are submitted *on time* to the main office. . .

As a First-Aider. Apply first aid *only* in emergency. Know the accident procedure completely and thoroughly.

As an Authority. Supervise carefully lavatories and *out-of-the-way* places. Do not permit marking on walls of buildings or fences. Eliminate all smoking, swearing, rowdyism and gambling, etc. . . .

As a Friend. One of your most important jobs as a leader is to be a friend to all who participate on your playground. . .

Program Functions

In organizing and carrying out the overall playground or community center program, the leader should follow a number of general guidelines or principles. First, he or she should provide a wide range of activities, including sports and games, creative activities and hobby and social pastimes. These should be suited to both sexes and to as broad an age range as possible. Many playgrounds and community centers serve neighborhood populations that run the gamut from pre-schoolers to senior citizens. The leader should seek to alternate strenuous with quiet activities, team games with individual play, and competitive with cooperative games and projects.

The program should be planned in advance for each day as part of an overall schedule of regular events and program features organized at the beginning of the summer. However, the leader should not hesitate to change this plan when special circumstances demand it. Weather should be considered when outlining the program schedule, with active sports planned for the morning or late afternoon and quiet activities held during the warmer part of the day. The leader should also consider the following suggestions:

Offer a diversified program, including both old and new activities. *Plan* special events at regular intervals to heighten interest and participation. *Strive* for maximum participation in such special events; they are not just for highly skilled "champions" but for *all* children or youth on the playground.

Plan a progressive program, with culminating activities at the end of units, tournaments in various sports and major events, such as festivals or carnivals, at the end of the summer.

Encourage informal, self-organized activity by providing definite times when no specific activities are scheduled but when play equipment is available. *Arrange* time periods so that if projects or activities are not completed within scheduled times, they may be carried over without interfering with the overall program. The leader's time should be divided fairly between different age groups, boys and girls, and different types of activity.

In planning program activities, all those concerned (including recreation aides or assistants, volunteers and the participants themselves) should be involved. Always *follow through* on all advertised plans or special features. If you are unable to do it yourself, make sure that another leader takes over responsibility for it. If it is absolutely necessary to cancel an announced activity or special event, make sure that everyone knows about it. It reduces interest to postpone events or fail to live up to promised program plans.

For specific examples of program schedules, the reader should consult other textbooks. This text is primarily concerned with the process of leadership rather than with program development.

PUBLIC AND COMMUNITY RELATIONS

The recreation leader plays an important role in promoting effective public and community relations. In any recreation department or agency, public relations are essential for the following reasons: (a) to create a favorable public image of the department and to encourage positive official or legislative support; (b) to encourage maximum attendance at regular programs and special events; (c) to enlist volunteers to help in the program; (d) to overcome public misconceptions or distortions about the program; and (e) to develop a public constituency that will support budget requests for facilities, staff, equipment or materials, or that will help the department attack its operational problems most successfully.

Public relations must not be left to chance. Individuals skilled in this field should be given the responsibility for arranging major public relations events, such as interviews, tours and radio or television programs, and for preparing newspaper releases, magazine articles, reports, brochures and other publicity materials. However, *all* public relations cannot be carried on effectively by central office specialists. Instead, they must also be the direct responsibility of recreation leaders on the grass roots level, in community centers or playgrounds.

How do recreation leaders carry out this important assignment? This is done in essentially two ways: (a) through personal relationships, and (b) through use of the formal media of public relations.

Personal Relationships

All recreation leaders should seek to do the following when dealing with the public:

1. Acquaint themselves with the neighborhood as fully as possible—its streets, buildings, businesses, churches and other organizations. Whenever possible, chat with parents and program participants. Special efforts should be made to help each participant feel that he or she is wanted in the program, and that there is a helpful, friendly and courteous attitude on the part of all staff members.

2. When there are requests or problems, treat them with sincere interest and respect. Each problem should be given prompt attention and handling. Policies should be explained fully and tactfully when they are challenged. Use all available information or resources to solve problems or meet requests of residents.

3. Set a positive image for the public. Neat appearance and responsible conduct on the part of recreation and park employees will help give neighborhood residents a favorable view of the department. Facilities and equipment should also be maintained in the best possible condition. If department morale is high and recreation workers project a strong, optimistic view of their program, public attitudes will reflect this.

Use of Public Relations Media

In addition, it is necessary for recreation leaders to take specific steps to bring information to the public. This may be done through the use of traditional publicity media—some of which the recreation leader may send out or initiate (subject to departmental policy), and some of which come from the central administrative office. These include the following:

Newspapers. Recreation leaders should submit, through regular departmental channels, suggestions for news releases or photographs that would make good publicity. They should keep the central office accurately advised of all games, tournaments and special events, with emphasis on good "human interest" stories. Guidelines for preparing newspaper copy are as follows:

a. Type all stories double-spaced.
b. Identify the name and address of the playground or center at the top of the sheet, along with the date of the release.
c. Keep stories brief, colorful and interesting.
d. Include the main facts of the story in the "lead," or first paragraph.
e. Keep a carbon copy of all stories for the file.
f. Know newspaper release deadlines and observe them.
g. When reporters are sent to cover stories, have accurate lists of participants, program events and other information that will help them prepare copy.

Magazine Articles. These are more difficult to prepare and not as timely in their impact as newspaper stories. However, they can be used to reach specialized audiences, either through magazines that serve a particular age group or region or through those concerned with a particular hobby or activity.

Brochures, Leaflets and Newsletters. Most recreation and park departments prepare brochures advertising seasonal programs on a citywide basis. However, the local leader should also prepare and publish such printed materials, advertising his or her own program or special events.

Bulletin Boards and Posters. These should be used to display topical and interesting announcements. In addition to locating them on the recreation department's facilities, posters may be placed in stores, schools, churches and other locations.

Audiovisual Materials. Many departments prepare color slides and films depicting department activities, facilities and programs. These may be used for presentations in schools, Parent-Teacher Associations, local service clubs and similar organizations to promote recreation programs.

Exhibits and Displays. Demonstrations of sports, dance, drama or music, as well as displays of arts and crafts, nature projects and similar program activities, offer an excellent means of publicizing a recreation department.

Tours and Open Houses. These are particularly useful in getting publicity for new facilities or unusual programs. Generally, a department arranges an interesting series of events or presentations, provides transportation and invites newspaper reporters (including reporters from schools and colleges nearby), television reporters, and news editors.

Although the recreation leader may not be able to carry through on all such public relations projects alone, the leader is the key contact person with the public and should constantly feed publicity ideas and program suggestions to those who do direct public relations. The importance of public relations is well illustrated by the emphasis given it by commercial recreation agencies. Talbot writes:

> Many commercial recreation organizations devote thousands of dollars to, and employ (personnel) whose sole responsibility is public relations. The management of commercial facilities clearly view public relations as a vital and necessary function. Public supported leisure services can improve their operations, generate more goodwill toward their agency and perhaps insure more funds (or avoid drastic cutbacks) if they follow the example of their commercial counterparts and initiate a sound public relations program.[1]

Community Relations

The recreation leader should also consult frequently with school principals, heads of civic associations and service clubs, and directors of other voluntary or commercial recreation agencies. Whenever possible, cooperative arrangements in sharing facilities, coordinating schedules, planning to meet com-

---

[1] Richard L. Talbot: "Marketing Leisure Services: A Hint from the Private Sector." *California Parks and Recreation,* August/September 1978, p. 15.

munity needs, and attacking social problems should be worked out with such groups.

One of the best ways in which recreation leaders can develop constructive community relations is by forming neighborhood advisory councils. Such councils are groups of citizens, both adults and youths, who are sincerely interested in the recreation program and are willing to assist it. Although local advisory councils have no legal status as boards and commissions do, they can be invaluable in determining the leisure needs and interests of the community and in interpreting these to playground or community center directors. They are helpful in advising the recreation staff on needed policies and in assisting in the development of programs. Similarly, they serve as a two-way communication link by helping to inform neighborhood residents about the objectives of the program and publicizing specific activities and events. When favorable testimony is needed before city councils or governmental officials, representatives of local advisory councils can play an important role. Finally, they can be extremely helpful in providing volunteer assistance or in raising funds to finance special projects or purchase needed equipment that is not included in the regular budget.

Members of advisory councils may be selected in a number of ways. In some communities there is a formal election process, while in others the procedure is to ask a number of neighborhood organizations or clubs to delegate representatives. In still others, members are simply informally invited by the recreation leader or supervisor to join the council. The quality of the members and their enthusiasm and willingness to work are more important than the way in which they are selected. Members need not be "key" people in the community; in fact it is often better to avoid such persons because they tend not to have enough time to give to the recreation council. Although political experience and contacts are helpful, they are not essential. The most important elements are leadership ability, good judgment and willingness to give time to the council's work.

It is up to the recreation leader or supervisor to work closely with such councils, assisting them in their work and seeking advice and help from them. Skill in community relations is one of the most important attributes a leader can have; it involves a willingness to listen, respect for the views of others and the ability to serve as an intermediary between the formal structure of the recreation and park agency and the people it serves.

BEHAVIOR CONTROL FUNCTIONS

An extremely important area of recreation leadership responsibility today relates to the supervision of participants' behavior and the handling of discipline problems. In any recreation situation involving youth, a certain number of participants are likely to be mischievous, destructive or hostile. However, in recent years this problem has become more severe. The increase in juvenile delinquency and antisocial gang activity has been accompanied in many communities by drug abuse and drinking among young people.

Any recreation facility should provide a safe and wholesome atmosphere for young people. There must therefore be certain rules of behavior that protect the safety and security of staff members and participants and prevent vandalism, destruction, theft and physical aggression. In general, such rules are directed at preventing or controlling the following kinds of misbehavior: smoking or drinking in the playground or community center, fighting or excessive horseplay, carrying or threatening others with weapons, destruction or defacement of property, profanity and the use of liquor or drugs.

How should the recreation leader deal with the problem of maintaining discipline? Essentially, there are two kinds of approaches. The first consists of categorizing certain forms of unacceptable behavior and outlining the specific steps that must be taken to prevent them or to punish those who are responsible for them. The other approach involves understanding the cause of misbehavior and developing a human relations philosophy that is basically preventative rather than punitive.

Disciplinary Guidelines

Most recreation and park departments provide specific guidelines for their staff members that outline procedures to be followed in case of violation of department rules. For example, the Oklahoma City, Oklahoma, Parks and Recreation Department makes clear that leaders must interpret departmental policies or city ordinances to participants on playgrounds or in community centers. The following steps are to be taken in the case of serious violation of rules:

1. One recourse in case of infraction of rules is dismissal from the playground. Leaders may not handle patrons with physical force.
2. Before dismissing a patron from the grounds be sure that he knew the rules. If he did not, he should be given a chance to prove himself.
3. The period of suspension should be based on the severity of the infraction of the rule. One effective plan is not to impose a specific length of time but require that the patron return with parent or guardian when he thinks that he is ready and have a conference with recreation staff before reinstatement.
4. The senior leader in charge should call the parents or guardian of all patrons suspended and outline reasons and ask for cooperation.

In Topeka, Kansas,

> Directors or managers of facilities under the jurisdiction of the Recreation Commission shall have the authority to suspend any person who violates the rules and regulations of the said facility for a period of not more than three activity days. Supervisors shall have the authority to suspend an individual for a period not to exceed ten days. Further banishment from the facilities shall be authorized by the Recreation Commission.

In some cases, specific departmental procedures are outlined to deal with special types of problems. For example, the Hollywood, Florida, Parks and

Recreation Department has a detailed set of guidelines dealing with problems of smoking, drinking and drug abuse. It makes clear that all staff members are expected to seek out and eliminate drug abusers from recreation programs. The following guidelines suggest actions that leaders may take:

1. Suspension from area, from one night to an indefinite period, as immediate action. Use your own judgment in dealing with each individual infraction.
2. Request those believed to be under drug influence to leave area immediately with friends, if one of friends is "straight." Keep girls in office until they can be released safely.
3. Call parents if they will not, or cannot leave. It is inadvisable to call parents and accuse youth of using drugs. Tell parent the child is acting ill and needs attention.
4. Do not hesitate to call police should any trouble occur.
5. If you believe someone is pushing drugs but cannot prove it, you should suspend him from the area for another valid cause. Immediately make a report of suspicions to office.
6. No unauthorized selling of *any* product on recreation facilities is permitted.
7. If definite selling of narcotics is noticed, call police immediately and make reports.
8. Take license number of any car you suspect of being a stakeout for selling drugs.
9. Watch for unusual signals (signs with thumb or feet, etc.). These may be signals to pass drugs or alcohol.
10. All reports to police and leader's reports should be filled out (see Incident Report) in duplicate. Keep one and send one to office.

Still other departments may outline a range of possible offenses or infractions and develop procedures for dealing with each level of antisocial behavior. The Recreation Department of the City of Oakland, California, has developed a manual describing three levels of problems: minor, serious and extremely serious. These are described as follows: (a) *minor* offenses are routine behaviors that are socially unacceptable or in violation of center or playground safety rules, such as fighting, attempting to enter facilities without authorization, destroying property or disturbing organized programs; (b) *serious* offenses are technically misdemeanors, such as using a gun or other weapon, committing morals offenses, being under the influence of intoxicants or refusing to leave the premises for violation of Recreation Commission regulations; and (c) *very serious* offenses involve more hazardous control situations, such as potential riots, rumbles or major incidents. The appropriate measures that should be taken for each level of difficulty are clearly outlined for recreation leaders.

Human Relations Approach to Discipline

A second major approach to the problem of controlling antisocial behavior places emphasis on understanding the causes of the problem and attempting to deal with them constructively. First, leaders are encouraged to understand the wide variety of children and youth with whom they must deal, including those who are relatively happy and well adjusted as well as those who are hard to reach or difficult to handle. They must understand that many children come from family backgrounds that have not nurtured them properly, and so are hostile, aggressive, unsure of themselves and insecure with others. They may also have physical or mental disabilities that have hampered their social development.

While it may be difficult to accept children who are frequently hostile or disruptive, the recreation leader must be patient in working with such youngsters and should never ignore or reject them. Whenever possible, the leader must show personal interest and concern for them and be generous with smiles, words, time and encouragement. Rules should be simple, clear and consistently enforced. Children and youth should have a voice in the making of rules, and should know why it is necessary to have rules and why certain forms of behavior are undesirable.

The leader who is consistent and fair, who knows individual children or youth well, who identifies and works with natural leaders in youth groups, and who is alert to the signs of unrest or difficulty, will usually succeed in averting serious behavior problems. Leaders must recognize that expulsion from a playground does not really solve the problem for an individual child. Every effort should be made to keep the child active within the program and to work constructively with him or her.

In most communities, the level of antisocial activity on playgrounds or in community centers can be tolerated and worked with. Particularly if the recreation leader is able to call upon a supervisor for assistance when necessary, and to get help from the police (some police departments maintain juvenile divisions that handle such matters), the problem is not excessive.

However, under some circumstances, discipline becomes a much more difficult task. This is true most often in the poorest areas of large cities, where, in crowded and run-down slum neighborhoods, teenage gangs and social pathology of all kinds tend to flourish. It is not at all uncommon to have delinquent groups of youth who dominate playgrounds or small parks and prevent others from using the facilities. If a leader attempts to oust them, they will often retaliate physically. Senior citizens often fear to use recreation centers or even walk along the streets after 3 P.M. because of teenagers who threaten or prey on them. Some small parks or playgrounds are so dominated by derelicts or alcoholics that it is not safe for children to enter them. In some community centers, older youth or adults sell drugs or "shoot up," again making such settings unsuitable for constructive recreational activity.

How do recreation leaders handle such situations? Ordinarily, physical enforcement of regulations should not be their responsibility, just as it would not be expected of bank tellers that they engage in pitched gun battles with hold-up men. Instead, recreation leaders should receive assistance from the police or, when appropriate, other agencies, such as youth boards or drug addiction agencies, in dealing with these problems. Similarly, when vandalism is severe—including damage and graffiti, thefts, break-ins, or other forms of destruction to equipment and facilities—leaders should not have to combat these alone. Departments should make organized plans for dealing with such problems and should develop guidelines and various support services to prevent vandalism. The City of Boston has carried out a planning study, with the assistance of the National Science Foundation, and has prepared an excellent report on this subject.[2]

SAFETY PROCEDURES AND ACCIDENT-PREVENTION FUNCTIONS

In any well-organized recreation program, safety and accident prevention are important responsibilities of all leaders and supervisors. Conscientious leaders should be aware of the dangers that may exist in play areas where children and youth participate in active games or use various types of equipment. Recent studies have shown that more than 1 million injuries a year occur in high school and college sports programs, and that more than 100,000 children are taken to the hospital each year because of accidents on playground equipment.[3] In 1975, the federal government's Consumer Product Safety Commission published "Hazard Analysis—Playground Equipment," and efforts have been made recently to develop federal standards for playground safety, particularly in the area of playground safety surfacing.

However, the problem is much broader than the matter of proper equipment. The following principles should be clearly established in all recreation programs.

General Safety Principles

1. Safety is a basic consideration in playground and pool operation, and well-managed recreation facilities must provide safe places to play.
2. *All* accidents have causes, and every effort should be made to prevent them before they can occur.
3. Professional recreation personnel should be safety-conscious and should instill this attitude in other leaders, volunteers and participants.
4. All recreation staff members should know their own responsibility and degree of liability with respect to accidents, and should also understand the department's liability.
5. All recreation staff members should know the procedures for han-

---

[2] *Managing Vandalism: A Guide to Reducing Vandalism in Park and Recreation Facilities.* Study Report, National Science Foundation and Boston, Massachusetts, Park and Recreation Department, May 1978.

[3] "Congress Gets Study on Injuries." *The New York Times*, February 25, 1979, p. S-7.

dling accidents and injuries. These procedures should be outlined in staff meetings or orientation sessions and should be printed in departmental leadership manuals.

6. Leaders should be trained in basic first aid techniques, and should be carefully informed of departmental policy about using these in case of accidents. Well-stocked first aid kits should be kept at all recreation facilities.

Specific Safety Practices

These general principles should be supported by a number of procedures that minimize the possibility of accidents. These include the following:

1. Prepare, post and enforce simple rules of safety for your playground or other facility.
   a. Prohibit climbing on fences, buildings or other structures not intended for this purpose.
   b. Prohibit bicycle riding on the playground, and restrict the use of skateboards, scooters, roller skates, jump ropes and similar equipment to specific areas.
   c. Prohibit climbing on apparatus when it is wet and slippery.
   d. Prohibit rough-housing, unnecessary pushing and throwing of sticks, stones or other objects.
2. Inspect all equipment, grounds and facilities daily, and carry out the following measures:
   a. If any piece of equipment or apparatus is not in working condition, place it "out-of-order," and notify the maintenance department immediately.
   b. Keep play areas and sanitary facilities clean at all times.
   c. Keep all pointed or sharp-edged tools out of reach when they are not in use.
   d. Restrict play activities in areas where surfaces are slippery or not suitable for use.
   e. Keep animals off grounds, except when they are part of organized playground activities, such as pet shows.
   f. Establish "safety zones" around areas such as swings, giant strides or merry-go-rounds, so children can move past them safely.
   g. Locate active games involving batted or kicked balls in areas where they will not interfere with or endanger "tot" playgrounds or other quiet activities.
   h. Generally, keep play areas free of congestion.
3. In carrying on active games, sports, gymnastics or similar activities, observe the following guidelines:
   a. See to it that children have proper conditioning or preparation before engaging in strenuous activity.

b. Require physical examinations before organized competition.

c. Require children to have suitable equipment and uniforms (such as batting helmets in baseball) for specific activities.

d. Exclude children who are recognizably ill from activity, and stop activities before fatigue sets in.

e. Gear activities to the physical capabilities and skill levels of groups.

It is a generally accepted principle that municipalities conducting playground or other recreation programs, and the individuals in charge of programs and facilities, are not liable for damages in case of accident unless negligence can be proved or equipment was known to be defective. Therefore, if recreation leaders take careful precautions to assure safe conditions for play, they should be reasonably assured that they will not be liable if accidents occur. However, it is essential that they be familiar with the necessary steps to be taken in case of accidents or other emergencies—and that they follow these exactly, both to assure proper care of injured persons and to avoid possible post-accident liability.

There is no single set of prescribed procedures that all public recreation and park departments follow in the event of accident. However, most departments require their employees to carry out the following steps:

Minor Injury. Most accidents on the playground will be of a minor nature. Within prescribed limitations (see page 156), the leader should apply first aid as needed, following procedures outlined by the National American Red Cross or departmental first aid guidelines. It is then customary to send the child home or have a parent or another responsible relative call for him.

Major Injury. In the event of a more serious accident or an injury that the recreation leader thinks *may* be more serious, the following steps should be taken:

1. Make the injured person as comfortable as possible, covering him or her to provide warmth. Do *not* move an injured person, because this may aggravate the injury.

2. In the event of severe bleeding or stoppage of breathing, apply emergency first aid measures. Do not apply any other treatment; do not probe injuries, test the movement of limbs or attempt to set fractures.

3. Immediately call for appropriate medical assistance if the injury appears to be of an emergency nature:

   a. In some departments, the procedure is to call the police or sheriff's office directly, to have them call for an ambulance.

   b. In other departments, the procedure is to call a special police emergency squad that normally transports individuals to hospitals after giving expert first aid.

   c. In other situations, the recreation leader must call the ambulance directly.

4. Call parents or guardians immediately. In some departmental guidelines it is required that this be done *before* sending for med-

ical assistance, so that parents can make needed decisions. If the injury is extremely severe, or if it is not possible to contact parents, the recreation leader must send for an ambulance first.

5. Notify the recreation department of the accident, and fill out a report form, giving full details of the incident. Meanwhile, other participants should be encouraged to continue with the recreation program.

Other Guidelines. Most departments stipulate that their employees should follow these procedures when injuries of any sort occur, chiefly to protect the individual leader and the department in the event of a possible lawsuit:

1. In the event of serious injury, be sure to secure signed statements from all witnesses, including other employees. This may be done by a departmental supervisor.

2. The playground leader must not use his or her own car, or that of any other private person, to transport an injured person to a physician or hospital.

3. Under no circumstances should the recreation leader discuss or promise financial reimbursement or municipal liability in the event of an accident; the accident should not be discussed with anyone other than appropriate departmental or municipal officials.

4. If the playground leader gives parents or relatives any information regarding doctors, clinics or hospitals where an injured person may be treated, it must be clearly stated that the department has no facilities or financial provision for paying for medical care.

5. The person in charge of the facility, the staff member in whose program the accident occurred and any other staff member who witnessed the accident should remain at the location until medical help has come and investigating officers have gathered all the information they need.

6. A follow-up telephone call or visit to the injured person and parents or family should be made after the accident, both as a matter of personal concern and interest and as a desirable departmental procedure.

7. When a child who has been injured returns to the playground after recovery, special care should be given to insure that he or she is brought back into participation as normally as possible.

It should be recognized that special circumstances may necessitate procedures different from those suggested here. For example, in California park and recreation programs, state law requires that parental permission be obtained *before* minors are given medical service. Therefore, in this state it is essential to notify parents or guardians before sending for an ambulance, or to make every effort to reach them at the same time that emergency medical assistance is being called.

First Aid Procedures

It cannot be overemphasized that there should be strict limitations to the actions taken by recreation leaders with respect to first aid to injured persons. First aid should be offered only under two circumstances: (a) if the injury is a minor one, of a type that the recreation leader is equipped for and authorized to deal with; and (b) if it is an emergency situation requiring immediate action while more expert medical assistance is on the way. It is essential that leaders realize that they are subject to a lawsuit if they apply incorrect procedures or if they violate policies governing the appropriate assistance that may be given.

Within these limits, a sound knowledge of first aid procedures is an important requisite for playground or other recreation leaders. When minor accidents occur, prompt and careful treatment may be invaluable in relieving the discomfort of injured persons and reducing or eliminating the danger of infection.

The most common types of injuries occurring in recreational settings are small cuts and abrasions, splinters, insect stings, animal bites, puncture wounds, more serious cuts or injuries causing bleeding, shock, heat stroke and heat exhaustion, fractures and dislocations. Appropriate procedures for dealing with such injuries are provided in many departmental manuals.

Problems of Liability and Lawsuit. Apart from the natural desire to avoid injury to participants, leaders and supervisors must be keenly aware of the problems of legal liability. A number of general guidelines are helpful in avoiding the possibility of claims for injuries to participants on playgrounds and in other recreational programs. These include the need to provide safe and well-maintained equipment and adequate instruction and supervision at all times, and to avoid dangerous conditions or challenges that might be inappropriate for participants at a given age level or level of physical condition.

Farina comments that, although the determination of negligence clearly depends on the specific facts of particular cases, in general

> Recreation leaders should remember that they act in the place of the parent, and in such capacity they must act as reasonably prudent parents would act. This means that recreationists must protect children from their own childish pranks.[4]

Van der Smissen points out that parental permissions and waivers do not protect recreation leaders or agencies against lawsuits for injury to young children. She stresses the need to have a basic, systematic risk management program, including procedures for accident emergencies; safety and first-aid education of personnel; regular inspections of facilities and equipment; appropriate progressions of activities keyed to stages of personal development,

---

[4]Albert M. Farina: *Accident Liability: What Is Your Legal Responsibility?" Parks and Recreation,* March 1979, p. 29.

skill and experience; and an overall effective public relations program. These should serve to minimize the risk of injury, and also are useful in helping to prevent lawsuits or in presenting a defense when necessary.[5]

Since an increasing number of departments have begun to sponsor high-risk recreational activities, such as ski trips and adventure programs, the question of negligence and possible liability has become increasingly important. Frakt points out that, although there should be no reason to fear "undue or excessive" liability, carelessly or foolishly run programs still run a high risk of lawsuits for injury. Liability is likely to be found, he concludes, when there is

> (1) a failure to fully and clearly explain the hazards of the activity to the participant, (2) a failure to limit participation to those who have attained the maturity, physical conditioning, and level of expertness that the particular activity demands, and (3) a failure to provide the kind of professional leadership and instruction that would meet the reasonable standards of those engaged in such activities generally.[6]

HOUSEKEEPING FUNCTIONS: CARE OF FACILITY, EQUIPMENT AND SUPPLIES

Although most recreation facilities have their own maintenance personnel (janitors, custodians or laborers) who are responsible for routine cleaning, repairs and other maintenance, it is the job of the recreation leader or supervisor to be certain that housekeeping duties are carried out properly.

The leader or supervisor is normally responsible for making inventories of supplies and equipment, requisitioning new materials, ordering repairs and storing supplies. It is essential to use all equipment and apparatus carefully, to have them repaired when necessary and to ration all supplies or expendable materials with care.

Care of Facility and Equipment

From a health and accident-prevention point of view, the following guidelines should be followed regularly. The recreation leader who is not directly responsible for doing these tasks should still make sure that they are being carried out properly.

1. All equipment must be safely checked before each opening of a playground (this means twice a day).
2. Storage facilities should be kept neat and in good order.
3. Play areas should be sprinkled to eliminate dust. Sand in the

---

[5]Betty van der Smissen: Presentation at Pennsylvania Recreation and Park Society Conference, Pittsburgh, Pennsylvania, April 1979.
[6]Arthur N. Frakt: "Adventure Programming and Legal Liability." *Journal of Physical Education and Recreation (Leisure Today)*, April 1978, p. 51.

sandbox should be sprinkled and raked each day, and loose sand should be swept up daily.

4. Lavatories, drinking fountains and showers (when available) should be inspected regularly and kept clean. Playground directors should encourage hand-washing and showering, when facilities are available.

5. The facility should be cleaned up daily, including arts and crafts scraps, paper cups and napkins, broken glass and other kinds of refuse.

6. Make sure that grass is cut regularly, broken windows are repaired and all problems are immediately dealt with or reported to the responsible office.

Supplies and Expendable Materials

Staff members are generally held responsible for supplies and materials in their work settings, including the process of requisitioning, storing, handling or returning all small pieces of equipment or materials that are not used. Supplies should be stored in such a manner that inventories can be carried out promptly and efficiently. Lost or stolen equipment should be reported immediately, and records kept until the needed item is replaced or a new inventory is taken. Generally, requisitioning major blocks of supplies and materials is done at the beginning of the summer or other seasonal program, when allocations are made to all playgrounds and centers in a community. However, it is usually possible to make additional requisitions on an emergency basis.

In some departments, supplies and materials are divided into two categories: expendable and unexpendable. Expendable items are those that are expected to wear out or be used up during the course of the season, such as arts and crafts supplies or tennis or ping pong balls. Although staff members are expected to exercise care in the use of such materials, they need not usually make a report as the supplies depreciate or are used up. Unexpendable items are those that are *not* used up and that must be accounted for in a final inventory at the end of a season. Whenever equipment is worn out or damaged beyond use, it is common practice to require that it not be discarded or disposed of by playground leaders. Instead, broken or damaged items should be exchanged for new ones, using the regular requisition process. This is intended to prevent casual disposal of equipment and materials, which might encourage participants or even staff members to "help themselves" to needed items, explaining their disappearance by saying, "It was broken, and we threw it out."

In general, the key guidelines with respect to the use and care of supplies and equipment are that they must be systematically stored and handled, given as long a life as possible and accounted for at all times.

PREPARING REQUIRED REPORTS AND PROGRAM EVALUATION FUNCTIONS

A final important function of recreation leaders in playgrounds or community centers is maintaining accurate records and submitting required reports to their departmental supervisors. Linked to this is the responsibility for evaluating programs regularly and systematically.

Weekly and Monthly Reports

Many departments require staff members to maintain accurate records of programs and to submit regular reports, usually on a weekly or monthly basis. In addition, special reports must be submitted under certain circumstances, as in the case of accidents or theft. Regular reports fall into the following categories:

Program Reports. These usually must follow prescribed formats, in which the individual responsible for a facility must describe the general activities that were carried on, special events and other matters of concern. Membership and/or attendance figures are usually requested, and any problems or suggestions should be noted. If these reports are routine, no action may be taken on them. If they raise serious problems or reveal inadequacies, they may become the basis of staff meetings or other supervisory action.

Personnel Reports. Individual staff members normally submit time cards, noting latenesses, overtime, illness, special leaves and similar information. Supervisors review these and, in addition, must submit reports dealing with problem situations, such as violations of departmental policies, infractions of rules or other information that should go into personnel records.

Attendance Records. Accurate attendance records should be kept for all recreation programs and should go into departmental files. This information is to be used in reviewing programs and providing the basis for future planning. In some cases, attendance records are not as accurate as they should be, either because of the desire of recreation leaders and supervisors to paint as favorable a picture as possible, or because of the difficulty in getting precise statistics of attendance.

In recreational situations in which each person is registered by name or must purchase an admission ticket or pay for transportation, it should be possible to keep a completely accurate record of attendance. In other facilities, such as community centers or club programs that only registered members may attend, it is also possible to get fairly precise head-counts of the participants involved in activity groups. Playground attendance is generally more difficult to record, because of the transient nature of much participation. Therefore, special formulas have been used to count attendance at the peak time in the morning and again in the afternoon and evening, with a specified percentage added to account for "come-and-go" participants. Obviously, such estimates amount to little more than guesswork, and stronger efforts should be made to get completely accurate figures of attendance.

Special Events Reports. These are reports of major programs that are carried on, usually on a districtwide or communitywide basis, as opposed to special events at a single facility. They should sum up the major details of the event, how it was planned and carried out, who participated and other relevant information. Such reports serve as a basis for helping to determine in the future whether given programs should be repeated and exactly how previous arrangements were made.

Other Reports. As previous passages in this text have indicated, most departments also require submission of reports dealing with the following: (a) accidents and personal injury, to either participants or staff members; (b) permission slips for trips; (c) vandalism, damage and theft reports; (d) reports of disciplinary problems on playgrounds or in centers, and of actions taken, such as suspension or expulsion; (e) inventory reports regarding equipment and supplies; (f) facility or apparatus condition reports; and (g) reports dealing with monies collected by the department (for memberships, transportation or other fees) or the use of petty cash funds.

Within each such area, departments usually have specific procedural guidelines, requiring precise reports. For example, one department has the following rules governing the handling of monies collected by employees and the reporting of such income:

> All employees who must handle City money as part of the job are personally responsible for following established procedures. No money is accepted by an employee without the proper financial records being completed.
>
> Under no circumstances may the employee spend city money, nor may he refund money previously collected.
>
> Copies of all receipts and forms properly completed, and all monies collected, must be turned in to the Treasurer's office daily. No money is to be retained on a recreation area overnight. Refunds may be transacted only through the City Treasurer.

While it *is* essential that accurate records be kept in each of the areas that have been cited, it is also important to keep "paper-shuffling" to a minimum, and to require only those reporting procedures that are really necessary and that make a contribution to the work of a department. A comparable example might be found in some hospitals, in which recreation staff members are involved in so many planning sessions and team meetings (interdisciplinary meetings, meetings of ward or unit teams, "grand rounds" to review individual patients, staff development meetings and so on) that little time is available during the week to provide actual programs and services for patients. Paper work should be completed as quickly and efficiently as possible, and either filed systematically or forwarded to the appropriate office.

Evaluation of Programs

This involves the process of determining how effective the recreation program is—at a single facility, within a district, or on a communitywide basis. At each level, an appropriate individual should be designated to carry out the evaluation, although persons who are higher in the chain of the command then review the analysis and conclusions.

Evaluation is made in a variety of ways. It may involve measuring the performance of individual leaders throughout the season or year and determining the success of all regular programs or specially scheduled activities. Some departments require that elaborate forms be filled out regularly for every playground or community center. For example, one municipal recreation department has its recreation center directors fill out narrative reports twice a month, dealing with points such as scheduling, attendance levels, publicity, and diversity and suitability of programs for the populations being served.

For departments that wish to carry out a thorough self-evaluation, the National Recreation and Park Association has formulated a detailed instrument for measuring all the major aspects of recreation and park operations, providing suggested standards and criteria for performance.[7] Although it would not normally be the responsibility of recreation leaders or supervisors to carry out such an evaluation, they might well be part of it, and would certainly be expected to assist in the evaluation of programs for which they are directly responsible. Such evaluation might be based on a variety of elements, such as (a) attendance, as a basic criterion of interest; (b) nature of participation by those attending; (c) interest and support by members of the community; and (d) success in achieving specific goals or carrying out desired projects and programs. On the basis of guidelines found in the literature, questions such as these might be asked:

> "Are diversified programs being provided that meet the needs of all age groups, both sexes and varied socioeconomic groups in the community?"
> "Have behavior and cooperation of participants generally been favorable, or have there been many instances of behavior problems, such as fights or tensions between groups?"
> "Have members of the community supported the program by serving as volunteers or in other ways?"
> "Have programs received public attention through favorable coverage by newspapers or other media?"
> "Has the program been carried out in cooperation with other public agencies or voluntary or private organizations?"
> "Has the net impact of the program been to enrich the leisure life of the community and to strengthen desirable human values and development?"

---

[7]Betty van der Smissen: *Evaluation and Self-Study of Public Recreation and Park Agencies: A Guide With Standards and Evaluation Criteria.* Arlington, Virginia, National Recreation and Park Association, 1972.

As indicated, an important element in program evaluation may be the observation and appraisal of *participants.* This is particularly true in hospitals or other treatment centers, where regular records are kept of the progress of individual patients. Their involvement in recreational activities, their social participation and their ability to function in such situations is recorded and related to treatment goals and recommendations for future involvement or recreation experience. Such records should be used in staff meetings that review patient progress and in conferences with patients themselves.

In general, whatever form of evaluation is carried out, it will be meaningful only if it is honest, thorough and systematic. When a recreation leader is called upon to present a report of his or her own programs and performance, the leader should feel free to point out all strengths and weaknesses rather than gloss over flaws and exaggerate successes. In order to do this, the leader must be assured that the self-evaluation will not be used destructively by his or her supervisors. Instead, it must be used constructively, both to help the leader improve and to upgrade the program.

CONCLUSION

This chapter has presented descriptions of the various functions of recreation leaders in addition to their familiar tasks of presenting program activities. It has given primary emphasis to playground and community center settings found in all public recreation and park departments, and it has dealt chiefly with children and youth as participants. However, many leaders must function in more specialized settings, dealing with populations of different ages and with special needs or interests. Often, these programs are sponsored not by public agencies, but by voluntary, private or other organizations. The chapter that follows examines a number of such settings, placing specific emphasis on their unique requirements for recreation leadership.

SUGGESTED EXAMINATION QUESTIONS OR TOPICS FOR STUDENT REPORTS

1. Apart from the obvious function of leading recreation activities, what are several of the other key responsibilities of recreation leaders in playgrounds and community centers? Which of these do you feel are of the greatest importance? Why?
2. Discipline and control of participants' behavior are key functions of recreation leaders. On the basis of this chapter and your own experience, what do you regard as the key elements in carrying out this responsibility successfully?
3. Outline a set of basic principles for promoting safety in recreation and park settings. On the basis of the text and your own experience, what are the most important steps to be taken when an accident does occur?

SUGGESTED ACTION ASSIGNMENTS OR GROUP PROCESS ACTIVITIES

1. Examine the specific guidelines for first aid outlined in the recreation leadership or summer program manual of your community, assuming that such guidelines are provided. Contrast these with recommended guidelines in American Red Cross manuals, and make suggestions for their improvement or correction.
2. As an exercise in public relations, plan a hypothetical event or recreation program, and carefully prepare several newspaper releases for it that would appear before, during and after the event.
3. Develop an evaluation guide, with criteria and standards, and then apply it to a local playground or community center program. Base your guide on examples appearing in books or published by professional organizations.

Leadership in Special Settings: Part One

Chapter Eight

Earlier chapters of this text deal with the most familiar aspects of recreation leadership, and with playgrounds and community centers operated by public recreation and parks departments, which serve primarily children and youth.

However, it is obvious that many recreation leaders are employed today in other types of agencies, such as voluntary organizations, industrial concerns, the armed forces, commercial and private organizations or colleges and universities. These situations often require special administrative or supervisory skills, or impose the need for new kinds of leadership approaches. Particularly when working with groups of disabled persons, leaders must assume functions related to counseling and guidance, social service or behavior modification. Increasingly, they must cooperate closely with representatives of other disciplines or services, such as psychologists, psychiatrists, social workers and penologists.

None of this is completely new. For decades, recreation leaders have worked with gang members in city streets or with the mentally ill in psychiatric institutions. However, a number of recent trends in community service impose new challenges and opportunities.

For example, the financial limitations that have affected many public recreation and park departments have meant that in some cases, the services that they traditionally offered are being taken over by other community organizations. Increasingly, public departments must cooperate with other private, voluntary or commercial agencies in synergistic programming; recreation today *must* be provided by a wide variety of such organizations, so that diverse community needs may be met. It is important that recreation leaders and supervisors understand fully the leadership approaches and methods found in such agencies.

Public departments themselves have taken on an increasing responsibility in many cities for human services programming, in some cases actually being transformed into departments of human services.[1] Some professionals have sharply challenged this trend, questioning whether such services are appropriate for leisure services departments and suggesting that the trend is operating to the actual detriment of recreation and park professionals. Two California professionals, Richard Johns and Cathy Pardee, have written,

> We suspect that many of those pushing the human services approach . . . are professing that leisure services be blended in with or subordinated to human services as a means to seize existing mechanisms, organizational structures and funding sources needed to put their concepts across. In short, parks and recreation are viewed as having a positive image and status, stability, facilities and fiscal resources, and the efforts of human services proponents are nothing more than a power grab.[2]

This text, however, takes a contrary position. Its authors believe that public recreation and park departments have a responsibility to provide leisure services for disabled, deprived or other special populations, as well as other related or supportive programs that will strengthen their overall contribution to community life. In so doing, it is necessary to recognize that recreation programs and approaches themselves have changed markedly in recent years, and that recreation leaders must have more specialized skills and a new degree of sophistication that will help them fulfill new service roles.

This chapter and the one that follows therefore examine ten specialized types of settings or areas of recreation-related service:

1. Recreation programs for teenage youth
2. Industrial recreation programs
3. Armed forces recreation programs
4. Commercial and private recreation programs
5. Senior center programs
6. Campus recreation programs
7. Outreach programs for "problem" youth
8. Therapeutic camping programs
9. Recreation in psychiatric treatment settings
10. Recreation in nursing homes

The first six categories, dealing with settings or agencies that serve so-called normal populations, are analyzed in this chapter. The last four categories, dealing with populations that have special recreational needs or disabilities, are discussed in Chapter Nine.

---

[1]For example, see the Department of Human Services, New Rochelle, New York, where Joseph Curtis, Park and Recreation Commissioner, has been made director of a Department of Human Services incorporating parks and recreation; the city office of aging; youth bureau; drug and alcohol abuse program; docks, harbors and marina; and other health and special-service or cultural programs.

[2]Richard C. Johns and Cathy Pardee: "Human Services: Can Parks and Recreation Afford It?" *California Parks and Recreation*, May 1978, pp. 10–11.

In each case, the nature of the participants, their unique needs and interests, the goals of the agencies serving them, and appropriate guidelines for leadership are presented. As the reader combines these two chapters with the preceding ones, it should be possible to gain a fuller understanding of the wide variety of functions that recreation leaders carry out in modern society—and of the kinds of skills and techniques they must possess. The basic principles of leadership, group dynamics, effective teaching and sound organization apply in all situations. However, the emphasis and methods used vary markedly from setting to setting.

RECREATION PROGRAMS FOR TEENAGE YOUTH

One of the most important contributions any recreation department or agency can make is to provide constructive and attractive programs for teenage youth. The period of adolescence is one in which many young people seek to affirm their identity and to establish themselves as autonomous beings. It is also a time in which many individuals are in a state of conflict or turmoil, in which they rebel strongly against adult codes or moral values. Many adolescents engage in forms of leisure behavior that express their rebellion in potentially self-destructive and negative ways: violent gang activity, dangerous car racing, promiscuous sexual involvement or the abuse of drugs and alcohol.

Helping teenagers move successfully through this period is obviously the responsibility of a number of community agencies or forces, including schools, religious authorities and parents. The special contribution of a community recreation program for teenagers is threefold: (a) it provides challenging and constructive leisure activities that may serve as an appealing alternative to the many forms of antisocial play that tempt adolescents; (b) it provides a specific form of release for many of the drives and energies of young people, and meets many of their psychological, social and physical needs; and (c) it provides an opportunity for teenagers to make their own decisions, gain experiences in self-government and contribute to society.

Many different types of agencies seek to serve teenage boys and girls. Of these, three models are described here: (a) religious youth-serving agencies, (b) public recreation departments and (c) independent youth canteens or "drop-in" centers.

Religiously Affiliated Youth Programs

Each of the three major faiths—Catholic, Protestant and Jewish—provides organized programs for youth. As an example, one might examine the work of the Catholic Youth Organization in the Archdiocese of New York. In this organization, recreation is regarded as an important need of young people and a crucial area of character development. For example, the CYO Pledge of Sportsmanship states

> I pledge myself, upon my honor, to be loyal to my God, to my Church, and to my Country. I pledge myself to live a clean and honest life and to fulfill all my duties as a Christian. I bind myself to promote by word and example clean and wholesome recreation. I shall work and pray to be in all things, a generous winner and a gracious loser.

Catholic Youth Organization leadership manuals stress that the very nature of one's daily leisure activity has serious religious meaning; play should be regarded as "spiritual sacrifices acceptable to God." Sports in particular are seen as a means of training young people in Christian behavior, fairness, teamwork, honesty, sportsmanship and other forms of virtue. At the same time, they provide a way of strengthening morale and a sense of affiliation in parish life:

> A spirit should be built up in each parish. Enthusiasm for the different teams, encouraging parents to come out to see their children compete; pulpit and parish bulletin announcements concerning parish team games; posters announcing different events; all contribute to good parish participation.
>
> Uniforms for a parish team can be a big boost to morale. Parish CYO banners help build a spirit. Parish cheers, songs, and . . . cheerleaders add a great deal to build up a good spirit.

Obviously, the program is not restricted to sports. CYO sponsors a five-fold program of spiritual, cultural, apostolic, social and athletic activities for youth in the Archdiocese. It maintains youth centers throughout the city that sponsor daily programs, as well as a number of summer camps open to underprivileged children, regardless of age or creed. It offers specialized group projects in 17 parish areas of the Archdiocese, in cooperation with the New York City Youth Services Agency. It sponsors numerous scout troops, special programs for handicapped youths and a wide variety of recreational activities. These include the following, as both regular activities and special events:

> Major sports programs in baseball, softball, basketball, soccer, track and field, swimming and "roller hockey."
>
> Oratorical contests; "Christmas Crib" contests; religious quiz contests; essay contests; music, art and theater programs.
>
> Social and club programs, leadership training seminars and projects, retreats, youth centers and numerous other activities.

The bulk of leadership throughout the CYO is provided by volunteers, in the form of interested adults coaching teams or working with young people in other special activities. However, the central Archdiocese staff and a number of the center directors are full-time professionals. They must provide extensive field services and act as consultants in helping local parishes establish their own programs as well as in setting up many Archdiocesan activities. Their role is predominantly an organizational one, and it is enacted within a highly structured system. They need to be able to work closely with parish priests or nuns, with other school personnel, with parents, with directors of other city agencies and with large numbers of volunteers.

The CYO recreation program places emphasis on traditional recreational activities carried out under Church auspices in carefully structured clubs, leagues or other groups. It is not a program that tends to reach out to troubled youths or is able to accept deviant behavior. The role of the professional leader is chiefly one of setting up large-scale programs; obtaining facilities; scheduling and publicizing events; arranging banquets, clinics and training sessions; and performing other managerial tasks.

Programs Sponsored by Public Recreation Departments

Many municipal recreation and park departments provide a broad range of activities specially designed for teenage youth. Although primary emphasis tends to be given to team sports principally designated for this age group, other activities are offered.

For example, the Phoenix, Arizona, Parks and Recreation Department offers the following categories of special "teen" activities: *Arts and Crafts*, such as girls' "fix-it" classes, woodworking, and other crafts; *Community Service Activities*, including a teenage volunteer service and employment program; *Dramatics*, including one-act plays, puppetry, stage shows and movie making; *Hobbies and Special Interests*, such as "charm" classes, sewing clubs, model car contests and boys' and girls' cooking classes; and various other musical, camping, physical fitness and hobby activities. The Phoenix program includes many social activities, such as dances, canteens and parties with special themes.

Municipal departments that wish to provide more extensive programs for adolescents often sponsor or encourage the formation of "teen clubs." For example, the Montgomery County, Maryland, Department of Recreation has sponsored or assisted a number of successful clubs that are organized by young people and adult advisors in local communities or school districts. This involves a number of important ingredients: *planning* by teenagers, their parents and the Recreation Department; *organization* and active committee work; *publicity;* the development of *community support;* well-planned *bylaws* and *regulations;* varied and attractive *programs;* and, above all, good *leadership.*

Programs of such teen clubs in Montgomery County fall under several headings: "at home" recreation events, "away" events and service projects. Examples are given of each.

> *At Home Events.*   Pizza parties, picnics, buffet suppers, table games, costume or holiday dances, band dances, talent shows, rock-and-roll contests, novelty dances and square dancing.
>
> *Away Events.*   Cookouts, roller or ice skating outings, swimming parties, bowling, visiting other teen clubs, attending athletic events, barge trips and visiting amusement parks.
>
> *Service Projects.*   Fund-raising drives or volunteer work for March of Dimes,

Heart Fund, UNICEF, American Cancer Society; or volunteer leadership with county welfare projects, summer camp for underprivileged children, summer playgrounds or programs serving retarded children.

Such programs generally tend to serve teenagers who are willing to enter into socially approved and constructive programs and who will accept the regulations imposed by adult authorities. For example, some public recreation and park departments or schools that sponsor teenage canteens and dances have rigid codes of admission, dress, behavior and other regulations. The departments believe these are necessary, although the regulations tend to restrict or exclude other adolescents who are not willing or able to accept these limitations.

New Approaches to Sponsoring Youth Centers

A final approach to serving young people today in organized programs may be found in a number of communities around the United States and Canada, in which attempts to provide more contemporary and realistic programs for teenagers have been made. The rationale for these programs is that young people have changed so radically in their interests and attitudes that the traditionally conceived recreation program, with its emphasis on carefully chaperoned social activities, is no longer acceptable or attractive to them. After making an intensive study of teenage recreation in Los Angeles County, the Los Angeles Recreation and Youth Services Council came to this conclusion:

> Traditional agencies created to serve the recreation needs of teenagers must pioneer a new form of program and administration, only partially comparable to teenage centers as we have known them in the past and as we know them today.[3]

A study of many teen centers around the United States, carried out by Springfield College, concluded that three major concepts should be recognized in planning teen centers:

1. Young people should take the lead in the responsibility for their own affairs.
2. The program should be based on the needs and desires of youth . . . as they see them.
3. Serious youth problems should be faced realistically.

The Springfield College report, *A Youth Center for the 70's*, stressed the need to serve diverse groups of young people with meaningful social experiences:

> A teen center should be for all young people in the community. There are those who believe that teen-age cliques exist which are as different from one another as the differences that exist between the generations.

---

[3]*A Profile of Recreation and Youth Services in the Pasadena-Foothill Area.* County of Los Angeles, Recreation and Youth Services Planning Council, February 1969.

However, a center should be diverse enough in its makeup, representation, and programming to provide for:

The Swingers and the Clingers
The Squares and the Long Hairs
The Blacks and the Whites
The Normal and the Handicapped . . .
The Junior High and the Senior High (although usually programmed separately), and frequently
Post-High School young people . . .[4]

Activities should provide the opportunity for social interaction and for young people to "do their own thing." Programs should be determined with the help of questionnaires, youth conferences, bull sessions, suggestion boxes and careful planning. They should include a wide range of informal, "drop-in" activities, such as listening to records; playing ping pong, pool or table shuffleboard; eating and talking; coffee house programs; and similar elements. Special events, including camping, skiing trips, theatre parties, fishing, surfing, picnics and similar outings, or carnivals, street dances, games, tournaments, skating, bowling or car rallies, are offered by many centers. In addition, special interest groups involving activities such as working with stereo components, photography, music, physical fitness, judo or karate, boating or other specialized areas are often found in teen centers.

Beyond this, if teen centers are to be fully meaningful to young people today, they must involve the opportunity to deal with real issues and problems. The Springfield report suggests that teenagers may want to have discussions about "pollution, drugs, ecology, population, women's liberation, materialism vs. humanism, the racial situation, youth involvement, war, etc."

Services offered in some communities have included the following:

Tutoring	Job Referral
Drug Counseling and Referral	Family Counseling
Rap Line (Emergency)	Welfare Assistance
Draft Counseling	Free School

Community involvement programs may include

Youth Government Day	Teen Council
Youth Conferences	Adult–Teen Dialogues
Anti-Litter Campaigns	Service to Handicapped or Elderly
Playground Assistance	Environmental Projects
UNICEF Drives	Information Service

In developing centers with such programs, much help is needed. They simply cannot be accomplished successfully by community organizations or departments that provide staff, set policies and dominate the entire operation.

---

[4]Donald Bridgman, Project Director: *A Youth Center for the 70's*. Springfield, Massachusetts, Springfield College Report, 1971, p. 7.

Instead, young people must take the lead in organizing the programs—although they will need considerable assistance from adults in terms of obtaining facilities and funding, getting legal advice, handling problems and insuring continuity. The Pennsylvania Youth Advisory Council, in a pamphlet, *Let's Listen to Youth*, sets the limits of adult involvement:

> Youth need the backing of adults. Successful youth councils have continuing adult assistance without adult domination. Adult advisors must be helpful, when needed, but must give youth great latitude in making plans, reaching their own decisions, and carrying out their activities. The quickest way to kill a youth council is to spoon-feed it with projects which adults think youth should carry out.[5]

Thus, the role of adult leaders will be to help teenagers carry as much of the responsibility as possible for planning their own programs and for center operation.

It is obvious that much of the self-destructive or hostile behavior of young people arises because they feel a sense of helplessness or frustration at being "irrelevant" to the adult society all around them. Teen centers may serve to provide both causes and meaningful tasks for young people that can absorb their energies and are relevant to their psychosocial needs. Taking responsibility for themselves and carrying out meaningful programs is essential to their own healthy growth, as well as to the success of the teen center itself.

Obviously, limits must be set by adults. Teen centers cannot be permitted to operate with members openly using alcohol and drugs, and regulations governing such behavior must be enforced. But, the Springfield report suggests, the existence of problems in this area does *not* mean that programs should be discontinued:

> Problems will arise from time to time in or around a youth center. Young people will appear on the scene obviously under the influence of alcohol or drugs; pushers might even show up. These problems are also found in schools, but schools are not closed; education, after all, provides an important and vital service. The contention here is that a youth center also provides an important and vital service that should not be jeopardized by the misadventures of a few. . .
>
> Our contention is not that drugs should be permitted. They should not. But we do make a plea for a realistic approach to the problem. *A youth center should not be abandoned as a failure because occasional problems arise.* It is at this very point that support for young people is most significant—after all, what support is required when things are running smoothly?
>
> A youth center is frequently sought out by the teen-ager who has problems and is not involved in traditional forms of recreation. If we accept the viewpoint that many young people try drugs as an escape from unpleasant realities and because they have not found meaning in life, a relevant youth center and wise, understanding leadership might contribute to the prevention of drug abuse . . .[6]

---

[5]*Ibid.*, p. 46.
[6]*Ibid.*, p. 49.

The implications here for leadership of teenage recreation programs are clear. Programs that are planned, organized and carefully supervised by adults can provide interesting and valuable recreation activities for a segment of the youth population. In order to serve a much broader segment, however, it is also necessary to provide activities and programs that significantly involve young people who are less conforming in their values and behavior, and who not only need the opportunity for meaningful involvement but who also can make an important contribution to community life. Although this represents a difficult challenge for recreation leaders, it is a challenge that must be met if this population group is to be served effectively. (A number of community recreation programs that use an "out-reach" approach to working with deviant youth and anti-social gangs are described in Chapter Nine.)

INDUSTRIAL RECREATION PROGRAMS

Industrial recreation is another important area of recreation service that is directed primarily at adults and is sponsored by non-governmental agencies. It consists of recreation programs that are offered by or in conjunction with companies, to serve their employees and, in many cases, their families.

Scope of Industrial Recreation

This form of recreation sponsorship has grown rapidly during the past three decades. Approximately a thousand major industries or companies provide extensive recreation programs, many under professional leadership. Essentially, their purposes are threefold: (a) to *improve employer–employee relationships* by developing attractive and comprehensive activity programs as part of the overall personnel services and "fringe" benefits offered by the company; (b) to *promote employee efficiency* by helping to reduce absenteeism, accidents or even sabotage (studies have indicated that these may stem from boredom and the psychological problems of workers), and by promoting the physical fitness of workers; and (c) to *improve the public image and recruitment appeal* of industries, which is particularly important for concerns that are located in remote geographical areas or that must compete with other companies for skilled employees who may be in short supply.

Robert Galvin, chairman of the board of Motorola, Inc., speaks for many business executives in this statement:

> The basic objective of industrial recreation is to recognize people's needs as a social entity. . . . Through recreation, employees become better acquainted. We all find that we have many interests in common with one another. We gain better understanding of each other. . . .
>
> Apart from personal development, recreation is also good for the corporation. Being known as a company with a varied recreation program helps in recruiting. Further, employee recreation is of great value to fam-

ilies and to the community. We hope that our recreation program helps bring family, community, and company closer together.[7]

Numerous studies by sociologists have shown that modern patterns of industrialization and automation have alienated many employees from their work and have created feelings of job dissatisfaction. Finney points out that a recent study of industrial recreation shows striking improvements in worker productivity, as a result of a newly instituted employee recreation programs.[8] Similarly, an Ohio-based jewelry manufacturing concern showed a striking decline in worker absenteeism after an employee recreation program was introduced in the home office.[9] Thus, there is growing evidence of the value of this form of organized leisure service.

Patterns of sponsorship vary considerably among different companies in the United States and Canada. In some cases, the industry may take full responsibility for providing facilities, leadership and financial support for a diversified program of activities; frequently this is done with the assistance of an advisory council of employees. In other cases, the facilities are provided by the company, while the employees, through a recreation association or council, take responsibility for organizing and staffing the program. In still other cases, the employees take the major responsibility for financing and operating the program, using facilities that are chiefly away from the place of employment.

Samuel C. Johnson, chief executive officer of the Johnson Wax Company, has made this comment:

> We believe the recreation program at Johnson Wax is successful for several reasons. Above all, we get our employees involved in the planning and administrative aspects of the various activities. Even though we have a professional recreation staff, we consider this degree of employee involvement to be vital. We want and encourage our employees to be in on the decision-making, in order that they may feel the recreation program is truly *their* program.[10]

Range of Program Activities

Industrial recreation typically encompasses a wide variety of activities. The Goodyear Company, for example, has a large gymnasium at its corporate headquarters in Akron, and sponsors active leagues in such sports as basketball, flag football, softball, bowling, volleyball and golf. In recent years, membership in skiing and tennis clubs has mushroomed. In addition, Goodyear

---

[7]Robert W. Galvin. Cited in "Top Management Speaks." *Recreation Management*, March 1979, p. 31.

[8]Craig Finney: "Recreation: Its Effect on Productivity." *Recreation Management*, December-January 1979, pp. 14–15.

[9]Jacqueline Erwin: "Organization Profile: Peoples' Jewelry Co." *Recreation Management*, April 1978, pp. 18–19.

[10]Samuel C. Johnson. Cited in "Top Management Speaks." *Recreation Management*, August 1977, p. 30.

sponsors more than 40 clubs serving a variety of interests, ranging from chess and bridge to gourmet eating and model railroading. Its facilities include a 75-acre employee park and a 1,400-seat theater for musical performances by employees. Goodyear also sponsors the world's largest hunting and fishing club, which has more than 5,000 members.

Numerous other examples of program activities in employee recreation might be given. Sometimes they are clearly of a "fun" nature, such as the well-known musical revue program sponsored by the Allen Bradley Company in Milwaukee, or the employee motorcycle club of the Jet Propulsion Laboratory in Pasadena, California. Sometimes they are concerned with employee retirement attitudes; for example, the Rockwell International Company is only one of many companies that have introduced workshops in pre-retirement preparation, placing emphasis on the constructive use of leisure, for older employees.[11] The American Stock Exchange has sponsored Outward Bound Expeditions for various groups of employees, producing positive effects on personnel morale and working relationships.[12] The functions of recreation personnel often include non-leisure services; for example, the Nationwide Insurance Company in Columbus, Ohio, operates a highly successful non-profit discount store for its employees.[13]

To illustrate the overall patterns of industrial recreation that are provided today, a detailed description of the program at one major industrial concern is provided here.

Xerox Corporation, Rochester, New York

The Xerox Corporation offers a leading example of how a major company provides outstanding recreation opportunities for its employees. The responsibility for organizing and carrying out this program is assigned to the Xerox Recreation Association. This incorporated, non-profit body was formed in 1965 through the combined efforts of the Xerox management and a number of interested employees.

Facilities and Funding. The Xerox Recreation Association offers programs at three company locations: at Xerox Square in the center of Rochester, and in two suburban settings, at Henrietta and Webster, New York. Xerox Square offers conference rooms, an executive fitness laboratory and lockers, physical fitness areas, saunas, gymnasiums, an auditorium and an ice skating rink. The Webster complex has a multi-purpose recreation building, including an exercise area with physical fitness equipment, lockers and showers, and a general purpose area for meetings of clubs and organizations. Its outdoor facilities include four lighted and two unlighted baseball diamonds, a putting green, a jogging and cycling path, lighted basketball and tennis courts

[11]James Patton: "Pre-Retirement Counseling at Rockwell International." *Recreation Management,* April 1977, pp. 12–13.
[12]"AMEX Builds Ties With Survival Trip." *The New York Times,* September 19, 1979, p. D-2.
[13]Bobbie Hildebrand: "Helping Employees Stretch Their Paychecks." *Recreation Management,* April 1978, pp. 20–22.

and facilities for horseshoes and archery. At Henrietta, there is an indoor recreation area with equipment similar to that at the Webster complex, in addition to a mile-long jogging path and two unlighted baseball diamonds.

In addition to providing and maintaining these facilities, the Xerox Corporation supports the Recreation Association in two ways—through total and partial subsidies.

Total Subsidy. This is given in the form of salaries for full-time professional personnel, payment of outside services, purchase of major equipment and similar costs.

Partial Subsidy. Fees are collected for participation in all recreation activities. However, these may not pay the full cost of conducting the activities. When a surplus occurs, money is returned to the Xerox Recreation Association's treasury. When a surplus does not occur, and when serious deficits are incurred in supporting certain activities, the corporation may assist in paying for instructors, umpires, supplies and other charges.

This arrangement, in which the employees and the company share the cost of operating the recreation program, represents a form of cooperative sponsorship in which employees not only pay for a major portion of what is provided them but also supply much leadership and direction, thereby gaining greater interest and desire to participate.

Program Elements. The Xerox Recreation Association offers a wide variety of opportunities in fields such as sports competition, physical fitness activities, cultural participation, special interest groups and clubs, travel tours and discount tickets to special events. An overall schedule for a recent year is provided in Table 8–1, which shows the activities offered, the seasons when they are available and the locations where they may be found.

In addition to the customary activities, several of the program elements deserve fuller description. These are (a) the travel program, (b) the inner-city youth program, and (c) the physical fitness program.

Travel Program. A wide variety of travel tours are planned as chartered discount flights to countries all over the world. These trips are formally sponsored by the Xerox Recreation Association; in a recent year, chartered jet flights were sponsored to Curaçao, Puerto Rico, Barbados, Disney World, the Costa del Sol (Spain), and the Soviet Union. In addition, the Xerox Ski Club sets up trips for a weekend or longer to outstanding ski areas in the United States and abroad, including Vermont, Lake Tahoe (in the High Sierras), and Innsbruck, Austria.

Inner-City Youth Program. The Xerox Corporation recognizes its obligation to assist the city of Rochester in a variety of social concerns. Although it is an attractive and economically viable community, Rochester has a seriously disadvantaged inner-city population, and has had summer disturbances related to this problem. Xerox therefore initiated a summer inner-city youth program called CONTACT. As part of its project, CONTACT took inner-city youth, mostly black, to the University of Rochester campus, where they participated in activities such as baseball, soccer, swimming and arts and crafts, which were planned for them by the Xerox Recreation Association staff.

TABLE 8-1. XEROX RECREATION ASSOCIATION PROGRAM SCHEDULE

Sports & Athletics	Location*	Season Available
Basketball—Leagues & Tournaments	1,3,4	November–March
Bowling—Leagues, Tournaments, & Fun Nights	4	September–April
Flag Football—Leagues	1	August–October
Golf—Instruction, Leagues, Putting Green, Tournaments	1,4	May–September
Horseback Riding—Open Riding & Instruction	4	Year Round
Horseshoes—Courts & Tournaments	1,4	May–November
Ice Skating—Rink, Open Skating & Instruction	2	November–March
Judo & Karate—Instruction	4	September–May
Physical Fitness—Executive, Men, & Women	1,2,3	Year Round
Roller Skating	4	Spring & Fall
Scuba—Instruction	4	October–April
Soccer Club	1,3	May–September
Softball—Slo-pitch, Men's & Women's Leagues & Tournaments'	1,3	May–September
Tennis—Exhibitions, Instruction, Leagues & Tournaments	1,2,4	April–October
Volleyball—Men's & Women's Tournaments & Co-Rec. Play	1,4	Year Round
Clubs & Special Interest Groups		
Antique Club	2,4	September–June
Archery Club—Ranges	1,3,4	Year Round
Auto Club	1,4	April–October
Bridge—Instruction & Club	1,2,3	September–May
Photo Club	2,4	September–June
Pistol Club	4	Year Round
Sailing Club	2,4	April–October
Ski Club	1,2,4	September–April
Table Tennis Club	1	Year Round
Xerox Players—Drama Club	2	Year Round
Social & Cultural		
Dancing—Ballroom	1	September–May
Dancing—Square Dance Club	1	Year Round
Education—Language, Music, Sewing	1,2,3,4	Year Round
Fashion Shows	1,2,3	Year Round
Health—Diet Workshop	1,2,3,4	Year Round
Picnic Kits	1,2,3	April–September
Ticket Sales—Athletic, Social, & Cultural	1,2,3	Year Round
Toastmasters	4	Year Round
Travel Tours—Domestic & Foreign	4	Year Round
Xerox Pioneers—Retirees Club	2,4	Year Round

*1 Webster, 800 Phillips Road
 2 Xerox Square, Rochester
 3 Henrietta, 1350 Jefferson Road
 4 Sites located outside Xerox property

Physical Fitness Program.   Recognizing that, in an age of mechanization and automation, many individuals get insufficient exercise, the Xerox management has strongly supported a sound physical fitness program for the prevention of cardiorespiratory diseases. It is provided on two levels: (a) an executive fitness program, and (b) a general fitness program for other employees.

The executive program is provided in Xerox Square. It offers an elaborate circuit interval training program that makes use of eight Universal weightlifting stations, a mechanical treadmill and a bicycle ergometer, along with an ultraviolet room and sauna. Medical diagnoses are made of the executives participating in the program, and the physical fitness specialist keeps a close check and maintains daily progressive records on each. It has been found that this fitness program is valuable in preventing the cardiovascular problems and other disabilities faced by executives, who are often challenged by stressful, deskbound daily routines. The general fitness program offered for other employees at all three locations provides basically the same indoor equipment for fitness along with guidance from a fitness specialist who maintains records of employees on a daily basis.

Incidentally, employee fitness programs of this type have become extremely popular with many major corporations, which have developed outstanding facilities and well-trained staff members to direct them.[14]

Leadership.   The Xerox recreation staff consists of seven professionally trained staff members, three of whom have advanced degrees in this field. In addition, there are full-time secretaries and a bookkeeper. Considering the number of employees served—at present, more than 8,000 persons—this is an excellent ratio of staff to participants. Detailed position descriptions have been developed for professional staff members on five levels: Recreation Specialist, Senior Recreation Specialist, Recreation Supervisor, Manager of Recreation Programs and Manager of Corporate Recreation Services. These position descriptions include the following statement of needed skills and abilities in industrial recreation:

> Foremost, the recreation professional must be able to deal effectively with men and women with varied ages, interests, education, economic levels, and abilities. He must be able to communicate effectively with superiors and subordinates, and to tactfully and diplomatically make constructive criticism. He also must provide the necessary encouragement to program participants and to generally make employee experiences with recreation enjoyable and beneficial. Natural leadership ability and knowledge of leadership skills cannot be overemphasized.
>
> Each professional staff member must be able to project a favorable image of his company and himself. In short, he must be skilled in all aspects of administration, with major emphasis in the management of finances. Additionally, he must be skilled in supervising subordinates while being able to take positive action with superiors. He must also be able to adapt quickly to new situations and to study and grow with new program, facility, and staff developments. . . . He must have a sound philosophy of

[14]See Gloria Geannette: "Inside the Corporate Gymnasium," *Recreation Management*, March 1979, p. 20, and Kenneth E. White: "Components and Staffing of an Employee Fitness Program," *Recreation Management*, July, 1978, p. 26.

recreation consistent with current trends in municipal and industrial recreation.[15]

A fuller statement of the skills essential for success as an industrial recreation professional would include the following elements:

1. The ability to work closely with all levels of management and to communicate effectively with line-level personnel.
2. The ability to make contact and work with community groups, school principals and similar officials, to make cooperative program or facilities arrangements.
3. The ability to be an "enabler," to help members get their own clubs or special interest groups formed and to take on many of their own responsibilities.
4. The ability to manage a variety of facilities—including assisting in the conceptualizing and designing of facilities, as well as maintaining and scheduling them properly.
5. The ability to develop and carry out a variety of sometimes complicated financial arrangements for the support of programs, and to make judgments about the allocation of company resources.
6. The ability to carry out effective promotional procedures. Just as in any other department, employee participation in recreation is not assured, and the leader must be highly skilled in publicizing the activities offered.
7. The ability to have the interests of both employees and management at heart; the leader must be able to represent both groups in an equitable and fair manner.
8. Finally, the ability to envision a program that incorporates a wide variety of recreation elements, but which may also include other personnel services that can legitimately be attached to this department.

ARMED FORCES RECREATION

Another special setting in which large numbers of recreation leaders are employed is the broad field of armed forces recreation. Both civilians and military personnel have the responsibility for providing recreation programs and facilities for men and women in the United States Army, Air Force, Navy and Marine Corps and, in many cases, for their families. The philosophy underlying this program may be seen in an official handbook outlining the Air Force Special Services program:

Mission of the Program

The Special Services program fulfills the recreation needs and interests of Air Force personnel and their families by providing maximum op-

---

[15]*Professional Staff Standards.* Rochester, New York, Xerox Recreation Association, June 1969.

portunities for them to participate in leisure-time activities that help to stimulate, develop, and maintain their mental, physical, and social well-being. Recreation is a fundamental part of the American way of life; and Air Force military personnel and their families need and deserve self-rewarding creative recreation programs and opportunities equal in variety and quality to the best offered in the most progressive civilian communities. Proper recreation activities improve the individual's mental state, character growth, and job performance. Moreover, military personnel and their families who participate in recreation activities are more likely to have favorable attitudes toward an Air Force career.[16]

The Air Force recreation program includes the following types of activities: (a) sports, including self-directed, competitive, instructional and spectator programs; (b) motion pictures; (c) service clubs and entertainment, including dramatic and musical activities; (d) crafts and hobbies; (e) youth activities for children of Air Force families; (f) special interest groups, such as aero, automotive, motorcycle and power boat clubs, or hiking, sky-diving or rod and gun clubs; (g) rest centers and recreation areas; (h) open messes; and (i) libraries. Base commanders are required to establish Special Service programs that are sufficiently diversified to provide a broad variety of activities for all those residents on the base, within manpower authorizations and available funding.

One of the key areas of armed forces recreation is sports, which are designed to accomplish the following objectives:

1. To promote physical fitness and dispel fatigue and boredom.
2. To assist in the adjustment of military personnel to the service.
3. To create a socializing influence among military personnel, counteracting possible feelings of isolation and loneliness.
4. To provide opportunity to express socially approved forms of aggressive behavior.
5. To promote healthy personality development.
6. To strengthen military morale, fighting spirit and esprit de corps.
7. To promote military discipline, respect for authority and acceptance of rules and regulations.
8. To encourage wholesome use of leisure.
9. To provide, through sports, entertainment of a satisfying, vicarious nature, for large numbers of spectators.

As in all specialized areas of recreation, the goals reflect the unique mission of the sponsoring agency. This is best demonstrated in the description in the Air Force Special Services Manual of how sports contribute to "fighting spirit," "unity and esprit de corps" and military discipline. The manual states

> *Fighting Spirit.* Morale is synonymous with fighting spirit. Its psychological basis is founded in the need for survival. Courage, determination, initiative, and aggressiveness are certainly desirable qualities for a

---

[16] *Air Force Sports Program Manual.* Washington, D.C., Air Force Publication No. 215-1, July 1966, p. 1.

soldier. They become mandatory in time of war. Nowhere is the fighting spirit and the will to win held in higher esteem than in the field of sports. . . . The will to win, to endure, the courage to carry on, is built continuously through a program of sport . . .

Unity and Esprit de Corps. Sports develop a spirit of unity. Social distinction, race, and creed are forgotten in the light of the common task. Nothing in the Air Force program will so unify an Air Force base, a flight squadron, or group, as sports. It is through participation on the base or squadron team that an airman may gain . . . identification with his squadron, with the base, and with the Air Force . . .

Military Discipline. Cheerful obedience to orders and to superiors is a military necessity. Discipline and respect for authority are a must in the service. Every agency which can make a contribution to discipline should be used fully. Respect for authority, acceptance of rules, and self-imposed obedience of the spirit of the rules are the essence of sports competition. . . .[17]

It becomes the responsibility of recreation personnel in the Air Force to promote these goals vigorously. This is done through an extensive program of sports, which includes six major elements: (a) *instruction* in basic sports skills; (b) a *"self-directed"* phase of informal participation in sports under minimum supervision or direction; (c) an *intramural* program, in which personnel assigned to a particular base compete with others at the same base; (d) an *extramural* program, which includes competition between the intramural teams of different Air Force bases, or with teams from neighboring communities; (e) a *varsity* program, which involves high-level competition with players selected for their advanced skills, who compete on a broader national or international scale; and (f) a program for *women* in the Air Force.

The task of organizing this extensive program is an extremely complex one. The individual serving as sports director must perform a variety of functions. Working with a sports council that consists of the squadron sports directors, members of base standing committees, team managers and squadron representatives, the director must formulate policies and be responsible for the proper conduct of the base intramural program. This includes the following responsibilities:

1. Plan, direct and supervise the general conduct of all intramural activities.
2. Assist group and squadron sports directors and team managers in an advisory capacity.
3. Develop intramural policies in collaboration with the base sports director, the sports council, the sports staff and the participants.
4. Systematically publicize and promote the program.
5. Draw up schedules; organize leagues, meets, and tournaments; and plan special events.
6. Select, train, assign and supervise intramural officials.

---

[17]*Air Force Sports Program Manual.* Washington, D.C., Air Force Publication No. 215-2, October 1966, p. 4.

7. Interpret the intramural program to base personnel.
8. Provide for the safety and well-being of all participants.
9. Evaluate the program.
10. Compile and publish game results and individual and team records.
11. Develop and publish rules relating to program administration.
12. Develop and supply to squadron sports directors and organization managers the necessary forms for reporting game results, signing out equipment, reserving practice areas, making a protest and so forth.
13. Control equipment furnished for contests.
14. Prepare budget estimates.

Although this listing of responsibilities refers to the intramural sports program in the Air Force, it provides a useful overall picture of the function of recreation personnel in all the armed forces. The tasks of recreation personnel include a number of key supervisory and administrative functions. Although many specialists are employed in specific areas of recreation interest, the general role requires the ability to organize, work through appropriate channels, motivate participation and carry out program elements within the total framework of the military structure. The successful recreation director in the armed forces must have enthusiasm, drive and imagination, and must be able to turn ideas into program realities through "know-how" of the bureaucratic structure. Great emphasis is placed on administrative efficiency in the armed services. In a *Special Services Manual,* published in the mid-1970's, that outlines U. S. Navy policy in this area, the point is made:

> Special Services in the Navy is not only important to the accomplishment of the Navy's mission, but in major Navy activities it is "big business," often involving budgets in excess of a million dollars. Consequently, the administration of both programs and funds should be viewed as a vital administrative function.[18]

In the Navy, Special Service Directors have responsibility for (a) developing and conducting programs and services to improve and maintain the morale of Navy personnel and their dependents; (b) operating recreational facilities; (c) developing a financial plan and administering the use of both appropriated and non-appropriated funds; (d) supervising the purchase, custody and issue of recreation gear; (e) training and supervising the personnel assigned to Special Services; and (f) coordinating relations with other commands and with adjacent communities.

In all, armed forces recreation personnel must possess many of the same qualities as industrial recreation professionals. They must be excellent organizers and administrators, in part because the task is so complex that it requires these skills, and in part because the organizations value these qualities highly. Finally, they must be initiators, self-starters and "do-ers."

[18]*Special Services Manual.* Washington, D.C., U.S. Navy, March 1974.

COMMERCIAL AND PRIVATE RECREATION PROGRAMS

As indicated earlier in this text, the commercially operated or private, profit-making recreation venture has become a major provider of leisure services in the United States and Canada during the past several decades. Although it would be impossible to describe all the different kinds of commercial and private recreation programs, they include travel and tourism; places of entertainment (including cultural activities and professional sports); places of instruction, such as dance studios or music studios; health spas and other fitness centers; residential communities of various types that offer elaborate recreational programs and facilities; and hundreds of other types of complexes, such as ski centers, bowling or billiards facilities, skating rinks, chess or backgammon clubs, "singles" clubs and many others.

In such settings, the purpose obviously is to provide attractive, efficiently run services that draw large numbers of participants and earn a substantial profit. Increasing numbers of resorts that formerly offered little more than entertainment, food and rooms today provide a wide variety of sports, hobbies and other pursuits, all of which must be carefully scheduled and supervised. For example, the Host Farm and Corral, a 225-acre resort in the Pennsylvania Dutch country, offers nightclubs and Las Vegas-style cabaret entertainment and other typical hotel attractions. However, it also operates a ski center with a chair lift and ski shop; indoor and outdoor skating rinks; indoor and outdoor lighted tennis courts; indoor and outdoor swimming pools; a PGA Championship golf course; saunas and steam rooms; facilities for volleyball, badminton, softball, handball, paddleball and basketball; and dozens of other sport and game activities. Guests may hike, bike, take Amish pony-cart rides through the countryside, take dancing lessons or enjoy indoor game arcades. There are separate teenage programs, with discotheques, folk-singers and other forms of entertainment, as well as day camp programs with skilled counselors for younger children.

At the Host Farm and Corral, as at other motel/hotel operations that seek to attract family vacationers along with conventions and other specially arranged tour groups, there are also many specially scheduled events, classes and programs. Evening dances and parties with special themes, carnivals, shows, game sessions and classes make up a busy schedule that must be carefully planned, publicized and coordinated.

In many privately operated residential communities, including retirement or "leisure" villages for older persons and condominiums or planned communities for persons of all ages, recreation has become an increasingly important part of the sales package. Such communities typically provide golf courses, swimming pools, tennis courts and club houses that offer social programs, hobby classes and a variety of special services and activities.

In Boca Raton, Florida, for example, the Boca Raton Club has a well-staffed Club Activities Department. Under the direction of a professional coordinator, this department operates major sports facilities, emphasizing golf and tennis, with top "pros," classes, tournaments and other special events. Yacht cruises, lectures and discussion programs, holiday and other children's parties, teen dances, trips and outings, and a variety of hobby groups and classes provide a wide range of activities. In such settings, the activity coordinator tends to be very much a "social" director, placing emphasis on purely fun-oriented programs. In senior residences or retirement communities, the coordinator's functions may include other human service responsibilities as well.

As such resorts and residential communities continue to grow, it seems clear that opportunities for employment in commercial and private recreation will expand. More and more college and university recreation departments are placing their field-work students in such settings to receive practicum experience, and increased numbers of professionally trained workers undoubtedly will hold these positions in the future.

In addition to growing as a field for potential employment of recreation leaders and supervisors, commercial recreation is likely to influence other areas of professional practice through its strong emphasis on business-like management procedures and aggressive marketing programs. In profit-oriented recreation enterprises, where the "name of the game" is designing and "selling" an attractive product, sophisticated and effective techniques have been developed that will be useful in many other types of recreation agencies.

COLLEGE RECREATION PROGRAMS

Another expanding field of recreation service is to be found on the campuses of colleges and universities throughout the United States and Canada.

All institutions of higher education today sponsor some form of leisure activity for their students, faculty and staff members, usually including recreational sports, cultural programs and social activities as primary components. Many of the larger colleges and universities have departments of student life or campus unions that provide a wide range of such activities. Often a dean of student life will be responsible for overseeing these programs and services, particularly on campuses that have many resident students. This diversified responsibility includes operating arts centers; planning performing arts series, film programs and forums with guest speakers; and managing student center buildings, which may include specialized facilities such as bowling alleys, coffee houses, game rooms, restaurants, bookstores and other activity areas.

Supervision of student government activities and the provision of counseling and guidance services are also important areas of responsibility in this field. From a recreational point of view, what are some of the major trends on college and university campuses today?

Expansion of Recreational Sports. There has been widespread growth in the area of sports participation, both on an organized, intramural level and in low-pressure, often coeducational athletic competition. Activities may include leagues and tournaments in team sports like basketball, volleyball and softball, or in other sports such as tennis, bowling and table tennis. When teams are mixed, the rules are often modified to equalize play between men and women. Similarly, sports clubs involving large numbers of students are becoming increasingly popular. For example, at West Chester State College in Pennsylvania, there are active student clubs in the following sports: boxing, horseback riding, fencing, ice hockey, karate, lacrosse, rugby, skiing, track and volleyball.

Haniford describes the diversity found in some college and university programs:

> Informal indoor sports participation opportunities typically embody, but are not restricted to, those of the intramural program. Additional offerings include roller skating, modern, square and/or social dancing, miniature golf, martial arts, small games (e.g. air hockey, skittles, Monopoly, etc.), shuffleboard, riflery, weight training, gymnastics, trampolining, and general exercise with and without special equipment.[19]

He points out that since Purdue University opened a $2.5 million center in 1957 to house coeducational recreational sports, hundreds of institutions of higher education have constructed multi-million dollar facilities designed solely or primarily for recreational sports participation. Many house billiard rooms, bowling alleys, saunas, Jacuzzis and similar special facilities. So extensive is the range of participation that a number of colleges and universities organize and schedule their activities—particularly intramural sports—through a campus computer system. Holley points out that at Brigham Young University, for example, where intramurals may include several hundred teams in a single sport, computers are used not only to schedule league play but to evaluate programs, prepare statistical reports and provide a detailed analysis of participation.[20]

Revenue From Game Rooms. Because of students' enthusiasm for pinball and electronic games, many colleges and universities today operate student game rooms or amusement areas that provide "vending" games. Football tables, air-hockey tables, pinball machines and various other types of electronic games provide the opportunity for casual play by students, faculty and staff—plus, on occasion, special events or tournaments. Such facilities can help to supplement recreation and student life budgets. Gage comments that at the University of Houston,

> . . . since "vending" has been initiated . . . we have had a steady increase in revenue and a tremendous increase in the number of people participating in the recreation area who may not have participated before.[21]

---

[19]George W. Haniford: "Recreational Sports: A Component of the Campus Leisure System." *Journal of Physical Education and Recreation (Leisure Today)*, April 1980, p. 48.

[20]Bruce Holley: "Computer Coordination for Campus Intramurals." *Journal of Physical Education and Recreation (Leisure Today)*, April 1980, p. 50.

[21]R. S. Gage: "Amusement Games Are In—Do I Buy or Lease?" Association of College Unions–International, *Proceedings, 57th Annual Conference*, San Diego, California, March 1977, pp. 99–100.

Outdoor Recreation. Another growing area of participation on many campuses is outdoor recreation, which includes a wide range of activities carried on in the natural setting, such as hiking, backpacking and river-running. These often are sponsored by campus outdoor clubs, sometimes affiliated with college outdoor federations, and may include clinics, workshops and short- and long-term outings as part of their programs. As a single example, in 1967 a handful of students at the University of Oregon began an activity-oriented outdoor recreation program. By the early 1970's it had grown to have nearly 5,000 participants, making more than 300 outdoor trips a year and sponsoring numerous other environmental, instructional and educational projects.[22]

An outstanding illustration of successful campus recreation programs today is provided by San Diego State University in California, where the Associated Students Organization sponsors a remarkable range of films, concerts, recreational and athletic programs, legal services and other activities. This multi-million dollar corporation, funded by annual student fees, operates the Aztec Center, the college's student union building. In addition, it runs a highly successful travel service, intramurals and sports clubs, special events, leisure classes, lectures, movies, concerts, an open-air theater, a large aquatics center, a campus radio station, a child-care center, a black students council, a general store, a campus information booth and many other services and activities. Within this spectrum, the bulk of the leisure activities on the San Diego campus are operated directly by the Recreation Activities Board, a unit within the overall Associated Students Organization.[23]

Professional Staff Responsibilities

Particularly when the campus union or student life program provides counseling and guidance services, it has traditionally been expected that members of the university's professional staff will have earned degrees in the field of student personnel work. However, with the trend toward developing more varied programs of student activities and the growing importance of recreation as a campus service, increasing numbers of persons with training in recreation leadership and supervision are entering this field.

Cashel and Krause write that professional staff members originally were responsible for organizing and carrying out campus recreation programs themselves. However, as the concept of student development emerged in the late 1960's, staff members moved away from direct leadership responsibilities and began to see their role as one of guiding and training students:

> This evolved into the concept of "programming or student union boards," where students were selected to be the program planners with

---

[22]B. V. Mason: "College Outdoor Programs." Association of College Unions–International, *Proceedings, 54th Annual Conference*, Toronto, Canada, March 1974, pp. 53–58.
[23]See *Break Away*, Recreational Guide to San Diego State University, San Diego, California, Spring 1979.

professional staff's role being that of training students in program design and production. The training of student leaders through their involvement in student government, program boards, and other campus organizations became the educational function of the college union staff.[24]

It is necessary to be certain that students plan, supervise, schedule, publicize and evaluate all activities in a manner that is efficient, fiscally sound and in accordance with university policy. To make this a reality, Cashel and Krause suggest, college union or student activity staff members must play varied roles as educators, researchers and consultants. The specialized nature of the programs being operated often requires that staff members have unique experience. Kennedy comments that in the supervision of a program emphasizing the performing and visual arts, for example, he would prefer to employ an individual with a strong background in the arts, rather than a generalist in leisure studies. He also points out that the successful college union or activities program will combine staff members who have different degrees and capabilities:

> Each union has its own particular mix of staffing with particular qualifications which require attention when hiring new staff. A staff of four professionals, each having a degree in Leisure Activities or Recreation, would not be appropriate if there were strong emphasis needed in union management, food sales, student government advising, fine arts programming, concert production, etc. However, the backgrounds of those people would weigh more heavily than a degree when it comes to determining "hireability."[25]

In general, Kennedy suggests, the trend in college union staff hiring is toward the acceptance of greater numbers of recreation-trained personnel, particularly because of their philosophy of active leadership and their organizational skills, as opposed to the somewhat passive or unstructured approach typical of many counseling or guidance-oriented professionals. Typically, as recreation specialists enter the college union field, they become affiliated with the professional societies, such as the Association of College Unions–International and the National Intramural and Recreational Sports Association, that are active in higher education programs.

LEADERSHIP IN SENIOR CENTERS

This chapter concludes with an examination of the types of programs provided for older persons in senior centers and of the leadership required in these programs. Today, about 25 million citizens of the United States are over 65, and this number will continue to grow throughout the remainder of the century. Although older citizens in some societies are highly respected and

---

[24]Christine Cashel and Lynne Krause: "College Union Staff: Leisure Educators, Researchers, Consultants." *Journal of Physical Education and Recreation (Leisure Today)*, April 1980, p. 53.
[25]John Dale Kennedy, University of North Dakota. Letter to Gay Carpenter, July 1979.

well cared for, this is not generally true in the Western world, which tends to be youth-oriented and to denigrate the aging person.

Social isolation becomes a particularly important problem for the elderly. Often, they are seriously disadvantaged economically, living on only a fraction of the income of younger persons. In recent studies, the United States Bureau of Labor Statistics found that 36 percent of all retired couples could not afford the recommended annual budget for even the lowest standard of living, while 56 percent could not afford the intermediate budget. Thus, it becomes difficult for the elderly to travel or to make use of commercial recreation opportunities. The problem of isolation is made more acute by the fact that so many older persons live alone, having been widowed or divorced and having lost many of their earlier friends and associations.

Health problems tend to be increasingly severe as one grows older. Limited mobility, poverty and fear of venturing out keep many elderly persons from securing the health services they need. Similar factors make it difficult for them to shop and cook properly, with the result that nutrition becomes a serious problem for older persons. Mental illness becomes an increasing hazard, and the availability and adequacy of psychiatric care for older persons are seriously limited.

However, there is also considerable evidence that aging need not be a process of inevitable deterioration, and that many of our preconceived notions about its limitations are false. Older persons are becoming increasingly active in sports and exercise programs. Throughout the country, they are taking to jogging paths, gymnasiums and health clubs in record numbers:

> An 86-year-old woman enters and completes a 26-mile marathon. A stroke victim, also a woman in her 80's, begins walking for exercise. Soon she is running and eventually settles on a comfortable three-mile jog every day. A 70-year-old man—who looks 20 years younger—bicycles 50 miles a day on weekends.[26]

"People are beginning to realize that they are going to get old. They don't want to find themselves in the same position that many older people find themselves in today," says Dr. Raymond Harris, a leading geriatric cardiologist. One important way for older people to continue to remain active and find interesting physical, social and creative outlets for their abundant leisure time is by attending senior centers.

Role of Senior Centers

For the past two or three decades, there has been an increasing trend toward the development of community-based Senior Centers or Golden Age Clubs that provide older persons with recreational opportunities and other badly needed social programs. Project FIND (Friendless, Isolated, Needy and Disabled), sponsored by the National Council on the Aging, sought to locate the

---

[26]Michael Clark: "Good Health for Folks Over 50." *Parade*, January 28, 1979, p. 7.

elderly poor and to learn the source and amount of their incomes; their problems related to health, housing and isolation; and similar needs. It was found that the most serious difficulties lay in the need of the elderly for social contacts and recreation. The National Council on the Aging, after evaluating data gathered by FIND, recommended the multi-purpose center as a way of meeting the social and service needs of the elderly and urged that such centers be established in all communities, along with national programs of volunteer "friendly" visiting and telephone reassurance for homebound older persons.

A number of organizations, such as the National Council on the Aging, the National Council of Senior Citizens, and the 1971 White House Conference on Aging, have developed guidelines for the establishment of Senior Centers. In 1971, the State of Michigan recommended to the White House Conference on Aging

> . . . that consideration must be given to multi-purpose senior centers in full recognition that such centers' activities are not only recreational, but an essential element in the maintenance of good mental and physical health for the older person.

The trend has been toward the development of multi-service centers that offer at least three of these five basic services: (a) recreation, (b) counseling, (c) nutrition, (d) health programs and (e) adult education programs. In defining such centers, the distinction has been made that Golden Age Centers generally hold meetings only once or twice a week, have programs that are primarily social or recreational and have volunteer or nonprofessional leaders. In contrast, Senior Centers generally hold meetings each day, provide a variety of recreational and other social services and operate under professional leadership.

Multi-purpose Senior Centers today are regarded as places where all elderly persons, particularly the economically disadvantaged, can find social contacts and the opportunity for self-expression and mental stimulation. Here, they may receive needed personal services, and they are offered the opportunity to play significant social roles and, generally, to find meaningful life enrichment.

Among the goals of Senior Centers are the following:

1. Providing older persons with the opportunity for meaningful and satisfying group and individual relationships.
2. Helping them learn new skills for enrichment and self-expression in the arts, music, drama, nature, language, current events, dance, crafts, games and similar activities.
3. Offering opportunities for them to be useful and provide service to others through volunteer action programs, thus reassuming a valued role in society and gaining a strengthened self-concept.
4. Assisting them in maintaining good physical health through programs of exercise, nutrition and medical and dental care.
5. Promoting mental health through the use and development of creative abilities, exposure to a healthy social environment that

counteracts social isolation, and provision of counseling services, when needed.

6. Helping the individual to keep informed about changes in the community and the world and to become active in programs and organizations serving older persons.
7. Giving older persons the opportunity to assume leadership roles, and strengthening their personal effectiveness in working with others.
8. Offering guidance and, when necessary, formal assistance in a wide range of personal or legal service areas, such as housing, Social Security or similar problems.

Typical Recreation Programs

The recreation activities found most commonly in today's Senior Centers are the following:

1. Arts and crafts, including oil and watercolor painting, sketching, woodworking, ceramics, needlepoint, sculpture, rug making, basketry, quilt making and jewelry making.
2. Games, mixers and social activities, including card playing, Bingo, parties, dances, chess, checkers and similar activities.
3. Physical activities, such as dancing, exercise groups, lawn bowling, shuffleboard, horseshoes or billiards.
4. Music, including community singing, small instrumental groups, choruses, music listening or entertainment by performing groups.
5. Literary activities, such as having a center newspaper, book review or current events discussion, writing classes, debates or visiting speakers.
6. Hobby and club groups related to interests such as sewing, knitting, photography, history, languages, stamp collecting or armchair travel.
7. Trips and outings to parks, scenic locations, major amusement complexes and beaches, or to concerts, plays, political rallies or conventions of older persons, boat trips, picnics and similar excursions.

Usually, such programs are scheduled so that the most popular activities are offered daily at a regular hour, while other activities are provided once or twice a week. Programs often reflect the particular ethnic or religious make-up of the group; for example, Senior Centers in some locations offer dramatic clubs, language groups and other activities related to particular nationality backgrounds. In some cases, individuals may be exposed to an activity or may attend classes in which they develop a strong interest, and may then be encouraged to attend the adult extension program of nearby colleges.

An individual center's program may be tied to events promoted for senior citizens throughout the city. For example, the Senior Citizen Section of the Department of Recreation and Parks of the City of Los Angeles offers many special events citywide or in individual districts. These promote the work of neighborhood centers and provide a second level of participation for active center members. In a recent year, the following events were scheduled for the month of June:

Senior Citizen Master Calendar for June

June 7—10	Citywide Art Finals, City Hall Rotunda
June 8	West Area Federation Meeting, Baldwin Hills Recreation Center
June 9	Citywide Federation Meeting, Hoover Recreation Center
June 15–17	Annual Shuffleboard Tournament, Sportsmen's Park
June 19	Citywide Talent Show Finals, Hollywood High School Auditorium
June 19	Senior Citizens Evening at the Hollywood Palladium, with Lawrence Welk and his TV Musical Family
June 21	Valley Area Federation Meeting, Van Nuys–Sherman Oaks
June 26	Disney on Parade
June 27	Mayor's Senior Citizen Day at the Greek Theatre
June 29	Senior Citizen Day at Hollywood Park

Health Services in Senior Centers

These may include classes, lectures and workshops or special clinics on all aspects of health, disease prevention, diagnosis and care. Specific health maintenance services may include any or all of the following: medical examinations, blood tests, X-rays and special eye, ear or dental clinics. Some multi-service centers have their own medical or dental facilities, provided by public or voluntary agencies that may open up a service center, for example, within a housing complex attached to the social or recreational center. In other cases, a visiting team of doctors or nurses may come to the center on a weekly or monthly basis. Still other centers may schedule organized trips to a nearby glaucoma inspection center or to other health facilities.

Multi-service centers may also provide home care or home health aides as part of their health service program. They may also provide assistance in Social Security, welfare, food stamps, housing, legal aid, Medicare and similar concerns. Nutrition programs may include cafeteria service at the center (for example, the Associated YMHA–YWHA's of Greater New York received a grant of more than $800,000 from the City of New York to develop seven Senior Citizen Centers to provide one hot meal a day to the needy, as well as for other social welfare and recreation programs). The programs may also deliver meals from the center to homebound elderly persons, provide surplus foods, arrange for supermarkets to accept food stamps, and set up food purchasing cooperatives.

Community Service Programs

There are many ways in which older persons accept important social responsibilities in a multi-service center. In addition to assuming leadership roles in the center itself, they may act as delegates to other citywide or statewide associations for the elderly or to senior center federations. They may engage in service projects such as making things for hospital patients, putting together Christmas packages for the homebound or institutionalized in cooperation with service clubs, telephoning voters on election days, raising funds for worthy causes, doing clerical work for social agencies or assisting in children's day-care programs.

In some cases, specially funded programs have been established through which older persons are paid to work with emotionally disturbed or mentally retarded children. The important element is that they are able to use their lives in productive ways—whether or not they are paid—and thus regain a sense of value and importance to society.

Organization of Senior Centers

Senior Centers operate under a variety of auspices. As they have grown in size and scope, and have received funding from government and community fund drives, they have tended to be sponsored by organizations that are capable of providing thorough and efficient administration. Many have assumed formal structures based on the model proposed by the National Council on the Aging (Table 8–2).

Many such centers are separate entities that operate under funds granted annually by the city or sponsored by voluntary agencies. In other cases, they are part of recreation and park departments with personnel hired through the Civil Service structure. They may use existing community centers in which special rooms are set aside for senior programs during the day, or they may operate in facilities that have been specially built for exclusive use by elderly persons. In many cases, these facilities are attached to low-income housing projects.

In some metropolitan areas, where many smaller communities or school districts are not equipped to take responsibility in this area, a larger township or county department of social services will take responsibility for operating a network of Senior Centers. In the town of Hempstead, New York, for example, the Department of Services for the Aging sponsors 11 large Senior Centers, scattered throughout the geographic area, each of which provides a full range of hobbies, social and cultural programs and nutrition services.

TABLE 8-2. ORGANIZATION CHART FOR MULTI-PURPOSE SENIOR CENTER, RECOMMENDED BY NATIONAL COUNCIL ON THE AGING

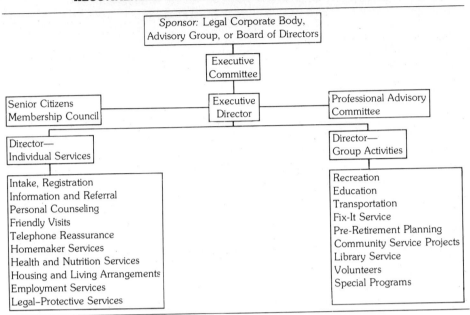

Intergenerational Programs. Senior Centers and program activities usually are kept sharply separated from other age groups being served—a form of segregation that many older people themselves seem to want. However, in a few cases, deliberate efforts have been made to break down this practice. In one unique example, the recreation director of Downington, Pennsylvania, established an innovative summer recreation program in which members of the city's Senior Center and Golden Age Club shared a short-term activity program with a large group of junior-high-school students. The Downington Intergenerational Group (DIG) participated in varied activities, including games, fishing, contests, crafts, slide shows, a picnic and a square dance, with members ranging in age from 10 to 81.[27]

Multi-Purpose Senior Centers. In multi-purpose Senior Centers, the following rooms are generally provided: a combination auditorium–social hall–dining hall, multi–purpose meeting rooms, craft shops, health maintenance offices, library, lounge, kitchen and administrative offices. Centers should be located with good accessibility to main roads or public transportation, and should be designed with ramps and other architectural features that make it possible for the physically disabled who need wheelchairs or who have other limitations to use them conveniently.

---

[27]Pamela F. Emory: "All Ages Dig 'Dig.' " *Perspective on Aging,* January/February 1979, pp. 22–23.

Some communities have constructed major facilities in the area of greatest population density of senior citizens, and then have established satellite programs in other neighborhoods. One such example is Vintage, Inc., a large multi-purpose facility in Pittsburgh, Pennsylvania. This outstanding center, sponsored with a combination of funding from United Way, church support and county grants, provides the following services: (a) recreation, in the form of parties, hobbies, trips, clubs and other social programs; (b) information and referral services; (c) transportation services, through which Vintage coordinates travel arrangements for older persons to needed services; (d) small businesses, in which the elderly can be employed to earn additional income; (e) "in-home services," such as meal delivery, friendly caller and visitation services, home health aides and housekeeping assistance; (f) health programs, including screening examinations and seminars, with physician back-up; (g) retirement, legal, housing and other counseling services; and (h) a free nutritional program.[21]

As the number of retired persons increases, we may rid ourselves of the last vestiges of the Protestant work ethic, which values only paid work and tends to make us feel guilt-ridden about leisure and play. In such a liberated society, older persons may be able to use their time more easily in a wide range of enjoyable ways that are not economically productive but that bring pleasure and a sense of self-worth.

The task of leadership in centers for the aging requires certain unique talents and abilities. The Milwaukee, Wisconsin, Department of Municipal Recreation and Adult Education operates an extensive network of Golden Age Centers. It describes the role of leaders in such centers in the following terms:

> The backbone of the entire program is leadership. Leaders must bring to their assignments sympathy, patience, humility, a willingness and capacity to understand the problems of the older person, and the ability to lead and guide.
>
> The same basic group-work philosophy and principles apply to the old as well as to the young. It is necessary that the leader develop a sensitivity to the needs, feelings, and desires of the individuals in her group and discover opportunities for their recognition and fulfillment. It is important that a leader know when and how and to what extent to gradually transfer this to the club officers and committees. Her professional knowledge and competence is always important in recognizing the sort of activities that will meet the interest span of members, that will obtain the highest degree of participation, that will help develop wholesome attitudes, that will fit into the time schedule and facilities available, and that will meet the physical limitations of the members.[28]

Beyond this, it is essential that center directors and leaders bring a strong degree of warmth and enthusiasm to their work, providing older persons with acceptance and support while building upon their strengths and capabilities.

---

[28]*Annual Brochure.* Pittsburgh, Pennsylvania, Vintage, Inc., 1980.

Leaders must be able to work effectively with representatives of different organizations and disciplines in a unified team effort. In addition to recruiting and sustaining membership, leaders must also be able to involve volunteers successfully and to obtain assistance in the form of financial contributions, gifts or other helpful services from many different sources. In a number of colleges and universities, special graduate programs in gerontology have been established through the funding of the Administration on Aging, to equip professionals to work with older persons. In many cases, such curricula have been attached to departments of recreation and park administration.

It seems clear that the specialized field of working with the aging will continue to be a more and more important aspect of recreation leadership, and will require an increasingly high level of expertise in the future.

CONCLUSION

This chapter has provided descriptions of a number of special types of agencies, in terms of either sponsorship or those served, that provide a considerable amount of leisure service today. Chapter Nine adds to this picture by describing programs and leadership techniques designed to assist individuals who have special forms of disability, such as psychiatric patients, the mentally retarded or dependent older persons.

SUGGESTED EXAMINATION QUESTIONS OR TOPICS FOR STUDENT REPORTS

1. Compare the traditional approach to working with youth to some of the newer, more innovative methods described in this chapter.
2. Both armed forces recreation and industrial recreation make certain demands upon professional leadership personnel that are different from those found in other types of settings. What are the key requirements, in terms of personal qualities and skills, of leaders in these two fields?
3. The needs of aging persons have become increasingly important in our society. Describe these in detail and then show how they are met by recreation personnel in senior centers.

SUGGESTED ACTION ASSIGNMENTS OR GROUP PROCESS ACTIVITIES

1. Select a commercial recreation agency that provides the opportunity for participation, such as a racquetball center, resort or similar facility. Examine its program and outline the staff's responsibilities and functions in detail.

2. Compare the ongoing recreation program on your campus (including recreational and intramural sports, campus union program and similar activities) with the program at a nearby college or university. Identify the strengths and weaknesses of each institution, and make recommendations for improving the operation on your own campus.
3. If you were to decide to prepare yourself for work in a non-public recreation agency, how would you go about developing your own competence and attractiveness to a potential future employer?

Leadership in Special Settings: Part Two

Chapter Nine

The previous chapter described varied recreation programs provided in special settings, such as industries, the armed forces, or commercial and private agencies, for the population at large. It also presented program and leadership guidelines for youth and the aging in community settings. This chapter deals with somewhat more special needs, within what has come to be known as therapeutic recreation service.

This consists of prescribed and voluntary activities that are designed to promote the constructive use of leisure time, physical well-being and resocialization for population groups that have special disabilities limiting their recreational involvement. Harsanyi points out that therapeutic recreation services are usually found in institutions such as

> . . . psychiatric hospitals, physical rehabilitation hospitals, chronic disease hospitals, convalescent and old age homes, schools for the mentally retarded and emotionally disturbed, special camps, group homes, and halfway houses. . . . Therapeutic recreation is also provided in the community, sponsored by private agencies, benevolent associations, and cities and towns. . .[1]

John A. Nesbitt, former president of the National Therapeutic Recreation Society and Project Director of the National Institute on Community Recreation for the Handicapped, points out that major breakthroughs are being made in this field:

> At the local level, recreation programs for handicapped are starting and expanding every year. Wheelchair athletes number 15,000. There are

---

[1]Suzanne Harsanyi: "Practice and Promise of Therapeutic Recreation." *Journal of Physical Education and Recreation (Leisure Today),* April 1979, pp. 19–23.

as many as 750,000 participants, parents and volunteers involved in the Special Olympics each year. The range of recreational activities in which handicapped are making breakthroughs to participation is inspiring and limitless. Recreation activities that are being pursued include skiing for amputees and blind, flying and horseback riding for paraplegics, skydiving for epileptics, and on and on goes the list of breakthroughs for handicapped in recreation.[2]

A number of important social factors and governmental programs have contributed to the awareness of disabled persons' needs for wholesome leisure opportunities. The Education for All Handicapped Children Act (P.L. 94-142) included recreation as a required service for the handicapped, and numerous state and local educational or social service organizations are working toward the goal of "mainstreaming" the handicapped in programs serving the general population. The Federal Administration on Aging, Rehabilitation Services Administration, National Endowment for the Arts, Comprehensive Employment Training Administration (CETA), Bureau of Education for the Handicapped and other offices have helped to support special services and research in this field.

Yet, by 1979, Nesbitt estimated that not more than 10 percent of disabled persons in the United States were involved in special recreation programs.[3] It seems probable that similar figures would apply to Canada as well, where Peter Witt and others have shown a need for improved leisure services for the disabled. One of the important factors that will assist agencies of all types in working with special populations is better leadership training. Those who specialize in therapeutic recreation, and community recreators as well, must become familiar with the needs of special populations and with general guidelines for serving them in both community and institutional situations. This chapter therefore examines the role of recreation leaders and therapists in several settings, such as outreach programs for problem youth in the community, special camping programs, psychiatric hospitals and nursing homes.

COMMUNITY OUTREACH PROGRAMS FOR PROBLEM YOUTH

In recent years, a serious problem has arisen in many community recreation departments that have been attempting to serve young people in disadvantaged, inner-city neighborhoods. Large numbers of teenagers in crowded, urban slums are school dropouts and, even at an early age, have been in trouble with the police because of delinquent behavior. Often they are alienated from any constructive contact with adults or community agencies and

---

[2]John A. Nesbitt: *New Concepts and New Processes in Special Recreation.* Iowa City, Iowa, University of Iowa, Report of Bureau of Education for the Handicapped Project, 1978, p. v.
[3]John A. Nesbitt: "The 1980's: Recreation a Reality for All." *Education Unlimited,* Boothwyn, Pennsylvania, Educational Resources Center, June 1979, p. 1.

are active members of anti-social gangs. It has been extremely difficult for traditional recreation programs or youth organizations to involve such young people.

In the late 1970's, this problem has become increasingly serious. Contrary to the popular viewpoint that teenage gangs in the United States periodically appear and disappear, Miller points out, gangs in our large cities have never declined. In a recent survey of gang activity throughout the country, he found that they have become increasingly violent and disruptive, more widespread and more dangerous to ordinary citizens. Operating chiefly in low-income urban areas,

> . . . youth gangs today typically consist of small, loosely organized groups of about a dozen teen-age males. Instead of confining their claims of control to local streets and parks, many gangs have taken over neighborhood schools and recreational facilities. . . .
>
> When we asked local officials to predict the future of teen-age gang crime and violence in the next few years, their outlook was grim. Nine out of 10 did not feel that gang problems would lessen during the next several years. About half predicted things would get worse.[4]

Obviously, the need for recreation programs is only a small part of the overall approach to work with urban youth gangs. These gangs have increasingly become involved in making money through protection rackets, shakedowns, mugging, robbery and guerrilla raids or gang attacks. However, it seems clear that at least part of the reason for juvenile delinquency lies in the boredom and lack of leisure opportunity for unemployed or school dropout urban youth.

Since the 1950's, cities such as New York, Philadelphia, Washington, Richmond and Los Angeles, plagued by increasing juvenile delinquency and warring gangs, have employed special workers to serve unaffiliated "problem" youths. A number of different titles have been applied to such workers, including "roving leaders," "outreach workers" and "street gang" or "street club" workers. Bannon describes such leaders in the following terms:

> A roving leader is an outreach worker assigned to a specific community to stimulate hard-to-reach youth to participate in wholesome recreation programs. A basic purpose of this outreach service is to help disadvantaged youth use their free time constructively and, at the same time, assist them in effectively using community resources in education, health, employment and related social service.[5]

The task of outreach workers encompasses far more than traditional recreation leadership. They have the mission of making contact with anti-social gangs, gaining their confidence and attempting to re-orient their values and behavior in more constructive directions. The Washington, D.C., Recreation Department, which has had such a program since 1956, sees its general func-

---

[4]Walter Miller: "The Rumble This Time." *Psychology Today*, May 1977, p. 52.
[5]Joseph J. Bannon: "The Roving Leaders: A New Look." *Parks and Recreation*, February 1972, p. 23

tion as preventing, neutralizing and controlling the hostile behavior of youth groups and individuals. The specific goals of outreach workers include the following:

1. To help adolescents make use of community resources that are available to them.
2 To encourage dropouts to return to school.
3. To direct youth behavior into more constructive social outlets, and to promote more productive and positive channels of communication between youth and the adult community.
4. To reduce the severity and frequency of offenses such as vandalism, theft and gang violence.
5. To intervene on behalf of youth with schools, police and the courts, and to assist youth in their relationships with all community authorities.
6. To help youth understand the consequences of their anti-social behavior, and to promote in youth a desire to become part of the larger society.
7. To identify conflict-producing elements in the community, and to work constructively with these.
8. To create opportunities for youth to assume more significant roles in society.

General Leadership Approaches

Outreach workers or roving leaders usually follow a somewhat similar plan of operation. Initially, the leader establishes informal contact with groups or individual youths in their neighborhoods, on the streets or in informal hangouts. The leader develops rapport with them, helps them in small ways and gradually attempts to gain acceptance as a friendly adult. Once a relationship has been established, the leader meets periodically with group members and attempts to lead them into constructive activities. Recognizing that they will distrust and resist any attempt at domination, the leader must employ a considerable amount of tact and discretion, and must adjust to the needs of the group, meeting them in places and at times convenient to them. The Richmond, Virginia, Department of Parks and Recreation describes the leader's functions as follows:

> Upon stimulating general interest among groups and individuals, the Roving Leader channels their interests and desires into constructive activities by organizing athletic events, securing employment for them, forming clubs and special interest groups, assisting them in developing hobbies, gaining admittance for them to movies, concerts, and to special events and activities sponsored by the Department and introducing them to recreation units where they may participate in organized athletics, social activities, arts and crafts, etc. He maintains continued close relationship and follow-up to assure their modification of attitudes and social behavior.

The Roving Leader maintains close relationships and has numerous contacts with such individuals, groups and agencies as the Juvenile Aid Division, Juvenile Court, Public Schools, Youth Councils and youth-serving agencies, civic organizations, churches, Parent-Teacher Associations, parents, public and private recreation centers, and the United States Employment Service.

The roving leader may also attempt to help individuals with personal problems or disability by referring them to group-work or family case-work agencies, to psychiatric, health and dental clinics, to public employment services, or to religious and educational institutions, and then by continuing to assist them in appropriate ways. In terms of specific recreation-related activities, outreach workers may involve youth groups in a wide range of sports, cultural and social programs. Typically, the Washington, D.C., Recreation Department's roving leaders involve disadvantaged, inner-city youth in summer activities such as trips and outings, classes, community service projects and sports events.

In most cases outreach workers are not attached to a particular facility, but are simply assigned to a neighborhood and are given responsibility for a designated number of groups. In Washington, for example, the workload of a roving leader varies from two to four groups, depending on the needs of the community and the severity of the problem. A worker may be assigned only two groups if they are extremely hostile and aggressive, but may have three or four if they pose less serious problems.

The Department of Recreation and Parks in Los Angeles, California, has a different approach. This department has a Special Problems Unit that is assigned the task of working with anti-social and disruptive youth in and around recreation centers. Customarily, Youth Counselors, as they are titled in Los Angeles, are assigned to two or more recreation facilities, which may include centers, swimming pools or other areas.

Qualifications of Outreach Workers

Formal qualifications for outreach workers and roving leaders vary from city to city. In some departments they are required to have college degrees; in others, they may be on a "career ladder" that permits them to work in this position while studying for a college degree. Specialized training in recreation is not usually required; in fact, the background and personal qualities of street workers are usually considered to be more important than formal credentials. Theoretical knowledge of group dynamics, juvenile delinquency or social work is not as important as knowledge of the slum milieu, personal experience and character traits that are needed to work with alienated and hostile youth. The Los Angeles Special Problems Unit has developed the following statement of the desired qualities and skills of its youth workers:

1. First of all, a Youth Counselor must have commitment. He must be committed to what he's doing and know above all else that what he's doing is most important for the youth.

2. A Youth Counselor has to have persistence. He needs the drive to go from hangout to hangout and from street corner to street corner—constantly talking to youth.
3. A Youth Counselor has to be tough enough to be forceful both with others and with himself, yet at the same time, he must be sensitive to the needs of those around him.
4. A Youth Counselor has to develop and encourage youth leaders in his group. This requires that he be tough on his ego and let others receive the recognition, and also be prepared for the day he must back out. He is not building his own organization, but an organization of the youth.
5. A Youth Counselor must build trust. He must trust the youth with whom he works and they must be able to trust him.
6. A Youth Counselor has to listen so he will know what's going on in his area at all times.
7. A Youth Counselor must not be a phony. He must be himself and be natural. He can have a "bag of tricks," but must be comfortable with them.
8. A Youth Counselor must learn never to make promises that he can't keep, or threats he can't back up.
9. A Youth Counselor must know his area inside and out. He has to do a lot of research to find out about his area, but must never let this be an excuse for not doing his work. He must train others by involving them in this process.
10. A Youth Counselor must get youth to work for him. He must be able to involve youth on a personal level.
11. A Youth Counselor must recognize self-interest as one of the important motivations for human action and must, therefore, give a service which is needed and of value.

Careful training and constant supervision are essential for outreach workers. They must be aware of clearly defined departmental policies governing difficult areas such as (a) how to handle threats from gang members; (b) how to deal with knowledge of a gang's past or present criminal activities; (c) what to do with respect to drug activities, possession of firearms, threatened gang "rumbles" and other critical situations; and (d) relations with the police and other community agencies. Whenever possible, the ultimate goal of roving leader programs is not only to use recreation as a positive tool for working constructively with problem youth but also to draw gang members and individuals into organized community programs.

Not all agencies that work with delinquent or pre-delinquent youth make use of the outreach worker approach. In some cases, special recreation projects are devised that have a unique appeal for young people and that may have remarkable benefits in helping to move them in desirable social directions.

YMCA Minibike Project. One unusual delinquency project, the National Youth Project Using Minibikes (NYPUM), was sponsored by the National Board of the Young Men's Christian Association. It made use of outreach methods to work with small groups of young people of junior high school age who had resisted other community recreation services. The "minibike" project involved forming groups of about fifteen 11- to 15-year-old boys who had been referred by schools or youth authorities for serious behavior problems. As a first step, they were taught how to ride minibikes and how to maintain them properly. An attempt was then made to channel the boys into other types of constructive activities.

The first successful pilot program using minibikes was sponsored by the Los Angeles YMCA. With the assistance of the American Honda Motor Company, which donated 10,000 minibikes to the National Board of the YMCA, a national project was initiated throughout the United States. Project funding was supplemented by a grant from the Law Enforcement Assistance Administration of the United States Department of Justice to begin new NYPUM's and to carry out scientific evaluation of the entire program.

Judges, probation officers and other community workers have concluded that NYPUM has been an effective way of reaching and influencing delinquency-prone youth. There is an extremely low recidivism rate among first and second offenders who have been involved in the program. Additionally, the evaluation carried out by Western Center Consultants in Los Angeles showed positive gains in behavior modification, community cooperation and safety training.

California Youth Gang Employment Project. In another innovative delinquency prevention project, the Boys' Club of El Monte, California, developed a program of finding employment for youth gang members, persuading businesses to give them a chance and providing continued guidance to make the experiment work. The National Boys' Club organization itself has sponsored a World of Work Project, funded by the U. S. Department of Labor.[6]

Both these projects show how recreational and social agencies may develop carefully designed programs to meet the needs of delinquent and socially alienated youth. It is important to recognize that it is not the individual activity that is the major factor in creating behavioral change. Instead, it is the quality of leadership, the bond built between the leader and the participants, the other services that are offered and the fact that ultimately the socially constructive and desirable program becomes more rewarding and attractive to the youngster than his former anti-social associations and behavior.

THERAPEUTIC CAMPING PROGRAMS

Another major area of specialized service in the field of recreation involves organized camping programs that serve the mentally, physically or psychologically impaired. Such programs have developed rapidly in recent years. They include several different types of camps; among these are resident camps, trip camps and day camps.

---

[6]"In California, Gang Members Punch Time Clocks." *Keynote* (Boys' Clubs of America), February 1977, pp. 4–5, n.a.

Resident Camps. More than 250 resident camps are listed in the *Easter Seal Directory of Resident Camps for Persons With Special Health Needs.* Residents stay at such camps for periods ranging usually from one to two weeks.

Day Camps. Although the precise number of such camps is not known, there are many to which campers come each day to participate in varied activities and return home each night.

Trip Camps. Trip camps do not use a central facility; instead, they set up temporary facilities to permit camping in natural surroundings.

According to a recent national survey of camping programs and services for the handicapped, sponsors of such camps fall into the following categories: (a) youth agency camps; (b) private independent camps; (c) church camps or those with religious affiliations; and (d) specialized camps. In those camps not specially designed for the handicapped, approximately three to ten percent of the campers have been identified as having some significant disability. Specialized camps tend to serve primarily those with physical disabilities, although many are designed for the mentally retarded as well.[7]

The rationale for providing therapeutic camping programs is that all handicapped individuals have the right to experience positive recreation and leisure pursuits, to grow in terms of independence and self-reliance, and to achieve satisfying peer relationships. A recent national conference identified the following specific needs of handicapped persons for camping experiences. These include the following:

> To experience the growth and development provided by camping which is normally denied the handicapped.
> To experience independence from the family, and build self-confidence.
> To experience successful activity, including satisfying and beneficial physical activity.
> To recognize his/her relationship to the natural world.
> To gain functional interdependence with others, and to experience relationships which extend beyond the camping opportunity.
> To learn carry-over recreation and leisure skills, and enrich one's lifestyle.[8]

A vivid example of how even the most severely physically disabled children and youth can adapt to the summer camp environment may be found in an unusual report that appeared in *Psychology Today,* "The Acorn People: What I Learned at Summer Camp."[9] Although it is true that only a small proportion of the nation's estimated 7 million handicapped children are today involved in therapeutic camping programs, there is growing pressure to ex-

[7]John A. Nesbitt, Curtis C. Hansen, Barbara J. Bates and Larry L. Neal: *Training Needs and Strategies in Camping for the Handicapped.* San Jose, California, Therapeutic Recreation Service for Handicapped Children Project. Center of Leisure Studies, University of Oregon, 1972, pp. 27–28.
[8]*Ibid.,* pp. 12–13.
[9]Ron Jones: "The Acorn People: What I Learned at Summer Camp." *Psychology Today,* June 1972, pp. 70–78.

pand such opportunities. A number of excellent therapeutic camps have been developed in the United States and Canada, two of which are described here.

Camp Spindrift, San Francisco

This outstanding day camp is sponsored by the Recreation Center for the Handicapped, a pioneering program founded in San Francisco in 1952 to provide year-round social, cultural and educational opportunities for children and youths with physical and mental disabilities.[10] Camp Spindrift is a carefully supervised program designed to provide a close-to-home camping experience for boys and girls who would not otherwise have camping opportunities. A recent camp report describes its program in the following terms:

> Activities for the Day Camp are selected, adapted, modified, or invented, to meet the needs of mentally retarded and handicapped children and to help them to grow and develop as individuals. Each child will have the opportunity to cook, and to eat, out-of-doors; to go on collection hikes, nature observation walks, exploring hunts; to become acquainted with trees, plants, animals, birds, and to enjoy campfires. They may go on field trips to the zoo, to a farm, to museums, parks and other areas which will expand their horizons and offer new living experiences. They will listen to stories and music, sing, dance, play games, participate in simple pantomime or drama activities, and enjoy worthwhile craft projects designed to be within the area of individual capabilities.
>
> The schedule is flexible and the program is carried out in an atmosphere of relaxed enjoyment . . .

Essentially, the camp's policies and operational procedures are not very different from those of a normal day camp, except that extreme care is taken to select mature and responsible staff members, with a ratio of at least one adult counselor to every four campers. Counselors are carefully trained and supervised throughout the camping period, and a strong effort is made to have a sufficient number of staff members returning from year to year to give stability, cohesion and continuity to the program. The program offers a wide variety of activities, as indicated earlier, with opportunity for individual participation, small group activities and events involving the entire camp. The tempo is leisurely, and campers have the opportunity to help plan activities and make their own choices. All camp procedures related to transportation, diet, medication, health and safety, and the modification of activities are carefully planned in advance. Detailed records are kept of the progress of all campers, and staff members are thoroughly briefed about their individual needs and capabilities, their health care problems and how to deal with emergencies that may arise, such as seizures.

Numerous other camps exist throughout the United States and Canada that deal either with mixed groups of disabled campers, as Camp Spindrift does, or with groups of persons who have a single major class of disability, such as blindness, mental retardation or a physical handicap.

---

[10]Janet Pomeroy: "The San Francisco Recreation Center for the Handicapped: A Brief Description." *Therapeutic Recreation Journal*, Fourth Quarter 1969, pp. 15–19.

Camp Confidence, Brainerd, Minnesota

Known officially as the Northern Minnesota Therapeutic Camp, this facility provides year-round camping and outdoor education opportunities for the residents of Brainerd State Hospital and for other mentally retarded individuals in the state of Minnesota. It represents a unique example of teamwork among many individuals and public and voluntary organizations in obtaining a large wilderness site on Sylvan Lake and developing an outstanding camping facility with docks, tent campsites, cabins, nature playgrounds, a ski slope and chalet, skating rink and warming house, nature trails, fish houses, wheelchair walks and numerous other special units. Camp Confidence is the only year-round camping and outdoor education program for the mentally retarded in the northern half of the United States. It provides the following different types of services:

1. *Day Camping.* Primarily intended as a camping experience from which to develop skills in camping and outdoor education in preparing for resident camping.
2. *Independent Living Skills Resident Camp.* Conducted at separate tent sites or individual cabin units, with emphasis on the camp living skills portion of the outdoor education curriculum.
3. *Wilderness Camping.* Considered an ultimate goal as individuals become proficient in various phases of the outdoor education curriculum.
4. *Recreation Camping.* Primarily intended for industrial residents who have little or no vacation opportunities.
5. *Vocational Training Center.* Located in a resort area, the camp provides skills training in various phases of resort work for selected individuals to assist them in finding appropriate employment.
6. *Family Tent and Trailer Camping Area.* Provides opportunity for parents of the retarded to enjoy family camping and meet other parents and friends of the retarded.

Leadership for the Mentally Retarded. In working with the mentally retarded, it is necessary to structure activities carefully and to involve participants in appropriate activities on the basis of their readiness and observed levels of capability. While trial-and-error and experimentation are necessary at all times, the Camp Confidence program has developed the following guidelines for leadership with the mentally retarded:

1. Verbal directions should be brief and simple, with a calm, well-controlled voice rather than a high-pitched, excited one. The leader's facial expression and tone of voice must convey a feeling of friendliness and warmth.
2. Present new skills carefully, efficiently and clearly, using demonstration as a teaching device and to motivate interest.
3. Praise and encouragement are essential at all times; even when an individual is unsuccessful, his effort should be given approval. Do not expect immediate results in the learning of skills.

4. Although it is generally believed that retardates necessarily have short attention spans, this often stems from disinterest, boredom or lack of understanding. When motivated and interested, and when they see progress in a meaningful activity, retarded children may show considerable interest and ability to stick to a task. When interest wanes, activities should be kept short and changed frequently.

5. Repetition, drill and review of skills are needed more than with the non-retarded. Keep the fun in fundamentals; the "game" approach in teaching fundamentals is effective. Visual aids of all types are valuable supplementary tools.

6. Activities should be constantly evaluated in terms of the individual's needs and objectives, and then modified as needed. The same activity with appropriate modifications often has possibilities for use over the entire range of mental retardation.

7. In presenting activities, the leader should attempt to stimulate as many of the participant's senses as possible—seeing, listening, feeling and touching are better than any of these alone. Since motivation plays such a key part in the retardate's participation and achievement, the leader must seek a variety of ways to stimulate his desire and interest in the program, and to reinforce learning.

8. Discipline must be consistent and firm, but without threats and within the understanding and capabilities of the retarded participants. There is no room for corporal punishment in this program at any time.

This set of guidelines shows how a particular disability calls for special leadership approaches. The same is true of a number of other major disabilities. For example, in working with the emotionally disturbed child an entirely different method is used.

Therapeutic Camping for Emotionally Disturbed Children

In working with emotionally disturbed children, it has been commented that non-residential treatment programs, such as those provided by guidance clinics, school counselors or group therapy sessions, often are ineffectual because they cannot control the child's total environment strongly enough to bring about positive change. On the other hand, residential therapeutic programs, which *are* able to control the total environment, have the disadvantage of separating the child from parents and peers over a period of time, and tend to damage the child's self-concept and create problems for adjustment upon his or her return to the community. Rawson points out that camping programs can represent a "compromise"—short enough to minimize the difficulties inherent in separation, yet controlled enough to permit a great degree of influence over environmental factors.

Short-term therapeutic camping programs have been used in a number of instances to serve emotionally disturbed children. One such program was first organized during the summer of 1970 at a church-owned facility, Englishton Park, which is operated by the United Presbyterian Church as a national service mission and is affiliated with Hanover College, in Hanover, Indiana. The program consisted of two intensive ten-day sessions, the first for boys aged 8 to 11, and the second for boys aged 11 to 14. Many of the participants were chronic school truants, highly disruptive when in school and often extremely weak in their academic work. They tended to have poor peer and adult relationships, with negative social prognoses if successful intervention did not take place.

Rawson described the goals of this therapeutic camping program, which has been held each summer since 1970 and which has now served several hundred boys and girls. Three specific goals were established:

1. The program would aim at significant alteration of specific behavior patterns which seemed to be causing the child the greatest difficulty in relation to others.
2. The program would make every effort to improve a child's academic skills and attitudes, since chronic frustration in school situations was probably aggravating the child's disturbance.
3. The program would direct itself toward highly reinforcing modeling and identification relationships with teachers and therapists in an effort to teach the child more effective skills of interpersonal relationships.[11]

Although the staff included a psychologist, an outdoor educator, an academic remediation specialist and several social workers, the bulk of the round-the-clock leadership was provided by four male and four female college-age leaders who acted as "teacher-therapists." These leaders, selected for their sex-typing modeling potential, strong interest in working with children and good interpersonal skills, were given a month-long orientation in program skills and methods before camp began. A man and a woman were assigned as a team to each group of six children to simulate a "family-type" situation, so children could relate to adults of both sexes in work, play, learning and other therapeutic activities. Male leaders took the dominant role with groups of male campers, and female leaders did the same with girls' groups.

Behavior Modification Techniques

Behavior modification, as a method, has been widely explored in recent years. A variety of techniques have been used in psychiatric rehabilitation, drug therapy, correctional and other settings. Rawson describes the rationale of behavior modification, as applied at the Englishton Park Therapeutic Camp:

> Behavior modification theory places heavy emphasis upon the early extinction of socially maladaptive behaviors and immediate and consistent reinforcement of socially appropriate behavior. Put in its simplest terms, the basic assumption of this theory is that most behavior, good or bad, is in fact learned, and it was originally learned because it was reinforced

---

[11]Harve E. Rawson: "Residential Short-Term Camping for Children With Behavior Problems: A Behavior-Modification Approach." *Child Welfare*, October 1973, pp. 511–520.

socially or otherwise. Therefore, deliberate, consistent manipulation of reinforcements as a consequence of specific behaviors leads to unlearning of previous behaviors (which no longer lead to positive reinforcements) and simultaneous learning of new alternate behaviors which now lead to positive reinforcements.[12]

Before each child arrived at the camp, an intensive "behavior prescription" was drawn up, based upon study of family case histories, school and teacher reports, psychometric test findings and parental reports.

On the basis of the behavior prescription, the teacher-therapists sought to achieve specific behavior modification goals, using a number of positive and negative reinforcements to either reward or inhibit behavior. Positive reinforcements included (a) verbal praise; (b) physical gestures of affection and approval; (c) award of candy pellets; (d) award of gummed stars on name badges, which could be traded for candy bars, soft drinks or ice cream; (e) fancy certifications of merit given in public ceremonies; and (f) the right to participate in highly desired activities, such as evening swimming or overnight camp-outs. Negative reinforcements were (a) complete ignoring (turning one's back on a child, despite his or her attention-getting pleas), and (b) withdrawal of the child from a highly desired activity for several minutes.

Rawson cites an example of a prescription for a hostile-aggressive boy with extremely poor interpersonal relationships, characterized by frequent fighting:

> *Primary goal:* to decrease fighting behavior. *Methods:* male teacher should be warm and supportive at all times and utilize a great deal of physical gestures of approval and affection, such as hugging, holding, etc.; set up token reinforcement system for self-control of overt aggression toward others, starting at 10-minute intervals and increasing to 30-minute intervals; reinforce immediately with verbal praise (and at first candy pellets) for any assertive positive social or work relationship with peers.
>
> If he fights, stand between him and aggressed, turning your back toward him in total ignoral and immediately reinforce aggressed for nonretaliation and others in group for not paying attention to the distraction; all attention-seeking behaviors, such as verbal annoyance, backtalking, talking too much, gross exaggeration, punching others, etc., should lead to immediate physical ignoral and reinforcement of others in the group for not paying attention; reserve leadership role as a coveted activity, but utilize immediately for socially desired behavior; be very firm and consistent with this camper at all times and make sure he understands your expectations, repeating them often; utilize maximum peer pressure where possible to alter inappropriate behavior, including halt of coveted activity for entire group.[13]

On the other hand, a prescription for a girl marked by excessive shyness, limited verbalization and extreme withdrawal might be as follows:

> *Primary goal:* to increase assertive behavior. *Methods:* female teacher should be very warm and supportive at all times and throughout

[12]*Ibid.,* p. 513.
[13]*Ibid.,* p. 514.

session, and utilize a great deal of physical gestures of approval and affection; set up token reinforcement system for assertive vocalization behavior. . .; reinforce immediately for any appropriate assertive verbalization response; reinforce immediately for any assertive positive social or work relationship with peers; make sure this girl gets appropriate public ceremonial awards for any social appropriate behavior; wait for all responses with no exhibit of anxiety or 'hurry-up' clues if this child stutters or stammers.[14]

Psychological tests administered to emotionally disturbed children in this therapeutic camping program demonstrated that they had improved markedly in areas such as response to authority, self-concept, frustration tolerance and attitudes toward parents and school. Although the behavior modification techniques used in this program might be regarded as controversial, they demonstrate how techniques for changing behavior and bringing about constructive change may be carefully designed to meet the needs of individual campers or patients.

An increasing number of short-term camping programs for adolescent or adult psychiatric patients have involved wilderness camping, backpacking and, in some cases, high-risk programs somewhat similar to Outward Bound experiences. Although the results of such innovative therapeutic camping programs are somewhat mixed, patients have tended to show remarkable ability to accept the challenge of the natural environment with realistic and responsible behavior. Thomas Stich, coordinator of a pioneering program at Dartmouth Medical school that uses a 150-foot backward rappelling task (going down a sheer cliff backward) as well as rock-climbing, canoeing, backpacking and skiing in wilderness trips with hospitalized mental patients, comments:

> The outdoors provides us with tough challenges and opportunities for emotional growth that simply cannot be duplicated inside four walls.[15]

RECREATION IN PSYCHIATRIC REHABILITATION

One of the major specializations within the broad field of therapeutic recreation service involves working with psychiatric patients. Until recently, mental patients constituted one half of all the hospital patients in the United States. In general, recreation has been accepted as one of the important rehabilitative services in psychiatric hospitals or treatment units, and is viewed as meeting the following important patient needs:

1. To help patients become involved in reality situations.
2. To help withdrawn patients become resocialized.
3. To provide emotional release and interests outside self.
4. To improve the self-concept of patients.

[14]*Ibid.*, p. 514.
[15]Marilyn Elias: "Out of the Ward, Into the Mountains." *The Philadelphia Bulletin*, November 18, 1979, p. 12.

TABLE 9—1. ACTIVITIES OFFERED IN RECREATIONAL THERAPY PROGRAMS*

Activity	Percent of Hospitals	Activity	Percent of Hospitals
Cards	97.3	Crafts	82.7
Sports	97.3	Bowling	81.3
Bingo	96.0	Hobbies	80.0
Music Listening	96.0	Music Classes	78.7
Social Activities	93.3	Cooking	77.3
Movies	93.3	Swimming	76.0
Arts	93.3	Talent Show	73.3
Professional		Drama	72.0
Entertainment	90.7	Gardening	71.7
Discussion Groups	89.5	Creative Writing	58.6
Game Room	89.5	Newspaper	54.7
Trips	88.0	Ham Radio	10.7
Television	86.7		

*Cited in *Recreation and Related Therapies in Psychiatric Rehabilitation*, p. 24.

5. To create patient awareness of leisure needs and improve motivation for participation.
6. To provide information useful for diagnosis or treatment.
7. To provide release for hostility and aggression.
8. To keep patient morale high.
9. To teach skills that will be useful for leisure after discharge from hospital.[16]

A recent study of recreation activities provided in psychiatric hospitals in the New York–New Jersey–Connecticut region indicated the program activities listed in Table 9–1.

In the past, such activities generally were organized carefully and scheduled in most hospitals. The hospitals' weekly calendars of activity were comparable to what might be found in most community centers or other large-scale recreation programs. They tended to be planned by professional staff members, and patients were expected to attend the programs they were assigned to; if they did not attend, or if they did not take part, it was regarded as evidence of their inability to function socially and a sign of continuing illness. In recent years, however, changes have occurred within the broad field of psychiatric care that have modified the nature of recreation—in terms of both its goals and its treatment methods.

Changes in Psychiatric Treatment Approaches

The most significant change has been the administrative shift away from large, custodial hospitals located at a considerable distance from the home

---

[16]Richard Kraus: *Recreation and Related Therapies in Psychiatric Rehabilitation*. New York, Faculty Research Award Program, Herbert H. Lehman College, November 1972, p. 23.

communities of many mental patients, toward smaller treatment units located in or close to the patients' places of residence. This has been accompanied by a much greater emphasis on short-term care. Instead of accepting as inevitable that the majority of patients must be locked up in hospitals where they remain for several months or years before being discharged, the effort today is to provide "crash" treatment, with an intensive effort made to get people out of the hospital as quickly as possible or, better than that, to avoid hospitalization completely.

By using a variety of new drugs, mental hospital authorities found it possible to have many patients reside in the community while attending day clinics, night clinics or even weekend programs in mental health centers. Increasing numbers of patients who have been discharged live in halfway houses or attend after-care centers or special social clubs for discharged mental patients. Many states and provinces have reduced their mental hospital populations sharply, and in some cases have eliminated the need for entire hospitals. Mentally ill individuals today live in the community—some in special hotels, others in apartment units where they have responsibility for self-care.

Within this new approach, recreation has come to be viewed in a new light. Several of the key aspects of the contemporary use of therapeutic recreation in psychiatric settings are (a) the milieu therapy approach, (b) the development of activity therapies, and (c) leisure counseling.

Milieu Therapy Approach

This approach is based on the conviction that the entire institution should provide a total environment in which the patient is respected as an individual, has a meaningful voice in developing hospital plans and programs and is able to play a real part in his or her own recovery. It argues that mentally ill individuals have lost their ability to relate effectively to others or to handle environmental pressures and demands in the outside world. The effort of the psychiatric hospital should be to provide a new setting in which the patient will be able to function meaningfully, and in which he or she will develop a sense of reality and ability to communicate with people, take part in social situations and deal with real challenges and responsibilities.

Within this framework, the mental patient should be able to make meaningful decisions about his or her own experiences while in the hospital. In some hospitals, patients take over responsibility for housekeeping or cooking duties. In others, they serve on hospital committees or councils and make recommendations to hospital administrators. On all levels, each member of the hospital staff is expected to play a significant part in the treatment program and in all contacts with patients. Obviously, within this approach, recreation therapy must assume new roles. For instance, patients are not *required* to take part in activity. They have a real voice in developing programs; schedules tend to be less structured and to involve new and different kinds of creative programming.

Development of Activity Therapies

Over a period of time, many psychiatric hospitals have developed a variety of different types of non-medical therapies, including recreational, occupational, physical, educational and industrial therapy, in addition to a number of other therapies in music, art and dance. By their very number, these services have tended to create confusion and overlap in many hospitals. For this reason, and for administrative efficiency, an increasing number of hospitals have been combining the various adjunctive therapies under the heading of "activity therapies."

This trend has generally meant that recreation workers have been assigned new kinds of responsibilities and are now expected to work much more closely with other staff members in other treatment disciplines. In many hospitals there is greater emphasis on recreation as a medium through which patients plan their own trips to the community or organize their own events or activities. Activities of daily living that are offered by activity therapies departments typically include the following elements: (a) grooming and self-care classes or sessions; (b) social awareness discussions or encounter groups; (c) home and family management discussion groups or projects; (d) clerical work groups, which do office work for the hospital and teach work skills; (e) "boutiques" or other sheltered workshops that produce craft articles for sale in the hospital; (f) ward clean-up assignments; and (g) shopping trips to the community to re-establish competence in dealing with typical tasks of independent living.

Such activities represent a conscious effort to make the program helpful in preparing people to return to the community. Instead of having them take part in recreational activities that, although enjoyable and constructive in the present, might not be readily available to them in the future, the effort is made to have them gain practical experiences that will be directly helpful in building competence for independent living.

Leisure Counseling

Leisure counseling (or recreation counseling, as it is sometimes called) is a process of working closely with patients to assure that they will be able to use their leisure constructively upon return to the community rather than become involved in negative or self-destructive patterns of free-time use. One of the first programs of recreation counseling for psychiatric patients was established at the Veterans Administration Hospital in Kansas City, Missouri, in 1955. The objectives of this program were as follows:

1. Assist the patient to maintain and strengthen existing affiliations with family, friends, church, lodge and civic groups.
2. Help the patient form new ties with individuals and groups.
3. Teach the patient how to make use of available community resources for recreation.

4. Stimulate the patient's awareness of his or her own recreational needs.
5. Mobilize community resources for fostering mental health.

Group therapy sessions with patients on the neurological ward were scheduled with a committee that included representatives of the psychiatric staff, psychologists, recreation therapists and a representative of the public recreation department. This program has been described by Olson and McCormack:

> It has been our experience that with sustained psychiatric treatment in the hospital environment, withdrawn patients have come to participate with apparent enjoyment in social-recreational activities. Contact with patients who have required rehospitalization here or at nearby psychiatric centers indicates that some tend to lapse into solitary ways on discharge and thus set the stage for reactivation of old pathological patterns of behavior. Our observations suggested that in several of these cases, specific guidance in this area—living through the non-working hours—was indicated. As a consequence, a new patient service was instituted which we called Recreation Counseling. . . .
>
> Recreation Counseling is available to patients on both an individual and a group basis. Individual counseling is done where the psychiatric staff feels that use of leisure time or need for social contact or group affiliation is a prime factor in the current illness. . . . The counselor and the patient explore the patient's needs in this area and work together toward its resolution. In this type of counseling, the patient contact is done by the psychologist. He is able to call upon the hospital recreation section for help with regard to the patient's current situation and on the city recreation worker for advice with regard to opportunities for the patient after discharge. The team members work together in helping the patient make contacts that can last after discharge. The therapist is able to follow up on these contacts and work through whatever practical difficulties might come.[17]

An important element in recreation counseling is the group discussion, in which patients are encouraged to discuss their experiences, problems and expectations for the future. Each staff member participating in these meetings clarifies problems or offers assistance on the basis of his or her own specialized expertise, while the representative of the city recreation department helps to provide knowledge of community programs and facilities. In addition, patients, through their counseling groups, visit many places in the nearby community, including sports centers, community centers, schools, clubs and similar facilities.

Evaluation over a period of years indicates that the Kansas City Veterans Administration Hospital recreation counseling program has been extremely effective in helping patients strengthen existing affiliations with community

---

[17]William E. Olson and John B. McCormack: "Recreation Counseling in the Psychiatric Service of a General Hospital." *Journal of Nervous and Mental Disease*, May-June 1957.

groups, form new ties and learn to avail themselves of facilities and programs that they had not formerly used.

Many other hospitals throughout the United States and Canada have developed leisure or recreation counseling programs in recent years. The Binghamton, New York, State Hospital, for example, has initiated a "Gateway Program," a pilot project intended to assist discharged patients in returning to the community through both a systematic and carefully designed selection of patients and a series of experiences and planned exposures that provide them with a solid base of recreational opportunity. A major element in this program was the preparation of the community to receive and work with the discharged mental patient:

> After some experience in Gateway's Community-Readiness phase, we became aware of a void in continuity which existed on the community side of our program. . . . It was felt . . . we should develop a network of communication and understanding between the institution and those individuals in the community who represent leisure-activity involvement for not only the convalescing mental patient but the entire "population at risk" within our institution's catchment area.
>
> In order to initiate this understanding, we began a series of educationally oriented workshops for community recreation agency personnel; administrators, as well as program people. Via these workshop experiences, an attempt was made to point out the responsibility the community has in dealing with *all* disabled individuals. Recreation professionals in the community presently make efforts to adapt their program to include the more obviously handicapped, and it therefore became our intention to point out the over-riding need that a similar effort be made on behalf of the convalescing mental patient. . . .[18]

Following these meetings, the Binghamton Gateway project developed a community referral plan, which involved cooperating groups that represented local, state and county recreation organizations, school and university representatives, public and private recreation agencies, church groups and community volunteer associations. This process included post-discharge communication, through which guidance was given to community agencies serving discharged mental patients, with the hospital receiving feedback on their progress. It was decided, as this system began to yield positive results, to establish a community-based, leisure-use education and adjustment clinic, which was to become the base of operations for an expanded system of community referral agencies.

A final example of the strong effort being made to equip discharged mental patients to use their leisure effectively may be found in the Mental Health Centre in Penetanguishene, Ontario, Canada. This regional mental health facility makes a clear distinction between three phases of recreational service: (a) general recreation activities, which are intended to make the patient's stay at the hospital as pleasant as possible but are not for achieving therapeutic

---

[18]*Report of Gateway Pilot Program.* Binghamton, New York, State Hospital, February 1969, pp. 5–6.

goals; (b) a therapeutic phase, involving assessment of the patient's status and needs, including development of a treatment plan, counseling services and effective referral; and (c) a carefully designed research program, which is carried on to evaluate needs and outcomes.

The Penetanguishene Mental Health Centre examines the social and recreational patterns, interests and needs of entering patients in order to provide a basis for developing treatment plans. Following an anonymous observation of the patient attending evening activities, a series of seven sessions is scheduled to explore the entire problem. The first session is a video-taped interview between the assessor and the client that examines the patient's general attitudes toward recreation, pre-hospital and present recreation activities and interests, and perception of future involvements. The remaining sessions include the administration of the Guilford-Zimmerman Temperament Survey, a psychological projective test designed to complement the assessor's observations, and a series of meetings that actually expose the patient to social situations, games and recreational areas, after which the patient's reactions and involvement are carefully analyzed.

Much of the information gathered through these sessions is used as the basis for counseling patients while at the hospital or for guiding them in the use of available recreational opportunities, both in the hospital and in the community. The Penetanguishene staff makes an intensive effort to involve patients in community programs throughout their treatment stay in order to avoid the harmful effects of institutionalization and to promote healthy ties with community leisure resources. Patients take bus trips to local community recreation events; they attend church, go shopping regularly in the community, use a local YMCA swimming pool and attend movies, harness racing events, wrestling matches and other entertainment activities in and around Penetanguishene.

At the same time, intensive efforts are made to help those in the local community become aware of the recreational needs of the Centre's patient population:

> Members of the recreation staff attend local community council meetings and take active roles in community affairs. Recreation staff have been used as recreation resource persons within the local communities of Penetanguishene and Midland as well as the Simcoe County area. The dual role as participants and resource persons within the community is an important facet that assists in the integration and education of the community toward the recreational needs of the patient population.[19]

The examples that have just been cited show how recreation professionals in the field of psychiatric care must today operate as "social systems" specialists. They help to prepare individuals for successful return to the community, involve community representatives in the hospital program, make extensive use of community resources and, through follow-up and referral

[19]*Staff Manual.* Description of Community Involvement Program at Penetanguishene, Ontario, Mental Health Centre, 1973.

programs, actually continue to sustain and assist patients through the difficult process of transition. Obviously, such programs tend to represent the vanguard of new treatment approaches in the most advanced states or provinces in the United States and Canada. They demonstrate one of the ways in which recreation leadership and supervision have adapted to meet pressing contemporary needs in an important area of public service.

RECREATION PROGRAMS IN NURSING HOMES

A major area of recreation service that has expanded markedly during the past several years consists of nursing homes serving individuals with a significant degree of physical or mental disability who are unable to live independently in the community. Depending on the nature and degree of disability and the level of medical and nursing care provided, such institutions may be called "extended care" or "health-related" facilities. Although in many cases they may also serve younger individuals who have suffered severe illnesses and are undergoing rehabilitation, nursing homes generally are for persons over the age of 65. In most cases, they are separate institutions, although some state hospitals operate geriatric units that house patients similar to the more regressed residents of nursing homes.

In earlier societies, little social assistance was given to poor, sick or aged persons. They were often placed in the poorhouse, or almshouse, which comprised persons of all ages and disabilities, including the mentally ill. Only later were special institutions developed to care for dependent children, the retarded, the mentally ill and similar groups in need.

Gradually, county poorhouses began to serve only aged, indigent persons in need of special care. Many other organizations, such as religious bodies or fraternal orders, also established group care homes for dependent older persons. Increasingly, private family homes also began to meet this growing need. In the United States, federal and state governments began to provide funding to assist older persons in paying the cost of such care. In 1954, for example, the Hill-Burton Law provided state and federal reimbursement to public old-age homes and voluntary nursing homes. Proprietary (privately operated) nursing homes were able to obtain loans guaranteed by the Federal Housing Authority beginning in 1959. With such assistance, nursing homes expanded rapidly and became much larger institutions, run by management-oriented personnel.

With the establishment of Medicare and Medicaid, which pay the major portion of costs for eligible persons, great numbers of elderly, indigent persons have been placed in nursing homes today. The monthly fees are paid almost completely by these agencies; individuals who have modest savings must use them up, and then are covered by local welfare programs, which, in turn, have federal subsidies supporting them. As a consequence, nursing homes have become a billion-dollar business. Although such facilities are regulated by municipal or state departments of health or social welfare, and are approved nationally by nongovernmental agencies organized under the American Medical Association, the American Association of Nursing Homes and the American Association of Homes for the Aged, too often they are shabby, unsanitary and unsafe and provide only limited health care and activity programs. This situation results from two factors: (a) the profit motive, impelling many unscrupulous home operators to skimp on essential services in order to clear the greatest margin of financial return; and (b) the fact that nursing homes are supervised by a bureaucratic maze of agencies, unclear standards and conflicting regulations, and have inadequate numbers of supervisors.

Nursing homes actually fall into several categories today: *governmental* homes (sponsored by state, county or municipal government), *voluntary* homes (sponsored by nonprofit agencies, usually of a philanthropic or religious type) and *proprietary* homes (privately operated for profit). They serve patients who have a wide range of disease or disability, including cancer, heart conditions, stroke, multiple sclerosis and other illnesses or impairments. Typically, patients have not only physical but also social and emotional problems. Aged persons often enter nursing homes or extended care facilities fearing that they have been abandoned by their families, and with a great sense of loss and despair. This is accentuated by the nature of life in a nursing home, where patients suffer a loss of privacy and independence and are too often cared for by untrained and inexperienced aides who lack sensitivity and compassion. Although medical and nursing staff members play a leading role in nursing homes, it is also clear that psychological, social service and recreational and occupational therapy are also key elements in meeting the varied needs of aged residents.

Stein and Sessoms comment:

> Nursing homes, hospitals, homes for the aged, and extended care facilities provide a protective environment for older persons unable to fully care for themselves due to some degree of physical or emotional disability. Recreation services can play an important and vital role toward the patient's return to a community situation by improving his physical, emotional, and mental health.[20]

Nursing homes are obligated to provide activity programs that permit each patient to be as alert and active as his or her individual physical and emotional health permits. The White Plains, New York, Center for Nursing Care has described the goals of its social rehabilitation program (which includes occupational therapy and recreation as key elements) in the following terms:

Purpose of a Social Rehabilitation Program

> *General Aim* of such a program is to help each patient to function to his or her optimal level—physically, emotionally and socially. The suc-

---

[20]Peter J. Verhoven: "Recreation and the Aging." In Thomas A. Stein and H. Douglas Sessoms: *Recreation and Special Populations*. Boston, Holbrook Press, 1977, p. 401.

cessful program assists patients achieve the most vital way of life commensurate with their illness and disability. It encourages both individual and group enterprise and motivation. As such, it is an important segment of the total rehabilitation process.

Specific Goals are as follows:

To alleviate patients' fears of loneliness, abandonment and impending death

To provide stimulation and pleasure

To discourage the withdrawal tendencies so prevalent in the elderly sick, by encouraging patients to share activities and experiences with their peers in group situations, thus fostering the we-are-not-alone feeling

To re-awaken latent skills and interests, and in this way help patients revive their normal life patterns

To build self-confidence and self-respect, and lessen self-pity, by encouraging patients to communicate and to function

To make patients feel that they are not forgotten but are still part of current life in the community, by bringing members of the community into the nursing facility to entertain, to instruct, to give volunteer services

To encourage patients' sense of responsibility toward others, and to demonstrate to them that they can still be useful to society, by providing opportunities for them to participate in civic projects

According to standards that have been developed for nursing homes and extended care facilities by the National Therapeutic Recreation Society, programs should include both active and passive pursuits, individual and group activities and varied forms of social, physical and creative recreation. Federal regulations for extended care facilities operating with Medicare funding include the following guidelines for patients' activity programs:

1. The person in charge of patient recreation uses, to the fullest possible extent, all community, social and recreational resources, including personnel, supplies, equipment, facilities and programs.
2. Patients are encouraged, but not forced, to participate in recreational activities. Suitable activities are provided for patients who are unable to leave their rooms.
3. Suitable space is provided for the conduct of daily recreational programs, including areas designated for: (a) individual recreational pursuits, and (b) privacy for visits with friends, relatives, or clergymen.
4. The facility makes available a variety of supplies and equipment adequate to satisfy the individual interests of patients. Examples are: books and magazines, daily newspapers, games, stationery, radio, and television.[21]

---

[21]Jean R. Tague: "The Status of Therapeutic Recreation in Extended Care Facilities: A Challenge and an Opportunity." *Therapeutic Recreation Journal,* Third Quarter 1970, pp. 13–14.

Specific examples of program activities in a given nursing home include the following:

Entertainment. Arrangements are made with many individuals or groups from the nearby community to provide dance, drama, vocal, instrumental or other entertainment. In some cases, groups that are preparing for formal concerts or shows elsewhere will hold their rehearsals at the home.

Parties. Several times each month, parties, teas or holiday or religious celebrations are held. Birthdays are celebrated en masse once a month, and frequent summer barbecues are provided.

Movies and Slide Presentations. Free movies are obtained from corporations and similar sources. Patients particularly enjoy travel films or films or slides that are shown by visitors to the home from the community.

Music. Record players or strolling players are used to provide music at special events or sometimes in the various living areas of the hospital.

Creative Arts. Patients enjoy arts and crafts, including painting and sculpture, as well as sewing and needlework, cooking and food preparation, assisting at barbecues, gardening and flower arranging.

Sports. These are necessarily limited but may include shuffleboard, ball tossing, rhythmic exercise or marching drills, dancing, a modified form of bowling and table games.

Spiritual and Cultural Activities. Religious services are held regularly; in addition, group discussions, lectures, a weekly story hour, a circulating book cart, reading therapy sessions and a "talking book" machine are all provided.

Outings. With medical and family approval, patients are taken on outings such as community picnics, boat trips, visits to museums or art shows, churches and synagogues or social occasions at local homes or organizations. Usually these events serve ambulatory patients, although special arrangements may be made for those in wheelchairs.

Patients who are capable of such activity are drawn into community service projects or into other roles that keep them active and provide them with meaningful responsibilities. In some institutions, patients have developed Welcoming Committees, which help to orient new patients to the nursing home and its program and assist with the social adjustment that is often so difficult for them. In other nursing homes, patients are responsible for planning and editing a newsletter or newspaper that comes out weekly or monthly. In still other settings, patient councils have been formed that represent the various wards or floors in meetings held with staff members to discuss patient needs and grievances, to make requests for change or to work cooperatively in planning new programs. At the White Plains, New York, Center for Nursing Care, community service-oriented programs include the following:

> *Civic Projects.* Patients who contribute to the community continue to feel a part of the community. Patient-volunteers make cancer dressings for a hospital, roll bandages for a church group, and stuff, seal and stamp envelopes for a fund-raising drive. These are good examples of useful services within the range of patient capabilities.

Fund-Raising. Fairs are held twice a year for a worthy community organization or, sometimes, for the facility itself. Although staff participation is heavy and welcome, patients themselves make many of the articles sold, help with decorations and, if able, serve as sales personnel. Many patients have been similarly involved with bazaars and fairs in the past, during their healthier years, and thus enjoy this type of endeavor.

Voting Participation. Good citizenship is encouraged, with shut-in patients voting via absentee ballots. Candidates for local offices are invited to present their platforms to patients. Representatives of the local chapter of the League of Women Voters visit to discuss issues; they return to assist with voting procedures. Civic leaders visit from time to time to discuss local problems and to report on progress in such areas as urban renewal.

Senior Citizen Visitors. A continuing effort is made to invite senior citizen neighbors regularly to the facility to join patients in activities. Following the formal program they are invited to stay for refreshments and conversation. In this way, patients have an opportunity to form friendships with local people outside the institution.

Many nursing home patients may not be capable of taking part in such activities. These patients may be severely withdrawn or regressed and unable to interact with their environments or to respond to stimuli. In some cases their behavior varies, and they are able to engage from time to time in meaningful activity or conversation, while also having intermittent periods of withdrawal or depression. Other patients will cry or babble continuously, strike their hand or arm or head regularly against a table or the wall, or simply sit or lie motionlessly. Patients of this type are generally referred to as "regressed," "disoriented" or suffering from "chronic brain syndrome." Their condition may stem from a variety of causes, including physical, psychological and social factors.

Whenever possible, these patients should be involved in program activities geared to their capabilities and interests, such as simple rhythmic activities or exercises, modified arts and crafts, singing or other participant or spectator pursuits. In addition to such approaches, two special methods have been developed for working with highly regressed and disoriented patients. These methods are known as "remotivation" and "sensory training."

Remotivation

This consists of a technique promoting group interaction that recreation leaders, nurses or specially trained aides may use with patients in both nursing homes and psychiatric facilities. When patients do not respond well to other types of therapy, remotivation is often tried. Its essential purpose is to improve alertness, involvement and communication, and thus to help the patient develop other involvements and interpersonal relationships.

Remotivation was originated by Mrs. Dorothy Hoskins Smith at the Philadelphia State Hospital in 1956. Smith, Kline and French Laboratories gave support to the program, and before long it was being used by hospitals, mental health clinics and nursing homes throughout the United States and Canada. With the assistance of the American Psychiatric Association, classes, seminars and demonstrations have been provided to train leaders in this method. By the late 1960's, it was estimated that more than 15,000 leaders were participating in remotivation programs.

Essentially, the method consists of a series of patient meetings held once or twice a week under the supervision of a leader. Usually, there are 12 such meetings, each session lasting from 30 minutes to an hour and involving from 10 to 15 patients. Patients are encouraged to come but should never be forced to do so. The basic method of remotivation involves an attempt to help the senile, regressed patient to come out of a shell and to become more fully aware of other persons and of things outside himself or herself. Remotivation sessions are highly structured and follow a five-step sequence, briefly summarized as follows:

1. *Climate of Acceptance.* The leader addresses the group and expresses appreciation to its members for coming to the meeting. The leader moves around the group greeting each member, calling them by name, or introducing herself to them. She compliments them on their appearance, or attempts to establish contact in similar ways. The purpose of this first step is to attempt to involve the group member in a social setting, and to provide a comfortable relaxed atmosphere.

2. A *Bridge to Reality.* The leader uses some sort of clipping, poem, or article to gain the attention of the group. She may read the poem slowly and rhythmically, or may move around the room asking each patient to read a line, or, if it is an article, to look at photographs it may contain, or read from it.

3. *Sharing the World We Live In.* This step seeks to develop a topic to be covered by the group, which may have been introduced in the previous step. The leader may bring some articles to show the group to provoke their responses, or may prepare a number of specific objective questions to ask them about it. Varied topics related to leisure, recreation, family life or personal interests may be developed; however, the method usually avoids topics which may arouse controversy or disturb patients, such as religion or racial prejudice.

4. *The World of Work.* Here the effort is to discuss work as a focus of activity, and (particularly in psychiatric hospitals, where patients may be returning to the community) to encourage patients to give their own perceptions of work and feelings about it. This step may be less relevant to senile, regressed patients. Whenever possible, similar themes or examples should be used through steps 2, 3 and 4, to establish a continuity in the session.

5. *Climate of Appreciation.* The leader thanks each patient for coming to the meeting and indicates that she is pleased with the group. She announces when the next meeting will be held, and urges group members to attend.[22]

In some institutions, evaluation reports and progress notes are kept for all remotivation group members. Groups on different levels of capability and

[22]Alice M. Robinson: *Remotivation Technique: A Manual for Use in Nursing Homes.* New York, American Psychiatric Association and Smith, Kline and French Laboratories, 1968.

participation may be established so that, as patients improve, they may be moved along to the next highest level. In many cases, remotivation sessions are held before patients take part in recreation programs.

Sensory Training

Sensory training is a method that was developed originally in the early 1960's for children with perceptual-motor impairment. It has since come to be used very widely in work with regressed and disoriented psychiatric patients or residents in nursing homes suffering from chronic brain syndrome. While it has some elements in common with remotivation, the basic emphasis is to rehabilitate function or prevent further deterioration of regressed geriatric patients by providing various types of stimuli that arouse the patient's various senses and promote awareness and meaningful responses. Richman describes the methods in the following terms:

1. Sensory training is designed for the patient who is regressed, blind, or wheelchair-bound, and does not participate in off-ward activities.
2. Sensory training is a structured, sequential process, which is a shared group/individual experience.
3. The program provides the person with differentiated stimuli to improve his perception and his response to the environment.
4. All sense receptors are stimulated: auditory, olfactory, tactile, vision, taste, proprioception and kinesthetic.
5. Sensory training is specifically ordered, structured and designed to increase sensitivity to stimuli by the individual's discrimination and response to stimuli. A "response-feedback" system is inherent in the group interactional setting.[23]

Customarily, four to seven patients are involved in each sensory training group. Sessions last from a half hour to an hour and may be held daily or less frequently. The general goals of each session are to stimulate the patient's awareness of self and of others, to orient him or her to reality, to increase his or her alertness to environmental stimuli and to improve his or her level of functioning, including such aspects as concentration, tolerance, judgment and manual dexterity.

To begin a session, patients are usually brought together and seated in a close circle. Both the leader and the patients are given name tags. The leader and the group members introduce themselves. The leader should shake hands with each patient, speaking loudly, slowly and clearly, and repeating phrases when necessary. If patients do not know their names, the leader should try patiently to get them to say their names. Tactile contact, with much hand touching, holding, shaking or clapping, is repeated frequently. When introductions are over, the leader begins to orient the group

---

[23]Leona Richman: *Manual of Sensory Training Techniques.* New York, Bronx State Hospital Geriatric Unit, 1968, p. 1.

to the time, the place, the date, the day and the fact that they are in the hospital because they are ill or need treatment and special care. The purposes of the sensory training session are explained and repeated carefully and slowly. Important ideas may be written on a blackboard or bulletin board. At this point, the leader should go through the following series of stimulation exercises:

> **Kinesthetic and Proprioceptive Exercises.** These exercises deal with awareness of the movement of the joint, and the awareness of different parts of the body. Patients are asked to identify and move different parts of their bodies—the should joint, arms, legs and head. In a sitting position, the patients go through various flexion and extension movements.
>
> **Tactile Exercises.** These exercises, which involve touching and identifying objects, are intended to sharpen patients' awareness of the environment and of their own reactions to it. The leader presents various types of materials or objects to patients for them to feel or touch, or may rub them or brush them with the objects. Examples of materials might include a piece of wood, sponge, brush, ball or piece of cotton. Patients are asked how they feel about the various objects or materials, what the sensation received from it is like and which ones they prefer.
>
> **Olfactory Exercises.** The leader presents patients with different substances or materials that have distinct odors, such as tobacco, mustard, perfume or garlic. In each case, the leader tries to get them to identify the substance by its odor, to indicate their feelings about it and possibly also to say what it is used for.

Other senses, such as *hearing, vision* and *taste,* are also focused on, using appropriate stimuli and exercises. Patients are worked with in terms of their level of capability and alertness; patients functioning at higher levels are pressed to respond more fully than those who are extremely regressed.

Often the leader may have mirrors in which patients may look at themselves. In every way possible, they are bombarded with stimuli—by touch, sound, sight, smell and taste—and with suggestions and nonthreatening opportunities for social interaction. At the end of the sensory training session, the group may join together in some simple, purposeful group activity, such as singing a folk song. The leader shakes hands with each patient, announces that the meeting has ended and reminds them of the date of the next session.[24]

Both "remotivation" and "sensory training" are techniques that are carried out by recreation leaders in many hospitals and nursing homes. Although specialized leadership training is needed for both methods, they are not highly complicated techniques and may readily be mastered with careful preparation and supervision. It should be noted that in many nursing homes, activity programs are directed by occupational therapists; in others, qualified therapeutic recreation specialists are in charge.

---

[24]*Ibid.*, pp. 1–4. See also Leona Richman: "Sensory Training for Geriatric Patients." *American Journal of Occupational Therapy,* May-June 1969, pp. 254–257.

SCOPE OF SERVICE IN SPECIAL SETTINGS

This chapter has demonstrated how recreation leadership today may require unique or special skills and abilities, depending on the type of setting in which the leader functions. The examples of "behavior modification," "remotivation" and "sensory training" demonstrate how new and sophisticated methods of leadership are constantly being developed, particularly within the field of therapeutic recreation.

Obviously, no recreation leader is likely to face all of the kinds of challenges or job demands described in this chapter. Instead, what is essential is that the leader develop broad-based competence and then move ahead to gain the kinds of special expertise or skills required within his or her unique job situation. Throughout this process, the role of the supervisor is an important one. It is the supervisor who is primarily responsible for guiding and directing recreation leaders and promoting their professional growth. The chapters that follow deal with the process and philosophy of effective supervision in recreation and parks.

SUGGESTED EXAMINATION QUESTIONS OR TOPICS FOR STUDENT REPORTS

1. What are the unique values in therapeutic camping for special populations? Describe some of the practices in camping for the mentally retarded or emotionally disturbed, as outlined in this chapter.
2. How does the role of outreach workers or roving leaders who are assigned to work with youth gangs in urban settings differ from the normal role of recreation leaders working with youth? Why is this an appropriate function for recreation and park departments, as opposed to other types of social agencies?
3. Recreation or activity leaders in nursing homes must often work with a population that is extremely limited in its potential for participation. Sometimes these individuals may be severely regressed or disoriented. How can the leader serve such a population and at the same time work with more normal patients?

SUGGESTED ACTION ASSIGNMENTS OR GROUP PROCESS ACTIVITIES

1. Select one of the four following methods or techniques: "leisure counseling," "behavior modification," sensory training" or "remotivation." Do additional research on it, either in the literature or by observation, and then write a brief manual indicating how it can be used in recreation or activity therapy programs.

2. Many psychiatric rehabilitation programs have been shifted to community mental health settings (day clinics, after-care centers, and so on). Carefully observe one such program, and gather as much information on it as you can. Then evaluate its effectiveness and review the use of recreation as a treatment method in this setting.
3. Select one category of physical disability, such as blindness or severe orthopedic disability. Analyze two or three frequently used recreation activities, and show how you would modify or adapt them for use with this special population.

Principles and Practices in Recreation Supervision

Part Three

Recreation Supervision: Philosophy and Process

Chapter Ten

Particularly in smaller communities or voluntary organizations with limited staffs, the major responsibility for planning, organizing and carrying out programs is held by supervisors, while the bulk of the actual program leadership is done by part-time or seasonal employees or volunteers. In almost all recreation and park departments, the supervisor plays a pivotal role in determining needs, carrying out middle management functions and mobilizing the total efforts of the agency.

This chapter deals with the basic concepts and process of supervision. It provides five elements: (a) a definition of supervision as a key function in governmental and voluntary agency management; (b) a general description of the roles of supervisors; (c) a more detailed description of such roles within typical recreation and park agencies; (d) a philosophy of supervision based on contemporary teaching in administration and human relations; and (e) a set of guidelines for effective supervision in recreation and parks today.

SUPERVISION DEFINED

The term "supervision" has, for some, a rather narrow connotation. Edginton and Williams, for example, prefer the term "manager," suggesting that whereas *managers* are selected for intellectual capability and behavioral flexibility and have a wide range of responsibilities, the *supervisor's* role is rather limited and is based heavily on technical capability.[1] This text takes a some-

---

[1]Christopher R. Edginton and John G. Williams: *Productive Management of Leisure Service Organizations: A Behavioral Approach.* New York, John Wiley and Sons, 1978, p. 6.

what more liberal view—that, in effect, supervisors *are* managers and are very broadly responsible for the success of the enterprises that they manage.

Supervision may be defined both in technical terms and with respect to its overall purposes. From a technical point of view, the National Labor-Management Relations Act has defined a supervisor as any individual having authority, in the interest of the employer, to hire, transfer, suspend, lay off, recall, promote, discharge, assign, reward or discipline other employees, or having responsibility to direct them, or to adjust their grievances, or effectively to recommend such action, if in connection with the foregoing the exercise of such authority is not of a merely routine or clerical nature but requires the use of independent judgment.[2]

Williamson defines supervision in the following terms:

> . . . any person who is responsible (1) for the conduct of others in the achievement of a particular task, (2) for the maintenance of quality standards, (3) for the protection and care of materials, and (4) for services to be rendered to those under his control.[3]

He suggests that supervision must be viewed as a process by which both paid and volunteer workers are helped by a designated member to make the best use of their knowledge and skills and to carry out their responsibilities more effectively. The ultimate objective of supervision is to improve the agency's total functioning through more effective employee functioning. Similarly, Ball and Cipriano state, "Supervision is a process through which leadership of personnel is conducted so that services may be offered most effectively. In this context the supervisor is the helper of the leader."[4]

Such definitions place emphasis upon the "personnel management" aspect of supervision. However, in many recreation agencies, the responsibility of supervisors extends beyond this definition to performing a wide variety of tasks of an administrative nature that are *not*, strictly speaking, personnel management functions.

In recreation and park service, supervision should be regarded as the administrative level on which professional employees assume responsibility for a major division of service. This may be a geographical area or district, an important unit of departmental operations or program service, or a key facility. Within this division of service, the supervisor is responsible for planning, organizing and carrying out program activities and for directing a variety of support services. It is his or her task to develop budget plans, carry out public relations and assist in facility planning. In addition, the supervisor has the major responsibility of helping to direct and assist all subordinate employees in the district or unit, improving their work attitudes and performance and building an effective work team. Finally, it is his or her function to serve as a channel for communication between top management and line employees.

---

[2]William R. Spriegel, Edward Schulz and William B. Spriegel: *Elements of Supervision.* New York, John Wiley and Sons, 1957, p. 1.

[3]*Ibid.,* p. 1.

[4]Edith L. Ball and Robert E. Cipriano: *Leisure Services Preparation: A Competency-Based Approach.* Englewood Cliffs, New Jersey, Prentice-Hall, 1978, p. 182.

Within recreation and parks, there are three distinct types of supervisors: (a) District Supervisors, (b) Supervisors of Special Services, and (c) Supervisors of Major Centers or Facilities.

District Supervisors. These are middle-management employees who are placed in charge of either recreation or recreation and park operations within a major geographical area of a community, such as a district, borough, sector or other political subdivision. Such individuals tend to have a generalist background, with an overall responsibility for coordinating program services, supervising personnel and carrying out budgetary, facilities planning, public relations and similar responsibilities.

Supervisors of Special Services. These individuals have responsibility for major areas of service, involving either a particular type of activity (such as performing arts, outdoor education or sports programs) or a population group to be served (such as the mentally or physically disabled, children and youth or the aging). In some cases, a supervisor of special services may be assigned responsibility for all playgrounds, community centers or pools within a city. In most cases, the supervisor of special services has an in-depth background of training and experience in his or her area of responsibility. It is his or her function to promote and carry on services related to this specialized program area throughout the city. For example, a Supervisor of Performing Arts in a typical, medium-sized city might be expected to plan music, dance, theater activities and special events throughout the city, to train leaders in this area and to coordinate departmental programs with other organizations active in the performing arts.

Supervisors of Major Centers or Facilities. Positions of this type involve the responsibility of administering a large recreation center with a diversified program and a substantial number of staff members. The center might consist of a large-scale arts and crafts operation, a varied aquatic facility, a senior center, a cultural arts center or a similar facility. In a sense, such supervisors are similar to each of the other two types in that they must fulfill the functions of the District Supervisor (although within a limited geographical setting) and must often have the in-depth capabilities of the Supervisor of Special Services.

GENERAL RESPONSIBILITIES OF SUPERVISORS

Although job functions may vary considerably in different types of agencies or departments, Edginton and Williams suggest that managerial functions may be categorized in three areas: interpersonal, informational and decision-making. *Interpersonal* roles encompass the development of a set of interpersonal relationships between the manager (or supervisor) and his or her subordinates and superiors. These include such roles as figurehead or symbol of authority, leader and motivator, and liaison among different individuals and groups. *Informational* roles involve receiving and sending information; the manager acts as monitor, disseminator and spokesperson for the organization.

Finally, *decision-making* has the manager serve as entrepreneur, promoter of change in the organization, disturbance-handler or conflict-resolver, resource-allocator and negotiator.[5]

In more concrete terms, a good example of the overall tasks of a recreation supervisor in a public recreation and parks department may be found in the following passage. It is excerpted from the *Job Manual* of the Recreation Department of the City of Long Beach, California, and describes the varied responsibilities of the Supervisor of District II in that city, an area that includes five parks, two recreation centers and two playgrounds.

District Supervisor, City of Long Beach

Major Responsibilities

1. *To the Public:* Surveys community attitudes and meets changing needs and interests of the public through provision of high quality, diversified, recreational activities within the district for all groups and individuals.
   a. Assists in establishing and maintaining communications with Advisory Councils. . .
   b. Maintains contact with community groups. . .
   c. Uses professional expertise and experience.
   d. Communicates with other recreation departments and individuals in the field.
   e. Sees that leaders in area are providing programs needed by residents of area.
2. *To Subordinates:* Recruits, trains, assigns, schedules, evaluates, counsels and supervises general and specialized personnel at recreation facilities within the district.
   a. Interviews and recommends for appointment to the Assistant Director for Programs and Facilities all applicants for positions in the district.
   b. Assists in setting objectives for each employee and evaluating him on achieving objectives and job performance.
   c. Conducts in-service training and staff meetings.
   d. Reviews employee schedules.
   e. Observes leaders' performance and counsels them on weaknesses and needed improvement; offers recognition for good performance.
3. *To Co-Workers and Administrators:* Coordinates all aspects of program with administrators and other supervisors, offering assistance wherever appropriate.
   a. Attends weekly staff meetings of Program and Facilities Division.
   b. Works closely with Program Section Supervisor to determine and meet needs and desires of community, and coordinates classes offered.
   c. Works with Publicity Supervisor in providing articles, tapes, programs.

---

[5]Edginton and Williams, *op. cit.*, p. 7.

    d. Works with Cultural Arts Supervisors to resolve problems in class scheduling or other difficulties.

    e. Works with Special Activities Supervisor in planning and staging special events.

4. *For Program:* Plans, organizes, promotes, coordinates, supervises and evaluates the city recreation program in the district.

    a. Inspects and evaluates adequacy of recreation services.

    b. Promotes and publicizes the program through brochures, public speaking, and other public information media.

    c. Is responsible for coordinating all playground program schedules with other departmental personnel.

    d. Reviews and approves new program ideas from leaders and other sources.

    e. Supervises and coordinates district special events, such as tournaments, beach days, etc. . . .

5. *For Facilities:* Oversees general development, use, and upkeep of recreational facilities, equipment, and supplies.

    a. Assists in developing long-range capital improvements.

    b. Prepares purchase requisitions and approves purchase of district supplies and equipment.

    c. Submits work orders requesting maintenance and repairs.

    d. Requests assistance from Projects Coordinator with small construction projects.

    e. Reviews use of facilities by "permit" groups.

    f. Coordinates supervision of caretakers with Superintendent of Building Services.

6. *For Administration:* Reviews and/or prepares all reports and documents produced in the district, maintaining necessary records, and managing district finances.

    a. Prepares district budget and continuously reviews budget status.

    b. Supervises use of district "incidental" funds and other special allotments.

Within each of these categories, the District Supervisor must follow procedures outlined in the departmental policy handbook and must work closely with other appropriate officials. In addition, the *Job Manual* describes the following responsibilities for this position:

    Attends conferences, workshops, and training sessions; prepares reports as requested by Assistant Director of Program and Facilities.

    Assumes supervision of additional areas during the absence of other District Supervisors.

    Supervises the assigning of substitutes for recreation areas, and coordinates the hiring, assigning, orientation, and supervision of Student Workers, Neighborhood Youth Corps Workers, and other special aides in district.

    Cooperates with Co-op Nurseries using recreation areas in district.

    Checks with "What's New," the departmental newsletter twice each month for accuracy and policy matters.

The Program Supervisor must also carry out a wide range of daily or weekly responsibilities related to receiving and acting on memoranda and requests; verifying and reviewing reports of income, time sheets and overtime reports; submitting publicity items; submitting employee evaluations and reports on seasonal programs; meeting with various departmental groups; and carrying out other, similar responsibilities.[6]

In addition to positions that are formally designated by the title of "supervisor," many recreation and park positions that are actually supervisory in nature may have other job titles. For example, in the organizational chart of the Tuscaloosa County, Alabama, Park and Recreation Board (Fig. 10–1), job titles include Athletic and Program Supervisor, Area Supervisor and Park Maintenance Supervisor. Other positions that involve supervisory functions have titles such as "director" or "center director," "specialist" or "coordinator." In each case, the individual is responsible either for overseeing a major unit of program service or a specific operational function or facility, or for directing the work of other subordinate employees. In other types of recreation organizations, such as voluntary agencies or therapeutic recreation settings, the terms "director" or "division head" may be used instead of "supervisor." However, the functions are likely to be essentially the same.

Supervisors Viewed as Middle Management

In a broad sense, supervision must be viewed as a somewhat lower, "action-oriented" level of management or administration. For the past several decades, business administrators have sought to have supervisors trained and officially recognized as representatives of management.

> Practically every supervisory training program emphasizes this fact. The National Labor-Management Relations Act recognizes the foreman as management's representative, and under this Act management is not required to recognize a union of foremen. The supervisor not only *represents* management to the men, but to the average employee the supervisor *is* the company. . .[7]

Because of their position midway between top management and line personnel, supervisors in effect share responsibilities of both groups. They work closely with administrators on policies, strategies, plans for budget development, major program development, facilities acquisition and similar departmental functions. At the same time, many authorities regard them as having a "secondary leadership" function, in which they supplement the work of primary leaders, assisting and guiding them, and acting as a helping person, counselor, problem-solver and, at times, a co-worker. This middle management role is described in the following terms:

> In the administrative process, the forces of leadership flow upwards, downwards, and sideways, and all lines of communication meet in the middle; in many respects, therefore, middle managers are the key people

---

[6]*Job Manual.* Long Beach, California, Department of Recreation, 1974.
[7]Spriegel, Schulz and Spriegel, *op. cit.,* p. 42.

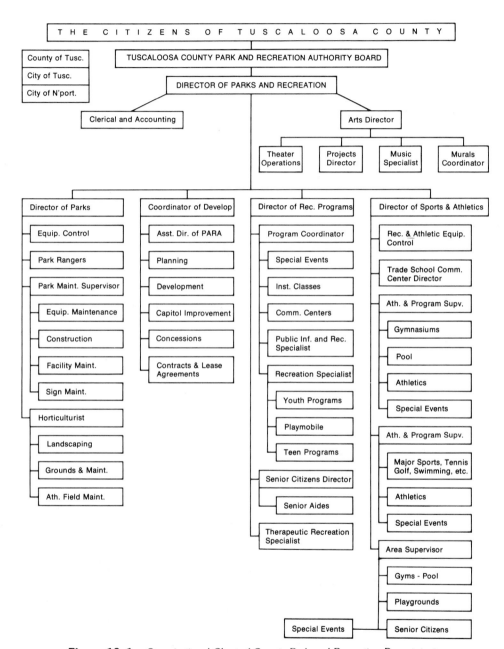

Figure 10-1. *Organizational Chart of County Park and Recreation Department.*

in administration. It is they who transmit orders, decisions, and guidance from the top down, and in turn, communicate problems, difficulties, viewpoints, complaints, and suggestions from the lower ranks to the top.[8]

Personnel Management Function

The most important single responsibility of supervisors is generally considered to be personnel management. Although we refer to individuals serving as supervisors of programs or facilities, their key role is as supervisors of *people!* The art of building creative and effective human relationships is at the heart of successful supervision. Specifically, the supervisor is called upon to do the following:

1. To regularly observe the performance of line personnel, and to provide technical assistance in helping them solve problems and carry out their assignments more effectively.
2. To provide leadership, in the sense of acting as a spokesperson for the organization and as a builder of incentives and positive motivation.
3. To act as a trainer and teacher of subordinates, both in formal training programs and in day-by-day contacts.
4. To help to resolve conflicts that may exist among personnel and to build cooperation and teamwork among them.
5. To help line personnel realistically understand their own strengths and weaknesses and work consciously toward improving their overall performance.
6. To serve as a key official in personnel administration, enforcing or communicating departmental regulations or policies, and assisting employees with respect to personnel requests such as leaves, vacations, reassignments or similar matters.
7. To make recommendations with respect to promotions, demotions, transfers or special job assignments.
8. To evaluate the overall performance of personnel, for use in service ratings and other departmental decisions.

It is essential that supervisors have technical competence, in the sense of knowing *how* the job is to be done accurately and efficiently. However, it is also necessary that they be able to operate within a total framework of intelligent, comtemporary philosophy that provides a sound basis for judgment and logical decision-making.

PHILOSOPHY OF EFFECTIVE SUPERVISION

Supervision, viewed primarily as the process of personnel management, has obviously developed a substantial body of literature during the past several

---

[8]Marshall E. Dimock and Gladys O. Dimock: *Public Administration.* New York, Holt, Rinehart and Winston, 1969, p. 350.

decades. Principles have been developed relating to structural patterns of administration and supervision, such as the "staff and line" concept, according to which those employees who are directly concerned with the delivery of service are known as "line" personnel, while those who assist them as planners, researchers, consultants and so forth are "staff" personnel.

A number of similar concepts of staff relationships and functions, such as "span of control," "unity of command," "delegation of authority," "chain of command" and the "scalar principle," generally describe how responsibilities are assigned within a department and how authority is exercised. Such principles are described in detail in other texts on recreation and park administration or on public administration in general, and will not be presented here.[9] Instead, emphasis here is given to alternative approaches to supervision. Dimock and Dimock describe three common models of supervisors:

> The *bureaucratic* type has a passion for detail, for reducing every aspect of his job to systems and minutely prescribed procedures: this man is tied to his desk and rarely has a chance to think beyond the demands of his daily schedule. The *crisis* type has more energy but seems to reserve it for crises and "drives," which he often deliberately arranges. Almost invariably he lacks judgment and the capacity to plan ahead. . . . Finally, the *strategic* type delegates as much detailed supervision as he can, plans his "drives" to synchronize with the rest of the work, and reserves his best energies for innovation and planning for the future.[10]

In general, the most effective supervisors are those who, as in the "strategic" model, have good judgment, plan ahead, work toward tangible goals and are able to motivate others to perform to their highest capacity. They are skillful in using group methods of supervision to build cohesive work groups with high performance goals, based on many of the principles of group dynamics that were described in Chapter Four.

The process of successful supervision involves several key elements. First, supervisors must be sharply aware of their objectives and those of their organizations, and must make every effort to work efficiently toward these. Second, they must concentrate on improving motivation and releasing the "will to work" of their subordinates. Third, they must make effective use of communication at all times, in order to improve their relationships with other staff members and to strengthen overall departmental performance. Fourth, they must develop specific techniques that are useful in directing and overseeing work performance. Fifth, they must be able to exert sufficient discipline and control (when needed), to compel adherence to the rules and practices of their organizations, to give reprimands when necessary and to deal with employee complaints and grievances. Sixth, they must be skillful in observing other employees at work and in making judgments regarding their

---

[9]See, for example, Richard Kraus and Joseph Curtis: *Creative Administration in Recreation and Parks.* St. Louis, C. V. Mosby, 1977, pp. 15–34.
[10]Dimock and Dimock, *op. cit.*, p. 352.

performance that will provide the basis for continuous counseling and guidance designed to improve their work.

Managing by Objectives

A frequently expressed principle is that managers must learn to "administer by objectives." The purpose of this approach is to define clearly and express all of the objectives of a department or agency. When objectives are understood and accepted by all staff members, it is possible to place less reliance on mechanical rules, procedural manuals and detailed instructions—which often tend to make an organization bureaucratic, sluggish and lacking in innovation. Instead, authority can be more freely delegated to a wide mix of staff members who have the right to make decisions at lower levels of responsibility.

To be meaningful, objectives cannot be determined solely by the departmental administrator or supervisor and then presented to employees. If this is done, employees will not necessarily understand or accept the objectives. Instead, all employees should be consulted and should participate in the development of objectives. Such discussions should extend to the best ways of achieving objectives—the most useful and effective techniques of working, organizing programs and delegating responsibility.

Glover suggests that in park and recreation departments, objectives are established at four hierarchical levels: *Level 1,* the top level, represented by the agency's director or department head; *Level 2,* the divisional level, represented by the recreation division director or parks division director; *Level 3,* the unit level, represented by various unit heads within the two divisions; and *Level 4,* the staff level, consisting of staff personnel working within their respective units. Broad, departmentwide objectives are established at Level 1. These in turn are translated into more specific divisional objectives at Level 2. It is at Level 3, the unit level, that the objectives are made more concrete and that supervisors may share meaningfully in the setting of goals. Glover writes:

> Management by Objectives (MBO) is one example of an increasingly popular management concept that has improved efficiency and organization in various types of private and public sector organizations, and which should prove to be similarly useful in the sophisticated new leisure service organizations.[11]

He concludes by providing several suggested guidelines for effective use of the MBO approach: (a) objectives must be quantified (that is, stated in measurable rather than general terms); (b) time limits should be established for all objectives; (c) staff members should be involved in setting their own goals; (d) there should be a limited number of objectives for each individual

---

[11]James M. Glover: "MBO: A Tool for Leisure Service Management." *Parks and Recreation,* March 1979, p. 26.

or administrative unit, focusing on critical tasks, rather than too many; (e) objectives must be realistic and attainable; and (f) objectives, once established, should be used as the basis for later efforts at evaluation.

Realistically speaking, if this approach—which has been enthusiastically supported by many authorities in personnel management—is to work, the key agent in carrying it out is the supervisor. His or her tact, judgment and skill in involving personnel in defining objectives and agreeing on work approaches are essential for team success.

Freeing the Will to Work

A traditional view of the supervisor's role was that he or she was an overseer, a sort of grim, coercive boss who had to watch constantly over other employees to make sure that they were not loafing and that they stayed on the job. It is often assumed that financial reward is the only important source of motivation—that employees work for an organization chiefly for pay. Although this may be true of many people who do not enjoy their work or who lack a sense of self-realization or meaningful involvement in it, it is not true of all forms of employment or job situations. Stahl points out that factors other than pay loom larger in personnel motivations:

> In an affluent society with a high minimum standard of "creature comfort," pay is rarely the number one motivator. Research studies time and again have shown that in public service and industrial environments in the United States pay usually ranks second or third, and sometimes lower, on a scale of morale factors. Ahead of it . . . are such factors as credit and recognition, challenging work, a congenial work group, freedom for decision-making, security of tenure, fair and equal opportunity for advancement, and the quality of supervision.[12]

Morale should then be regarded as a key factor in whether or not individuals in any work setting are highly motivated and able to be fully productive. Morale has been defined as the capacity of a group to pull together persistently and steadily in pursuit of common goals. It is based very heavily on the confidence that individual members of a group have in their leadership and in each other, the degree of support they give to the group's goals and the extent to which the group has been efficiently organized to carry out its work functions. Probably the key factor in achieving favorable motivation is whether or not the basic emotional needs of workers are being met. As suggested earlier, they must have a strong sense of security, of success based on achievement and recognition, and of belonging.

Workers respond favorably to supervisors who consult with them frequently, who have high standards of performance and who evidence concern for their welfare. The landmark study in the field of human relations in work settings was the experiment carried out at the Hawthorne plant of the Western

---

[12]O. Glenn Stahl: *Public Personnel Administration*. New York, Harper and Row, 1962, p. 199.

Electric Company in Chicago, beginning in the late 1920's.[13] This research revealed that, more than any other factor, the motivation and productivity of employees was improved when they were given the feeling of being important, of not being "bossed" arbitrarily, of being consulted and cared about. In terms of encouraging the will to work, the physical factors of the work environment were not as important as the emotional climate. Horney sums up the point:

> The improvement of working conditions, raising salaries or shuffling work assignments alone will not motivate employees. The motivating factors that are intrinsic to the employee's job assignment are: achievement, recognition for achievement, the work itself, responsibility and advancement.[14]

This concept is based on the views of McGregor, Herzberg, Maslow, McClelland and a number of other social psychologists who studied personality in its relation to work and other forms of achievement and self-actualization. For example, McGregor outlined two theories, X and Y, which depicted traditional and contemporary assumptions about workers and work attitudes.

According to Theory X, the average human being has an inherent dislike of work and will avoid it if possible. Because of this attitude, most people must be coerced, controlled, directed and threatened with punishment to put forth adequate work efforts. Beyond this, Theory X concluded that the average individual prefers to be directed, wishes to avoid responsibility, has relatively little ambition and wants security above all. This approach was the basis for older organizational policies and procedures in personnel management, which treated workers in an authoritarian, rigid fashion.

In contrast, Theory Y holds that people in general do not dislike work, and that for many, work is a source of real satisfaction. Accepting this, it is not necessary to rely on external control or the threat of punishment to make people work; instead, they will exercise self-direction and self-control in the pursuit of objectives to which they are committed. If they regard work goals as meaningful and challenging, people will not only accept but will seek responsibility. Finally, Theory Y holds that the ability to exercise imagination and creativity in solving departmental problems is widely, not narrowly, distributed in the population.[15]

Herzberg points out that we have typically believed that the only way in which workers could be motivated was to improve the work environment or to increase work rewards. The potential motivating power of work was limited by the fact that many jobs were not at all stimulating or challenging, and

---

[13]Descriptions of this study have appeared in many social psychology texts. A useful summary appears in Stuart Chase: *Men at Work*. New York, Harcourt, Brace, and World, Inc., 1941, Chapter Two.
[14]Robert L. Horney: "Administration by Motivation." *Parks and Recreation*, August 1968, p. 15.
[15]See Douglas MacGregor: *The Human Side of Enterprise*. New York, McGraw-Hill Book Co., 1960.

therefore external pressure—either positive or negative—was needed to get people to perform them, almost as an unpleasant necessity. However, Herzberg points out that it was necessary to improve the motivation of workers by enhancing their feelings of accomplishment, professional growth and recognition and by offering jobs with sufficient challenge and scope. His analysis focused on job design. Pointing out that most jobs in modern industry were designed primarily from the standpoint of efficiency and economy, he stressed that it was necessary to "enrich" jobs to make them more appealing and interesting, and that this could be done without loss of productivity or greater cost.[16]

Another who contributed to the growing body of theory supporting a new philosophy of personnel management was Abraham Maslow, who developed a hierarchy of human needs that led to "self-actualization," or fullest realization of one's potential. Within this framework, work provided an important means of meeting human needs for physiological maintenance (shelter, food and clothing), social or belonging needs (social involvement in work groups), esteem (titles, status or other recognition), and finally self-actualization (sense of achievement, competence and creativity).[17]

A final behavioral scientist who explored the concept of "achievement motive" was McClelland, who suggested that this drive was extremely important in work accomplishment. Although he identified a class, representing about 10 per cent of the overall population, that has a strong achievement motive, he also concluded that there are considerable untapped reserves of achievement motivation in many organizations. To realize these reserves, McClelland suggested that it was necessary to build more "achievement characteristics" into more jobs by providing personal responsibility, individual participation in developing job targets, attainable goals and quick, easily recognizable feedback on each employee's accomplishments. Although highly specific directions and goals are not necessary, McClelland indicated that if the job does not provide its own feedback mechanism regarding the worker's performance, it is important that supervisors or other administrative workers give frank, detailed appraisals of how well the worker is performing on the job.[18]

These theories of personnel management have had a considerable impact on supervisory approaches in many business, governmental and recreational agencies. Although it would be incorrect to say that all administrators and supervisors today accept this philosophy of management, there is widespread recognition that the traditional approach of the "carrot or stick" style of supervision is no longer acceptable, and new forms of supervisor–worker relationships that promote a high level of job motivation and effective performance must be established.

---

[16]Frederick Herzberg. Cited in Edginton and Williams, *op. cit.*, pp. 84–87.

[17]Abraham H. Maslow: *Motivation and the Personality.* New York, Harper and Row, 1954.

[18]David C. McClelland: "That Urge to Achieve." In David Hampton (ed.): *Behavioral Concepts in Management.* Belmont, Cal., Dickenson Co., 1972.

Communication Process

One of the key factors in establishing constructive relationships between supervisors and line personnel, and in promoting favorable "team" attitudes, is effective communication. Too often, people are unable to communicate their feelings, ideas and wishes and, although they think they are making themselves clear, are not actually doing so. Effective communication is essential in all staff development and supervisory processes.

Communication involves far more than the transmission of verbal or written messages. It is a basic tool of understanding, agreement, discussion and decision-making within any organization. Horney points out that faulty communication is responsible for most human relation breakdowns, and that when it is not corrected, rumors develop, staff efficiency drops and frustrations, mistrust, insecurity and fear result. Stahl sums up the following important elements of communication:

1. Communication—oral and written—is the lifeblood of an enterprise. It is the means by which human beings work together.
2. Communication is a two-way process. Employees should know the goals of the organization, why management is proceeding the way it is, what changes are in the works. Management should know what employees are thinking and feeling, what ideas they have to get the job done.
3. Communication involves *receiving* and *understanding* as well as *telling*. Words, ideas, or proposals do not always mean the same thing to the receiver and the transmitter. A breakdown in understanding can occur because the communicator does not put himself in the other fellow's shoes. . . .
4. Normally, the more freedom and encouragement given to self-expression and the more care taken to provide people with the reasons for action, the less communication difficulty there will be.
5. Good communication is an essential concomitant of delegation of authority and reliance on the good sense and good intentions of the staff. Along with participation, it is the "stuff" of the decision-making process.[19]

Within traditional administrative theory, a number of basic principles of effective communication were established. Barnard, for example, developed the following rules based on administrative practice: (a) the channels of communication must be definitely known; (b) a formal channel of communication must extend to every member of the organization, and it must be as direct and short as possible; (c) the lines of communication should generally be respected (people should communicate through formal channels); and (d) lines of communication should not be interrupted during exchanges, and every communication should be authenticated or confirmed.[20] These some-

---

[19]Stahl, *op. cit.*, p. 211.
[20]Chester Barnard: *The Function of the Executive.* Cambridge, Massachusetts, Harvard Business School, 1938, pp. 175–180.

what formal and limited approaches to communication have gradually been expanded into a broader understanding of communication as a process that is greatly affected by the previous experiences and expectations of the parties involved, the methods used to communicate, the language used and the emotional tone of the exchange. Dooher and Marquis have developed a set of guidelines that should be helpful to supervisors in improving their communicative skills:

1. *Seek to clarify your ideas before communicating.* The more systematically we analyze the problem or idea to be communicated, the clearer it becomes. . . . Management communications commonly fail because of inadequate planning. Good planning must consider the goals and attitudes of those who will receive the communication and those who will be affected by it.

2. *Examine the true purpose of each communication.* Before you communicate, ask yourself what you *really* want to accomplish with your message—obtain information, initiate action, change another person's attitude? Identify your most important goal and then adapt your language, tone, and total approach to serve that specific objective. Don't try to accomplish too much with each communication. . . ,

3. *Consider the total physical and human setting whenever you communicate.* Meaning and intent are conveyed by more than words alone. . . .

4. *Consult with others, where appropriate, in planning communications.* Frequently it is desirable or necessary to seek the participation of others in planning a communication or developing the facts on which to base it. Such consultation often helps to lend additional insight and objectivity to your message. Moreover, those who have helped plan your communication will give it their active support.

5. *Be mindful, while you communicate, of the overtones as well as the basic content of your message.* Your tone of voice, your expression, your apparent receptiveness to the responses of others—all have tremendous impact on those you wish to reach. . . .

6. *Take the opportunity, when it arises, to convey something of help or value to the receiver.* Consideration of the other person's interests and needs—the habit of trying to look at things from his point of view—will frequently point up opportunities to convey something of immediate benefit or long-range value to him. . . .

7. *Follow-up your communication.* Our best efforts at communication may be wasted, and we may never know whether we have succeeded in expressing our true meaning and intent, if we do not follow-up . . . by asking questions, by encouraging the receiver to express his reactions, by . . . subsequent review of performance. . . .

8. *Communicate for tomorrow as well as today.* While communications may be aimed primarily at meeting the demands of an immediate situation, they must be planned with the past in mind if they are to maintain consistency in the receiver's view; but, most of all, they must be consistent with long-range interests and goals. . . .

9. *Be sure your actions support your communication.* In the final analysis, the most persuasive kind of communication is not what you say but what you do. When a man's actions or attitudes contradict his

words, we tend to discount what he has said—and perhaps to view it as an attempt to mislead us.

10. *Seek not only to be understood but to understand—be a good listener.* When we start talking we often cease to listen—in the larger sense of being attuned to the other person's unspoken reactions and attitudes. . . . Listening is one of the most important, most difficult— and most neglected—skills in communication. . . .[21]

Directing Work Performance

One of the key responsibilities of the supervisor in recreation and park agencies is the task of organizing and assigning work to subordinate employees. The International City Manager's Association's guidelines for effective supervisory practices suggest that supervisors need to think in advance about *what* shall be done, *how* it shall be done, and by *whom, when, where* and *why.* It is essential that work directions be precise and clear, involve a reasonable level of accomplishment and give the employee receiving them the opportunity to use judgment or initiative in carrying them out. Directions may be given in several forms:

> Commands or orders, which are usually used only when there is some immediate danger or urgency, or when an employee has been lax or insubordinate about carrying out assignments.
>
> Requests, which are the most appropriate form of direction for routine work. Often these are put in the form of a question, like, "Would you be able to get the bleachers set up by this afternoon?" These are generally as explicit as commands, but give the subordinate worker some input and show some fuller respect for his role.
>
> Suggestions, which permit the worker flexibility in carrying out the assignment, are particularly useful when he is more knowledgeable than the supervisor about how it should be done. However, not all employees will respond favorably to them, and they should be used only with workers who consistently show their responsibility and initiative.
>
> Volunteer directions, in which the supervisor asks for subordinates to volunteer to carry out an assignment, tend to be used only when there are assignments that are difficult, dangerous or disagreeable, or beyond the normal range of job expectations. They should therefore be used sparingly.[22]

After work directions have been given, supervisors should attempt to follow up to determine whether they are being carried out properly. Without actually hanging over the employee's shoulder in a threatening or repressive way, the supervisor should review the assignment at an early point in order to determine whether the directions have been understood and the work

---

[21]M. Joseph Dooher and Vivienne Marquis, eds.: *Effective Communication on the Job.* New York, American Management Association, 1956, pp. 21–23.

[22]Robert E. Bouton: *Effective Supervisory Practices.* Washington, D.C., International City Management Association, 1971, Bulletin 1, "The Supervisor Looks at His Job," p. 3.

performed properly. If not, the supervisor should consider (a) whether the directions were not clear, (b) whether the task itself was too difficult or unreasonable, or (c) whether the employee simply had not carried it out with sufficient effort and understanding. In general, as the supervisor learns that a given employee carries out routine tasks successfully, less supervisory follow-up will be called for.

Several devices or techniques usually are used to review performance in a systematic way. These include the following:

1. *Direct inspection of the program or other work situation* is the best way of getting information about how assignments are being carried out.
2. *Measurement of work output* through quantitative procedures, such as measurement of attendance, games played, sessions held or similar elements.
3. *Reports from employees, advisory groups or program participants.* These may be written or oral.
4. *Flow charts,* or other forms of "production measurement" devices, in which the specific steps needed to carry out an assignment or develop a project are outlined, along with deadlines for each step of the process.
5. *Employee diaries or project books.* Some organizations require employees to keep track of their time and tasks accomplished by maintaining personal record books showing their schedules. In general, this method has not been used in municipal government, where it smacks of a "time-clock" approach. However, organizations such as the United States Forest Service have used individual field diaries as techniques for reviewing the work of field supervisors.

In general, the most useful approach, as suggested here, is direct observation of the employee at work. This, in turn, provides not only information about the immediate work being done in response to supervisory directions but also general information that will be useful in staff conferences and meetings.

Maintaining Control and Dealing with Problems

Just as the playground leader or other fact-to-face recreation leader must be prepared to maintain control and proper behavior among recreation participants in a group situation, so must the supervisor expect from subordinate employees a level of responsible compliance with departmental policies. If this level is not met satisfactorily, it is the supervisor's responsibility to apply needed disciplinary action. Discipline, positively conceived, means that workers are aware of the right and wrong ways of doing a job, have good work attitudes and conform to departmental expectations and regulations. If this is not the case, the supervisor should attempt to determine why there is a problem, rather than automatically assume that the worker is at fault.

The first question to be asked in reviewing a problem of inadequate employee performance is, "Was the individual's responsibility clearly assigned, and did he or she know how to carry it out?" Through organization charts, job descritpions, flow charts showing work processes, procedural manuals and orientation and in-service training, staff members should be fully aware of their responsibilities. The supervisor should have made clear to the leader or other employees how specific tasks were to be performed. Departmental policy statements or manuals should also make absolutely clear the rules regarding work performance, hours of work, behavior on the job, use of department vehicles, handling of money, drinking and similar concerns.

If, despite these factors, employees have continued to perform inadequately or to disregard or fail to live up to personnel regulations, the supervisor should attempt to determine *why*. A number of factors may be responsible. In some cases, workers fail to do the job properly because of boredom, lack of interest in the work, inadequate supervision, unclear directions or poor communications. In such situations, the supervisor should attempt to remedy the situation by getting at the specific causes of difficulty.

Often, disciplinary problems occur because of friction between or among groups of employees. If this cannot be solved through the supervisor's intervention and team meetings devoted to improving staff relations, it may be necessary to reassign workers to other job settings. In some cases, when it is apparent that an employee is emotionally disturbed, the supervisor should set up personal counseling sessions to give whatever assistance is possible. If the problem is a severe one, the department's administrator or personnel director should be advised of it, and the possibility of recommending that the individual seek skilled counseling or psychological help should be considered.

When, despite these efforts, disciplinary problems continue, the supervisor has a responsibility to act. Many departments have guidelines that suggest procedures to follow; for instance, when an employee has failed to perform adequately over a period of time or has broken departmental regulations, the supervisor should plan to meet with the individual, not with the automatic intention of imposing a penalty, but rather with the purpose of attempting to improve the worker's behavior and work attitudes. Specific guidelines would include the following:

1. Arrange for a private meeting in a location where the discussion will not be heard by other employees.
2. Try first to get all the pertinent facts. Begin with a question or series of questions that will give the employee the opportunity to give his or her side of the case rather than starting immediately with criticism or accusations.
3. Maintain your own calm, regardless of the employee's behavior. Never lose your temper, become impatient or angry, or "bawl out" the employee.
4. Face the issue by outlining clearly the problem as you see it rather than skirting around it. Make sure that the employee has a chance

to know the full extent of the problem as it is viewed by management and to respond to it completely.

5. If the problem is fairly simple and the solution self-evident, action may be taken immediately in the form of a reprimand, set of suggestions or other supervisory action.

6. If the problem is more complex, the supervisor may suggest that a second meeting be held to explore the problem further. This may give him or her the opportunity to consult with other departmental administrators or personnel officers.

7. Whatever action is taken, close the meeting as pleasantly and positively as possible, making an effort to restore the employee's self-confidence, if necessary.

Possible actions to be taken in the case of serious employee infractions or poor job performance include the following: (a) *warnings*, either written or oral, which tell the worker that his or her behavior or job performance must improve, or other action will be taken; (b) formal *reprimands*, which inform a worker of the serious nature of failure to perform or violation of departmental rules and warn that more serious action may be taken; (c) *fines, assignment to overtime work, reassignment* to other duties or various forms of *demerits;* (d) *loss of seniority* rights or *negative service ratings;* (e) *suspension without pay* for a set period of time or subject to a hearing before a personnel board or review by top management; (f) *demotion or discharge,* with continuing disqualifications for re-employment; and (g) most serious of all, *judicial prosecution,* which obviously would be applied only to misbehavior involving criminal action.

Although it is desirable to avoid the more serious kinds of punitive action, in some cases there is no choice and it becomes necessary to suspend or discharge an employee. At this point, the possibility of a grievance procedure should be considered and the effect of the union contract and possible intervention by the union reviewed. Usually, at this level of concern, problems of appeals, grievance procedures or lawsuits become the responsibility of departmental personnel officers rather than of the supervisor.

Supervisory Conferences

In general, supervisors attempt to forestall such problems by carrying out a continuing process of employee observation and conferences that are intended to maximize job output and improve staff morale, motivation and relationships, Typically, supervisors seek to *avoid* grievances and difficulties by keeping on the lookout for lack of enthusiasm for the job or department; excessive complaints; lateness, loafing, absenteeism or excessive short-term illness; an abundance of errors on the job; or a marked decline in work output or efficiency.

When such situations occur, the supervisor should deal with them by speaking with employees as frequently as possible, trying to know them as individuals and improving communications with them. He or she should examine working conditions, review work assignments, be alert to staff relationships and consider other possible causes of difficulty.

Such conferences fall into several categories: (a) initial meetings with new employees; (b) individual conferences between supervisor and subordinate worker, which may be held at regular intervals or may be specially requested by either party; (c) group conferences, in which several employees meet with a supervisor to discuss staff progress and problems; and (d) evaluation conferences, which are held for the specific purpose of reviewing the worker's performance.

Such conferences should contain a number of important elements. They should be viewed as sessions in which the job itself and the work setting are examined in a constructive but analytical way. The employee should feel free to make suggestions in these sessions—or question why certain procedures or policies are followed—and to make alternative suggestions for other approaches. They should involve teaching, when appropriate, in the sense that the supervisor helps subordinate employees review their own work and shows them how certain tasks can be accomplished more effectively. They should include personal counseling in areas of job attitudes, relations with other workers or similar matters that are within the reasonable range of the supervisor's capability and judgment. Finally, the sessions should represent an opportunity for the supervisor to act as the "middle-management" employee mentioned earlier, in order to relay administrative concerns or directives to the employee and to transmit the employee's views and suggestions to higher administrators.

At all times in such conferences, the supervisor should attempt to be courteous, friendly and cheerful, and to show respect for the individual employee and his or her opinions. The supervisor should seek to develop a spirit of shared concern and responsibility, a tension-free atmosphere and a sense of confidence on the part of the employee that both the supervisor and the department he or she represents have confidence in the employee and want to work to help him or her become as effective and successful a worker as possible.

Only within such a framework can supervisors use conferences to their maximum benefit to improve employee performance and achieve departmental goals.

Guidelines for Supervisory Action

Summing up this chapter, the following guidelines represent a total approach to effective supervision. The successful supervisor observes these guidelines:

1. Establishes high but attainable expectations for staff in terms of work standards and goals, and makes sure that these are designed to achieve the goals of the department itself.
2. Places staff members in jobs in which their individual abilities are most likely to be fully utilized.

3. Recognizes the universal need for approval, and helps staff members meet this need by (a) bestowing credit and praising accomplishments, (b) showing consideration toward staff members, and (c) acknowledging their share in the total enterprise and their contribution in making it a success.
4. Seeks to help staff members become more effective, and removes obstacles to success by providing technical assistance and emotional support.
5. Avoids ego-threatening behavior, and uses the mistakes of subordinates as a basis for counseling and improving performance rather than as an opportunity for threats and punishment.
6. Clearly defines the responsibilities and accountability of staff members and shows confidence in their ability to carry out these tasks.
7. Encourages staff members to participate in policy-planning, decision-making and program development, not as a "token" gesture but with serious weight being given to their contributions.
8. Exercises leadership when necessary, asserting rank, making decisions and exerting force to achieve departmental goals.
9. Is an effective link between management and leadership, communicating information helpful to their psychological well-being and morale and to their awareness of total departmental developments.
10. Appraises employees on the basis of objective and measurable performance elements, taking into account differences in the qualities of individual workers and different levels of task difficulty.
11. Does not play favorites, but seeks to reward all workers equally and to provide tangible rewards and status symbols, particularly for high-level performance.
12. Is friendly, sympathetic and approachable, yet also maintains a sense of dignity based on the rank he or she has been assigned and the authority vested by the department.

According to Engle, those who are able to develop new products and programs, generate action and move enterprises forward possess the following characteristics: (a) a drive for dominance and the need to excel; (b) self-reliance and the willingness to accept responsibility and make decisions; (c) creativity and the ability to implement good ideas; (d) strong self-concept and confidence in own judgment and standards; (e) openness to diverse friends and to current events and new developments; (f) the drive to accomplish and the willingness to take risks; (g) intelligence, although not necessarily the kind measured by IQ tests; and (h) tact, persuasiveness and humor, as well as the ability to overcome resistance to change.[23]

---

[23]Peter H. Engle: "Movers and Doers: Anatomy of a Successful Manager." *TWA Ambassador*, October 1977, pp. 55–56.

SUPERVISORY SELF-MANAGEMENT

Finally, the effective supervisor must be able to manage himself or herself in order to be as productive and well-organized on the job as possible. Most recreation and park supervisors are required to work on a number of different programs at the same time, coordinating the work of many employees with different types of job specialties and cooperating with other municipal departments or commununity agencies. Clearly, this can be a difficult assignment, and it is not at all unusual for individuals who have been highly successful on the leadership level to discover that supervision poses many frustrations and problems for them.

In part, the problem is one of organizing one's own time, developing a workable set of immediate and long-range goals and concentrating on major responsibilities rather than wasting effort and time on unimportant or extraneous tasks. The Boys' Clubs of America have published a set of guidelines for effective self-management that are intended to assist their professional employees.[24] The following suggestions are drawn from these guidelines. The guidelines recognize that many individuals on the supervisory level find difficulty in overcoming inertia and in using their time most profitably.

Twenty Ways to Get Things Done

1. *Make a list of things to do, and cross off each item as you do it.* Crossing off an item when you complete it shows that progress has been made, and also calls attention to tasks still to be done.
2. *Keep the work you have to do right in front of you.* This helps to eliminate competing distractions. Instead of having four projects on your desk at once, clear away everything except the one task that should be done first.
3. *Break tasks down into segments.* If a task is particularly long or laborious, break it down into segments and tackle them one at a time; that way, it can be handled by stages and will not appear to be too overwhelming.
4. *Have an effective reminder system.* Develop a self-reminder system of events, deadlines and tasks to be accomplished, and keep these notes in a place where they can be regularly checked.
5. *Be decisive.* Once you have all the facts on a given matter, take action on it. Don't bother to worry about whether or not your decision was the best possible one; move on to other tasks.

---

[24]Adapted from "20 Ways to Get Things Done." In *National Orientation Program Manual*, New York, Boys' Clubs of America, 1973.

6. *Don't exaggerate a job's difficulties in advance.* Avoid building up all the problems in a given assignment beforehand, and you will find it easier to get at it and to carry it out successfully.

7. *Don't overplan.* Although it is necessary to plan carefully for each new project or task, excessive planning may be an excuse for not taking action. It is like the writer who keeps doing research and avoids getting down to writing.

8. *Set specific time limits for tasks.* Be definite, rather than vague, about when projects should be undertaken and completed. If there are several activities to be done, put them in a time sequence based on their order of priority, their possible deadlines and the degree and kinds of work it will take to carry them out.

9. *Don't be a perfectionist.* If you expect yourself to do everything perfectly, you may avoid new challenges for fear of failing. Although your standards should be high, they should also be realistic, and should recognize that you, like others, have the right to make mistakes.

10. *Strengthen your weak points.* Recognize your areas of weakness or performance skills in which you lack confidence. Concentrate on improving your skills in these areas.

11. *Know when you work best.* Many people function differently at different times of the day. Analyze your own energy, alertness and "ups and downs" throughout the day, and plan your most demanding tasks for the times when you will be best able to meet them.

12. *Learn to say "No."* When you are able to make a choice, avoid taking on commitments that you would rather not have or that are not essential.

13. *Listen attentively.* Avoid errors, backtracking and repetition by getting pertinent information right the first time.

14. *Do it now.* Many people put off getting started by sharpening pencils, day-dreaming or window gazing. Avoid procrastination—use your working time to the fullest.

15. *Seek short-cuts.* This does not mean to "skimp" on doing a job right, but rather looking for the most effective and efficient way to carry out an assignment, no matter how it was done in the past.

16. *Anticipate.* Look forward to the next day and make sure that all necessary arrangements have been made. Keep extra change, keys, eyeglasses and stamps in your office, and in other ways eliminate minor frustrations that waste time and energy.

17. *Make fullest use of time.* Use travel time and similar periods to think out problems, read reports, make plans or jot down ideas for future implementation.

18. *Vary your activities on the job.* Many jobs become tedious because of repetition. It is best to alternate tasks in order to fight off fatigue and keep mentally alert. Most supervisors do not have to worry about this; their jobs are seldom boring.

19. *Get an early start.* Many supervisors find that they can get a great deal of paper work and planning out of the way by starting early in the day, before distractions and other job demands begin.

20. *Gain a healthy respect for your own time.* Recognize that your time is an immensely valuable asset; use it as fruitfully as possible.

In a similar analysis, Simpson urges that managers map their work patterns, set their priorities and then take control of their habits. If necessary, they must learn to delegate responsibilities more fully, eliminate time-wasting or unproductive jobs, group activities to gain momentum and maximize effectiveness, develop new work habits and even concentrate on improving essential skills through study techniques like speed-reading, in order to accomplish work successfully.[25]

These guidelines would, of course, be helpful to administrative or management personnel in many types of job settings. They are particularly relevant to recreation and park supervisors who, at the same time they are responsible for the work of others, must also be responsible for themselves.

SUGGESTED EXAMINATION QUESTIONS OR TOPICS FOR STUDENT REPORTS

1. Make a case for the argument that the supervisor, rather than the leader or administrator, represents the key level for effective delivery of service in recreation and parks.

2. Select one type of supervisor from those presented in the text, and prepare a detailed statement of functions and responsibilities, based on job descriptions, observations and interviews.

3. It has been pointed out that personnel management is a major aspect of supervision today. Outline a detailed philosophy of modern supervision, with emphasis on such personnel-related concerns as freeing the will to work, management by objectives, improving communication and counseling employees. Base this on the literature in this field as much as possible.

---

[25]B. G. Simpson: "Effective Time Management." *Parks and Recreation*, September 1978, pp. 61–63.

SUGGESTED ACTION ASSIGNMENTS OR GROUP PROCESS ACTIVITIES

1. Interview a recreation supervisor and do a detailed breakdown of his or her functions within a given season or program area. Determine the areas in which the individual feels he or she is performing successfully and those in which he or she is experiencing difficulty. Develop a set of recommendations to improve performance in the latter areas.

2. Although you may not be a supervisor at present, do an analysis of your own "self-management" performance, based on the guidelines at the end of this chapter. Carry this on systematically for a week, and report your findings. How do you measure up? What can you do about it?

3. Write a paper describing your personal philosophy of supervision, and show how it is compatible with your general philosophy of human relationships and your past and present recreational and work experiences. Explore the ways in which you might expect your philosophy to change as you move into a supervisory position. Finally, discuss how effective your approach might be within an actual work situation.

4. Examine your own value system in relation to McGregor's Theory X and Theory Y by responding to the questions on pages 290–291 and discussing them with your classmates.

Supervisory Roles in Program and Facility Management

Chapter Eleven

Chapter Ten dealt with the overall process of supervision in recreation and park agencies, and with the philosophy that underlies effective supervision. This chapter examines some of the specific applications of supervision in the conduct of leisure service programs and the management of recreation and park facilities, giving examples of the roles of supervisors in a number of areas of responsibility.

It should be stressed at the outset that supervision represents a form of *middle-management staff function*. It is a bridge between administrative and leadership levels of responsibility. Typically, recreation and park supervisors work with agency or department directors in developing priorities, objectives and policies and in making major decisions about programs, budgets, personnel assignment and facilities management. On the other hand, supervisors also work directly with face-to-face activity leaders, as they schedule and carry out programs and fulfill responsibilities related to promotion and community relations, safety and accident prevention or the maintenance and use of recreation areas and facilities.

Recognizing that supervisors have both administrative and leadership functions, what are their *unique* responsibilities? It was pointed out earlier that supervisors are of essentially three types: (a) those responsible for areas or districts within a community; (b) those in charge of a single major facility or complex that offers varied programs and employs a number of leaders; and (c) those who direct a single major area of service within a community, such as sports programs or services for special populations. To this breakdown might be added the supervisory functions of individuals working in voluntary, therapeutic or other specialized agencies who are responsible for a major division of service or unit of an organization, but who are not technically regarded as administrators.

In each such role, supervisors have a major responsibility for providing professional leadership and, in essence, coordinating and giving direction to the recreation enterprise. Unlike the top administrator, who must deal with all aspects of the department's operation and who must relate to boards, commissions, trustees or the heads of other agencies, the supervisor is able to focus rather directly on the success of the recreation program. Similarly, unlike leaders, who tend to focus sharply on the activities they conduct (including clubs, tournaments, classes, special events and similar responsibilities), the supervisor must view the program within the total context of the sponsoring agency and the surrounding community.

Essentially, then, supervisors have the task of providing inspiration and leadership to the programs they direct. They must maximize productivity, insure that leaders and other staff members are functioning to their fullest capability, provide a free flow of communication both within and without the department and coordinate all elements of the operation to insure success. There tends to be a chain of responsibility, almost a "pecking order," in leisure service organizations, in which the public and its representative boards, commissions or other sponsoring groups hold the department executive responsible for the success of the program; the executive holds his or her department or division heads responsible; they in turn hold the supervisor responsible; and so on. But, in reality, it is the *supervisor* who is primarily responsible for initiating and publicizing programs; training, scheduling and guiding leadership personnel; and, in effect, maintaining an effective operation.

NEED FOR SKILLED MANAGEMENT

Within the field of leisure service in a rapidly changing society, we cannot continue to rely on traditional approaches to managing recreation facilities and providing programs. Jubenville points out that there is a critical need to find managers who have new strategies for solving tomorrow's problems today. Positive and innovative action, rather than strategy based solely on established principles and practices, is necessary to cope with recreation management problems. To illustrate, Jubenville describes the task of managing outdoor recreation facilities as an extremely complicated one, including resource management, visitor management and development of appropriate services. This requires, he states, a unique individual who has the interest, background and skills to deal responsively with the outdoor recreation system:

> . . . the manager must have an understanding of the visitor—background, desires for certain types of experiences, and reasons for participation. . . [and] of the resource in terms of both its durability for recreational use and its perceptual effects on the user's enjoyment of the

site. . . [and of] service management, which basically relates to the provisioning of services so that the user can enjoy the social and resource environs . . . often determined by . . . institutional, fiscal, and legal constraints. . .[1]

Within many other types of leisure settings, such as community centers, hospitals or industrial or armed forces recreation programs, although the components may vary somewhat, the challenge is still the same. Supervisors must, in all situations, provide an element of creative thinking and analysis, and management expertise, that welds the operation into a successful whole. A number of examples of newer trends in different areas of supervisory responsibility follow.

SUPERVISOR'S ROLE IN PROGRAM DEVELOPMENT

Recreation programs are developed in a number of ways. They may come about as a result of following traditional program-planning patterns or by inviting the views of participants through interest surveys. They may also be established as a reflection of current trends throughout the field or by unilateral decision of the administrator. They are obviously influenced by social and political trends and pressures, and by the economic realities that affect staff, equipment and facilities.[2]

It should be recognized that the task of planning recreation programs has frequently been regarded as of secondary importance. Rankin comments that too often the view is expressed that "anyone could organize a volleyball tournament, but that only a select few know how to fertilize a park." She goes on to present the position of the National Committee for Leisure Programming of the National Recreation and Park Association:

> . . . that professional programmers are an absolute necessity if the field
> is to make a meaningful contribution to the quality of life of our society,
> and that additional research and information sharing will assist in the de-
> velopment of more professional programmers.[3]

Supervisors must strive to promote innovative, imaginative and thorough program planning in all types of facilities. Too often, the use of a center is limited to a casual lounge program or a pick-up basketball game in the gym. Instead, a community center should be a place where various sport, social, creative and other community-service activities are provided, and should have a full calendar of well-publicized and well-attended programs.

Similarly, the use of a community swimming pool is too often limited to free swimming or an occasional beginners' swimming class. With a little plan-

---

[1] Alan Jubenville: *Outdoor Recreation Management*. Philadelphia, W. B. Saunders, 1978, p. 8.
[2] See, for example, Richard Kraus and Joseph Curtis: *Creative Administration in Recreation and Parks*. St. Louis, C. V. Mosby, 1977, pp. 113–120.
[3] Janna Rankin: "Perspectives on Programming." Editorial. *Parks and Recreation*, June 1979, p. 23.

ning and organizational effort, the pool could also be used for lifesaving classes, age-level competitive teams, classes in skin- and scuba-diving, special programs for the handicapped, water carnivals, water ballet shows and a host of other activities. The job of the supervisor is to be fully aware of the possibilities inherent in the center, geographical district or unit of special service that is his or her responsibility—and then to stimulate other staff members to plan and carry out the richest program possible.

Several guidelines for effective program planning follow:

1. Supervisors should use departmental goals and priorities as guide-posts for considering all program activities. Different activities may meet different priorities, in that some may be particularly strong in terms of attracting great numbers of participants, whereas others may have more limited attendance but be of very important social purpose, and still others may have special value because of their publicity or public-image potential. In all cases, the supervisor should be certain that program activities being considered meet the standards and important goals of the department.

2. Program-planning should not be a one-person operation. It is important that different staff members have the opportunity to contribute ideas and suggestions, within a brainstorming framework, and that the ideas of participants or potential participants be solicited as well. Good ideas frequently come from professional publications, workshops or special clinics, visits to other departments or agencies and professional conferences. When a new program works within one area or district of a large community, it often makes sense to try it on a citywide basis.

3. The supervisor should strive for creative and innovative thinking in the development of new programs, and should not be afraid to terminate older programs when they have lost their appeal to the public. Crompton points out that in the field of marketing generally, the "product life cycle" concept has become widely accepted. He writes:

> The evolutionary process of recreation programs is similar to other types of products. Recreation programs are discretionary consumer product purchases subject to replacement by newer, better, superior programs. Leisure services offered by public recreation and park agencies change in response to consumer demand and, hence, exhibit distinctive life cycle forms.[4]

According to Crompton, program life cycles include the following stages: (a) *introduction,* when support and acceptance for new programs are developed; (b) *take-off,* the period in which interest and enthusiasm grow rapidly; (c) *maturity,* the stage in which participation continues to grow but at a slower rate; (d) *saturation,* when few new participants are entering the activity, although increasing numbers of programs in it may continue to be offered; and (e) *decline,* in which public interest and participation drop off sharply. At this stage, Crompton points out, it may be possible to extend the activity

---

[4]John L. Crompton: "Recreation Programs Have Life Cycles, Too." *Parks and Recreation,* October 1979, p. 25.

by using new marketing strategies or by continuing it at fewer locations and with smaller numbers of participants—or it may be necessary to terminate it.[5]

The basic point is that supervisors should review all programs systematically, evaluate their degree of vitality and "life cycle" stage and make intelligent decisions about activities that appear to be growing obsolete.

4. Beyond this, supervisors should monitor or audit programs regularly to determine their effectiveness, appeal, appropriateness for the neighborhoods in which they are offered and, finally, their cost-benefit rating. This represents a process in which the costs and benefits of all program elements are determined, and thus their relative values established, as an aid to budgetary decision-making. Webster and Reich point out that many communities or agencies budget for recreation and park services on the basis of past accounting records, showing little concern about the present evaluation of returns for the dollars invested. They write:

> For greatest management efficiency, managers and supervisors of parks and other specialized recreation facilities must be able to compare high- and low-cost activity functions within and between designated facility and program divisions. For example, how does the cost per user-hour of service from the after-school activities at a center compare to other activities within the center operation; and to other centers; and to other programs in sports leagues, swimming pools, arenas, art centers, etc.?[6]

Pointing out that cost-benefit data of this sort are essential to continual evaluation of existing policies, procedures and programs, Webster and Reich urge that fuller use be made of this approach, along with information on user-satisfaction and cost-sharing and cooperative agreements among different agencies that make possible more economical service to the community.

SUPERVISOR'S ROLE IN FACILITIES PLANNING AND MANAGEMENT

Another major area of responsibility for recreation supervisors is in the planning, design, construction and operation of varied recreation facilities. Too often, these are constructed on the basis of recommendations of planners or architects who may have a limited understanding of recreational needs and behavior.

Frequently, facilities-development decisions are made at a level removed from those who actually staff the programs, and buildings or other leisure complexes are designed by individuals whose primary expertise is in other areas. However, more and more recreation and park departments—particularly those in large cities—have recently begun to employ their own planners. Increasingly, they are coming to recognize that it is necessary to develop an

---

[5]*Ibid.*, p. 54.
[6]Bill Webster and Chuck Reich: "Benefit/Cost Analysis—Its Use in Parks and Recreation." *Recreation Canada*, January 1977, p. 25.

understanding of the programs that will go on in buildings, as well as the patterns of use, including such elements as access, safety, vandalism prevention, the need for supervision and similar factors that make for efficient management.

In such situations, recreation supervisors should have input into the planning process to insure that the facility will be able to house the appropriate kinds of activities and serve the needed populations. Obviously, designing entries, walks, ramps, lavatories and other elements of the overall plan to permit full access by the handicapped is an essential concern today. Frequently, recreation supervisors will have observed outstanding facilities in other communities or will have become aware of innovative design approaches through professional conferences or publications, and can suggest these during the planning process. In addition, they often are in a position to involve members of the community in the planning process, thus insuring that the final design meets community approval.

Policies for Management of Recreation Facilities

Recreation supervisors play an important role in coordinating the actual operation of recreation facilities once they have been constructed. They are customarily responsible for developing policies (subject to the approval of their administrators) concerning hours of use, scheduling of various activities and availability of areas for use by other organizations. Many departments offer their athletic fields, gymnasiums and other special facilities to sports leagues or other organizations within the community. This is often done within a system of priorities, in which the department itself has the first priority for use of its own facilities, followed by other public agencies, such as the schools. These in turn are followed in order of priority by non-profit community organizations, service organizations and the like. Supervisors must make sure that such policies are carried out impartially on a first-come, first-served basis.

Furthermore, they must implement other policies relating to permit arrangements for obtaining use of fields or indoor facilities, signing of contracts and payment of fees, safety and control measures, clean-up, use of alcohol, gambling activities and similar matters. Beyond this, supervisors are generally responsible for insuring that facilities are properly maintained and that equipment is kept in proper working order to prevent safety hazards. Areas and equipment should be inspected regularly, and work orders for needed repairs must be promptly processed.

Well-organized departments and agencies have detailed procedural manuals for the operation of swimming pools, skating rinks and similar special facilities. These manuals usually specify exact maintenance schedules and standards, and it is up to the district or facility supervisors to be sure that these are observed. Equipment damage, acts of vandalism and accidents involving staff members or participants must be reported promptly.

Supervisors should, however, be concerned with more than routine reports and administrative responses to such events. Instead, they should be alert to the *causes* of vandalism or accidents and should constantly attempt to prevent such incidents from recurring. When problems go beyond what might normally be expected at a given facility, the supervisor must call them to the attention of administrators and other personnel and take prompt action to investigate and remedy the problem.

Supervisors also have a responsibility for developing suitable departmental policies and procedures in areas such as requisitioning of supplies and equipment, using department vehicles, maintaining inventories and similar tasks.

BUDGETARY FUNCTIONS OF SUPERVISORS

Supervisors are also responsible for fiscal management. As indicated earlier, they are typically called upon to prepare preliminary budgets for their districts or other units of service as part of the total departmental or agencywide budget planning process. In so doing, they obviously must take into account the costs of personnel, supplies and materials or other expenses related to programming. Supervisors often must revise budget requests in accord with departmentwide cuts or budget revisions or as the overall request goes through the fiscal hearing process.

A second important phase of the supervisor's budget responsibility is in maintaining appropriate fiscal controls. Typically, procedures must be developed and enforced for collecting fees and charges, handling petty cash, turning receipts over to the designated office, approving expense items or minor purchases, and similar tasks involving monies. Laxity in this area can be dangerous, and well-run departments have clearly outlined controls that supervisors must apply consistently. Similarly, other procedures for auditing budget expenditures and keeping appropriate accounting records are essential for efficient operations.

Beyond this, supervisors should be alert to opportunities to save money where possible and to supplement the regular assigned budget of the department or agency through other means. As a rule, recreation organizations have regular sources of income, either through tax funds, as in the case of public departments; through membership fees, United Fund allocations and other fund-raising efforts, as in the case of voluntary agencies; or through other appropriated sums, as in armed forces or employee recreation programs. However, in all types of recreation settings, there are usually additional ways of obtaining revenues, and alert, imaginative supervisors can propose approaches suitable for their organization.

Identifying Supplementary Finance Sources

As a single example, one might examine the budgetary support of college or university intramural sports and other campus recreational activities. Customarily, such programs should be supported in the same way as other educational activities. However, Colgate makes this point:

> . . . the recent trend in raising costs and decreasing support (taxes or student-fee funds) have once again brought about a financial squeeze on the budget for intramurals. Because most intramural programs are conducted after school hours, individuals responsible for allotting funds [may] believe these are extracurricular activities and, therefore, an unnecessary expenditure of educational funds.[7]

Thus, in addition to relying on regular forms of support such as general college funds, student fees or entry fees and dues, those in charge may wish to identify other possible means of developing financial support. Colgate suggests several other ways that income may be generated:

1. Charging admission to intramural tournaments or other special recreational events, such as sports nights, carnivals or exhibitions, showings of sports films or combined dances and game nights.
2. Special sales of such items as T-shirts, candy, magazine subscriptions, school stationery or gift items; often this may be done in a cooperative arrangement with distributing companies that give intramural or recreation departments a percentage of the income raised.
3. Intramural programs may sponsor one-day special projects, such as car washes, paper drives, collections of bottles and cans for recycling and other community-service activities that may be used to raise money.

Automatic vending machines, pinball and other electronic machine game rooms, equipment rentals, pancake breakfasts, cake sales and special trips are other ways of raising supplementary funds to support intramural and campus recreation programs. Supervisors of such programs should be alert to the possibilities of such ventures in supplementing their regular budgets.

Finally, recreation supervisors should explore cooperative or synergetic forms of programming as a way of compensating for budget limitations in a period of austerity. Ways must be found of co-sponsoring programs with other community agencies, both to avoid duplication and to pool joint resources in providing needed services. In addition, supervisors may take the lead in having their departments sponsor sports or hobby-related activities such as the Punt, Pass and Kick Contest sponsored by the Ford Company, Junior Tennis clinics and tournaments sponsored by Pepsi-Cola, and the Ken-L Ration Pet Show promotions. As middle-management personnel, supervisors are in an excellent position to suggest such program innovations to their administrators and also to follow through on organizing them in local programs.

---

[7]John A. Colgate: *Administration of Intramural and Recreational Activities.* New York, John Wiley and Sons, 1978, p. 26.

CARRYING OUT DEPARTMENT EVALUATIONS

Another important responsibility of supervisors is gathering accurate information about the success and effectiveness of their programs. This process, commonly referred to in the literature as program evaluation, is an often discussed but rarely used technique. Theobald writes:

> . . . [despite recent] trends toward accountability, only a handful of recreation programs operating at any level have undergone evaluation in any but the most cursory manner. As often as the need for evaluation is verbalized, it is seldom accomplished.[8]

In part, this is because the goals and objectives of recreation programs—particularly those operated by public or voluntary agencies—have tended to be of a rather general or subjective nature. Theobald makes this point strongly:

> . . . public recreation programs have their primary justification in human and social values, and not exclusively in economic terms. For example, a commercial amusement park may be assessed in terms of its net profit. However, it is quite different to assess the behavioral benefits of a public park. This latter resource must be viewed in social, not economic terms.[9]

Nonetheless, it is possible to evaluate all types of recreation and leisure service programs objectively. This may be done on a variety of levels: (a) assessment of the success of single program units or events, such as tournaments, playdays or carnivals; (b) assessment of the success of broader ranges of program activities in meeting stated objectives; and (c) assessment of the effectiveness of total departments in meeting pre-established standards and criteria of quality.

Evaluating Program Units or Events

Many departments and agencies have developed rating scales or checklists for use in evaluating the success of program activities on a limited scale. For example, at the end of an instructional course, sports tournament, ski trip, in-service training program or similar activity, it is highly desirable to carry out a systematic review procedure. Participants and staff members may both be asked to fill out a rating form asking questions such as the following:

Was the program well-planned and efficiently carried out?

Was attendance satisfactory, both at the outset and throughout the experience?

Were physical arrangements (for the hall or field, needed equipment, loudspeaker system, parking, etc.) satisfactory?

---

[8]William F. Theobald: *Evaluation of Recreation and Park Programs.* New York, John Wiley and Sons, 1979, pp. 4–5.
[9]*Ibid.*, p. 106.

Was there adequate publicity before the event?

Was leadership effective in achieving a high level of group participation?

What were the strengths of the program? What were its weaknesses? How could it be improved, if repeated in the future?

In order to evaluate any program systematically, Nolan suggests, it is necessary to consider the program's input, process and goals and the organization in which it exists. All these elements must be included in the evaluation in order to get a complete picture of what actually occurred. Nolan writes:

> Every recreation program consists of three parts: the input, or planning phase; the process, or period of time in which the program is run; and the outcome, or result. Methodical appraisal means formulating an outline beforehand as to how the administrator is going to evaluate each of these phases.[10]

Ideally, all three types of evaluation should occur throughout the programming process. Evaluation that takes place during the planning stage is usually referred to as *formulative evaluation.* During this phase, the supervisor should ask, "Will the program that is being designed meet our department's objectives?" The second type is called *concurrent evaluation.* Here, the supervisor asks, "Is the program that is going on now actually meeting our objectives?" The last, *summative evaluation,* takes place when the program has been completed and the supervisor is able to ask, "Have objectives been met?" Using a continuous evaluation process of this sort allows the supervisor to make adjustments in the program at various stages, rather than only at the end.

Supervisors can assist in the evaluation process by being certain that specific objectives are established when programs are planned. On the basis of these objectives, evaluation forms can be prepared in advance, which will make it possible to evaluate the success of the program at various key stages. Ideally, evaluation forms should not ask for "yes" or "no" answers, but should provide for a gradation of responses, such as *Excellent, Good, Fair* and *Poor.* Supervisors should then be sure that evaluation forms are tallied and reviewed, that staff members have the opportunity to discuss the results, and that the evaluations are used to prepare specific recommendations for future events.

Evaluating Broader Ranges of Program Activities

This type of evaluation is geared to measuring the success of larger program units, such as a summer playground program throughout a district or a performing arts program involving various groups and performances. Here, the

---

[10]Monica M. Nolan: "Evaluating Recreation Programs." *Parks and Recreation,* December 1978, p. 40.

overall success of the total program can best be measured by examining its various components. Overall attendance and and participation in the separate programs should be analyzed, as should the performance of different staff members, community reaction to various events, safety and accident records and similar factors.

As much as possible, behavioral and operational objectives should be established in advance and should then serve as the basis for measuring the program's success. Theobald points out that these should be made as concrete and measurable as possible. For example,

> . . . the stated goal: "Making children safe while in, on, or about the water" may be translated to the specific objective, "Each third-grade child will successfully complete the Red Cross Beginner Swimming Program."[11]

Within a complex program, such as a summer playground operation in which several different sites are staffed, it is necessary to evaluate each separate playground as well as the systemwide services such as transportation, use of specialists, lunch programs, aquatic activities or other arrangements. In such a situation, evaluation should not be reserved for the end of the summer program. Instead, it should take place regularly throughout the period, so that the supervisor is in a position to make recommendations for change and improvement while they still can be put into effect. Although this may be viewed as a normal part of the supervisory process, identifying it as a formal evaluative procedure tends to make it a more serious and effective supervisory tool.

Specially funded programs or experimental or demonstration projects usually include a separate evaluation component. Normally, the evaluation would not be *internal;* that is, department staff members would not be expected to evaluate their own programs. Instead, impartial outside experts would normally be employed to carry out such evaluations.

Assessing the Effectiveness of Total Departments

The third aspect of evaluation involves examining the quality and effectiveness of total departments. Here, the common procedure is not to attempt to measure success in achieving objectives, because these tend to be too broad and varied to be measured precisely. Instead, the most useful approach is to apply an instrument that measures a number of major aspects of the department or agency, such as philosophy and goals, administrative structure, program, personnel policies and similar elements. Two such instruments are *The Evaluation and Self-Study of Public Recreation and Park Agencies*[12] and *Recommended Standards With Evaluative Criteria for Recreation Services*

---

[11]Theobald, *op. cit.,* p. 108.

[12]Betty van der Smissen: *Evaluation and Self-Study of Public Recreation and Park Agencies: A Guide With Standards and Evaluative Criteria.* Arlington, Virginia, National Recreation and Park Association, 1972.

in Residential Institutions.[13] Both are manuals that list recommended standards and evaluative criteria, and are useful in obtaining a picture of the strengths and weaknesses of an overall department.

On a more limited scale, supervisors may also choose to examine specific aspects of their departments or agencies as a guide to more effective programming in the future. For example, the staff of the Xerox Corporation's Recreation Association recently carried out an intensive study of employee participation in that company's recreation program. A sample of 1,000 representative employees was chosen at random and given a questionnaire that sought information in four areas:

1. Employees' awareness and usage of Xerox Recreation Association facilities and activities.
2. The level of satisfaction or dissatisfaction with XRA facilities and activities.
3. Employee attitudes toward the XRA, and thus the effect of Xerox Corporation's sponsorship and support of the program.
4. Information regarding activities employees would like to see offered in the future.[14]

Similarly, the Cummins Employees' Recreation Association, in cooperation with Indiana University, carried out an extensive employee recreation interest survey designed to assess the level of participation and interest in various programs offered at Ceraland Park, a 345-acre family recreation complex close to the company plant in Columbus, Indiana. Approximately 1,000 employees were surveyed to gather information regarding the number of families that visited the park, the types of activities engaged in and suggestions for future programming, including emphasis on meeting the recreational needs of retired employees.[15]

A final example of agency studies of effectiveness may be found in a national Programs and Services Survey carried out by the Boys' Clubs of America. In this national research and evaluation study, several hundred Boys' Clubs executives were surveyed regarding their most popular activities, specialized and innovative areas of programming, problems pertaining to youth and the effectiveness of the national organization's services provided to local clubs.[16]

Such studies can be extremely useful to recreation agencies of all types in evaluating their own effectiveness and determining policies for future improvement. They represent an important area of responsibility for supervisors, many of whom have had professional study in the field of recreation and

[13]Doris L. Berryman, Project Director: *Recommended Standards with Evaluative Criteria for Recreation Services in Residential Institutions.* New York, New York University School of Education, 1971.

[14]Hal Scheinkopf and Michael Whitlock: "Conduct Your Own Research." *Recreation Management,* November-December 1978, pp. 13–14.

[15]W. Donald Martin and Stephen D. Waltz: "Surveying Employee Recreation Interests." *Recreation Management,* October 1977, pp. 27–30.

[16]"Relevance and Vigor Reflected in Programs and Services Survey Results." *Keynote* (Boys' Clubs of America), Winter 1976-1977, pp. 3–5.

parks and have taken courses in research and evaluation techniques. It is sometimes possible to have faculty members or graduate students from nearby universities assist in such studies, or to employ visiting teams from research and planning firms to assist in evaluation.

SUMMARY OF SUPERVISORY ROLES

This chapter has outlined a number of the ways in which supervisors can make an important contribution to the overall functioning of their organizations. Without question, however, their most critical responsibility is in the area of personnel management. Personnel management includes recruiting and selecting personnel, orienting and counseling new employees, carrying on an ongoing program of staff development and in-service education, and a number of related functions. These functions and guidelines for their successful accomplishment are presented in detail in Chapter Twelve.

SUGGESTED EXAMINATION QUESTIONS OR TOPICS FOR STUDENT REPORTS

1. Explain the concept, presented in this chapter, that recreation programs typically have a "life cycle" of increasing and then declining popularity. Illustrate it with a discussion of specific activities, either on the national scene or in your own community. What are the specific implications of this concept for recreation supervisors?
2. Assuming that effective programming is at the heart of the recreation enterprise, show how it relates to, or influences, several other important supervisory responsibilities, including (a) public relations, (b) facilities planning and maintenance, (c) personnel management and (d) budgetary functions.
3. Develop a method for carrying out a cost-benefit analysis of the major elements in a recreation program. In doing this, also develop a plan for getting additional fiscal support or maximizing revenues from specific program activities.

SUGGESTED ACTION ASSIGNMENTS OR GROUP PROCESS ACTIVITIES

1. Identify a recreation and park facility that has been developed or built within the past several years. Find out the role that the agency's professional staff played in planning and designing the facility, and determine whether there are specific ways in which the facility might have been more useful or successful if the professional staff had had more input in this process.

2. Analyze the role of a supervisory-level employee in a voluntary, therapeutic or industrial recreation program, with emphasis on its "middle-management" aspects. Develop a diagram showing graphically how this supervisor interacts with both administrative and leadership personnel in different areas of job responsibility.
3. With a group of classmates, interview two or more recreation supervisors in different agencies to determine how they carry out their program evaluation functions. Compare their methods, and develop a set of guidelines for doing such evaluations.

Supervisory Role in Staff Development

Chapter Twelve

This chapter deals with staff development, a key area of responsibility for supervisors employed in leisure service agencies. Typically, staff development is thought of as in-service education, consisting of formal training programs, such as workshops, conferences and clinics, or of individually planned development programs based on assessment of personal needs.

The staff development process actually is much broader than in-service education. It begins with recruitment and selection of suitable personnel and goes on to include (a) orientation and introduction to the organization; (b) formal in-service activities and opportunities; (c) continuing supervisory functions such as counseling, staff meetings and individual conferences; and (d) evaluation and follow-up processes. Although these services are generally found within any large business or governmental organization, they are particularly essential within the field of recreation and parks, for the following reasons.

Need for Staff Development Programs in Recreation

1. Many individuals entering work in recreation and parks tend not to have been prepared specifically in this field. Although they may have the needed leadership skills and personal qualities, it is important that they be given a fuller understanding of the goals of recreation and of the agency that has employed them.

2. Recreation involves many different settings and types of services, all of which require knowledgeable and responsive leadership. In many cases,

it is necessary to provide ongoing training in specific areas of leadership methodology, group dynamics and human relations. Because departmental approaches constantly undergo change to meet new community needs, personnel must also be encouraged to stay up-to-date and able to function meaningfully.

3. Evaluation is particularly crucial because work output in recreation is not as readily determined as in other fields in which it may be easier to measure an individual's accomplishment (e.g., caseload handled, number of insurance policies sold or amount of products manufactured). Therefore, it is important to evaluate the competence and overall performance of recreation and park personnel so the results can be used for counseling purposes and making personnel decisions.

For readers of this text, an understanding of staff development practices such as orientation, in-service training or evaluation is important for two reasons: (a) it is helpful for a new employee to know what kinds of supervisory assistance are provided in a well-organized department; and (b) they outline the methods used in many agencies, and so are helpful to those who are expected to provide these functions.

Example of Staff Development in Action

As an example of how a large, national voluntary organization approaches the task of helping staff members develop to their fullest potential, the Young Women's Christian Association encourages local and regional offices to provide the following services:

1. *Orientation of New Staff.* The executive director works with appropriate board and committee members in [introducing] new staff members to the community and the Association. . . . The National YWCA offers orientation institutes and basic training each year for staff who have been on the job for two years or less.

2. *Supervision—a continuous process.* It begins with orientation as a new staff member is helped to become acquainted with the Association and the job. The supervisory person related to each staff member is indicated on the job description. Regular supervisory conferences are planned for in the time schedule. . . .

3. *Staff Meetings* help all staff to see the program as a whole and to understand their various roles. They provide, too, the points to be followed up in supervisory conferences and are the place where problems from the supervisory conference relating to entire staff are worked on further.

4. *Opportunities for Staff* to participate in and carry leadership responsibilities in YWCA conventions, conferences, institutes and workshops are allowed for in time schedules of staff members. Educational or study leave on pay is usually earned after 3 to 5 years of employment, or schedules may be rearranged to allow time to take courses relating to the job.

    Special training for experienced administrative and/or program staff offered by the National YWCA provides opportunities for staff development and help in coping with current problems of the Y.

5. *An annual job performance appraisal* is a formalized part of the whole supervisory process—a time of stocktaking and deciding where emphasis shall be put. Both supervisor and supervisee will prepare for this conference constructively by pointing up progress or lack of it . . . .[1]

Many organizations provide similar services and opportunities. Before *any* staff development processes can be initiated, however, employees must be hired! Technically, recruitment and hiring are part of personnel management and *precede* the staff development process. However, recruitment interviews and related procedures help to acquaint prospective employees with the overall agency, and so might be regarded as part of orientation. In addition, choosing the right person for the right job is critical to the entire personnel management process and should be done in a way that is consistent with the staff development process that is to follow. It is therefore described in the following section.

RECRUITING, SELECTING AND HIRING NEW EMPLOYEES

The first step involved in recruitment, once a job opening has occurred and the go-ahead has been given to hire a new employee, is to prepare a job description. This should be concise, accurate, clearly written and up-to-date. It should provide potential candidates with a thorough understanding of the scope of the position, which will assist the employer by eliminating a flood of unqualified applicants.

Once the job description has been written, it must be used to actively recruit the best-qualified potential employees. This may be done in a number of ways. First, copies of the job description and invitations to apply may be sent to colleges and universities or distributed at professional meetings and conferences. Files of previous applicants or part-time or seasonal employees may be reviewed. Word-of-mouth advertising, leads requested from professional acquaintances and public service announcements of job opportunities may all be used.

In the case of major national federations, such as the National Council of YMCA's or the National Jewish Welfare Board, personnel services listings or newsletters may publicize the opening. The National Recreation and Park Association's *Employ* listing may be used, assuring national exposure. Federal recreation opportunities are frequently listed in announcements printed by the U. S. Civil Service Commission, including positions in Veterans' Administration Hospitals and the Department of Defense. Newspaper advertising may be used—and in some cases may be required by law—to announce job vacancies. Customarily, public agencies (and many private or voluntary agencies as well) stipulate that they follow "affirmative action" hiring policies, meaning that they do not discriminate in hiring for reasons

---

[1]*Personnel Administration Manual.* National YWCA, n.d.

of race, sex, age or similar characteristics. In many organizations that depend on special federal grants, a deliberate effort must be made to seek out qualified candidates from "minority" populations, for example.

When the deadline for applications has passed, the selection process begins. Each applicant's personal information, educational background, employment history, references and specific interests and skills are reviewed. In screening applications, it is important to be on the lookout for gaps in employment history, too-frequent "job-jumping" and other signs of possible problems—as well as for other, more positive attributes. If tests are part of the selection process, these must be given, graded and used to identify the leading applicants. The final step of the process is interviewing the most promising candidates and making a final selection.

Recognizing that a number of candidates may have the necessary professional qualifications, experience and skills, the task is to select the individual who best suits the agency's needs in terms of personality and motivation to perform at a high level of commitment. Rosenberg comments that in the hands of individuals untrained in personnel work, interviewing may turn out to be a "great guessing game" and result in unfortunate choices. She suggests that it is necessary to determine the *kind* of person who is called for in the situation and then to probe to determine whether each candidate has the needed qualifications. According to McClelland, there are essentially three different motivational types: those who are achievement-oriented, those who are affiliate-oriented, and those who are leadership-oriented. Asking questions such as the following will help the interviewer determine the orientation of each candidate's motivation and move toward a wise choice:

> "Tell me about your most recent job."
> "What aspects of your job do you enjoy doing most?"
> "Why does this kind of work interest or appeal to you?"
> "What kinds of things make your work difficult?"
> "Give me an example of a difficult problem you solved, or decision you had to make."[2]

Interviewers have essentially three functions: (a) to probe further into the appropriateness of the candidate's experience and education for the position under consideration; (b) to assess the individual's personality and character; and (c) to evaluate his or her intelligence, analytical ability and skill at performing under pressure. In getting at these points, interviewers may choose to follow a heavily structured format, using a list of prepared questions that are asked of each candidate. Or, the interviewer may allow the candidate free rein, asking a minimum of questions and encouraging him or her to ramble quite spontaneously. In either case, it should be recognized that the interviewer's judgment is likely to be somewhat subjective, so it is essential that it be supplemented by references from former employers and, if necessary, follow-up inquiries about the candidate's most recent job performance.

[2]DeAnne Rosenberg: "Take the Guesswork Out of Job Interviewing." *California Parks and Recreation*, December-January 1978-1979, pp. 22–25.

When the selection process has been completed and the leading candidate selected, it is essential that there be a full understanding of the nature of the job commitment, the work schedule and all relevant information regarding personnel policies, employee benefits and similar details. Although the job description and the interview process have provided the new employee with a degree of orientation, there should also be a formal and complete introduction to the job situation.

ORIENTATION IN PERSONNEL MANAGEMENT

Orientation may be defined as the process of introducing new workers to a department by familiarizing them with its philosophy, policies and working procedures, the overall structure and physical setting and their co-workers and supervisors. Its fundamental purpose is to provide new employees with the skills, knowledge and basic abilities needed to carry out work assignments during the initial period of employment, until they have participated in a fuller program of staff development.

The first days and weeks of any employee's beginning job experience should include a thorough exposure to (a) the department or agency, which may include a tour of the department's offices or facilities and familiarization with its various divisions and functions; (b) a detailed outline of all responsibilities and duties, including instructions for carrying these out, when necessary; and (c) a clear presentation of personnel policies relating to hours, sickness, leaves, vacations, health and medical insurance and similar areas of personal responsibility or company benefits.

How is all this to be accomplished? There are two methods that may be used separately or in combination. These are *printed manuals* and scheduled *orientation sessions or meetings*.

Personnel Manuals

Most cities and large organizations give all employees general personnel manuals that cover regulations and general information applicable to all departments. For example, the city of St. Petersburg, Florida, presents all new employees with a general manual that covers 21 major topics, including employee performance evaluations, classification plan, pay plan and safety regulations.

Many departments also publish printed manuals that cover such matters but also include special information relating to the recreation and park function. For example, the town of Hempstead, New York, presents new employees in its Parks and Recreation Department with a *Recreation Staff Handbook*. This manual includes general information on administrative policies and personnel procedures and on many elements related to leadership in recreation and parks, including regulations dealing with dress and appearance, staff meetings, in-service training, work schedules, inclement weather arrangements and similar matters.

Printed staff manuals may also deal with leadership methods. This is particularly true in therapeutic settings, where it is essential that new workers understand the institution's philosophy and method of operation. For example, the Recreation Therapy Department of the Evansville, Indiana, Psychiatric Children's Center issues a detailed Policy and Procedure Manual to new employees. This includes the following major sections:

1. Organization of Recreation Therapy Department
2. General Staff Relationships and Responsibilities
3. Program Responsibilities and Specific Job Assignments
4. Responsibilities of Supervisors
5. Time and Hours
6. Attire While on Duty
7. Responsibility and Relation to Volunteers
8. Responsibility With Patients
9. Equipment, Supplies and Area Requisitioning
10. Professional Attitude and Conduct

Under the final heading, the Evansville staff manual includes guidelines of this type:

> It is the aim of this department to improve and raise its standards of operation to the level whereby it will become a more professional service. . . . The overall conduct and attitude displayed by the Recreation Therapy Staff members as a whole or individually . . . reflect on the department and affect its function. Following are guidelines each staff member will be expected to follow.
>
> No discussion is to be held outside the hospital about a patient's history and/or illness. This includes indiscreet remarks to any of our public about any information concerning patients.
>
> Show each patient respect and courtesy regardless of how ill he is, just as you would any other human being. Do not play jokes on patients or mimic or make fun of patients. Expressions of this type often reflect your attitude toward the patient. Never argue with a patient. . .

Similarly, the National Boys' Clubs of America publishes a manual of suggested personnel policies for new employees, which includes a detailed section on the history, philosophy and goals of the Boys' Club movement, as well as other information regarding the probationary period, professional responsibilities and the employee evaluation process.

In some organizations, personnel manuals are given to new employees and a supervisor reviews and discusses each area of information. For example, the Hampton, Virginia, Recreation and Park Department has a New Employee Orientation Checklist, which specifies the following points that must be fully covered with the new worker:

1. Who his/her immediate supervisor is.
2. The purpose of the whole division; what part his/her job plays in the whole division.

3. The duties of his/her position.
4. Who the employee should go to for instructions and help in learning the job.
5. Performance requirements—what will be expected in terms of quantity and quality of work, manner of performance, relationships with co-workers and public, etc.
6. Evaluation process and probationary period (purpose and length).
7. Duty hours and lunch period; requirements for regular attendance and punctuality.
8. Procedure in case of sickness or inability to work.
9. Leave request and paydays.
10. Safety rules.
11. Where and how to report job-connected injuries.
12. Driver responsibility in case of vehicle accident.
13. Facilities of the division—lavatories, storage room, bulletin board, eating places.
14. Dress code.
15. Proper methods of handling cash transactions and accounting for funds.[3]

This checklist briefing is also accompanied by the supervisor's taking the individual on an orientation tour of the agency or its facilities and introducing him or her to other employees.

Orientation Meetings and Courses

Although manuals are helpful, they cannot do the job by themselves, and not all agencies are able to assign supervisors to orient new employees to the job on a one-to-one basis. Instead, well-planned orientation sessions are called for. Such sessions vary; they may be either formal or informal, may last several days or simply for a portion of one day and may involve only one new employee or a large number of new employees.

The Parks and Recreation Department of Phoenix, Arizona, for example, holds a special orientation session in September for all new employees. During this meeting, key staff members make presentations designed to acquaint the new employees with the history, structure and goals of the department, the functions of the Recreation Division, personnel policies and similar matters. The advantage of such meetings is that they provide the opportunity for give-and-take, for exploring problem areas in detail and for helping new workers identify individuals associated with different administrative and program areas.

Another form of orientation would be to assign the beginning worker to an experienced employee who has been specifically trained to "break-in" new staff members by working side-by-side with them for a period of several weeks.

---

[3]*New Employees' Orientation Checklist.* Hampton, Virginia, Department of Parks and Recreation, 1979.

IN-SERVICE TRAINING

Following the orientation period, there should be a well-organized program of in-service education that heightens employees' understanding of their work, improves their skills and generally enhances their professional growth. Authorities agree that it should be an important function of administration to provide such programs. The nature of professional responsibilities changes so rapidly in our society that it is necessary for most people to continue to learn and to change if they are to be successful in their work.

Dimock and Dimock write:

> The psychologist, Donald Michael, in *The Next Generation*, predicts that soon most people will regard education as a life-long pursuit. For one thing, continuing rapid social, economic and political change will mean that no one can afford to stand still. . .[4]

Another authority on personnel management, Nigro, agrees, and points out a dozen techniques that are widely employed to promote staff development. These include internships prior to formal entry into service, apprenticeships after entry, direct counseling, rotation and transfer of employment, opportunity for observation of other workers, supervised reading, lectures, discussions and group dynamics meetings.

If in-service training is to be successful, it must be made a serious responsibility of supervisors and must receive strong staff support from personnel administrators in research, advice and planning. In planning in-service training programs, a number of specific guidelines should be established. The following guidelines are drawn from the general literature on personnel management and from specific examples of in-service training in recreation and park departments in the United States and Canada.

Guidelines for In-Service Training

Identify Objectives. Each department should clearly identify specific objectives for each aspect of the program. These goals should be developed not by department administrators or supervisors alone but in collaboration with all staff members. It is common practice to conduct surveys to determine staff training needs. They may reveal that a variety of problems, such as accident records, absenteeism, resignations or poor production, stem from a lack of adequate training, and they may identify clear objectives for such training. Review of personnel evaluation records may also indicate specific in-service training needs.

Assign Responsibility. Instead of being everyone's responsibility, the task of planning and organizing in-service training should be assigned to one or more supervisory-level individuals. They should be allowed an adequate

---

[4]See Marshall E. Dimock and Gladys O. Dimock: *Public Administration.* New York, Holt, Rinehart and Winston, Inc., 1969, p. 235.

amount of time apart from their routine work. To assist them, a committee of employees should be established to help plan and carry out specific in-service training projects.

Select Appropriate In-Service Training Projects.   Those responsible for in-service training should determine which types of training projects should be selected to meet the specific needs of the department. An overall plan for a given year should be established, including all of the types of programs that have been selected.

Develop a Schedule.   The exact dates and times of in-service programs must be established. At this point, a major policy question must be faced. Will in-service training meetings be held outside of work hours, with employees attending of their own volition? If so, they will lack status in the eyes of the staff, and attendance is likely to be weak, although the department may find ways to motivate people to attend by giving special certificates, by recording attendance in personnel records and by using similar devices.

A more constructive approach is to schedule in-service training sessions as part of the regular job commitment of employees. This may be done in a variety of ways. In some situations, a period of required attendance on a non-paid basis may be scheduled before the actual work period; this is commonly done with summer playground leaders. In some departments, one morning each week is devoted to in-service training. In others, a particular group of employees may be selected for full-time intensive training workshops and released from other job responsibilities while these are held.

Plan Sessions.   The specific content of each workshop, clinic or other training session should be carefully planned to meet departmental needs, focus on special problems or prepare for new programs or responsibilities. Training sessions should be brief rather than drawn out. They should stimulate action rather than restrict it. The sessions should deal with real rather than theoretical concerns. They should make use of techniques that involve, interest and influence participants rather than be passive, lecture-type methods that are dry and boring.

Arrange Staffing.   Many departments use their own staff members to give courses or special training workshops, particularly if they have workers who are strong specialists in various program areas. Use is frequently made of personnel from other city departments or agencies, such as police officials, fiscal officers, youth board workers or other specialists. Faculty members from nearby colleges or universities and representatives of professional organizations may be drawn in as paid or unpaid speakers. It is essential that persons who conduct training sessions have something significant to offer; *nothing* is more disheartening than to have those attending a training session feel that they know more or are more highly skilled than the persons presenting the material.

Evaluate Programs.   It is essential to evaluate all in-service training programs to determine their effectiveness and to help in making recommendations for future activities. Too often there is little systematic evaluation of in-service training. Pfiffner and Fels comment, "Training conducted without research is like an automobile without a driver."[5]

In a simplified version of this analysis, in-service training in the Boys' Clubs of America has been analyzed as having five major stages: (a) assessing training needs, (b) defining objectives for the program, (c) designing in-service training, (d) holding training sessions, and (e) evaluating and redesigning the training program. In a suggested training unit intended to help staff members work with new club members by orienting them to the program, involving them in activities and helping them make new friends, evaluation was carried out by having staff members appraise the training when it was completed and by evaluating their performance with new members of the club during the following weeks.[6]

Summing up the development of in-service training programs, it is essential that there be well-defined training objectives that are based on self-diagnosed needs. The program should have top-level concern and support, with organization administrators or supervisors included as trainees. Course materials or modules should be well-designed and should be presented by qualified experts, whether "in-house" or drawn from the outside. Varied techniques should be used, including lectures, discussions, practice, role-playing, films or filmstrips and other special techniques described later in this chapter. There should be provisions to maximize feedback from participants, with all employees encouraged to take the initiative in their own self-development processes as well as in formal courses and staff development activities.

Types of In-Service Training Programs

A wide variety of methods may be used to conduct in-service training. For example, the Richmond, Virginia, Department of Recreation and Parks lists 11 specific methods used for staff development: (a) special institutes; (b) citywide and neighborhood staff meetings; (c) interchange of departmental personnel for special purposes; (d) regular in-service training meetings for staff (including roundtable discussion, demonstration and workshops); (e) monthly evaluations and follow-up; (f) meetings with advisory councils and volunteer groups; (g) bulletin service; (h) professional library service and magazines; (i) planned visits to other units or activities; (h) provision of opportunities for sharing experiences; and (i) research and study.

Several of these will now be described in greater detail, followed by actual examples drawn from departments and organizations in the United States and Canada.

---

[5]John M. Pfiffner and Marshall Fels: *The Supervision of Personnel: Human Relations in the Management of Men.* Englewood Cliffs, New Jersey, Prentice-Hall, 1965, p. 270.

[6]Frederick T. Miller: "National Training Plan." *Keynote* (Boys' Clubs of America), April 1975, pp. 26–28. See also "The Five Elements of In-Service Training." *Keynote*, Fall 1977, pp. 18–21.

Staff Meetings

In various ways, staff meetings make an important contribution to in-service training. The staff of a large center or district, or even the entire recreation staff of a department, may meet regularly to be informed of departmental plans and policies and to take part in problem-solving discussions or project planning. Individual members of the staff may be requested to report on their work, or committees may be appointed to study special problems and make recommendations at such meetings. Individuals who have attended professional conferences may be asked to share their experiences with the staff at the sessions.

Pre-Season Training Institutes

Customarily, pre-season training institutes are held before the summer, in the latter part of June. They are used to train seasonal employees for work on playgrounds or in other special programs.

In some settings, such workshops are held not only before the summer season but also before any major new programs are initiated, in order to train all personnel in their new responsibilities.

Special Workshops

These are special short-term, intensive in-service training programs that may last from a single afternoon or morning to several days of full-time attendance and participation. They may be concerned with the improvement of professional skills, involving clinics in major program areas such as sports, nature activities or the performing arts. They may serve to introduce new program features such as mobile recreation units and services. They may be concerned with problems of community relations, youth discipline, vandalism or other social problems. They may also be intended to improve personnel performance, encourage innovation or improve morale in a department.

In-Service Training Courses

These are similar to special workshops, except that they usually extend over a longer period of time and cover more varied topics. Many departments offer one or more training courses on a given morning or afternoon of the week, throughout an entire season, for 12 or 15 weeks. Normally, attendance is compulsory when such courses are offered during working hours, although in some departments they are given on evenings or weekends, and attendance is voluntary.

Other Methods

In addition to the preceding approaches, other recreation agencies use the following methods:

They may encourage staff members to attend national or regional conferences by giving them professional leaves and even assisting them financially with travel and registration costs.

Staff members may also be encouraged to attend college or university courses in recreation and parks and to work toward appropriate degrees; some departments help to pay tuition costs and arrange work schedules to facilitate attendance.

Professional libraries of books and magazines in the recreation and parks field may be maintained and staff members encouraged to read these or use them as planning resources.

Staff members are usually encouraged to join professional organizations and take part in their activities as an important stimulus to professional growth.

Departments may arrange visits and tours for staff members to observe recreation and park agencies in neighboring communities or special agencies as a form of in-service education.

Examples of Specific Training Programs

Several examples of specific training programs provided by public, therapeutic and voluntary agencies follow.

Pre-Season Training Institute: Reading, Pennsylvania

The Bureau of Recreation of Reading, Pennsylvania, sponsors an annual Pre-Season Playground Leaders' Workshop on three days in mid-June. All summer playground personnel are expected to attend. The schedule includes a variety of speeches, demonstrations and participation in playground activities. The staff of the institute includes supervisory members of the department, who conduct workshops in special activity areas, and guest speakers, including a newspaper reporter, police official, city attorney, city councilman and physician. The schedule is tightly organized and includes a wide variety of presentations and clinics. In a recent year, it followed this plan:

Monday

9:00 A.M.	Introduction and welcome address.
9:30 A.M.	Playground Administration.
10:15 A.M.	Responsibilities of playground leaders; safety on the playground.
11:00 A.M.	Introduction to folk dancing.
1:00 P.M.	Opening exercises.
1:05 P.M.	Legal responsibilities.
1:20 P.M.	Introduction to tournament games.
3:00 P.M.	Introduction to athletic events; organization of tournaments.
4:00 P.M.	Playground publicity.
4:15 P.M.	Distribution of supplies.
6:30 P.M.	Dramatic activities: singing games.
7:30 P.M.	Introduction to handicrafts.

Tuesday

9:00 A.M.	Opening ceremonies.
9:15 A.M.	Police and the playgrounds.
9:30 A.M.	Explanation of departmental forms.
9:45 A.M.	Active and quiet games for small groups and places.
11:00 A.M.	Problems on the playground: panel discussion.
1:00 P.M.	Opening exercises.
1:10 P.M.	Handicrafts.
3:00 P.M.	Folk dancing; athletic games.
4:00 P.M.	First aid on the playground.
6:30 P.M.	Music and drama.
7:00 P.M.	Planning a program.
7:45 P.M.	Playground publicity.
8:00 P.M.	Playgrounds in action.

Wednesday

9:00 A.M.	Opening ceremonies.
9:15 A.M.	Summer playground program.
10:00 A.M.	Advanced handicrafts.
11:00 A.M.	Dramatic activities; singing games.
11:30 A.M.	Low organized games.
1:00 P.M.	Opening exercises.
1:15 P.M.	Staff photo.
1:45 P.M.	Structure of athletic leagues and track meet.
2:45 P.M.	Advanced folk dancing and athletic games.
3:45 P.M.	Playground associations (neighborhood advisory councils).
4:00 P.M.	Playground assignments and conference.
5:30 P.M.	Playground federation picnic.

This institute is an example of an intensive in-service workshop for playground personnel. Many recreation and park departments have much less crowded schedules, cover a shorter period of time and have more flexibility in the choice of sessions. In some cases, a county recreation and park department may offer such a workshop for a number of different communities or school districts within its boundaries, and thus provide a richer pre-season training program than the smaller, separate departments could develop independently.

Pre-Season Training Program: Hewlett-Woodmere, New York, Leadership Course for High School Students.

An interesting approach to in-service training may be found in the Recreation Division of the Department of Community Services of the Hewlett-Woodmere, New York, public schools. The Department is responsible for four major areas of school services: Recreation, Adult Education, Senior Citizens and Coordination of Drug Programs. The Recreation Division operates a major summer program, including morning playground activities for elementary school children at four school sites and day and evening programs for junior and senior high school students. Teacher, college students and high school students are employed as leaders in these programs.

The Recreation Division makes use of several different training approaches in preparing personnel for summer work, including a six-week course conducted for high school students who hope to work in the summer program. This is held weekly during the spring and covers the following topics:

1st week: Philosophy of recreation and leisure; introduction to playground leadership.

2nd week: Playground directors in charge of the previous summer's centers present slides of past programs, facilities and equipment and discuss their programs.

3rd week: Safety and first aid, accident procedures and general responsibilities of playground leaders.

4th week: Games and sports: demonstration of leadership methods by staff and students.

5th week: Arts and crafts session, with demonstration of methods and student participation.

6th week: Discussion of overall workshop; question-and-answer period and examination.

On the basis of their performance during the six weeks, several of the most capable students are hired to work during the summer, filling vacancies created when members of the previous year's staff do not return. Other forms of in-service education include meetings and planning sessions with the college students, teachers or playground specialists who will be in charge of programs during the summer.

In-Service Training Courses in Large Cities

During the regular year, a number of large municipal recreation and park departments sponsor weekly in-service training courses for their personnel.

One example is Detroit, where the department has offered training courses in different districts of the city from 12:30 to 2:30 P.M., three days a week. Examples of the topics dealt with in these courses include "Alcoholism," "You and Your Police Department," "Mental Health Program," "Personnel Policies and Procedures," "Vest Pocket Parks," "Recreation Advisory Committees," "Special Events," "Mobile Programs" and varied courses dealing with program activities and how to conduct them. Obviously, these sessions cover a wide range of subjects, including specific leadership skills, human relations, professional development and community relations responsibilities.

Another example is Philadelphia, where the Recreation Department has offered a diverse list of in-service training institutes, including courses that each employee is required to take in order to develop professionally and to be eligible for promotion. For example, individuals seeking eligibility for promotion to *Recreation Leader II* have been required to take basic courses such as "Recreation Programming," "Facility Planning and Maintenance" and "Camping Organization and Administration." On a higher level, to qualify for promotion to *District Supervisor* or *Senior Recreation Leader,* employees have been required to take courses in personnel practices, fiscal planning and management, and supervision and public relations.

Probably the most ambitious single in-service training course to have been offered by a municipal recreation and park department was sponsored during the early 1970's by New York City's Parks, Recreation and Cultural Affairs Administration. This course was designed to give a thorough professional "re-treading" to selected supervisory or senior recreation directors as preparation for new assignments as "district superintendents" in areas throughout the city. The course involved attendance three full days a week over a period of several weeks from early February to mid-April. Held at Teachers College, Columbia University, it was staffed by faculty members from that institution and by dozens of speakers and consultants from varied government agencies in New York City, consultant planning firms, professional organizations and representatives from other cities.

The curriculum of the course was a total examination of urban recreation service, including study of the urban environment, the administrative structure of the recreation and park department in the city, administrative principles, staff development methods and other aspects of community life. Other class sessions dealt with problems of public and community relations, facilities design, program development and the proposed new district plan of decentralized recreation administration. The overall group of approximately 80 students was divided into four sub-groups, each of which was assigned to a community planning district in the city. Members of each sub-group did extensive field observation, developed master plans for their assigned districts and presented recreation events in various institutions as part of their "action-oriented" experience in this course.

During the past few years, elaborate in-service training programs of this sort have been eliminated in many cities for financial reasons. In some cases, they have been replaced by special recreation trainee programs, funded by the Federal Comprehensive Employment Training Act (CETA), which have combined work on the job with classroom experience for CETA employees.

In-Service Training in Other Settings

Obviously, other types of recreation agencies and departments also provide their personnel with in-service training opportunities. Examples are now given of four such settings: federal, voluntary, commercial and therapeutic recreation.

National Park Service

This major agency in the Unites States Department of the Interior operates a huge network of national parks, seashores and recreation areas. In order to provide ongoing professional development for its personnel, it sponsors a number of special training centers, including the Stephen T. Mather Training Center at Harpers Ferry, West Virginia; the Horace M. Albright Training Center at the Grand Canyon National Park; and the National Capital Parks Center in Washington, D.C.

Employees elect to take courses that will help them both in their present positions and in career advancement. If approved, they are sent to take courses that include practical management workshops and high-level executive development institutes given at appropriate training centers. Most such courses require full-time attendance, ranging generally from five days to two weeks; some longer courses permit employees to remain on the job while undergoing training. Typical course titles include the following:

"Dealing With Unions at the Park Level"
"Executive Management Seminar"
"First Line Supervision"
"Basic Law Enforcement for Seasonal Park Rangers"
"Introduction to Park Planning"
"Introduction to Maintenance Management"
"Standards for Operations: Historical Areas"
"Environmental Interpretation"

In addition to these training opportunities, employees of the National Park Service are also encouraged to attend other centralized training programs provided by the federal government for employees from various federal agencies and departments.

Girl Scouts of the United States of America

This leading voluntary youth organization maintains an intensive training program, both for its professional staff and for the tremendous number of volunteer leaders who direct Girl Scout troops. In part, this training is done through workshops and institutes. However, because of the numbers involved and their scattered location throughout the United States and other countries, the organization must also rely heavily on printed training materials.

For example, in a pamphlet titled *Just Tell Us How*, the Training Division of the Girl Scouts lists a number of major questions about objectives and techniques: "What is Scouting supposed to do for girls?" "How does a leader really get acquainted with so many girls at once?" "What do we do in meetings?" "What are some good program activities?" "How do we carry on ceremonies?" "How do we keep the group from getting out of control?" It provides answers to these questions and suggests additional training resources, such as packets, film strips, leadership handbooks and similar materials. The Girl Scouts also publish and distribute materials intended for professional staff development, in which they outline goals and executive improvement techniques for their paid professional workers.

Boys' Clubs of America

Another outstanding voluntary agency is the Boys' Clubs of America. This organization's rationale for conducting in-service training programs has been stated in the following passage:

> Competent leadership is the key to the success of the entire Boys' Club movement. To achieve and maintain high leadership standards, it is essential that all professional workers constantly increase their knowledge and understanding of boys in the Boys' Club setting and stay relevant to the demands imposed by a rapidly changing society. They should also continue to acquire better methods and techniques for organizing, operating and managing the Boys' Club itself, so as to achieve goals in the most efficient manner.
>
> Education and experience are important requisites for professional Boys' Club staff. However, every person should understand that he cannot get enough education and training before taking his first position to last his entire career. He should strive continually to improve those skills and abilities related to his present job. Also, whenever possible he should add layers of new skills and experiences which will equip him for advanced positions in the Boys' Club field.
>
> Professional workers, of course, form only a part of the staff team. They are the nucleus, but the successful Boys' Club also utilizes part-time paid employees (who may be professionals in other settings), volunteers, junior leaders and supporting staff, as maintenance and clerical personnel, to achieve its objectives. All of these people must be developed to their fullest along with the professionals.
>
> As the attitudinal and skill needs of an entire Boys' Club staff are considered, it becomes apparent that different kinds and different levels of training are required. One of the best ways to provide this is through an organized program of in-service training.[7]

Careful guidelines are prepared by the National Boys' Club headquarters to assist local directors in developing in-service education programs. Extensive manuals have been prepared to guide them in assessing needs and available resources and in developing staff training models. Training personnel are guided in the use of innovative techniques such as audiovisual materials, case studies, buzz groups, panels, programmed learning techniques, role playing, debates and a variety of other methods.

In the early 1970's, the Boys' Clubs of America embarked on an elaborate plan for national upgrading of staff development programs. National conferences were held and major committees appointed to implement this effort. At present, employees are involved in a five-phase plan of professional training:

> *First Phase: New Worker Briefing and Registration.* New employees receive extensive orientation materials outlining information about the Boys' Clubs and informing them of training opportunities.
>
> *Second Phase: Orientation Seminars.* Preferably during the first year of em-

---

[7]*National Orientation Program Manual.* New York, Boys' Clubs of America, 1973.

ployment, Boys' Club workers participate in a five-day Orientation Seminar, designed to serve 20 to 50 participants and scheduled each month as part of a National Professional Training Plan in several different cities around the United States.

Third Phase: Advanced Program Seminars. After two or three years in the field, professionals participate in Advanced Program Seminars, dealing with subjects such as program planning, principles of supervision and intensive work in discipline and guidance.

Fourth Phase: Management Preparation Programs. After about three years, workers are encouraged to begin professional preparation for administrative responsibility. They take part in pre- or junior executive conferences concerned with such problems as working with boards of directors, fund raising, staff development, budgeting and problem-solving.

Fifth Phase: Executive Training Programs. These are continued training experiences for executive personnel to refresh them on basics, bring them up to date on new trends and approaches and teach new job behaviors.

Commercial Recreation: Walt Disney World

Walt Disney World, in Lake Buena Vista, Florida, like its California cousin, Disneyland, operates a giant outdoor show on more than 27,000 acres of resort-hotels, campgrounds, golf courses and the "Magic Kingdom Theme Park." In this huge undertaking, with thousands of employees and millions of patrons, very little is left to chance. Orientation, in-service training and supervision of personnel are carefully planned and carried out. New employees are given colorful manuals welcoming them to Walt Disney World and outlining the organization's philosophy and working operation—as well as their own responsibilities. They learn quickly that they are part of "show business," on the "world's largest stage," and that the show is expected to be spectacular, fresh, new and unique, every day of the year.

Employees must learn a new language as part of Walt Disney World's formula for "creating" happiness. Their role is to help their "guests" shed the problems of the outside world and enter into a land of fantasy and excitement. They are "hosts and hostesses," "on stage at all times," following a careful code of costuming and appearance, speech, behavior, teamwork and showmanship.

Each new employee goes through a careful training program conducted through the "University of Walt Disney World." This University is a non-accredited training aspect of the company, and all employees take one, two or more of the training programs each year. Beginning employees go through a one-day training program, called *Traditions I,* at the University center, which is equipped with training facilities, conference rooms and special theater rooms. *Traditions I* is an eight-hour orientation to the company's tradition, history and philosophy—and to the basic concepts employees must follow in their contacts with the public.

On the second day of initial training, employees go to their respective Divisions for *Traditions II,* which covers all the information they need about their respective jobs. Little use is made of printed materials; instead, teaching aids, flow charts, talk boards, talks with various management personnel and walk-throughs of the areas under the Division's responsibility are used. On the third day of training, each employee reports to his or her assigned area:

> He meets the individual department head, and then is assigned to a qualified trainer (an employee who has proven himself capable, responsible and knowledgeable about a certain position). Each position from a Captain Nemo submarine operator to a lifeguard or a campground host has been assigned a certain number of training hours. The trainer works on a one-to-one basis with the employee, using a trainer check sheet, and the particular position's Standard Operation Procedure, in guiding the employee through the training period which goes anywhere from four hours to 110 hours.

Other training programs operated by Walt Disney University include classes to instruct teacher and "leads" (hourly employees who supervise other workers); *Disney Way*, a six-day familiarization program for all salaried personnel; a *Disney Way Seminar*, a seven-day seminar for key managerial staff that is conducted at corporate headquarters in California; a *What Can I Do For You?* series of half-day sessions for all supervisors and managers that deals with basic concepts of human relations; a *Management Awareness* program of management education in the area of minority relations and sex discrimination for all salaried employees; and a number of other specialized training programs.

In-Service Training in Therapeutic Settings

Programs of in-service training in the field of therapeutic recreation are developed, in some cases, on a systemwide basis in order to meet statewide requirements and guidelines. In others, they are planned and carried out by individual institutions. Several examples of such staff development programs follow.

Rainier School, State of Washington

This special school for the retarded provides a week-long course to prepare all new personnel to work effectively with residents. Trainees come from all school departments, and the purpose is to equip workers with a basic understanding of the Rainier School's objectives, philosophy and working procedures. The approach is chiefly through lectures, discussion and observation of facilities and programs. The basic training course follows this format:

> Day I. Orientation to resident care; routine hall duties; dental care and procedures; education department program; forms, records and record-keeping procedures.
>
> Day II. First aid methods; special hall programs; supervision of residents; handling of keys; planning the future for residents; medication and treatment procedures.

Day III. Resident life rules, regulations and procedures; laundry processing; vocational experiences for residents; understanding the mentally retarded; commissary tour; adult education program; understanding basic human needs.

Day IV. Housekeeping service; farm tour; recreation services; resident training methods and behavior modification; basic nursing techniques; safety.

Day V. Normalization and dehumanization; restraints and isolation; seizures; pre-placement and placement (discharge) procedures; contacts with public and residents' families.

Regional In-Service Training Program: Province of Ontario

A growing trend in the staff development of rehabilitative personnel is to provide in-training courses on a statewide or regional basis. In the Province of Ontario, Canada, the Ministry of Health has sponsored regional training programs with the purposes of upgrading the work of personnel employed in provincial institutions and of equipping staff members who have less than a two-year College Diploma in Recreation with formal training and an equivalent standing in this field.

As an example, a series of workshops was held in the Western Ontario Region, each course covering a five-day period and one or more major topics. Topics dealt with such concerns as philosophies of recreation, play and leisure; the needs of special groups; leadership and group dynamics; the evaluation of recreation programs; community recreation programs; and Canadian social problems. They were given at the campus of the University of Waterloo, and the lecturers were drawn chiefly from the therapeutic recreation specialists in that institution's Department of Recreation.

Another important innovative development in the Province of Ontario (although not directed exclusively to therapeutic recreation practitioners) has been the establishment of a unique professional education institution called the College of Recreationists of Ontario. Capling writes that although this college employs a full-time Director and has a Provincial Board of Directors and seven Regional Councils,

> . . . it conducts no classes, and has no faculty. Like other colleges, it is supported by a combination of Government grants and student fees. The most remarkable thing about the College of Recreationists of Ontario is that learners plan and carry out their own studies, and select their own teachers.[8]

A government grant through the Ministry of Culture and Recreation supports the program, which is based on the philosophical position that learners are capable of taking responsibility for carrying out their own developmental programs throughout their careers without earning traditional diplomas and degrees. With the help of Regional Councils, printed materials and workshops, participants set objectives for their learning, select advisors and de-

---

[8]Dick Capling: "Professional Self-Directed Learning." *Recreation Canada,* April 1979, pp. 42–43.

velop written plans for continuing education. These may include readings, workshops, courses, consultations and a variety of other experiences, which culminate in Board reviews and, if satisfactorily accomplished, certificates attesting to the work done. Practitioners in a variety of specializations, including therapeutic, outdoor, educational, private and commercial recreation, are involved in the College of Recreationists.

State of Maryland: Department of Mental Hygiene

This department operates an extensive training program for Rehabilitation Therapist trainees, including recreation personnel. In the past, this program involved a year-long sequence that included a pre-class orientation, lectures, practicums and finally a clinic assignment. Heavy emphasis was given to instruction in clinical subjects such as understanding of psychoneuroses and personality disorders, medical aspects of illness and psychometric evaluation. Trainees were exposed to techniques of patient assessment, counseling and group dynamics methods, specific skills in art and occupational, industrial and recreation therapy.

More recently, this statewide training program has been reduced to a six-month period, which places less emphasis on theory and more on practical applications.

State of Minnesota: Department of Public Welfare

This final example of an institutional in-service training program illustrates changing approaches in the field of staff development in rehabilitation service. On various levels, such as *Human Development Services Specialists, Rehabilitation Therapists* or *Rehabilitation Therapy Supervisors*, staff members must meet statewide training requirements for certification in their current positions or for promotion.

For example, the *Human Development Services* career ladder requires a minimum of 120 hours of training in basic methods, which may be taken through relevant college courses or through approved in-service courses. Those promoted to supervisory positions are required by the State Commissioner of Personnel to take a minimum of 48 hours of training in supervisory principles and methods through two three-day courses provided by the Training Division of the State Department of Personnel. There is an increasing attempt to make these requirements more meaningful to individual employees. Thomas Jung, the Rehabilitation Director of Hastings State Hospital, writes:

> The State of Minnesota is currently revamping its entire personnel system. Individual job descriptions are to be worked out by each employee and his supervisor. Standards will then be worked out and each employee will then be evaluated at least once annually against his job description and standards. The gap between what his job calls for and his performance will constitute his in-service training needs. The State has put together a

management training course which all administrative types must take and a course on supervision which all supervisors must complete.

This system leaves almost total freedom to the employee and supervisor in working out position descriptions. . .[9]

This attempt to individualize in-service training programs represents a desirable direction in current staff development approaches. However, it poses serious difficulties with respect to providing training, in that a wide variety of workshops or courses would be needed to meet the full range of individual needs.

Other Special Approaches to In-Service Training

A number of specialized approaches to in-service training have been developed recently; these have grown out of experimental group processes associated with encounter groups and the human potential movement. A number of these methods, such as "values clarification," "assertiveness training," "behavior modeling" and "stress management," are described in the following section.

Values Clarification

This is a group process designed to help participants—usually part of a professional team involved in a staff development program—come to grips with their own values or attitudes and see how they relate to those of their co-workers. Before constructive behavioral change can occur, it is often helpful to perceive the basis for one's customary approach in different work situations. Values clarification may deal with one's goals and social values, attitudes toward leadership or supervisory styles, or other relevant concerns. Often, it promotes better communication and understanding among staff members, and helps them work more effectively together. Exercises related to clarifying one's values can be useful in assisting supervisors to understand how their values affect their behavioral styles. After coming to understand his or her behavioral style, a supervisor can begin to modify that style in order to become more effective in performing job responsibilities.

Values clarification uses a number of different approaches, including the following.

Supervisory Style Questionnaires

Questionnaires may be devised that offer alternative responses illustrating different supervisory values and styles. In using the following questions, which are presented as illustrations, participants would have the opportunity to hear or read each question in turn and then draw a colored slip of paper,

---

[9]Letter from Thomas Jung, Hastings State Hospital, December 1973.

keyed to their response to the question, from one of three piles of different-colored slips on a table in the center of the group.

1. Operational guidelines for a new playground or center that is about to open in your district must be established. You should: (a) sit down with other staff members and jointly develop policies with them (Blue); (b) allow other staff members to make up the policies themselves (Gold); or (c) give staff members a set of guidelines which you have already established for other playgrounds or centers (Red).
2. At district staff meetings, you would: (a) separate yourself inconspicuously from other employees (Gold); (b) place yourself at the head of the group, with them all facing you (Red); or (c) place yourself on an equal basis with other group members (Blue).
3. A new position has opened up for a staff member in your department. You would: (a) interview applicants yourself, without others taking part (Red); (b) have members of your staff who would be working with the new employee take part in the interviews (Blue); or (c) have other staff members do the interviewing, rather than yourself (Gold).
4. You have the following approach to staff work schedules: (a) you do not check on employees or care when they come and go, providing that their work is done (Gold); (b) you establish precise work schedules and check regularly to make sure they are lived up to (Red); or (c) you work out appropriate schedules with other staff members and encourage them to work on a "trust" basis (Blue).[10]

These and similar questions are color-coded so that those with *red* slips reveal authoritarian or directive attitudes; those with *blue* slips tend to be democratic, participative managers; and those with *gold* slips have laissez-faire, "hands-off" leadership styles. To understand the meaning of their own choices, participants may be encouraged to discuss each question in turn and their reasons for choosing as they did. Or, each colored slip may be assigned a value (red being given a 1, blue a 2, and gold a 3). Participants total the value of all their slips, and as the discussion develops it is revealed that those with the lowest number of points tend to have authoritarian attitudes, those with the highest number, permissive attitudes, and those in a middle range, democratic or participative attitudes. Follow-up discussion should be carried on not in a spirit of "blaming" people or suggesting that one leadership style is less acceptable than others, but rather in a spirit of group interpretation. The member themselves, rather than the session leader, should draw conclusions from the process.

A different questionnaire may be used to help leaders or supervisors determine where they stand with respect to McGregor's Theory X and Theory Y analysis of management styles. A number of questions may be devised. Some examples follow[11]:

---

[10]Adapted from graduate course assignment at Temple University by Gary Harris, 1979.
[11]Adapted from graduate course assignment at Temple University by Gary Harris and David Coyle, 1979.

1. Most people need to be directed in their work.

   | 1 2 3 4 | 5 6 7 8 | 9 10 11 12 | 13 14 15 16 |
   | Strongly Disagree | Disagree | Agree | Strongly Agree |

2. The expenditure of physical and mental effort in work is as natural as play or rest.

   | 1 2 3 4 | 5 6 7 8 | 9 10 11 12 | 13 14 15 16 |
   | Strongly Disagree | Disagree | Agree | Strongly Agree |

3. The average human often wishes to avoid responsibility.

   | 1 2 3 4 | 5 6 7 8 | 9 10 11 12 | 13 14 15 16 |
   | Strongly Disagree | Disagree | Agree | Strongly Agree |

4. Most people have a high degree of creativity in the solution of organizational problems.

   | 1 2 3 4 | 5 6 7 8 | 9 10 11 12 | 13 14 15 16 |
   | Strongly Disagree | Disagree | Agree | Strongly Agree |

Following the application of these and similar questions, a scoring system would be presented to show participants whether they accept assumptions underlying Theory X or Theory Y, or tend to be somewhere in the middle. Again, this would be used as a basis for group discussion and to help leaders or supervisors examine their own attitudes and approaches constructively.

Assertiveness Training

A second special technique that is widely used in many staff development programs is known as assertiveness training. This approach is based on the concept that many individuals tend to be polarized in either "fight" or "flight" behavior. These two styles may be characterized as follows:

The *"fight"-oriented* individual tends to be aggressive in many relationships and to believe that life is a constant battle, in which attack is the best defense. Aggressive verbal behavior tends to be an attempt to "win" by humiliation or to "put down" others and so gain one's point. Leaders and supervisors using this approach usually believe that winning is necessary to maintain one's place in a competitive world—and that this in turn necessitates someone else's losing. Although aggressive individuals appear to be extremely confident, this is often a cover-up for feelings of insecurity.

In contrast, the *"flight"-oriented* individual tends to back off, to give in and to fail to stand up for his or her rights. Such individuals are usually reluctant to say or do anything that might upset others, or hurt others' feelings and/or lead to a confrontation. Passivity and withdrawal from possible conflicts are typical of this behavioral style.

The basic point of assertiveness training is that there is a third alternative—learning to stand up for oneself and making one's position clear without violating the rights of others. The purpose of training is to help individuals express their feelings, opinions and needs directly, honestly and appropriately, particularly in areas of disagreement or conflict situations. Unlike the aggressive approach, which is characterized as a *win-lose* style, or the passive style, which is a *lose-lose* stance, assertiveness training should result in *win-win* outcomes, with everybody gaining and no one losing.[12]

Originally, assertiveness training was widely used with people who had marked psychological problems in an effort to help them behave more effectively and solve their interpersonal problems. It has gradually come to be used as a training technique with across-the-board work forces as part of the employee development process. Different approaches may be used, but a common method is to prepare a full outline of course objectives and to have the training manager discuss these personally with all participants. O'Donnell and Colby describe an assertive management course sponsored for middle-level managers and directors by Minnesota Mutual Life Insurance Company:

> Although the instructor presents conceptual material on assertiveness, communications, motivation, teamwork, the managerial role, and goal-setting, it is clear from the outset that participants are responsible for their own learning. Action Contracts are set at the end of each three-hour class session so participants can begin practicing human-relations skills and/or behavior changes.
>
> Examples of such contracts were: "to express my feelings more openly, more often"; "to deal directly, this week, with an employee's erratic performance"; "to learn to say no"; "to give negative feedback without feeling guilty"; and "to stop talking and start listening."[13]

Through regular feedback in the group sessions, participants share their experiences and progress, and a sense of teamwork and mutual support is engendered. Follow-up sessions and evaluations conducted several months after the conclusion of the six-week course described by O'Donnell and Colby have shown that it had lasting value; people were still thinking about and applying the skills developed in the course. Clearly, this approach represents a useful tool for staff development programs in many recreation and park departments and agencies.

---

[12]Margaret P. O'Donnell and Lee Colby: "Developing Managers Through Assertiveness Training." *Training and Human Resource Development*, March 1979, pp. 36, 41.
[13]*Ibid.*, p. 41.

Other special techniques include (a) training programs based on *behavior modeling principles,* in which role-playing, demonstration and videotaping are used to show effective and ineffective leadership and supervision methods, with models of effective interaction being shown by the training leader;[14] (b) *stress-management* workshops, in which participants learn to recognize the causes and effects of stress, both in their personal lives and in the work environment, and to deal effectively with them;[15] and (c) *human-relations training programs,* which are geared to help participants become more sensitive to their own attitudes and interaction with others, to relate more meaningfully with them and to supplement their activity-leadership or program-oriented abilities with important human-relations skills.[16]

These and other special training approaches may be used by recreation and park or other leisure service agencies to improve the quality of their staffs' performance. Obviously, these approaches should not be the sole focus of in-service training, but they do provide a valuable ingredient.

Throughout all in-service training programs, emphasis should be placed on having participants play a meaningful role in the process and on drawing from their experience and capabilities in developing workshops and courses. Knowles writes that adult employees must be addressed as responsible, self-directing persons who have a deep psychological need to be treated with respect and perceived as having the ability to run their own lives. They must not be told what to do and what not to do, talked down to, embarrassed, punished or judged. He emphasizes:

> As a trainer, your role is more as a resource person than a teacher. Work with your learners to translate diagnosed needs into specific educational objectives and then to design learning experiences to achieve these objectives. Breaking the staff into small groups, such as planning committees, project teams and task forces, is one way to help learners share the responsibility of learning. . . Greater emphasis should be placed on tapping the experiences of your adult learners. Employ group discussion, the case method, the critical incident process, simulation exercises, role playing, skill practice exercises, field projects, action projects, laboratory training, demonstrations, group interviews, seminars, and audience participation patterns.[17]

---

[14]Terence O'Connor:"How to Set Up, Run and Evaluate a Training Program Based on Behavior Modeling Principles." *Training and Human Resource Development,* January 1979, pp. 64–67.
[15]Linda Standke: "The Advantages of Training People to Handle Stress." *Training and Human Resource Development,* February 1979, pp. 23–26.
[16]Paul R. Smith and Judith I. Futch: "A Human Relations Training Program for Leaders." *Therapeutic Recreation Journal,* First Quarter 1978, pp. 33–39.
[17]Malcolm S. Knowles: "Four Keys to Better Staff Development." *Keynote* (Boys' Clubs of America), September 1976, pp. 3–5.

Evaluation of In-Service Training Programs

As suggested earlier, it is essential to evaluate all in-service training programs. The professional literature in the field of personnel management suggests that the best way to do this objectively is to assess the on-the-job performance of those who have taken in-service courses or workshops in order to determine whether their work has improved within these three specific areas: (a) improvement in general knowledge, awareness of professional principles and program needs; (b) direct improvement in job skills and daily performance; and (c) improvement in attitudes toward the job and in relationships with co-workers.

In some situations, efforts have been made to determine the effectiveness of in-service training programs by observing the work performance of participants who have gone through the program, or by having them report on the effects of the training after a period of time has elapsed. Kirkpatrick, however, points out that such efforts tend to be rather subjective and inconclusive; instead to *prove* the value of training programs it would be necessary to measure the performance of leaders and supervisors *before* the training sessions and then *later*, in controlled situations.[18] Such measures, typical of what one might find in experimental research studies, would be extremely difficult to apply in most recreation and leisure service agencies.

Ideally, a training program should be designed to develop specific abilities in each staff member that might be consistently applied on the job. Training should give each individual the opportunity to develop his or her potential to the fullest. However, the practicability of assessing such "ideal" programs is remote. Trainees often vary considerably in skills already acquired, experience, motivation and trainability. Differences in job performance are affected by a great many factors other than the efficacy of training. Finally, there is rarely the opportunity to assess directly the effects of training by comparing those who participated with those who did not ("experimental" vs. "control" groups), since in most cases all persons within an agency are required to participate in training sessions.

Therefore, the method generally used to evaluate in-service training is to have those who have gone through courses or workshops fill out anonymous ratings forms or questionnaires. These usually ask questions about the value of the workshop, the contributions made by individual speakers or resource leaders and the overall worth of the training experience. Two examples of such efforts follow.

Milwaukee, Wisconsin, Department of Municipal Recreation and Adult Education

This school-sponsored recreation department makes a consistent effort to evaluate all phases of its program, including leadership training. For example,

---

[18]Donald L. Kirkpatrick: "Evaluating Training Programs: Evidence vs Proof." *Training and Development Journal*, November 1977, pp. 9–12.

Area Supervisors and District Directors are asked to evaluate In-Service Education Sessions with questionnaires covering the following points:

I. *Preparation for Playground Season*
   a. Was the April Preparatory Week of value?
   b. Was the teaching program as made out by the various committees satisfactory—or would you rather make out your own teaching plans?
   c. Pre-Season Staff Meeting—do you feel that this meeting is of value in clarifying procedures, policies, etc.?

II. *Opening Day Institute*
   a. Was the one-day session as valuable as the previous two-day sessions in: (1) lack of strain and pressure; (2) general preparedness of first-year leaders; (3) inclusion of pertinent information.
   b. General comments regarding this year's session: What did you like about it? What did you not like about it?

III. *Saturday In-Service Education Sessions*
   a. Were sessions planned to take care of play-leaders' needs in relation to timing?
   b. Did you see evidence of teaching on the playgrounds of activities taught on Saturdays? If no such evidence was found, why was this so, in your judgment?
   c. What features of the in-service education sessions do you feel were good? What features of the in-service sessions do you feel should be deleted or improved?

Alexandria, Virginia, Department of Recreation and Cultural Activities

The Department of Recreation and Cultural Activities of the city of Alexandria, Virginia, carries out an extensive program of employee orientation and in-service training, including a pre-summer Recreation Workshop. All leaders attending this workshop in a recent year were required to evaluate the program anonymously. Examples of the kinds of comments made by participants follow:

"I thought that the sensitivity groups and discussion groups were well worth the time. I enjoyed most of the speakers, but I felt that we did not have to have someone go through the manual for us. *We can read!*"

"In my opinion, the Summer Workshop was generally successful and beneficial to the recreation staff. This is probably mainly due to the good organization, which is in contrast to last year's Workshop. The arts and crafts and games demonstration were especially beneficial, although I think more time could have been spent in these two areas. . . . Also, less time probably could have been spent with the speakers on the first day."

"In general, the workshop was more beneficial than any I've attended in the past (this is my fourth). Although the structure and 'disciplinary' attitude seemed harsh at first, I've come to realize that this was essential to the noticeable improvement; I actually learned things."

"I am new to this program, and I felt that more time should have been spent on explaining the manner in which our part of the overall program interconnects with all of the other programs. A clearly organized timetable of events within and without our program should have been formulated. Each playground should have a schedule of events during the length of the program. I still am not sure who are my district supervisors, and who I go to for help in securing resources and program planning. . ."

Similarly, both the supervisor responsible for in-service training and the director of the department filled out detailed analyses of the strengths and weaknesses of the Summer Workshop and the contributions made by each of its session leaders. When these evaluations were combined with the frank comments made by the participants, it was possible to develop useful guidelines for future workshops.

EVALUATION OF RECREATION AND PARK PERSONNEL

A final important concern of this chapter is the process of evaluating departmental personnel. This is generally the responsibility of supervisors, who must assess the ability and performance of leaders. However, supervisors themselves are evaluated systematically by administrators, just as administrators must be evaluated in turn by city managers or mayors. Thus, on every level, personnel evaluation is a key aspect of recreation and park service.

Personnel evaluation may be defined as the process of appraising the quality of work performed by a member of the professional staff of an organization. Normally, it is reduced to a series of statements or conclusions that provide a general picture of the worker's strengths and weaknesses and areas in which improvement may be needed.

In well-administered departments or organizations, it is customary to have supervisors fill out personnel rating forms for each employee on a regular basis, such as every six months or once a year. These forms are customarily inserted in the individual's personnel file. They provide information that may be used in making personnel recommendations or decisions regarding an individual's move from probationary to regular employee status, transfer, promotion or other changes in status.

A second purpose of evaluation is to help supervisors do an informed and intelligent job of counseling staff members. Simply put, if evaluation demonstrates that a recreation leader has certain consistent weaknesses, these should become the focus of supervisor–leader conferences, in-service training or other purposeful efforts to improve the leader's performance.

Many departments require that workers be shown their evaluation ratings before the ratings are inserted in their personnel files, and that they be given the opportunity to discuss them and express their views on them. Although one might think that it would be the worker who is to be evaluated who dreads this process, research in the field of public personnel administration has shown that actually many supervisors find this task difficult and unpleasant. Often they resist the idea of sitting in judgment and, in effect, of "playing God." Specifically, they tend to dislike having to give *negative* judgments, while they enjoy being able to give *positive* ratings. Stone comments:

> . . . while people dislike playing a *punitive* God, they tend to enjoy playing a *benevolent* one.[9]

In general, supervisors have consistently expressed a wish for help in this process, so that their judgments are objective, detailed, consistent and based on sound evidence. Similarly, research has shown that workers who are evaluated are not only concerned about whether their ratings are favorable but also that those evaluating them be well-qualified, knowledgeable and unbiased.

Methods of Personnel Evaluation

What are the most common methods of gathering and reporting information for the purpose of personnel evaluation? Several approaches are used.

Direct Observation.   The best way to determine the effectiveness of a leader is to observe him or her at work in a variety of situations. Such observations may be casual and informal or may be regularly scheduled. The supervisor should keep notes of observations, especially of "critical incidents" that are particularly revealing about the worker's performance.

Supervisory Conferences.   Another important means of gathering relevant data for evaluation is through supervisory conferences with individual employees. These should be held regularly for the specific purpose of discussing the employee's performance and progress on the job, not in a threatening or judgmental way but as part of an open and frank process of two-way communication.

Reports From Participants or Co-Workers.   Another source of information to be used in the evaluation of personnel utilizes reports from individuals who participate in the program or from co-workers in the department. Obviously, these may reflect bias, either because of special friendship with the worker involved or because of antagonism or hostility. At the same time, they obviously have some merit, and if all participants and co-workers agree that a staff member has been doing an excellent job, their views must carry weight.

Review of Accomplishments.   A final basis for personnel evaluation may be a careful review of work done by an individual over a period of time. What has his or her job performance been like, in terms of successful projects (tournaments, special events, attendance on the playground, relations with community people or similar criteria)? Are programs well attended? Have

---

[19]Thomas H. Stone: "An Examination of Six Prevalent Assumptions Concerning Performance Appraisal." *Public Personnel Management*, November-December 1973, pp. 408–414.

they achieved their objectives? Much of this information may be found in departmental records, with some of it in the form of reports submitted by the worker or by his or her direct superiors on the job.

In making use of all these techniques for gathering information, it is customary to fill out a rating form that gives a total picture of the worker and his or her performance. Customarily, such forms present a number of important qualities or descriptive terms. The supervisor is asked to rate the individual on these traits, making use of a scale with a series of ratings, such as "excellent" through "poor" or "outstanding" through "unsatisfactory." These ratings may then be assigned point values, which may be used to develop a total performance rating for the individual as well as a profile of his or her strengths and weaknesses.

Several examples of rating forms or approaches in municipal recreation and park departments follow.

Montclair, New Jersey, Recreation and Parks Department

Name: _____

Position: _____

Location: _____

Date: _____ 19____

	Unsatisfactory	Below Standard	Satisfactory	Above Standard	Outstanding

Factors Evaluated

1. *Personality:* appearance, dress, poise, and tact.
2. *Cooperation:* cordial relations with staff and public.
3. *Initiative:* works effectively without detailed instruction.
4. *Organization:* plans and implements program according to needs and objectives.
5. *Leadership:* rounded leadership ability.
6. *Promotion:* submits timely, well-written publicity.
7. *Dependability:* punctual, carries out assignments.
8. *Emotional Stability:* can objectively accept suggestions and criticism.
9. *Enthusiasm:* interested in work and reflects interest to others.
10. *Reports:* submits reports correctly and promptly.
11. *Skills:* knowledge and ability in varied activities.
12. *Safety Hazards:* recognizes and eliminates them.
13. *Facility Upkeep:* bulletin, play equipment, supplies and apparatus.

Overall Evaluation:

Evaluated By: _____   **Employee Signature:** _____

Figure 12—1. Leadership performance evaluation form used by the Montclair, New Jersey, Recreation and Parks Department.

The leadership rating form (Fig. 12–1) used by the Montclair, New Jersey, Recreation and Parks Department is a fairly simple one that makes use of a standardized set of ratings for each trait to be evaluated. In other departments, the evaluation form may provide illustrative comments that assist the evaluator in making judgments.

Richmond, California, Recreation and Parks Department

This department has developed an Employee Performance Record form that has eight personality items to be measured: Knowledge of Work; Initiative and Application; Quality of Work; Quantity of Work; Relations With Other Workers; Dependability; Leadership; and Punctuality. Each of these must be rated according to its own set of five descriptions. For example, under *Initiative and Application*, the descriptions are:

Exceptionally industrious. Highly resourceful and self reliant.   ____

Energetic and conscientious. Goes ahead on own judgment.   ____

Steady and willing worker. Requires little direction.   ____

Inclined to take things easy. Requires occasional prompting.   ____

Wastes time. Needs close supervision.

In addition to rating each of the eight items based on such descriptive phrases, the supervisor must respond to a set of questions that include the following:

Employee's strong points: _____

Progress made since last evaluation
    or beginning of employment: _____

Areas of needed improvement: _____

Mutually agreed-on goals:
    Short-term: _____

    Long-range: _____

Employee development plan: _____

Supervisory recommendation: _____

St. Louis, Missouri, Department of Parks, Recreation and Forestry

In a variation of this type of form, the evaluation rating sheet used by the St. Louis Department of Parks, Recreation and Forestry asks a number of open-ended questions about the employee's attitude and cooperation. Some of these follow:

How many extra projects has the employee attempted during the
    period? _____

How many compliments have been received from supervisors, fellow
    employees and the general public regarding the employee's
    performance? _____

How many complaints have been received regarding the employee's
    performance? _____

Upper Dublin Township, Pennsylvania, Department of Parks and Recreation

In another personnel evaluation form used by the Upper Dublin Township Department of Parks and Recreation, park superintendents are rated on a considerable number of specific areas of job performance. They are graded on a five-point scale, ranging from "unsatisfactory" to "outstanding," on parks maintenance functions such as tree care, mowing and trimming, care of athletic fields, supplies storage, equipment repair and maintenance, safety and training program and trash removal, and on administrative functions such as report preparation, budget control, planning techniques and staff scheduling. As many as 35 different areas of performance are rated in this system.

Long Beach, California, Recreation Department

This department's Employee Appraisal System carries these evaluation approaches somewhat further. Each worker is asked to determine, in conference with his or her immediate supervisor, several "challenging, specific objectives" to be achieved during the next rating period. Such objectives should involve both regularly assigned tasks and new projects or measures for self-improvement. Estimated dates of completion should be given and, when possible, measures of successful performance included. Examples of possible objectives are given in the appraisal report:

> "Develop effective demonstration materials to aid teaching of new crafts skills."
> "Organize a soccer team in the fall."
> Contact fifty families in the area within the next six months."
> "Eliminate a safety hazard."

A second interesting element in the Long Beach appraisal system is that employees are asked to evaluate their supervisors anonymously and to forward the confidential statements to the supervisors for their personal use. Questions such as the following are asked:

> "In your opinion, what kind of job is this supervisor doing? Consider both his or her good points and weaknesses or areas needing improvement."
> "Were you in his or her position, what would you do to improve and to bring about improvement in your employees?"
> "How do you think your Area, District, or the Recreation Department as a whole could become more effective?"

This evaluation approach shows clearly how the review process may be used not only to put ratings of employees' work in their personnel folders, but also to provide positive and helpful input that will assist them in growing as professionals.

Edmonton, Alberta, Canada, Parks and Recreation Department

In this department's employee evaluation system, both leaders and supervisors play an active role.

Leaders' Responsibilities. Edmonton recreation leaders are required to fill out extensive forms that list their job responsibilities under a number of major headings, and to assign to each responsibility a percentage figure, representing the amount of time given to each responsibility during the week. They must describe their work in detail, including (a) statements about those who supervise them and with whom they work in the department; (b) responsibility for financial matters or other administrative functions; (c) role in making or explaining policies; (d) personal schedule, and role in supervising other employees; and (e) difficult or abnormal working conditions and similar information. This form provides a detailed record of employees' job functions, as they perceive them.

Supervisors' Responsibilities. Edmonton recreation supervisors must list six of each employee's major responsibilities and evaluate how well they are being performed. Statements must be written describing employee performance in the areas of *Knowledge, Planning, Organizing Work, Personnel Management, Control, Communications* and *Problem-Solving.* Supervisors must then indicate their plans to promote improvement in each of these areas, listing methods, giving a priority to each and providing a tentative timetable for action. Methods such as the following are suggested:

1. Directed self-development (reading, self-study, and so on).
2. Formal training program (department courses).
3. Outside educational programs (seminars, courses).
4. Counseling and coaching.
5. On-the-job training.

The entire plan must be discussed with the employee, and both employee and supervisor must sign it. Another section of the report requires appraisal of the employee's personal qualities, such as appearance, energy, adaptability, initiative, strengths and areas requiring improvement. A final, confidential section describes the "promotional potential" of the employee and gives the supervisor's judgment as to the best ways in which the individual can be used in the department.

At this point, it becomes clear that employee evaluation is not just something that happens once or twice a year, at the end of a period of work; rather, it is part of a continuing process in which the supervisor attempts to help the leader evaluate his or her own performance and work toward improvement. In effect, the supervisor uses a coaching and counseling process regularly, as part of an ongoing, informal staff development process. Buzzotta, Lefton and Sherberg distinguish between the two, pointing out that *coaching* focuses on improving job skills and job knowledge, whereas *counseling* focuses on problems of attitude and motivation or on interpersonal hangups. They write:

Coaching and counseling is (1) the use of *managerial* (supervisory) *power* (2) to elicit *self-analysis* by the subordinate which (c) combines with the manager's *own* insights and knowledge (4) to produce *self-understanding* on the part of the subordinate, *commitment* to mutually acceptable goals, and a *plan of action* for achieving them.[20]

Evaluation in Other Types of Agencies

Evaluation methods in other types of recreation agencies tend to follow the systems just described, although the qualities or performance criteria reflect the specific objectives of each agency. For example, in therapeutic agencies such as psychiatric hospitals or community agencies serving the mentally retarded or physically disabled, evaluation forms might examine traits such as the employee's understanding of disability, ability to promote constructive participation, rapport with patients or effectiveness as part of the treatment team.

A final example of evaluation forms is drawn from a major youth-serving voluntary organization, the Young Men's Christian Association. In this example, it is possible to see how the items being rated are based on the overall goals of the organization.

Nassau-Suffolk County, New York, Young Men's Christian Association

A recent statement of operational goals of this large, suburban YMCA included the following priorities:
1. Developing and implementing sound and progressive fiscal policies and practices.
2. Giving active leadership and support to closer collaboration with YMCA's and other public and private agencies on a local and regional basis for the purposes of planning, programming and funding.
3. Broadening present membership principles and implementing a unit program fee structure.
4. Recruiting, training and rewarding staff who are able to produce positive results.

These and other "Y" goals are directly reflected in the evaluation form (Fig. 12–2), which deals specifically with characteristics regarded as essential for success in this agency. At the end of the form, if the candidate is rated *Below Average* or *Not Acceptable*, the evaluator must indicate what action is being taken or what training is recommended for the employee. He or she must also give a statement concerning the promotional potential of the individual.

---

[20]V. R. Buzzotta, R. E. Lefton, and Mannie Sherberg: "Coaching and Counseling: How You Can Improve the Way It's Done." *Training and Development Journal*, November 1977, p. 50.

YMCA OF NASSAU-SUFFOLK

INDIVIDUAL PERFORMANCE—PROMOTABILITY RATING

BRANCH: _____ PERSON BEING RATED: _____ DATE: _____

EMPLOYEE'S AGE· _____ YMCA TENURE: _____ SEX: _____

CURRENT POSITION TENURE: _____ PRESENT POSITION: _____

(DO NOT CHECK ITEMS UNLESS YOU ARE CERTAIN)

	Does Not Apply	Not Accept.	Below Avg.	Avg.	Above Avg.	Out-standing
PERFORMANCE						
RESPONSE TO COMMUNITY NEEDS						
PEER WORK GROUP COOPER-ATION						
WORKING RELA-TIONSHIP TO SU-PERIORS						
WORKING RELA-TIONSHIP TO SUBORDINATES						
USE OF RESOURCES						
WORKING WITH BOARDS AND COMMITTEES						
FOLLOW THROUGH						
SUPERVISORY SKILLS						
EMOTIONAL STABILITY						
PROGRAM SKILLS						
RACIAL SENSITIV-ITY						
FUND RAISING ABILITY						
PLANNING ABILITY						
BUILDING ACCOUNTABIL-ITY						
STATISTICAL ACCOUNTABIL-ITY						
INITIATIVE						
FINANCIAL ACCOUNTABIL-ITY						
COOPERATION WITH COMMU-NITY AGENCIES						
INVOLVEMENT OUTSIDE REGU-LAR POSITION						
INNOVATION						

Fig. 12—2. *Voluntary Agency Rating Form*

EVALUATION OF OVERALL PERSONNEL EFFECTIVENESS

As a final aspect of staff development and evaluation processes, it must be pointed out that supervisors should not only evaluate individual employees, but should also be concerned about the overall effectiveness of leaders and other staff members. Alexander cites a single example of how a systematic analysis of the weekly activities of personnel in the Canyonlands National Park in Utah enabled district managers in the park to "pick up literally hundreds of man-days for visitor services." By documenting the weekly activities of each employee in the district, including daily patrols, projects or programs and completed assignments, it was possible to identify both productive and non-productive uses of staff time. In one district, for example, Alexander writes,

> The increase in available days came when this district manager found more days were spent in the contact station than were needed to serve visitors. Hence, he let contact station personnel handle administrative duties when no visitors were present; he got rid of pet projects of marginal value when he found they were absorbing large numbers of man-days; and he more closely controlled patrol activities to curtail excessive patrols in "favorite" areas.[21]

Thus, evaluation may be a useful tool not only for measuring and improving the performance of single staff members but for promoting overall staff interaction and effectiveness. Similarly, the supervisor should be concerned about measuring the effectiveness of his or her own performance on various levels and of the way he or she is being used within the total departmental or agency structure.

SUMMARY OF STAFF DEVELOPMENT PROCESSES

This chapter has provided a detailed analysis of several of the key processes of recreation and parks staff development, with chief emphasis given to orientation, in-service education and evaluation. It has provided general guidelines as well as examples of manuals, courses and forms used in each of these processes. Such staff development functions are extremely important to developing the maximum performance and effectiveness of all employees on leadership and supervisory levels. In addition, they provide a solid basis for supervisory recommendations in the areas of promotion, raises and shifts in assignment—although evaluation should be kept somewhat separate from such administrative procedures if it is to be done within a climate of mutual trust and cooperation.

---

[21]Glen D. Alexander: "Evaluate Your Personnel Services for Greater Productivity." *Parks and Recreation*, October 1978, p. 30.

SUGGESTED EXAMINATION QUESTIONS OR TOPICS FOR STUDENT REPORTS

1. Make a strong case supporting the need for carefully organized and well-supported orientation and in-service training programs in recreation and parks.
2. Several different types of in-service training programs are described in the text. Describe several specific kinds of problem situations or needs for staff development as they might occur in a given agency, and show how a different kind of in-service training program might be planned to meet each need.
3. Develop a philosophy of personnel evaluation that you believe is constructive and in harmony with modern principles of personnel management. Then show, specifically, how this philosophy would be carried out in the evaluation process in a given department.

SUGGESTED ACTION ASSIGNMENTS OR GROUP PROCESS ACTIVITIES

1. Attempt to obtain a personnel manual for a recreation agency. Review the contents and decide whether this agency is one in which you might like to be employed.
2. Try to get permission to attend a regular staff meeting or in-service training session at a recreation agency. Record your reactions in writing, and share them with the supervisor.
3. Contact your college's instructional media or audiovisual center to find out whether videotaping facilities and help are available. If so, team up with a classmate to role-play a hiring interview. Exchange roles, so you each gain experience in interviewing and being interviewed. Play back the videotape, and make a careful critique of your style, reactions and skills in interviewing. Have the class review and discuss the interviews.
4. Select a large municipal, voluntary, therapeutic or other agency, and examine its existing program of staff development. On the basis of principles presented in this chapter, present recommendations for improving this program.
5. Develop a three-part evaluation form for a given agency, including these elements: (a) evaluation of leader by supervisor; (b) evaluation of supervisor by leader; and (c) self-evaluation by each individual.
6. As part of your own self-development process, fill out and review the Leadership-Supervisory Ability and Skill Analysis form on page 375 and share it with your classmates as indicated.

Supervision of Recreation Volunteers

Chapter Thirteen

Volunteers traditionally have been an important part of organized recreation and park programs. In part, this has been because so many people have skills in hobbies, sports or the arts, which have lent themselves to program leadership. It also has been because volunteer leadership has played an important role in the American way of life, with many charitable and public-service organizations counting very heavily upon volunteers to assist their professional staff workers.

Volunteers, simply defined, are individuals who perform services without financial remuneration. They may, however, receive payment in other ways. Some volunteers give their time in order to receive public recognition and approval. Others volunteer to obtain early training for a career, often as part of college field work or internship. Great numbers of individuals volunteer because they are interested in supporting programs that serve members of their families, such as Little League or the Boy or Girl Scouts. Many volunteers work with special organizations that serve the disabled, because they have family members or friends who have a particular type of disability.

Religious denominations in particular make a major contribution to community life through the use of volunteers. The National Council of Jewish Women, for example, has more than 200 local volunteer Councils which, with the assistance of national officers, committees and professional staff, support over 1,200 community service projects plus numerous educational and training activities. The Council's advocacy programs on behalf of the aged, the poor, the ill and children and youth are justified in the following passage:

> Voluntarism is in the finest tradition of Judaism. To volunteer one's time and talents to help a neighbor or advance the common good is to

fulfill one of the basic tenets of our faith. Voluntarism is also uniquely American. In our country the tradition of voluntarism goes back to the very first settlers who fashioned a society based on their joint efforts as volunteers working together cooperatively to develop this new land. Voluntarism is a strong and vital force in our society and must remain so.[1]

Thus, the motivations for volunteering are varied. What types of roles do volunteers assume?

ROLES OF VOLUNTEERS

Generally, these are divided into three categories: (a) administrative or advisory volunteers; (b) program-oriented volunteers; and (c) service volunteers.

Administrative volunteers in recreation and parks generally tend to work closely with the professional executive staff in helping to determine policies, assisting in fund-raising or other fiscal matters, or advising on program or community relations problems. They are often members of boards, commissions or advisory councils. Other individuals, such as business people, architects, professors, planners and psychologists, may also provide volunteer assistance to recreation and park administrators, although they may not be formal members of boards or commissions.

Program-oriented volunteers accept responsibilities for helping to plan, carry out or support direct program activities. Many coaches in youth sports organizations such as Little League, the Catholic Youth Organization or Biddy Basketball are volunteer leaders. In public or voluntary recreation agencies, volunteers may provide transportation, chaperon social programs for teenagers, offer entertainment to nursing homes and hospitals or perform a variety of other tasks essential to carrying out programs successfully.

Service volunteers are those who assist in clerical or other auxiliary functions. In some cases, professional persons who give direct guidance or help to staff members on a volunteer basis—such as journalists who help with public relations, or lawyers who provide sessions of advice on legal liability as part of in-service training—might also be considered service volunteers.

VALUES OF VOLUNTEER LEADERSHIP

Obviously, volunteer leaders hold a wide variety of responsibilities. Often they carry out routine, unchallenging, time-consuming tasks that offer little glamour or excitement, but that must be done. In some cases, however, they undertake difficult and extremely challenging tasks. In general, their values are considered to be the following:

1. Providing assistance in areas where it would be impossible to offer programs without a substantial corps of unpaid workers.

---

[1]National Council of Jewish Women: *Personal Career Portfolio*, 1977, p. 1.

2. Offering special skills, expertise or leadership talents not possessed by regular professional staff members.
3. Providing an emotional ingredient—such as freshness of outlook, enthusiasm and interest—that regular staff members, because of their length of service or heavy work load, often cannot match.
4. Serving as a special link between the community or neighborhood and the recreation department or agency. Volunteers can help professional staff members understand the needs and wishes of community residents and can help interpret department goals to local people.

These values of volunteer recreation leadership are well summarized in section entitled "The Why's and Wherefore's of Volunteers" in the Recreation Manual of the Penetanguishene Mental Health Centre in Ontario, Canada. This manual points out that the volunteer movement seeks to meet two important human needs—the needs of hospital patients for added, personalized human contact and the needs of volunteers themselves for the opportunity to give altruistic service to the community. It suggests that volunteers are particularly able to help long-term patients in mental hospitals, because they do not accept the "dull, gray life" of the institution as the only reality, and because they are part of the outside world:

> Volunteers can give individual attention and personal contact. They can assist at different levels. . . They can help the staff to do the extra jobs for which there is seldom time—reading, writing letters, tidying and sorting personal belongings, playing games, planning and organizing outings and excursions. They must be able to supply specialist help or instruction—in Braille, in languages, piano playing, etc. . . . .

One of the important values of volunteer leadership is the fact that many individuals find leisure fulfillment themselves through community service. Since volunteers *do* accept unpaid positions very largely to meet their own psychological or social needs, it is important to recognize that they may pose a number of serious problems to recreation and park administrators who seek to use them.

Although some volunteers have a high level of ability, others may volunteer for assignments that they are not equipped to handle satisfactorily. Some volunteers cannot be counted on for regular and responsible involvement. In some circumstances, volunteers may be in conflict with the basic goals or philosophy of an organization or may be unwilling to abide by its leadership guidelines or principles. Because they are not regular employees, discipline or other forms of corrective action are difficult to apply.

Even those volunteers who carry out work assignments satisfactorily may pose special problems. They sometimes are resentful of the fact that regular employees are being paid for work that, in their judgment, they are performing more effectively—on an unpaid basis. Too often, the very reasons that compel individuals to volunteer, such as need for approval or recognition, stem from the fact that they may be basically lonely or insecure people. Thus, personality problems may prevent a volunteer from doing an effective job. It sometimes happens that volunteers demand so much of the professional recreation leader's time and attention that they represent a non-productive drain upon the department rather than contributors to its success.

Recognizing these possible difficulties, it is nonetheless true that volunteers have a great deal to offer, and the recreation and park agency that is able to use them effectively should take full advantage of this potential resource. As an example of the kinds of contributions that volunteers can make when well coordinated and directed, the Heritage Conservation and Recreation Service has published a handbook that cites leading examples of citizen-contributed efforts:

> A community center operated for seniors by the Department of Parks and Recreation in *Eugene, Oregon* uses approximately 200 volunteers a year at a value of some $100,000 in volunteer services.
>
> During the 1976–1977 fiscal year, 62,421 volunteers in *Baltimore County, Maryland* served 77 different recreational programs for a total of 856,664 hours.
>
> During a recent ten-month period, some 1,670 *San Leandro, California* volunteers donated almost 19,000 hours of labor to the Recreation Department—all under the coordination of one paid staff person.
>
> In *Seattle, Washington*, the Department of Parks and Recreation recorded 50,000 volunteer-hours during the first six months of 1978.
>
> Over 1,000 school children regularly maintain selected sites in *New York's* Central Park. Elsewhere in New York City, 1,500 volunteers worked on 174 different projects coordinated through the non-profit Parks Council in 1977.[2]

However, to help such programs work, a serious effort must be made in working with volunteers in the following areas: (a) recruitment, (b) selection and placement, (c) orientation and training, (d) ongoing supervision, (e) evaluation and (f) recognition. All of these are essentially supervisory responsibilities and should be carried out, not on a piecemeal or scattered basis, but through intelligent communitywide or agencywide planning and direction.

RECRUITMENT OF VOLUNTEERS

First, it is necessary to determine the need for volunteers and the kinds of functions they may fulfill. Any agency that uses volunteers should define their potential roles and determine the kinds of individuals they need to carry out these unpaid assignments. It should then identify the possible sources for volunteers. Recruitment may use either the "rifle" or the "shotgun" ap-

---

[2]Heritage Conservation and Recreation Service: *Volunteer Handbook: A Resource Guide.* Washington, D.C., U.S. Department of Interior, September 1978.

proach. That is, recruitment appeals may be directed to the public at large or to groups or agencies serving special populations. Examples of techniques for recruiting volunteers fall under the following categories:

1. General publicity addressed to the community at large, through such media as television, radio, newspapers, advertisements in subways or buses and similar methods.
2. Appeals in the form of letters, invitations or speakers who target such organizations as service clubs, Parent-Teacher Associations, hospital auxiliaries or sports groups as potential sources of volunteers.
3. Emphasis on the need for volunteers in the bulletins, newsletters or brochures published by an agency as part of its overall public relations effort.
4. Development of special cooperative programs with appropriate organizations, such as a nursing home having a special arrangement with a community-based Senior Citizens' Club that furnishes volunteers on a regular basis.
5. Seeking direct volunteer assistance from those who have an important stake in the work of an agency—such as youth recreation programs obtaining parent volunteer help.
6. Development of continuing field work relations with nearby colleges or universities, and particularly with their departments of recreation or social work.
7. Affiliation with a central recruitment and referral agency in the community that coordinates the assignment of volunteers to varied social agencies.

Customarily, many agencies begin with a generalized use of the media to reach the public at large and then "zero-in" on more selective groups.

Much information has been gathered about the types of motivations that affect the willingness of individuals to volunteer. For example, a recent conference of public and private agencies identified the following reasons for *not* being willing to volunteer: (a) timidity, shyness or lack of confidence; (b) fear of taking risks; (c) reluctance to associate with certain types of clients, such as the physically disabled, aged or mentally retarded; (d) a feeling of not really being needed; (d) fear of being insufficiently qualified; (e) laziness or lack of motivation; (f) the fact of not having been invited personally to volunteer; and (g) the view that the volunteer assignment would not be interesting enough.

On the other hand, it has been found that positive factors in recruitment include the following: (a) a feeling that the job to be done is an important one; (b) a sense of participating in community programs; (c) agreement with the basic objectives of an organization; (d) a feeling that volunteer work would contribute to one's self-development, and particularly to professional ambitions; (e) the wish to make a contribution to society or to other human beings in need; and (f) other psychosocial rewards, such as approval and recognition by others.

In view of these factors, it is clear that recruitment should not be carried out casually and should in fact be made the responsibility of a knowledgeable and capable individual. Some organizations employ volunteer coordinators, usually on the supervisory level. The Volunteer Coordinator Guide, published by the Center for Leisure Study and Community Service of the University of Oregon, states this about the volunteer coordinator:

> . . . he is responsible for developing and implementing the volunteer program within his organization. . . . He may recruit, interview, select, orient, train, place, supervise, motivate, recognize and evaluate volunteers. He may also be responsible for public relations, funding, budgeting, and record-keeping. . . .

Such individuals should be in close touch with community groups and organizations and should be highly knowledgeable about the agencies they represent. They should be good "salespersons" in terms of being able to convince people to invest their time and energies in volunteer work. They should be able to work effectively with the groups that have traditionally provided the bulk of social service volunteers as well as with others that have been relatively untapped but could be useful sources of volunteers, such as blue- or white-collar workers, teenagers and retired citizens.

SELECTION AND PLACEMENT OF VOLUNTEERS

When individuals volunteer for unpaid work with a recreation and park agency or department, it is important that they meet with the staff member responsible for coordinating volunteer services, so that their background and qualifications can be reviewed and the wisest possible decision made about accepting their application and placing them within the agency. At this point, there should be a careful examination of the volunteer's background, experience, skills, motivation for volunteering and similar information. A well-organized volunteer service will ask the candidate to fill out a detailed background form that systematically supplies the following kinds of information:

1. Personal information (name, address, telephone number, closest relatives).
2. Club or organization memberships.
3. Past experience in volunteer work.
4. Past experience or skills in dramatics, games, music, hobbies or other recreational activities.
5. Educational background.
6. Clerical skills.
7. Schedule of availability (time preferred).
8. Occupation.
9. Transportation capability, including ability to transport others.
10. Source of referral.
11. Additional relevant information, including personal references.

In addition to this information, some agencies, particularly those concerned with health care, also ask for information about the health of the prospective volunteer and include a permission form to be signed by parents or guardians so that volunteers who are minors may be given emergency medical care, if necessary.

In a thorough personal interview, the volunteer coordinator should explore the individual's motivations and get a general picture of his or her personality. It is at this point that the coordinator makes a judgment as to whether the candidate would make a contribution to the department or might pose problems. As an example of the qualities sought, the Penetanguishene Mental Health Centre seeks the following personal qualities or attitudes in volunteers:

1. Maturity and stability.
2. Positive work motivations and self-directed manner.
3. Quality of being perceptive, but not rigidly judgmental.
4. Empathy, but not excessive sentimentality.
5. Willingness to learn.
6. Being a "doer," a normally busy and active person, and having a strong sense of identity.

At the same time, the volunteer should be given a thorough picture of the agency itself—its history, organization, goals and philosophy—as well as a basic understanding of the kinds of persons it serves. This would be particularly important in the case of therapeutic agencies serving special populations, for which it would be desirable that the potential volunteer have a detailed understanding of the individuals with whom he or she would be working. A third element in such conferences would be a review of the types of positions that the volunteer might hold and areas in which he or she might be of service. These vary widely according to the type of agency or department.

For example, the Richmond, California, Department of Parks and Recreations makes use of volunteers in a variety of special roles and settings. The classifications of these volunteers and their duties include the following:

Equipment and Supplies Assistants: (a) keeping supply room in order; (b) keeping equipment in working order; (c) dispensing various types of tools or supplies; (d) dispensing and controlling suits and towels at swimming pools; and (e) keeping inventories and records of supplies and equipment.

Technicians in Performing Arts Programs: (a) movie projector operator; (b) phonograph operator in dance classes; (c) lighting or stage manager in drama productions; and (d) accompanist for musical activities.

Assistant Recreation Leaders: (a) helping club or special interest group leaders; (b) acting as monitor for large play areas such as playgrounds or gyms; (c) leading special activities such as story-telling; (d) serving as officials or judges for contests or games; and (e) maintaining bulletin boards.

At the White Plains, New York, Center for Nursing Care, youth and adult volunteers assist in the following program areas:

Art cart	Religious services—assisting clergy
Arts and crafts	Sensory training sessions
Book cart	Serving refreshments
Bulletin board posting	Sewing circle
Civic projects	Escort service
Current events discussion	Flower arranging
Driver corps	Games and cards
Newsletter assistance	Hostessing
One-to-one visiting	Strolling with patients
Plant care	Showing slides and movies
Reading aloud	Talking book machine

At the Penetanguishene Mental Health Centre, volunteers assist in both ward and outside activities. Examples include a wide variety of roles:

> *On the Ward:* answering telephone, clerical assistance, bathing patients, bedmaking, escorting patients, feeding patients, giving massage and exercise, library trolley, messenger service, providing entertainment, playing checkers and chess, organizing bingo, reading to patients, talking to lonely patients and writing letters for patients.
>
> *Outside:* assisting staff with patients on holidays or outings, helping in social club for discharged patients, inviting patients home, making survey of lodgings for discharged patients, providing transportation for outings and bringing family or friends to hospital and visiting discharged patients.

In the field of employee recreation, DeFranco suggests that volunteer assignments may include the following: (a) *administrative or advisory help,* usually involving responsibilities on boards, councils or committees or tasks such as carrying out surveys of recreation interests; (b) *group leadership,* involving a direct role in designing, organizing and carrying out varied program activities; (c) *non-leadership roles,* such as officiating at sporting events, furnishing transportation or acting as stage crew or ticket-takers in drama programs; (d) *clerical or maintenance work,* including registering participants and other office duties; and (e) *miscellaneous services,* such as preparing publicity material, participating as a guest speaker or providing other needed expertise.[3]

At the same time that the possible roles are laid out, the Volunteer Coordinator should describe fully the regulations governing the use of volunteers, the expectation that the department or agency has of volunteers and the possible benefits that may be provided, such as meals or other "fringe" items. It is at this initial meeting that the volunteer coordinator should attempt to screen out those who appear to be unstable, who have unrealistic goals or expectations or who seem to lack needed skills or personal qualities.

---

[3]Peter De Franco: "Recreation Volunteers." *Recreation Management,* April 1978, pp. 12–14.

ORIENTATION AND TRAINING OF VOLUNTEERS

When a definite commitment has been made, the volunteer should receive a careful orientation to insure that he or she knows exactly what is expected, as well as the basic information about the department or agency he or she will be working in. Typically, the following areas should be covered in orientation meetings (those that were dealt with during the initial interview and selection process need not be repeated):

1. Introducing new volunteers to the physical layout of the department, agency or facility where they will be working.
2. Having them meet the people they will be working with, and giving them an understanding of their functions and responsibilities.
3. Reviewing the basic philosophy and objectives of the organization, and making these as specific and factual as possible, in operational terms.
4. Outlining the specific tasks and functions of volunteers in precise terms, including time schedule, individuals to whom they will be responsible and how each task should be carried out.
5. Giving background information about the clientele they will be working with—their characteristics, background, limitations, needs and other useful information.
6. Other regulations or legal limitations to the work of the volunteer, such as elements of safety, accident prevention, first aid or rules relating to discipline or behavior control.

Following the orientation period, volunteers should receive continuing assistance in the form of in-service training programs, although it may not be feasible to involve them in the full range of staff development activities that are provided for regular paid workers. These activities are intended to strengthen their leadership skills and give them a fuller sense of involvement in the agency's work.

SUPERVISION OF VOLUNTEERS

Too often, volunteers are not given the same degree of conscientious supervision that professional workers receive. They should, however, be regularly observed and assisted by professional staff members. Such supervision will indicate to volunteers that their contributions are being taken *seriously*—that they are not being ignored or treated in an off-hand manner simply because they are *giving* their time. The assignments must be meaningful, not just "busy work."

Supervisors should meet with volunteers at regular intervals to review their work and to discuss problems that may have developed. When problems *do* occur, they frequently stem from the following causes: (a) poor communications, (b) lack of adequate job descriptions, (c) inadequate screening or inappropriate assigning of volunteers, (d) misconceptions held by the volunteer about the agency and (e) conflict with other staff members.

The solution to such difficulties should be arrived at by the supervisor and volunteer meeting together, discussing the problem and attempting to reach improved understandings that will solve it. It may be necessary to give additional training, to give the volunteer different responsibilities or to terminate the volunteer arrangement.

The key factor in the volunteer–agency relationship is *motivation.* If volunteers are properly motivated and have a sense of satisfaction in working at a significant job, as well as faith in the program to which they are assigned, it is usually possible to keep them enthusiastic and interested in the volunteer assignment.

EVALUATION OF VOLUNTEERS

An important element in the volunteer process is the evaluation procedure. Accurate records of the volunteer's work should be kept, including careful reports of attendance and participation. The Volunteer Coordinator Guide, prepared by the Center for Leisure Study of the University of Oregon, provides an excellent volunteer evaluation form that covers many of the same points usually found in regular staff evaluation forms (see pages 298–303).

Such evaluation forms and procedures are helpful in providing a concrete basis for counseling volunteers and helping them improve their work. They also are useful in making out reference statements for individuals who do volunteer work with an agency and, years later, request that personal references be sent to a college or university or to a potential employer.

RECOGNITION OF VOLUNTEERS

A final important guideline for the effective supervision of volunteers is that they must receive recognition and rewards for their contribution.

Rewards come in a number of ways. For example, some elements of the on-the-job experience may serve to encourage and motivate the volunteer from the outset. These include having a uniform (a practice in many hospitals or nursing homes); having benefits such as meals, a transportation pool and insurance coverage; and gaining professional skills through in-service training. Beyond the concrete advantage of volunteer work, unpaid workers also may achieve personal satisfaction from the knowledge that they have done a worthwhile job and have contributed significantly to the lives of others or to community well-being.

In addition, volunteers who have performed successfully should be given evidence of this in the form of concrete tokens of recognition. There are many ways in which an agency can make its appreciation known to volunteers, including the following:

1. Regular praise and encouragement, given by supervisors or other key professional workers.
2. Publicity, through mention of the volunteer's work in department newsletters or releases to newspapers or other media.
3. Letters of commendation, or special mention of volunteer contributions at board or staff meetings or at annual meetings of the organization.
4. Increased responsibilities, or change of title.
5. Award of pins, plaques or special certificates of appreciation.

Some organizations have "volunteer recognition days" or other events at which they single out for praise all those who have provided assistance to their programs throughout the year. The American Hospital Association encourages such events, and some state Departments of Health, as in Connecticut, make available several different achievement certificates, based on length and type of service in health-related facilities. In one form or another, recognition is essential to the successful use of volunteers in recreation and park service.

SUGGESTED EXAMINATION QUESTIONS OR TOPICS FOR STUDENT REPORTS

1. What are the major reasons that volunteers are so essential in many public and voluntary recreation programs? What unique benefits do they provide?
2. Identify and discuss some of the major problems involved in working with volunteers. How can these best be overcome?
3. Outline a careful, detailed process of selecting, training, supervising and providing recognition for volunteers as it might be carried on within a specific community agency.

SUGGESTED ACTION ASSIGNMENTS OR GROUP PROCESS ACTIVITIES

1. Examine a specific agency, such as a hospital, nursing home or youth organization, with respect to its use of volunteers. Do a detailed report of its recruitment and assignment methods and the level of supervision given to its volunteers.
2. Prepare a handbook for a specific organization or public recreation and park department to orient volunteers to the agency and to their roles.
3. Brainstorm (see Chapter 14) with several classmates on the topic "Why do people volunteer?" in order to identify the variety of motivating factors that lead people to take volunteer assignments.
4. Explore (in your own mind first) whether you would supervise volunteers differently than you would paid staff. Then, in small groups, discuss your opinions and those of your classmates.

Problem-Solving in Leadership and Supervision

Part Four

Problem-Solving in Recreation and Parks

Chapter Fourteen

Throughout this text, a number of guidelines have been presented for effective leadership and supervision in recreation and parks. These guidelines provide useful directions for handling most routine situations or responsibilities. However, it is probable that other situations that call for special solutions will arise from time to time. Situations of this type demand creative and intelligent decision-making and problem-solving.

These two terms are often treated synonymously in popular usage. Actually, they are not identical. Jubenville suggests that there are several levels of decision-making, ranging from *primary decisions,* which are the strategic decisions made in determining long-range directions an agency will follow, through so-called *reflex decisions,* which are decisions made every day in the operation of recreation systems.[1]

This text takes the position that *decision-making* is often of a routine nature, involving the application of basic departmental policies and sound judgment to choosing among alternatives. In contrast, the term *problem-solving* implies that there are barriers to an easy solution, or that a series of actions must be carried out over time before the matter can be successfully resolved. Obviously, effective problem-solving should lead to intelligent decision-making.

THE PROBLEM-SOLVING PROCESS

Exactly how are problems dealt with in most public or voluntary organizations? Several basic approaches may be identified.

---

[1]Alan Jubenville: *Outdoor Recreation Planning.* Philadelphia, W. B. Saunders, 1976, pp. 29–30.

Authoritarian Action. Here, the administrator or supervisor simply makes a decision on a unilateral basis, without consulting other subordinate employees or program participants.

Group-Centered Problem Solving. In direct contrast is the approach in which the members of the team become involved in a process of group discussion and analysis that examines alternatives and ultimately decides on an appropriate course of action. Such team-oriented approaches to problem-solving have become increasingly popular in recent years.

Analysis by Planning Specialists. In some recreation and park departments, problems of a special nature or of a high level of importance are assigned to special teams of planners or experts in systems analysis. Such teams do a careful analysis of the problem and arrive at recommended solutions.

Decisions by Higher Authorities. One way of dealing with difficult problems is to automatically "pass the buck" by moving them up the chain of command. This may be done either because lower-level employees do not want to take the responsibility for handling more serious problems or because administrators have made clear that they *wish* to be consulted on all such matters.

Avoidance. A final approach is simply to avoid the problem and hope it will go away. Although there is some justification for letting difficulties work themselves out and for not making an emergency out of every momentary problem, this ostrich-like approach is obviously not a desirable course of action.

Stages of Problem-Solving

Six stages are essentially involved in effective problem-solving. These are (a) recognizing the problem, (b) assigning responsibility for it, (c) gathering relevant data, (d) identifying and analyzing alternative courses of action, (e) selecting an alternative and (f) implementing the decision and following up on it.

Recognizing the Problem

As indicated earlier, many routine difficulties can be solved by ordinary, day-by-day decision-making processes through the automatic application of departmental policies or procedures. For example, in most recreation and park departments, drinking on the job would normally call for a warning, followed by suspension if it continued. However, unless the problem were very severe and touchy (if, for instance, the individual involved brought political pressure to bear to protect himself, or if it involved a large number of employees), it would not call for special problem-solving attention.

On the other hand, problems that are severe, of long duration or concerned with controversial areas call for a problem-solving approach. Examples of such problem areas follow:

1. Problems of staff functioning—personality conflicts, consistently poor work records, serious insubordination, grievance cases or matters affecting the unity of the group.
2. Problems with participants, such as low levels of attendance; unwillingness to accept rules dealing with fighting, drinking or drug use; antagonism toward staff members; and so on.
3. Problems of co-worker relationships involving difficulties between peers or between supervisors and subordinates, that are based on disagreements about responsibilities, conflicts between cliques of employees or departmental policies.
4. Problems of interdepartmental relationships. The conflict may involve a disagreement as to objectives or jurisdictional rights of a public recreation and park department and another municipal department, or it may occur between different departments in a single institution, such as activity therapies and nursing in a hospital.
5. Problems of community relations, such as complaints by parents, community councils or local business persons or serious difficulties in obtaining public support, cooperation or volunteer assistance.

In all such cases, it is essential first to recognize the severity of the problem in order to determine whether it requires special attention rather than routine decision-making procedures. Next, it is important to recognize the problem for what it is. This means that attention too often is paid only to the symptoms stemming from a problem rather than to the problem itself. This is like paying attention only to the small portion of an iceberg that is visible and ignoring the much greater bulk beneath the waves. It is essential to recognize and to zero-in on the real difficulty and not merely deal with the symptoms.

Assigning Responsibility

The second stage of problem-solving is to determine who should be responsible for tackling a particular difficulty. This usually depends on the level of concern that is involved. For example, if the matter involves a single playground or community center or a small group of participants, it is likely that it would be assigned to a local recreation leader for solution. If the problem were a more persistent or widespread one, it would probably become the responsibility of a district supervisior. If it were more serious, it is probable that the departmental administrator would assume responsibility or would ask a staff assistant to take over the task of investigation and problem-solving.

In general, it is best to handle such matters on the lowest possible level of staff operations, both to avoid overloading administrators with unnecessary responsibilities and to build a sense of authority at lower levels. However, since administrators will ultimately be held responsible for all staff decisions or actions taken to solve problems, it is usually wise to inform them of all such matters and to consult them when controversial issues are involved. In any case, it is essential to make a clear assignment of responsibility for a particular problem. Making it "everyone's responsibility" in effect makes it "no one's responsibility."

Gathering Relevant Data

The third step is to investigate the problem thoroughly, gathering all relevant information. This should involve getting a precise picture of what has happened, who the concerned individuals are, the related circumstances, the possible causes of the difficulty and appropriate solutions for it.

This may be done in a variety of ways: (a) by direct observation of the situation; (b) by discussing it with the individuals involved; (c) by examining case records; (d) by interviewing other individuals who are not directly involved but who are familiar with the situation; (e) by informal investigation, such as sending to a community center a group of "participants" who do not identify themselves; or (f) by a formal investigation. In some cases, it may be necessary to gather considerable amounts of statistics (as in the case of departmental efforts to reduce vandalism or accidents) and to analyze them through computer program methods. In other cases, observation and discussions will be sufficient to get the needed information.

Once the needed information has been gathered, it must be analyzed. Jubenville suggests that for this to be done effectively, planners or managers must have a clear sense of the total system within which decisions must be made, as well as the conceptual framework that should govern it. He writes:

> *Models.* Before someone attempts to solve a problem, he must first understand the total system—subsystems, phases, and interrelationships—with which he is working. One has to understand the potential effects that a problem-oriented decision may have on other parts of the system. . . without using the "trial and error" process.[2]

The manager must also analyze the data within a relevant conceptual framework, either derived from education, experience and observation or established through formal agency guidelines. These help the manager see beyond details, understand the dynamic process at work and apply principles that govern effective professional practice in the field.[3]

Identifying and Analyzing Alternative Courses of Action

When the data have been analyzed, it is time to determine what the alternative courses of action may be and their relative merit. Occasionally the

---

[2]*Ibid.*, p. 30.
[3]*Ibid.*, p. 30.

answer seems crystal clear; there is only one logical solution. However, such cases are rare. Instead, in most situations, several possible courses of action are likely to appear. For example, if the problem concerned extremely poor participation in recreation activities in a given area of a city, alternative solutions intended to promote better participation might include the following:

1. Changing the program entirely by eliminating all existing activities and introducing an entirely new schedule of activities and events.
2. Building several new facilities to increase interest and attendance in appealing new programs.
3. Changing the leadership and supervisory staff, with the view that new faces and leadership approaches might attract large numbers of fresh participants.
4. Carrying out a comprehensive survey of community residents to gather their suggestions for improving and strengthening the program.
5. Eliminating all fees and charges, based on the possibility that these are discouraging large numbers of participants from attending program activities.
6. Mounting a large-scale publicity campaign to draw attention to the program and increase attendance.

Any or all of these alternative approaches *might* be helpful in solving the problem. Obviously, they are not all feasible or likely to be of equal value. The following questions must be asked in examining alternative solutions to a problem:

Is a solution feasible, in the sense that it can be done within departmental limitations on funding, staff facilities, or other "cost" areas?

Does it seem to get at the heart of the problem rather than just the outward symptoms? Is it likely to be effective?

Is it an appropriate or desirable solution, in terms of basic departmental philosophy or policies?

What barriers stand in the way of each solution that must be overcome if it is to be successful?

Selecting an Alternative

In arriving at a decision, the manager or planning group must carefully scrutinize each alternative in order to determine whether it is a logical and appropriate one. Sometimes a choice must be made between "playing it safe," by making a decision that goes by the books and represents a literal, strict interpretation of agency policy, and "taking a flyer," in the sense of making a more experimental or risky decision. The probability of success must be balanced against the measurable cost and desirability of each solution being considered. Finally, a decision is made in favor of one of the alternatives.

Implementing the Decision

The final stage in problem-solving is to take action to carry out the approved alternative. Often, this cannot be done without careful preparation and briefing of all those concerned.

For example, a severe problem of low personnel morale might result in a plan to shift a number of individuals from one job to another, to promote some workers while demoting others and to initiate a general realignment of staff responsibilities. Once the decision is made, to move ahead directly with these actions might result in even lower morale, lawsuits, a work stoppage or similar reactions. Therefore, before this plan could be implemented, it would be advisable to hold a full-scale briefing of all individuals as to the actions being taken and the reasons for them. It would also be advisable to present and discuss the plan with the municipal personnel department, legal counsel and the labor union involved. In some cases, these parties would have been involved in earlier discussion and may have contributed their views about the appropriate action to be taken.

Finally, each individual involved should be given the reassurance that the department is concerned with improving its overall functioning and is interested in working with each employee from this point on to develop his or her career potential. If the problem-solving process has involved consultation with all staff members, with effective two-way communication throughout, this sort of preparation should make it possible to put the plan into effect. Once this has been done, it is obviously important to give it all the departmental support possible, to monitor it regularly and to evaluate its success.

THE GROUP-CENTERED APPROACH TO PROBLEM-SOLVING

Obviously, the manner in which a supervisor or administrator approaches the task of decision-making and problem-solving reflects his or her entire leadership style. Tannenbaum, Weschler and Massarik list a series of personal statements that reflect different administrative viewpoints on problem-solving:[4]

> "I put most problems into my group's hands and leave it to them to carry the ball from there. I serve merely as a catalyst, mirroring back the people's thoughts and feelings so that they can better understand them."
>
> "It's foolish to make decisions oneself on matters that affect people. I always talk things over with my subordinates, but I make it clear to them that I'm the one who has to have the final say."
>
> "Once I have decided on a course of action. I do my best to sell my ideas to my employees."

---

[4]Robert Tannenbaum, Irving R. Weschler, and Fred Massarik: *Leadership and Organization: A Behavioral Science Approach.* New York, McGraw-Hill Book co., 1961, p. 67.

"I'm being paid to lead. If I let a lot of other people make the decisions I should be making, then I'm not worth my salt."

"I believe in getting things done. I can't waste time calling meetings. Someone has to call the shots around here, and I think it should be me."

These differences of opinion may be illustrated in a diagram that shows the range from one extreme of authoritarian, "boss-centered leadership" on the left to the other extreme of "subordinate-centered leadership" on the right (Figure 14–1).

Most authorities today agree that the group-centered appraoch to decision-making and problem-solving is a constructive and useful method. Generally, group problem-solving serves to bring a greater wealth of information and judgment to bear upon a problem. As pointed out earlier, it helps the morale of staff members to be consulted and drawn into a meaningful process of planning and decision-making. Shared decision-making is likely to result in a greater consensus in reaching the final solution, which should make it easier to develop support for the solution's implementation.

A number of special techniques may be used in group problem-solving. The first of these, and the most widely used, is the group discussion process. Other methods include sensitivity training, the use of encounter groups, "brainstorming" and role-playing. Each of these is discussed in the concluding section of this chapter.

Boss-centered leadership						Subordinate-centered leadership
Use of authority by the supervisor						Area of freedom for subordinates
Superior makes decision and announces it.	Supervisor "sells" decision.	Supervisor presents ideas and invites questions.	Supervisor presents tentative decision, subject to change.	Supervisor presents problem, gets suggestions, makes decision.	Supervisor defines limits; asks group to make decision.	Supervisor permits subordinates to function within limits set by superior.

Figure 14–1. *Supervisory Behavior in Decision-Making (Robert Tannenbaum and Warren H. Schmitt: "How to Choose a Leadership Pattern."* Harvard Business Review, March—April, 1958, p. 96.)

Group Discussion

Group discussion relies on the orderly but informal interchange of ideas among a number of individuals. (There are usually 12 persons or fewer in the group situation.) As opposed to an arrangement in which a supervisor or administrator might stand before a group of subordinates who are sitting in rows facing him or her, the group discussion method works best when all members have equal status in the situation. A face-to-face arrangement is best achieved by having all participants place their chairs in a circle. There are no special rules for group discussion beyond those of simple courtesy. Each member of the group is expected to contribute, when he or she has something to say, and to address his or her views to the entire group rather than to the leader. A conscious effort is made to get all members of the group to participate as fully as possible, and therefore group members should avoid dominating the discussion through overly long statements.

In most group situations, different members of the group tend to assume various roles that reflect their individual personalities, and which are needed to promote the effective functioning of the group. These roles are likely to include the following:

> *Initiator.* This is the person who gets things started—either the formal head of the work team who issues a formal request or order, or an informal member of the work team who mobilizes others to begin to plan together.
>
> *Information Seekers and Opinion Seekers.* These individuals elicit fuller understanding of the situation through their questions. The information seeker is concerned chiefly with facts, whereas the opinion seeker asks others for their views and values. Both tend to promote full communication within the group.
>
> *Elaborator.* This individual develops the meaning, explains the rationale or gives examples that enrich the contributions that have already been made by others.
>
> *Coordinator.* The purpose of this role is to help orient the group to its goals and enable it to understand the direction in which it is heading in the discussion. The coordinator also may evaluate the group's performance or may help others do so.
>
> *Energizer.* This individual urges the group toward action, fuller involvement or a higher quality of discussion and participation.
>
> *Procedural Technician.* This role involves routine tasks that assist group functioning, such as distributing writing materials; arranging chairs, blackboards or other visual materials; or providing other resources needed by the group.
>
> *Recorder.* This individual keeps a record of the discussion, not in the sense of formal "minutes" (since group discussions do not rely on parliamentary procedure) but rather as a report of the major ideas covered or suggestions made.

Other roles that are normally played in group discussions include the following: an *encourager*, who provides praise, agreement and acceptance; a *critic* and a *discipliner*, who point out negative contributions or inappropriate behavior within the group; a *harmonizer*, who mediates conflicts among individuals; a *compromiser*, who reconciles different points of view;

an *integrator*, who helps to build a common group-will and sense of unity; and an *expediter*, who moves the group toward action or helps it arrive at a common decision.[5]

Particularly when there is a need to develop highly innovative solutions, one or more members of the group should have the psychological capacity to apply creative thinking to both the identification and the solution of a problem. Gerald Gordon, Director of the Center for Applied Research at Boston University, concludes that there are two measurable characteristics, which he refers to as *social differentiation* (the ability to discriminate among stimuli) and *remote association* (the ability to find similarities among apparently different and unassociated items), which determine the limits of an individual's ability to use information creatively.[6] Although it may not be feasible to screen group members scientifically to identify these qualities, it is usually possible to recognize those members of the planning team who tend to think innovatively and to encourage their creative input.

Within this framework, although democratic participation is the keynote, a skilled leader can help the group move more efficiently through the process of sharing views and achieving a consensus. Because they are usually vested with authority, in terms of their formal positions within the job hierarchy, supervisors and administrators are often called upon to provide such leadership. Although there are no precise guidelines for group discussion leadership in all situations, a number of general suggestions may be made. The discussion leader, or group chairman, should do the following:

> *Help* group members define the limits of the problem they face.
> *Help* group members define and select the elements of the problem area which are most important and real to them; as they move into the discussion, these may be extended.
> *Encourage* all participants to share their information and views on the problem.
> *Keep* the discussion focused on the problem the group is dealing with rather than on extraneous matters.
> *Help* clarify the contributions to the discussion, and relate these to the short-and long-term goals of the organization.
> *Help* maintain an atmosphere in which cooperation and maximum group productivity can be achieved. Is there freedom of expression and freedom from unhealthy anxiety or other pressures?
> *Help* group members keep the line of discussion clear and moving from a general exploration of the problem toward practical planning and decision-making.
> *Make Use* of all the experiences of group members, and special skills or resources they may have.

---

[5]See Frank P. Sherwood and Wallace H. Best: *Supervisory Methods in Municipal Administration*. Chicago, International City Managers' Association, 1958, pp. 62–65.
[6]Gerald Gordon, quoted in "How to Boost Group Problem-Solving Creativeiy." *Training HRD*, November 1978, pp. 16–17, n.a.

Strive to build a cohesive and productive team, not only to be more successful in this discussion, but in other work experiences and assignments.[7]

Obviously, such group discussions can be extremely helpful in defining the issues, exposing all relevant facts and information, identifying alternatives (and their strengths and weaknesses) and arriving at a decision that appears to have the greatest potential for success. It is important to avoid a situation in which, in a very cohesive group, participants feel strong pressure to agree with others rather than to state their real views. Rivchun describes the process of "groupthink," in which members of a planning committee or task force are reluctant to disagree with each other in front of the group:

> In addition to not voicing concerns because of pressures to agree, other characteristics of groupthink include . . . self-appointed mind guards within the group who cut off any challenging concerns, and a shared feeling of unassailability and self-righteousness. Perhaps most destructive, however, is . . . the tendency for members of the group to think the proposal is a good one without even attempting a critical scrutiny.[8]

At the other extreme is the situation in which longstanding conflicts may exist among group members, preventing them from being able to share effectively in group discussions. Such conflicts, when they exist, are often continuing sources of difficulty within an organization and hamper its overall functioning to a marked degree.

When fundamental disagreements of this type exist, it is necessary to deal with them before attempting to resolve other difficulties. Since the early 1960's, many organizations have made use of newly developed "sensitivity training" or "encounter group" methods to overcome such problems and to build more positive and effective team relationships.

Sensitivity Training

This approach to developing more effective work groups stems from research done at the National Training Laboratories at Bethel, Maine, during the 1950's and 1960's. The research consisted of promoting awareness of group processes and individual behavior through unstructured group experience. By means of a series of stages of development, in which detailed analysis is carried out concerning how individuals behave, how they relate to each other and how they affect the overall functioning of the group, participants are helped to become much more aware of their own psychosocial needs, the meaning of their own behavior and the behavior of others and how to operate most effectively, both as a person and as an individual within an organization or team.

---

[7]Ken Herrold: *Group Problem-Solving Manual*. New York, Teachers College, Columbia University, Center for Improving Group Procedures, pp. 1–2, n.d.
[8]Sylvia Rivchun: "Group Decision-Making." *Leadership*, November 1978, pp. 23–27.

In essence, the sensitivity training process is intended to help people become more aware, more alert, less defensive or aggressive and better able to contribute meaningfully to group processes or ongoing organizational tasks. As an extension of this approach, a variety of organizations, including the well-known Esalen Foundation on the West Coast, developed new group techniques for helping people achieve a state of openness, trust and security with each other. Such "encounter" groups have made use of a wide variety of techniques, including many playlike or social experiences involving physical contact, creative expression, "marathon" sessions and other similar techniques.

Both methods have been used in modified forms by many organizations to improve staff relationships and facilitate group problem-solving processes. To be carried out effectively, they usually require specially trained workshop leaders.

Role-Playing

Another technique that has been widely used in problem-solving situations—particularly those situations involving sharply opposed groups or cliques—is role-playing. This is a device or method that helps group members to explore the interpersonal dynamics of a problem situation. Typically, members of the group assume different roles and act out specific scenes related to the problem as they understand it. Herrold describes some of the basic elements in role-playing, describing it as the "unrehearsed, free expression of individual and group personalities involved in a problem situation":

> The *role-players* are participants on stage in the situation and are taken from the group in an unrehearsed sociodrama.
> The *director* starts, interrupts, resumes, and ends the drama proper; he adds or subtracts actors, shifts roles and situations.
> The *stage* is the locus of the situation, with or without appropriate properties.
> The *situation* is the topic or problem of vital interest; in defining this at the outset, time, place, roles, and relationships are included.
> The *audience* (observers) is comprised of participants off-stage who actively communicate their feelings and responses, and are dependent upon the situation.[9]

Essentially, there are two types of role-playing events: *psychodramas* and *sociodramas*. Psychodramas are essentially concerned with problems in which single individuals or groups of individuals are privately involved. Sociodramas deal with problems in which the private relations of individuals are less important than collective or social factors. Either type may be pre-

---

[9]Ken Herrold: *Role Playing Manual.* New York, Teachers College, Columbia University, Center for Improving Group Procedures, pp. 1–2, n.d.

sented on three levels: (a) totally spontaneous, (b) partially planned and prepared and (c) totally planned and rehearsed presentations.

The major purpose of role-playing as a tool in problem-solving is to give participants—both those actually involved in the acting experience and those who are observing—a fuller sense of involvement and a heightened awareness of the various points of view in a situation. Not infrequently, those taking part in a psychodrama or sociodrama may be asked to take roles that contrast sharply with their own identities. For example, a district recreation supervisor might be asked to play the role of a teenage boy who has been causing problems in his community center, or the departmental director of personnel might assume the identity of a labor union organizer.

Thus, participants are compelled to examine and express—as freely and spontaneously as possible—points of view that are different from their own. Ideally, role-playing helps to create a situation in which there is fuller understanding of the issues, acceptance of both sides of a dispute and awareness of the motivations underlying the points of view of different protagonists. Often, both humor and more serious emotions are vividly expressed in psychodramas and sociodramas.

It should be clearly understood that role-playing does not provide solutions to problem situations by itself. Instead, it helps to develop a climate of understanding, a feeling of cooperation and sympathy, a greater readiness to develop acceptable solutions and perhaps a fuller understanding of what the real issues are. Typically, a group might move from role-playing as an interlude or preliminary stage in its problem-solving process to group discussion aimed at developing alternatives and making a decision for action.

Brainstorming

A final technique that is used to develop a large number of possible solutions to a problem in the most creative and spontaneous way possible is known as "brainstorming." It is based on a town-meeting type of session, in which participants throw rapid-fire suggestions for solving a problem into the hopper. As each idea is suggested, it is immediately written down on a large blackboard; to keep things moving at a fast pace, two recorders may alternately write down the suggestions. A tape recorder may also be used to record suggestions. Certain basic principles apply in brainstorming sessions:

1. All group members are encouraged to make whatever suggestions seem to them to have merit—no matter how far-fetched or unusual they are. They make one suggestion at a time, without long-winded justification or arguments.

2. No one may criticize or analyze previously made suggestions, since this might result in inhibiting new ideas or cutting off the flow of group creativity. Goble suggests a number of "killer phrases" that are to be avoided:

   a. "We've never done it that way before."
   b. "It won't work."

c. "We haven't the time . . . or the manpower."
d. "It's not in the budget."
e. "We've tried that before."
f. "All right in theory but can you put it in practice?"
g. "Too modern."
h. "Too old-fashioned."[10]

3. Individuals may "piggy-back" on previous suggestions by immediately throwing fresh ideas, based on preceding ones, into the session.

After a good number of ideas have been suggested (creativity becomes infectious, and it would not be unusual for a group to present 100 or more suggestions in a half-hour meeting), various procedures may be followed. Customarily, the majority of the group takes a "break" while a small committee goes over the list of ideas and places them into appropriate categories. In a second meeting of the entire group, participants review the suggestions and select those which appear to have the greatest merit. From these they develop actual alternatives for action and arrive at a decision for solving the problem.

The obvious virtue of this process is that it serves to stimulate a wide variety of imaginative ideas, many of which may have rich possibilities.

It should be stressed that every problem, large or small, should not be regarded as requiring a fresh sequence of collecting information, analysis and group decision-making. Instead, an intensive effort should be put into the formulation of policies that will deal with the bulk of possible problems and difficulties in a routine way. Group problem-solving should be reserved, as suggested earlier, for more serious, complex or sustained problems that are not adequately covered by existing policies or procedures.

CONCLUSION

Johnson and Johnson point out that there are several different methods that a group may use in trying to arrive at a decision. These include the following: (a) seeking agreement of the entire group; (b) accepting a majority vote; (c) accepting a minority opinion; (d) developing a compromise based on the individual opinions of group members; (e) relying on the opinion of the group member with the most expertise; (f) accepting the view of the group member with the highest status or level of authority, after a group discussion; and (g) accepting the view of the member with the most authority, without a group discussion.[11]

Obviously, a number of factors influence the choice of each group's decision-making method. These may include the type of decision that has to be

---

[10]Frank Goble: *Excellence in Leadership*. New York, American Management Association, 1972, p. 24.
[11]David W. Johnson and Frank P. Johnson: *Joining Together: Group Theory and Group Skills*. Englewood Cliffs, New Jersey, Prentice-Hall, Inc., 1975, p. 59.

made, the kind of climate the group wishes to establish, the amount of time and other resources available or the setting in which the group exists. In general, however, supervisors and leaders should consistently strive to achieve the maximum level of group participation in the problem-solving and decision-making process, both to improve the quality of group cohesion and to insure support for decisions once they have been made.

SUGGESTED EXAMINATION QUESTIONS OR TOPICS FOR STUDENT REPORTS

✓ 1. What are the differences between problem-solving and decision-making, as outlined in this chapter? How do they relate to the development and use of departmental or agency policies?
2. Outline the specific steps or stages of problem-solving. Show how each of these might be approached differently, according to whether one used the group-centered approach or more authoritarian methods.
3. Select one of the following techniques for problem-solving: "group discussion," "brainstorming" or "role-playing." Do additional research on this method, and then prepare a set of guidelines that will be useful in employing it in recreation situations.
4. When personality problems or conflicts cause staff difficulties, sensitivity training may be useful in developing more constructive attitudes and behavior. What are some of the key elements in this method and what, in your opinion, are some of its limitations?

SUGGESTED ACTION ASSIGNMENTS OR GROUP PROCESS ACTIVITIES

1. Interview a recreation professional on a leadership or supervisory level, and identify the most common types of problems he or she must deal with. Then, as a class exercise, use appropriate problem-solving techniques in a role-playing situation to solve these problems.
2. Using the group discussion method in solving one of the case studies in Chapter 15, identify the individual roles (i.e., initiator, encourager, and so on) that emerge. Discuss these with other class members after the group discussion has concluded.

Case Studies in Leadership and Supervision

Chapter Fifteen

One of the most effective ways of developing one's understanding of leadership and supervision is to examine and analyze case studies dealing with actual problem situations. This method is often used in college courses in recreation leadership, supervision or administration as well as in departmental in-service training workshops. It represents a useful means of learning more about the kinds of problems that are faced in real job situations and of developing techniques for effective group problem-solving and decision-making.

This chapter presents 24 case studies based on incidents or problem situations described by graduate students in courses at several colleges and universities where the authors of this book have taught. The first 12 are presented in full detail; the second 12 are much briefer. The cases deal with four types of problems: (a) those having to do with relationships between leaders and participants; (b) those analyzing problems between leaders on approximately the same level of authority; (c) those concerned with problems between leaders and supervisors; and (d) those focusing on problems between recreation and park administrators and their boards or community groups.

In several cases the problem sequences have been "played out," in the sense that they have been described fully, including the actions taken by those responsible and their apparent outcomes. In others, the cases are described, without a final action having been taken; alternative solutions may or may not appear in the presentation of the problem.

ANALYSIS OF THE CASES

In reading the 12 fully detailed case studies as class assignments, students may be asked to submit individual papers analyzing the cases and responding to the questions that follow each one. Or, they may volunteer to take part in team problem-solving groups to report on and fully analyze some of the more complicated cases. If such assignments are undertaken, students may wish to make use of some of the problem-solving or decision-making methods described in the previous chapter, such as brainstorming or role playing.

Obviously, there is no single "best" solution to any of these problems, nor is it possible to present a set of universal guidelines for problem-solving. Different organizations have widely varying philosophies, and the unique differences among communities, as well as the variations among personalities, mean that each case must be assessed on its own merits, and individual solutions developed. In general, the guidelines presented throughout this text that deal with group dynamics, the goals of recreation and specific methods in various types of settings should be useful in analyzing these cases.

In analyzing the 12 shorter case studies, students and instructors may elect either to develop them more fully (adding hypothetical details to them) as individual or small group assignments or simply to discuss them on the basis of the information that is given.

For both groups of problems, it is essential to recognize that all problem situations have both *symptoms* and *causes*. It is not enough to deal with the most obvious aspect of problems—their symptoms. These may be attacked easily enough, but such action does not provide lasting solutions. Instead, it is essential to understand and deal with the fundamental causes of each problem situation.

Now—read and analyze the cases!

DETAILED CASE STUDIES

Case No. 1. Counselor at the Youth Home

Tom D. was employed as a youth counselor at Carter Village, a large home for disturbed and dependent youth situated on its own property of 150 acres and located close to a large city. He was put in charge of a group of 10- to 12-year-old boys. By the time the first week of the summer had passed, Tom felt rather smug in the belief that he had struck it off very well with the boys and that few difficulties were likely to appear.

On Tuesday afternoon, he took the boys on a hike in a county park adjacent to Carter Village. While on the trail, several boys confided in Tom, telling him their personal feelings about the Village, discussing their problems with him and generally showing their trust in him. Other than being aware of certain cliques within the group, Tom felt the situation was well in hand. That evening, after supper and general assembly, he took a final headcount of the group and walked with them toward their cottage. At this point, one of the boys, Freddy, came up to Tom and said, "Mr. D., you don't have to take the roster in to Mr. L. (the cottage parent). We're all here—why don't you let me take it in for you?" Without questioning the situation, and feeling in full command, Tom handed the roster slip over to Freddy and headed for his car.

While traveling home, Tom mused that this summer job was quite satisfying—both challenging and professionally rewarding—and a good assignment for a college physical education instructor with a special interest in youth work. At 9 o'clock that evening, however, he received a call from Carter Village's night supervisor, asking if he knew where the group had gone. Apparently, when he left the boys without escorting them directly into the cottage, Freddy and eight of the other boys had decided to take off for "greener pastures," and the cottage parent had not discovered immediately that they were missing.

It took the staff of Carter Village three days to round up the scattered group. Several of them returned to their old neighborhoods in the city, while others hung out in the woods near the Village, playing a game of cat-and-mouse with the searchers. At the expense of a deflated ego, Tom D. concluded that he would never again underestimate a child—normal, disturbed or otherwise.

Questions for Discussion

What were the basic causes of this incident, in your judgment?

How might it have been avoided, i.e., what policies on the part of Carter Village's staff director might serve to prevent this or similar events from taking place again?

Case No. 2. Making Contact With Billy V.

Jeff R., a white college student working as a summer counselor at Camp Stony Creek, a non-sectarian coeducational camp operated by the Federation of Neighborhood Houses, was place in charge of eight boys ranging in age from 12 to 14 years. The boys were mixed in background. Five were white (three were Protestant and two were Jewish) and three were black. All were from low-income families.

During the first week of camp, most of the boys seemed to be getting along well with each other and with the counselor. However, Jeff soon realized that he would have trouble with one of the black boys, Billy V. Billy seemed to have no friends and was constantly picking fights with other campers. Over a three-day period, Jeff tried several ways of controlling Billy's behavior. He punished him by ordering him to "police" the area, by having him do push-ups and, as a last resort, "docking" him by prohibiting him from attending an evening movie with the other boys.

That night, after the boys had gone to bed, Jeff and another counselor went into town, returning to camp about 1 o'clock in the morning. When Jeff returned to his tent, one of the other campers awoke and told him that Billy had urinated in Jeff's cot. Jeff was shocked. The thought of someone deliberately urinating in another person's cot was foreign to him. Furious, he aroused Billy and ordered him to strip the cot and to re-make it with fresh linen. Billy did so sullenly, cursing liberally as he yanked the wet sheets and blanket from the cot. However, since Jeff was much bigger and stronger, Billy obeyed him. When the cot was re-made, the counselor asked Billy why he had done this, but the boy refused to talk.

The following day, Billy had two more fights with other boys and had to be physically restrained each time. Jeff felt that he was reaching the end of his rope with Billy and that he might have to recommend to the camp director that Billy be sent home.

After dinner, the boys decided to play Bombardment (a form of dodge ball). As a last resort, Jeff decided to try a different approach with Billy. He gave him his whistle and asked him to referee the game. At first Billy hesitated. But Jeff told him that he would be completely in charge and announced to the other boys that whatever Billy said counted. What followed in the next few minutes struck Jeff as amazing. Billy went ahead to referee the game efficiently. He made the other boys follow the rules strictly and tolerated no nonsense from any of them.

From that moment on, Billy became a self-appointed assistant counselor. He and Jeff got along very well, and there was no friction between them for the remainder of the camp season.

Questions for Discussion

Without knowing the full background of Billy V.'s behavior problem, why do you think he urinated in his counselor's bed?

How do you regard Jeff's efforts at controlling Billy during the first few days of camp? What else might he have done? In your judgment, what assistance should be given to young camp counselors, in terms of understanding and working with such problems?

What was the key event that turned Billy's behavior around? How do you interpret the cause of this radical change? What principle might Jeff draw from it for his own professional growth?

Case No. 3. Maria's Little Ritual

Nancy W., a nurse who had married and was no longer working, decided to do volunteer work as a recreation aide in a psychiatric hospital. She was accepted at Woods Island Hospital, a large state facility, where her responsibilities consisted chiefly of talking to patients, playing table games and sports with them, helping the occupational and recreational therapists and assisting at parties. She had worked in a state hospital before and was familiar with psychiatric patients.

The staff member responsible for supervising Nancy was a young man, Alex M., who was working for his doctorate in psychology. On the first day she reported for work, he took her, along with another volunteer, to see the ward where they would be assigned and to meet the staff members and some of the patients. As they were leaving the ward after this meeting, they passed the lunchroom where the patients were eating. Alex said, "Wait, there's something I'd like you to see." He called to a woman patient, asking her to come out. When she did not rise, he went in to the lunchroom to bring her out.

Alex introduced her to Nancy by saying, "This is Maria S. She is a catatonic schizophrenic and displays all the classic symptoms of the disease." He asked Maria to show them her little "ritual." When the patient did not respond, he took her hand and said, "Show us your hand ritual." He made a sudden spastic gesture with his hand, and she copied the movement. He commented that this was a very common gesture among catatonics, and they left the area.

On the basis of her past experience and personal philosophy of patient care, Nancy felt that this was inappropriate behavior on Alex's part. She asked him why he had done it. He replied that he did this sort of thing to "shock them out of it." Nancy replied that she felt that it was destructive to patients to put them up for show and that she understood that it was customary hospital policy not to let psychiatric patients know their diagnosis, because they frequently misinterpreted the information or were frightened by it.

Alex grew angry and said that if Nancy did not like his methods, she should resign as a volunteer. However, Nancy remained on the job. When she saw Alex again the following week, he said curtly that there was a universal law that one should never criticize a staff member in front of another staff member. Nancy agreed that she could understand his becoming upset, because other staff members had observed the episode. She apologized and said she hoped they would be able to start over again, although she could not accept the principle of not criticizing another staff member as a "universal" law. Alex replied, "If you can't accept it, you should not be working here." Nancy felt that they were not getting anywhere and merely stated that she wanted to continue to work as a volunteer in the hospital.

Although she did not have frequent contact with Alex, whenever she did, Nancy felt very uncomfortable. Although their relationship improved slightly, they were never really able to get along with each other.

Questions for Discussion

What is your reaction to Alex's asking Maria to show her little "ritual"? In your judgment, why did he become so upset when Nancy criticized him?

Although Nancy might have been justified in her criticism, in what way could she have behaved more constructively?

What recommendations could you make that might help to prevent this type of problem situation?

Case No. 4. Juan's Grand Strategy—The Fake Trip

Juan R. was recreation director in a center run by the Youth Aid League, a voluntary agency operating in a disadvantaged area of the city. One of his responsibilities was to work with a group of boys and girls who ranged in age from the early teens to about 18 or 19. There were approximately 40 participants in all. He was assisted by a woman leader, Luz S. Both Juan and Luz were in their mid-twenties, and neither was professionally trained for this work.

During the summer, most of the members of the group were not in school or working and therefore spent most of their time at the Youth Aid League center. The program went fairly well. Most of the group members were cooperative, except for five older boys, all of whom were about 18 or 19 years old. They occasionally caused difficulty for Juan because they refused to obey center rules, particularly with respect to drinking. However, there were no serious incidents, and they took part satisfactorily in most activities. Because of their age and aggressive behavior, they were regarded by other group members as leaders.

Juan and Luz planned three bus trips to nearby resort areas such as beaches and amusement parks during the summer. They set out in the morning and returned to the city in the late evening. The first bus trip went well. However, on the second one, the five older boys brought some liquor with them, became drunk and caused some difficulty on the beach by getting into a fight with local boys. Although Juan and Luz got them all back safely in the bus for the return to the city, Juan felt that the five older boys would have to be barred from making the last bus trip of the summer.

Plans were announced to the youth group that this trip would be made to Pine Shelter Beach, a popular resort area about 40 miles from the city— and that the clique of older boys would not be permitted to go with the group. However, one of the girls told Luz that the older boys were planning to follow them in a car to Pine Shelter Beach and disrupt the outing. In fact, she disclosed that some younger members of the group had lent them money to help them with the expense of making the trip on their own.

Juan decided to outmaneuver the group. The day before the trip, he announced to several members of the group that he and Luz had changed their plans and that the trip would be taken to Atlantic Knolls, another popular beach. As he had expected, the word of this "secret" plan quickly filtered through to the older boys. On the morning of the trip, Juan quietly gave the bus driver directions to take the group to Pine Shelter Beach, as originally planned. The older boys drove their car to Atlantic Knolls and spent the day fruitlessly searching for the group. That night, when the bus returned, the older boys were waiting at the Youth Aid League center. They threatened and cursed Juan and Luz and threw garbage on Juan's car, although they did not attack him directly.

Throughout that fall and winter, the older boys continued to be a problem. They took part in the activities of the youth group but frequently showed up drunk or stoned, were hostile and often refused to cooperate. When two of their members joined the Army, the clique broke up and the older boys stopped attending the center.

Questions for Discussion

What do you feel were some of the basic causes of the problem Juan and Luz faced with respect to the older group?

Juan's strategy of changing the destination of the bus trip to send the older boys on a "wild-goose chase" avoided an immediate problem at the beach. How do you view it as an example of long-range leadership tactics?

Do you see anything about the make-up of the group that might account for some of its difficulties? What fundamental recommendations could you make that might be helpful in working with a group such as this?

Case No. 5. The Youth Leadership Conference

Leona W., a physical education instructor at Miller College, volunteered to go along as one of the faculty members accompanying a large group of sophomore students to a special leadership training conference in the Pocono Mountains, about 100 miles from the college. In all, there were four men and four women faculty members and about 120 students. A professor in the psychology department, John R., was coordinator of the conference.

The busses left on schedule, arriving in the late afternoon at the isolated motel facility where the conference was being held. Students were assigned to rooms—girls in one wing of the building and boys in another. (Note: This conference took place in the late 1960's, before many colleges shifted to co-ed dormitory arrangements.) As Leona W. toured the girls' wing, she found that there were two to five girls in each room.

Immediately after checking in, dinner was served. At dinner, Professor R. briefed the other faculty members on the plans he had developed for the conference. Later, the group assembled to hear a guest speaker lecture on leadership. It was necessary for the faculty advisors to patrol the room during the talk because many students were noisy and inattentive. The remainder of the evening was devoted to having a dance in the motel lounge. Two men and two women faculty advisors were assigned to supervise this activity.

Leona W. was not involved, and played bridge until 3 o'clock in the morning with the other advisors. The dance was poorly attended, and many of the male students began wandering in and out of the girls' wing. Some of the girls complained that the boys were bothering them and would not leave; other rooms were completely quiet. Because their leadership function was not clearly defined, Leona and the other woman faculty member did not try to interfere with the activity, but made checks when there was excessive noise and tried to keep the area quiet.

After breakfast, group meetings were set up and the conference progressed. During the morning, Leona W. went to Professor R. and asked him whether any action should be taken to control the nighttime activity in the girls' dorm area. It was apparent that several of the boys had spent the night in girls' rooms. Professor R. replied only that he hoped that no one would become pregnant.

However, at dinner that night, Professor R. announced that all students would have to be in their own dormitory areas by 12:30 A.M. When many students protested that this was unreasonable, he agreed that the lounge could be kept open all night.

Leona announced that she would be making a check of the girls' wing to make sure that all male guests left by 12:30. Faculty and student leaders of the various workshop groups had a lengthy meeting that evening that ended at midnight. At 12:30, Leona and one of the male faculty members went off to clear the girls' wing. As they went from room to room, a large group of girls followed them. When doors opened, one by one, and boys came out (some in various stages of undress), the girls cheered. The boys went smilingly off to the lounge. Finally, when all the boys had left the girls' wing, the majority of girls took their pillows and blankets and stayed in the lounge with them. Only three remained in their rooms throughout the night.

The question of college policy regarding male–female relationships or personal standards of sexual behavior was not discussed by the conference, which ended the next day. Leona W. wondered whether she might have played a more effective role in this area.

Questions for Discussion

Could you analyze Professor R.'s role in organizing and directing this leadership conference, based on information you are given in the case study? How might the conference have been held more effectively?

Recognizing that this conference was held at a time when college policy toward the sexual involvement of students was less permissive than it is today, what steps might have been taken to anticipate and plan for the problem of who would be sleeping where? What else might Leona W. have done?

In general, what sort of guidelines would you suggest for planning a youth leadership training conference of this type?

Case No. 6. Hospital Security and Staff Morale

In a psychiatric unit of seriously disturbed patients in a large State Hospital, the supervisor of the activity therapy department, Tom L., emphasized at a staff meeting that it was essential to keep careful control of all keys for offices, equipment rooms, wards and elevators. Although many halls and buildings were kept unlocked, it was necessary to lock others for security reasons. Tom then returned a set of keys to Alice M., a staff member who had misplaced them. Tom again warned those present of the dangers of misplacing or losing keys and threatened to keep the keys the next time a staff member misplaced them.

The next week, another recreation therapist, Jean B., lost her keys. Tom found them and put them in his office. He told Jean that it was essential that she locate them, and she continued to search the building and question patients to see if they had taken her keys. Some of the patients began getting upset over this incident. Finally, another staff member who knew the facts told Jean that the activity therapy supervisor had taken the keys because Jean had carelessly laid them down in a patient area.

Jean confronted Tom in front of several other staff members, crying and swearing at him. She then went to the Assistant Director of Rehabilitation to voice her complaint against Tom and to ask for a transfer. The Assistant Director of Rehabilitation called for a meeting of the entire activity staff assigned to the unit. The various incidents leading to the episode were reviewed. It became apparent that Jean felt she had been unfairly treated by Tom and other staff members. Racial prejudice was hinted at, because Tom was black and Jean was white. She also made clear her feeling that because she had a master's degree in therapeutic recreation, she should not be supervised by Tom, who had only a bachelor's degree (although he had several years of experience and had come up through the Civil Service career ladder). Other staff members supported Tom and indicated that they found Jean a difficult person to work with.

Tom's reaction at this meeting was to say nothing against Jean or in his own defense. He apologized for hiding the keys, saying that he now realized that this was an inappropriate action.

However, Jean kept criticizing him and was unwilling to accept his apology. The final tone of the group appeared to be one of supporting Tom and indicating diapproval of Jean. A week later, she was transferred to another unit of the hospital. After this episode, there seemed to be a stronger feeling of cohesion and improved communication among the remaining staff members. Tom indicated that he would seek to avoid unilateral disciplinary action in working with staff problems and would hold group meetings to deal with problems when they arose.

Questions for Discussion

What do you think of Tom's action in hiding Jean B.'s keys without telling her? How else might he have handled this situation?

In what way might the hostility between the recreation therapist and her supervisor have been improved? What did Tom apparently learn from the situation? How effective was the Assistant Director of Rehabilitation in dealing with the problem?

What general principles or guidelines regarding staff relationships can you draw from this case?

Case No. 7. The Leader Faces Herself

Dawn R., a college junior majoring in sociology, took a part-time job leading a group of 10- to 12-year-olds in a Girls' Club. The club was scheduled to meet three afternoons a week.

It appeared to Jane M., director of the club, that Dawn was uncertain about her leadership approach from the very beginning. On the first day she let the girls run wild and do whatever they wanted in the game room. The next time they met, she was extremely harsh, spending most of her time disciplining and scolding the members. At the third session, she again exerted strict controls, and the group took part fairly well in craft activities. But, at the beginning of the next week, she was again highly permissive, and the group members responded in a wild and uncontrolled manner.

Jane held a supervisory conference with Dawn to talk over her experiences thus far. The club director got the impression that Dawn was aware of the problem and extremely sensitive about it. She seemed to be defending herself by saying that she was a good leader, but was "stuck" with a group of uncooperative, immature girls.

Jane was concerned, in part because she wanted the girls in Dawn's group to have a better experience than they were having, and in part because she feared that this club's disruptive behavior might affect other groups in the Girls' Club. In dealing with the problem, from a sound human relations point of view, she felt that it was important for Dawn to recognize that she was contributing to the problem—but this would have to be done without scolding or lecturing her. In addition, Dawn would have to be involved in developing possible solutions to improve the situation.

The director met again with Dawn and made it clear that she felt that Dawn's club was not functioning as well as it should. Without giving her views about the cause of the difficulty, she again asked Dawn what she felt was the basic problem. No clear answer emerged. Jane then asked Dawn to observe a similar club that was directed by a more experienced leader, Phyllis D.

Dawn observed this club, which met on a day when her group did not. She recognized that Phyllis D. had structured the program, with a major part of the meeting devoted to games of low organization and craft activities, but with a good amount of time given to a members' planning session. All of the group members were active throughout the session. The leader was firm but fair with them, reminding the club members of certain basic rules of conduct at the beginning of the meeting and repeating them when necessary, but allowing most of the discipline to emanate from the group members themselves.

Dawn met again with Jane. The director asked her what differences she saw between Phyllis' group and her own. Dawn commented that it was obvious that the program was more structured and that the group members appeared to be more cooperative than the members of her own club were. Jane asked whether Phyllis' greater involvement with the group (she had taken part in the games with them) might have contributed to a better feeling of rapport. Dawn agreed that this was so. She also volunteered that the way Phyllis had quietly presented rules of conduct, reminding the group members of them when necessary, had apparently helped them gain a sense of responsibility for their own behavior and to do their own "policing."

Jane then asked Dawn what changes she thought she might make in her own leadership. Dawn indicated that she would probably try to structure activities more carefully and have a plan of activities made up in advance of each session. The club director suggested that it might be a good idea for her to meet with Phyllis to discuss her approach to planning the program. Later that day, the two club leaders met and discussed the problem. Phyllis suggested several activities that she had found useful. She also suggested that once the group had gotten successfully under way, the club members themselves might be involved in planning future sessions, as her girls did.

Dawn took careful notes on the meeting and then outlined some plans for herself. She reported back to Jane and discussed the plans with her. Jane agreed that they seemed suitable and suggested some additional ideas. She also asked Dawn whether she would mind being observed for the next two session. Dawn agreed, saying that she felt the director's presence would help her maintain better control and that she would welcome Jane's comments and suggestions after the meetings. She seemed much more optimistic about her club than she had been before.

Questions for Discussion

Do you feel that Jane's approach to helping Dawn become a more effective leader was generally sound?

Isolate the specific concepts of supervision or methods of counseling that Jane used in helping Dawn understand the problem. Why was it logical for her to observe Phyllis and then meet with her?

What other approaches could you suggest that would be helpful to Dawn?

Case No. 8. The Coach Says "No!"

The Recreation Department in the town of Parksville obtained permission to use the local high school's gymnasium for an open sports program for teenage boys, to be held on Friday nights during the spring from 6:30 to 10:30 P.M. The two leaders placed in charge were Bill S. and Roy D., physical education teachers from the high school and junior high school. In this situation, they were hired and paid directly by the Recreation Department.

On the first evening of the program, more than 70 boys from both school levels attended. They expressed an interest in forming a basketball league. They were assigned to teams and took part in practice, and league play was scheduled to begin on the following Friday. The operation would be quite informal: there would be no uniforms or outside officials, games would be played by "running time" rather than by a clock, and several parents agreed to serve as coaches.

There was considerable enthusiasm throughout the week, with the boys looking forward eagerly to playing. It appeared as if the Friday night open gym program would be a success.

However, late on Friday afternoon the varsity baseball coach of the high school arrived back at the school with his team, which had just played a league baseball game. When he saw many of his boys preparing to stay for evening basketball, he promptly announced that they would not be allowed to participate. When Bill asked him why, he indicated that he did not want any of the boys to sustain an injury that might prevent him from playing baseball. He added that the boys on the junior varsity and freshman baseball teams also would not be allowed to play basketball.

It was clear to Bill and Roy that the baseball coach's decision posed a real problem. The evening basketball teams had been matched so that they were composed of players of roughly comparable age and ability. With many boys removed from play, the teams would be poorly balanced, and it would be necessary to set up the entire team structure again. This, however, was not the main point. The real question was whether a coach should be permitted to restrict players on his team from taking part in other wholesome sports activities during their leisure hours.

The baseball coach insisted that it was Roy's and Bill's responsibility, as school physical education teachers, to prevent any baseball players from taking part in the evening program. He made it clear that this was an order. The two leaders felt that this was unfair because they were being employed in the Friday evening program by the Recreation Department, not by the school district. They considered it their responsibility to allow as many youngsters to play as possible. Although they respected the wish of the baseball coach to keep his team intact, they questioned his reasoning. Roy pointed out that it was just as likely that boys would get injured in pick-up basketball games on neighborhood playgrounds—which no one could prevent—as in an organized league game.

Furthermore, if the baseball players were not allowed to take part in the open gym program, what would they be doing in their free time? Many Parksville teenagers sat in the woods near the high school on Friday and Saturday nights, drinking beer and wine or smoking "pot." Others drove hot-rods on the narrow, unlighted roads near the town. Was it really better—and safer—for them to be doing these things than to be taking part in a basketball league on Friday nights?

When Roy and Bill presented these arguments to the baseball coach, he replied that he simply did not care. He did not want his players to take part in the basketball league, and if they were permitted to do so, he would report the two teachers to the chairman of the school's physical education department as having ignored his request. There was an hour to go before the games were scheduled to begin. Roy and Bill discussed their alternatives.

They could refuse to honor the order the baseball coach had given them.

They might accept it for the varsity baseball team but insist that the junior varsity and freshman players be permitted to take part.

They could telephone the department chairman, or even the school principal, for a ruling.

Or, they could take the position that they had no responsibility for telling the boys whether or not they could take part in the basketball games, and insist that if the coach wanted to restrict them, he would have to do it himself.

Questions for Discussion

What do you see as the fundamental issues in this disagreement?

From the point of view of what is best for the boys, do you feel that the coach or the recreation leaders are in the right?

Which of the possible alternatives do you see as the course of action to take? Can you suggest any other solution for Bill and Roy? How might interjurisdictional problems like this be settled in the future?

Case No. 9. Volunteers in Trouble

The West Greenville YWCA conducted an after-school sports and physical fitness program in the gymnasium of the Crawford Elementary School located in a nearby community. It was held once a week at the school, on Wednesday afternoons from 3 o'clock to 5 o'clock, and involved approximately 80 fifth- and sixth-grade girls. The program was free, since the YWCA relied for leadership on three recreation majors from nearby Edgemont College, who participated in the program as part of a required field-work assignment. These three young women were assigned by the Y's program director, Alice P., to organize an intramural sports program at the Crawford School.

The program was held for the first time on February 3. Girls were organized into groups according to age, and they took part in volleyball, badminton, gymnastics and group games. A mother, who represented the Crawford Parent-Teachers Association, helped in the organization. Things seemed to be going fairly well that afternoon when Alice P. dropped by to see how the program was faring.

Two weeks later, however, a complaint report was submitted by the building custodian to the school principal. Entitled *Report of After-School Program,* the complaint stated

> On February 17, the Y.W.C.A. was in our building. When they left the gym was in a mess. These people leave the gym in a mess every time they are here. The girls are always running in the hallways. They spit water at each other in the halls. They also leave the gym mats thrown about. Mr. La Vena (physical education teacher) reported that two mats were ripped. On the same day, someone opened the gate that is across the hallway, left through the side door, and kicked a barrel of trash down the stairs into the basement. There is very poor supervision at this activity. The three people in charge cannot control the activity.

Immediately, Alice drove to the school and met with the principal and custodian to discuss the matter. She later met with the three volunteer leaders and the mother who assisted them. She concluded on the basis of these talks that the young women involved had never had experience with large groups of children before and lacked the ability to carry on the program in an orderly manner. They did not exercise disciplinary control successfully and spent a good deal of time chasing the less cooperative children through the hallways. When they did this, the sports activities began to fall apart and all the children started to act up. The mother had been helpful in keeping the girls in line during the first two sessions. However, she had been late in arriving on February 17, and by the time she did arrive, things were well out of hand.

When Alice reviewed the situation with the Executive Director of the YWCA the major causes of the problem appeared to be the following: First, there had been inadequate training or screening of the three field-work students from Edgemont College. It had been assumed that because they were recreation majors, they would be able to handle the situation. The students had received only a brief orientation session before beginning the Wednesday program, and the mother had no preparation or training at all. Finally, the children had been recruited in a completely haphazard fashion, and no attempt had been made to determine their previously learned skills or interests. When they saw how informal and permissive the sports program was—compared with their carefully structured and supervised daytime physical education program—they began to challenge the leaders and misbehave whenever possible.

Because of the damage that had been done and a lack of confidence in the ability of the three field-work students to carry on the program successfully, the program was terminated without meeting again.

Alice developed the following set of recommendations after this experience:

1. All volunteers for such programs should be carefully screened. Care should be taken to select individuals who have had experience in the appropriate activities and in working with children.
2. Volunteers should be given a detailed orientation before beginning the activity. They should be given a written job description and a list of objectives to be accomplished. They should be informed that this is an important job and that tardiness or absenteeism is not acceptable.
3. Appropriate disciplinary measures must be taken against those who hinder the operation of the program or who seek to destroy school property.

Questions for Discussion

Do you feel that blame for this unsuccessful program should be assigned primarily to the volunteer field-work students from Edgemont College, or should it rest primarily with the YWCA?

How adequate were the recommendations developed by Alice P. to improve the use of volunteers in future programs?

Could you suggest other procedures that would assist volunteer programs of this type, which are situated in decentralized operations that are not in the YWCA building itself, and that therefore are not easy to supervise regularly?

Case No. 10. Sharing the Load

At a meeting of about 40 recreation leaders and supervisors employed by the Allentown County Park and Recreation Commission, the bulk of the time was given to planning several special events due to occur during the fall season. The Recreation Division Director asked at the end of the meeting if there were any problems anyone wanted to bring up before it was adjourned. One of the leaders, Sharon S., stood up and presented the following problem:

As Sharon saw it, the workload of various recreation leaders throughout the county was not shared equally. Some leaders, she said, were assigned to do a greater amount of work than others, no matter what the season or program. Besides handling assignments on their own facilities or in their own special programs, they were often assigned to be in charge of special county events, workshops or competitions. Often, because of this increased workload, their own programs tended to suffer. The reason for this, Sharon said, was that these men and women were recognized as more productive and efficient than other leaders in the division. Supervisors tended to choose them for special assignments, since they were more likely to do a good job, and this would reflect on the supervisors and the Commission as a whole.

"What this means," Sharon concluded, "is that the reward for good work is more work. Conversely, if you want to get paid and do very little work, just do a poor job."

A heated discussion followed. Some leaders and supervisors agreed with Sharon. Others said that she had exaggerated the problem and that if some leaders were doing a poor job, all the department had to do was fire or suspend them. However, it was agreed that this was not easily done if the leaders lived up to the minimal requirements of the job (once they had passed their probationary periods), because the labor union contract and Civil Service procedures made it very difficult to take such action. In addition, it was agreed that the fact that some leaders got by with comparatively little effort hurt the morale of the more dedicated and capable leaders and kept them from extending themselves. The frustration of seeing others work very little for the same salary tended to lead even competent and highly motivated leaders down the road to mediocrity.

Gradually, it was agreed that something had to be done to help less productive leaders work more effectively if the entire department's program was to be carried on properly. Some leaders suggested that the most obvious method—that of promoting the best workers to supervisory positions—had limited potential, because within the Civil Service structure there were only a few supervisory positions, and these openings appeared very infrequently.

The alternative of trying to fire the poorest leaders, as a drastic measure, also had its weakness, because a job freeze was in effect in county government and it was unlikely that these individuals would be replaced. The question of concern was, "Is a warm body better than no body at all?"

The meeting finally adjourned without any conclusion being reached.

Questions for Discussion

Do you think that the kind of problem described by Sharon S. is a real one, particularly in large bureaucratic organizations? Have you seen examples of it in your own experience?

What steps would you take to improve motivation and performance of the weaker leaders in the Recreation Division and to help them share the workload more equally? Be specific about the actions that might be taken.

Case No. 11. Swimming Pool Fees—Who Pays?

Frank M., Director of Recreation and Parks in the village of Dobbstown, held a meeting with his advisory board, which was composed of five elected members and two trustees appointed by the village mayor. The board reviewed his plans for the coming summer program, including schedule of activities, hiring plans and budget, because it would be necessary shortly to send a brochure for the summer events to the printer. Frank described the swimming program, which involved busing children from various playgrounds to a nearby county swimming pool for instruction and free swimming. Because Dobbstown did not have its own swimming pool, this busing arrangement had been used for the past two years, and each family that wished to have its children take part in the program paid a special fee of $15.

Frank pointed out to the board that, although Dobbstown was a fairly comfortable community, a number of families were poor; some were on welfare. In the past, he had permitted children from these families to take part in the swimming program without paying the special fee. Would this policy be acceptable again this year?

Immediately, several of the trustees raised questions:

"Who or what determines if a family cannot afford the fee?"

"Do you just use your judgment, or is there a screening system to check financial ability?"

"Is this policy generally known in the community? Perhaps some families do not have their children take part in the swimming program because they do not know that the fee might be waived."

A heated discussion followed. Various points of view were expressed. Some board members felt that any family or individual who could not afford to pay a fee for any fee-bearing activity offered by the department should be permitted to take part in it, without any formal screening action or application being necessary. In contrast, others took the position that if some people were permitted to take part in activities without paying fees, many others would take advantage of it. In addition, they felt that waivers would pose a special problem in the winter program, when many activities were carried on in which the leader's fee was dependent on the amount of fees paid. However, it was agreed to confine the discussion to the summer swimming program, which was seen as vitally needed by all families in the village.

Gradually, the different points of view narrowed down to two positions: "idealist" and "modified realist." The attitudes of these groups were the following:

Idealist: Anyone who requested to have his or her child admitted to the swimming program should have the fee waived on the basis of a verbal request. There would be no investigation, and parents would not be asked to sign any type of paper. It was felt that (a) people were basically honest and would not take advantage of this policy, and (b) to require them to sign a statement of financial need would be humiliating and might prevent some children from taking part in the program.

Modified Realist: Parents who wished their children to be admitted to the swimming program without charge should be asked to come to the recreation office to sign a statement to the effect that they could not afford to pay the fee. This policy would be printed in the Summer Program Bulletin, which was distributed to all families in the village.

Again, the argument boiled over. Some felt that families that really needed the aid would be too proud to accept it. It was feared that if the fee were eliminated without any formal request of waiver, it might cause a serious financial burden in the department. The argument was made that the policy should not be printed in the bulletin, since it might encourage too many families to apply, and all those in need would probably hear about it by word-of-mouth.

Throughout the discussion, Frank M. did not state his opinion, other than to answer questions raised by members of the board. Finally, he was asked directly to give his recommendations, based on his view of what would be most workable for the department and fairest to all the citizens of Dobbstown. He made the following suggestions:

1. The fee would be waived for any family requesting it. No screening system should be used, and there would be no need to sign any type of statement or to prove financial need.

2. The policy would not be printed in the Summer Program Bulletin but would appear in the minutes of the Commission, which were available to all residents at the Village Hall.

Questions for Discussion

What are some of the fundamental issues regarding the role of community recreation and parks programs that the Dobbstown advisory board was grappling with?

What do you think of Frank M.'s approach in presenting the problem but withholding his views until asked to give a recommendation at the end of the discussion?

On the basis of the arguments that have been summarized, do you believe that his proposal was a sensible one?

Case No. 12. A Parking Lot—or Trees?

The Yorktown Park District recently expanded its athletic facilities at Secor Woods Park by constructing a new ballfield and six additional tennis courts. When the volume of use of these facilities began to grow, it became apparent that there was a serious parking problem, particularly on summer and spring weekends. Often, residents who wished to use the facilities were forced to park along Secor Road and adjacent residential streets, and sometimes they parked illegally along the entrance road into the park, creating a safety hazard.

The Yorktown Park Commission members reviewed the problem and determined that the best solution was to make use of an adjacent parcel of land, approximately 130 feet by 175 feet and situated under high-tension wires, which was owned by the local utilities company, United Electric. After considerable negotiation, United Electric gave its approval for the use of this property for overflow parking. The negotiations took some time to complete, and even after they were approved, engineering plans had to be drawn up. Meanwhile, a number of citizens began to protest the use of this site for parking. It was quite a wild area, with considerable bird and animal life in the shrubbery, although there were no tall trees because of the high-tension wires. Several environmentalists wrote letters to the town newspaper, protesting the plan to blacktop the area.

When the specifications were completed and approved, the town highway department was assigned to do the job. On a Monday morning, they moved in with bulldozers to clean off and grade the site. That afternoon, several truckloads of crushed stone and gravel were dumped on the side of the property.

On Tuesday at noon, with the grading work half completed, the commissioner of the park district suddenly received an emergency call from his supervisor, the town manager, Bart F. Mr. F. indicated that a number of influential citizens had come to his office with a petition containing several hundred names, which demanded that work on the parking area be stopped. Students in the high school had held a protest meeting the day before, had circulated the petitions and had aroused the concern of many adults. Bart was in a serious bind, as he explained to the Park Commissioner. As he saw it, there were three pressures being exerted on him.

First, there were the local residents in the Secor Woods area, who had been demanding action on the parking area for the past year because of the congestion the new facilities had caused in their neighborhood streets.

Second, there was the problem of public opinion. Bart did not want to have the label of "anti-environment" or "nature-spoiler" attached to him, and he assumed that the Park Commissioner did not want it either.

Third, it would be extremely difficult to stop work on the site, leaving it partially graded, particularly since he had been negotiating with United Electric for several months for a right-of-way into another town park that was to be developed. If the Secor Woods plan fell through, he was afraid that the other project would be jeopardized.

It was a difficult choice to make. The town manager turned to the Park Commissioner. "What do you think we ought to do?" he asked.

Questions for Discussion

What are the key issues in this controversy? What weight do you give to the arguments for and against clearing the land for the overflow parking area?

How might the Town Manager and Park Commissioner have avoided the difficult situation in which they found themselves?

What action should be taken in order to salvage the situation and make the wisest possible decision, in terms of both solving the parking problem at Secor Woods Park and maintaining effective community relations with town residents? In other words, what is *your* recommendation?

SHORT CASE STUDIES

The following 12 cases are presented much more briefly and may be used as the basis for individual student assignments or class discussions. One way to approach these is to have role-playing sessions—either psychodrama or sociodrama—in which the players add details to the problem situation, improvising them on the spot. Following this, both players and audience may analyze the problems and develop alternative solutions for them.

Case No. 13. A recreation facility (softball diamond) has existed for years in a residential neighborhood that has gradually grown up around it. A number of residents in the area have petitioned the municipal council to stop softball league play in the evenings because they regard it as an intrusion on their privacy. Yet there is no comparable facility in this area of the township. What position should the recreation and park director take before the municipal council?

Case No. 14. A therapeutic recreation worker in the admissions unit of a psychiatric hospital is confronted by a new patient who refuses to participate in the activities treatment plan recommended by her treatment team. Despite the strong encouragement of other staff members, over a period of weeks she has simply stated, "I do not want to do anything," and does not become involved. How should the therapist handle this situation?

Case No. 15. As part of a cost-cutting process in the city's recreation department, consideration is being given to having the electricity used to light outdoor facilities such as tennis courts or basketball courts be paid for by the participants, through coin-operated meter systems. What factors should be considered in deciding whether to approve this policy or to keep the night-lighting free, as it has been in the past?

Case No. 16. A staff member who has recently been hired for your agency through a government grant has been absent quite frequently. All absences are apparently justified, and the individual is not paid for workdays missed, because of the nature of his job. However, these frequent absences are causing a morale problem with other employees. How should the supervisor handle this problem?

Case No. 17. The recreation supervisor of a small community interviewed and selected approximately 15 leaders for the summer playground program, notifying them in mid-April that they had been hired. However, several of these new employees continued to "shop" for other jobs and informed the supervisor just a week before the summer began that they would not be working in his program. What went wrong in this situation? What procedures would you implement to prevent its happening again?

Case No. 18. A number of teenagers in a recreation center decide to operate a "snack bar" in their center, both as a convenience and as a money-making operation. When announcement is made of this, local restaurant owners complain that it represents unfair competition with their businesses. They threaten to take the matter to the recreation board. As supervisor of the center, how do you deal with this problem?

Case No. 19. The supervisor of a recreation program in a psychiatric hospital operated by a Catholic order schedules a weekly showing of older movies. The films are usually of a "family entertainment" type. However, one week she scheduled a showing of *The Notorious Landlady*, featuring Kim Novak. On the evening the film was shown, several nuns were in the audience. The audience appeared to be enjoying the film, which was slightly suggestive. However, during one scene that showed the star in a bubble bath, the projector developed "technical" difficulties, which did not clear up until the scene was over. The next day, the recreation supervisor was informed by the hospital administrator that there had been a number of complaints about the film and that in the future all films would have to be submitted in advance for approval. Should the supervisor take a strong stand on this matter?

Case No. 20. The young director of a special two-week therapeutic camp program is concerned about enforcing the camp board's policy against drinking alcoholic beverages on the campgrounds. She foresees two difficulties: (a) although she has a master's degree in therapeutic recreation, many of the camp's staff members are close to her age, and some are older; and (b) in past summers, the no-drinking policy was not enforced. She anticipates a problem in enforcing the rule, especially with older counselors who have been at the camp in previous years. What should she do?

Case No. 21. A local community center has extremely poor attendance at program activities for high-school-age youth. Not enough teenagers attend the programs to make them worthwhile. Yet youth in the community continue to complain that there is nothing for them to do and no place to go. What can be done about this?

Case No. 22.　A new therapeutic recreation specialist has been hired to work in the pediatric unit of a large hospital. One of the first patients to come to his attention is a 6-year-old who has been in a car accident, had a subsequent operation and is now in a body cast, flat on his back, for a period of six to eight months. This child is extremely demanding, spoiled and hyperactive (considering his immobility), and the director of the pediatric unit wants him to have special, personalized attention several hours a day. The new recreation worker gradually realizes that his role is thought of as a "baby-sitting" function; he does not join doctors on their rounds or share in treatment-team meetings and is not expected to work toward significant therapeutic goals. How can the recreation specialist develop a stronger image in the hospital and assume more meaningful functions?

Case No. 23.　Three of the most effective members of the park and recreation advisory board tell the department's director that they are planning to resign because of what they regard as the "futile" role of the board. How does he deal with this situation?

Case No. 24.　The director of a summer camp operated by a large voluntary agency is beginning to have serious difficulty with a counselor responsible for one of the major camp units. This individual is highly competitive and keeps charts and records of the young campers, constantly reprimanding them and demanding higher achievements. At a field day with another camp, he upset staff members and campers with his authoritarian tactics and quarreled angrily with the other camp's director. For him to be replaced in midsummer would be disruptive to the program. What should the camp director do?

CONCLUSION

In addition to analyzing these cases or using them as the basis for class problem-solving sessions, students may be asked to develop their own case studies, based on problems they have experienced as either workers or participants in recreation programs. Such group sessions provide an excellent means of helping students gain needed group-dynamics skills. In actual on-the-job situations, problem-solving group approaches may be used both to develop appropriate policies or decisions as a routine supervisory method and as a teaching technique in special in-service education programs.

Appendix A—Bibliography

GENERAL BOOKS ON RECREATION

Edith L. Ball and Robert E. Cipriano: *Leisure Services Preparation: A Competency Based Approach.* Englewood Cliffs, New Jersey, Prentice-Hall, 1978.

Joseph J. Bannon: *Problem-Solving in Recreation and Parks.* Englewood Cliffs, New Jersey, Prentice-Hall, 1972.

George D. Butler: *Introduction to Community Recreation.* New York, McGraw-Hill, 1976.

Reynold Carlson, Janet MacLean, Theodore Deppe and James Peterson: *Recreation and Leisure: The Changing Scene.* Belmont, California, Wadsworth, 1979.

Joseph E. Curtis: *Recreation: Theory and Practice.* St. Louis, C. V. Mosby, 1979.

Charles E. Doell and Louis F. Twardzik: *Elements of Park and Recreation Administration.* Minneapolis, Burgess, 1973.

Christopher R. Edginton and John G. Williams: *Productive Management of Leisure Service Organizations: A Behavioral Approach.* New York, John Wiley, 1978.

M. J. Ellis: *Why People Play.* Englewood Cliffs, New Jersey, Prentice-Hall, 1973.

Arlin F. Epperson: *Private and Commercial Recreation: A Text and Reference.* New York, John Wiley, 1977.

Geoffrey Godbey: *Recreation, Park and Leisure Services: Foundations, Organization, Administration.* Philadelphia, W. B. Saunders, 1978.

Thomas L. Goodale and Peter A. Witt, eds.: *Recreation and Leisure: Issues in an Era of Change.* State College, Pennsylvania, Venture Publishing, 1980.

Peter J. Graham and Lawrence R. Klar, Jr.: *Planning and Delivering Leisure Services.* Dubuque, Iowa, William C. Brown, 1979.

George Hjelte and Jay S. Shivers: *Public Administration of Recreational Services.* Philadelphia, Lea and Febiger, 1978.

Douglas M. Knudson: *Outdoor Recreation.* New York, Macmillan, 1980.

Richard Kraus: *Recreation Today: Program Planning and Leadership.* Santa Monica, California, Goodyear, 1977.

Richard Kraus: *Recreation and Leisure in Modern Society*. Santa Monica, California, Goodyear, 1978.

Sidney G. Lutzin and Edward H. Storey, eds.: *Managing Municipal Leisure Services*. Washington, D.C., International City Management Association, 1980.

Susanna Millar: *The Psychology of Play*. Baltimore, Penguin Books, 1968.

Jean Mundy and Linda Odum: *Leisure Education, Theory and Practice*. New York, John Wiley, 1979.

James F. Murphy: *Recreation and Leisure Service: A Humanistic Perspective*. Dubuque, Iowa, Wm. C. Brown, 1975.

James F. Murphy, John G. Williams, E. William Niepoth and Paul D. Brown: *Leisure Service Delivery System: A Modern Perspective*. Philadelphia, Lea and Febiger, 1973.

John Neulinger: *The Psychology of Leisure*. Springfield, Illinois, Charles C Thomas, 1974.

Jesse A. Reynolds and Marion N. Hormachea: *Public Recreation Administration*. Reston, Virginia, Reston Publishing Co., 1976.

H. Douglas Sessoms, Harold D. Meyer and Charles K. Brightbill: *Leisure Services: The Organized Recreation and Park System*. Englewood Cliffs, New Jersey, Prentice-Hall, 1975.

Edwin J. Staley and Norman P. Miller, eds.: *Leisure and the Quality of Life*. Washington, D.C., Association for Health, Physical Education and Recreation, 1972.

William F. Theobald: *Evaluation of Recreation and Park Programs*. New York, John Wiley, 1979.

Betty van der Smissen: *Evaluation and Self-Study of Public Recreation and Park Agencies: A Guide With Standards and Evaluative Criteria*. Arlington, Virginia, National Recreation and Park Association, 1972.

Donald C. Weiskopf: *A Guide to Recreation and Leisure*. Boston, Allyn and Bacon, 1975.

GROUP DYNAMICS, SUPERVISION AND LEADERSHIP

Lester R. Bittel: *What Every Supervisor Should Know*. New York, McGraw-Hill, 1974.

Dorwin Cartwright and Alvin Zander: *Group Dynamics: Research and Theory*. New York, Harper and Row, 1968.

H. Dan Corbin: *Recreation Leadership*. Englewood Cliffs, New Jersey, Prentice-Hall, 1970.

Howard Danford and Max Shirley: *Creative Leadership in Recreation*. Boston, Allyn and Bacon, 1970.

Myrtle Edwards: *Recreation Leader's Guide*. Palo Alto, California, National Press, 1967.

Patricia Farrell and Herberta M. Lundegren: *The Process of Recreation Programming: Theory and Technique*. New York, John Wiley, 1978.

Frank Goble: *Excellence in Leadership*. New York, American Management Association, 1972.

Margaret E. Hartford: *Groups in Social Work*. New York, Columbia University Press, 1972.

Israel C. Heaton and Clark T. Thorstenson: *Planning for Social Recreation*. Boston, Houghton Mifflin, 1978.

Bernard L. Hinton and H. Joseph Reitz: *Groups and Organizations*. Belmont, California, Wadsworth, 1971.

David W. Johnson and Frank P. Johnson: *Joining Together: Group Theory and Group Skills*. Englewood Cliffs, New Jersey, Prentice-Hall, 1975.

Gisela Konopka: *Social Group Work: A Helping Process*. Englewood Cliffs, New Jersey, 1963.

Richard Kraus: *Recreation Leader's Handbook*. New York, McGraw-Hill, 1955.

Richard Kraus: *Social Recreation: A Group Dynamics Approach*. St. Louis, C. V. Mosby, 1979.

Douglas McGregor: *The Professional Manager*. New York, McGraw-Hill, 1967.

Dorothy Roberts: *Leading Teenage Groups*. New York, Association Press, 1963.

Bill D. Schul: *How to Be an Effective Group Leader*. Chicago, Nelson-Hall, 1975.

Marvin E. Shaw: *Group Dynamics: The Psychology of Small Group Behavior*. New York, McGraw-Hill, 1971.

Ivan D. Steiner: *Group Process and Productivity*. New York, Academic Press, 1972.

Ralph M. Stogdill: *Handbook of Leadership: A Survey of Theory and Research*. New York, Free Press, Macmillan, 1974.

Albert Tillman: *The Program Book for Recreation Professionals*. Palo Alto, California, National Press, 1973.

Maryhelen Vannier: *Recreation Leadership*. Philadelphia, Lea and Febiger, 1977.

Margaret Williamson: *Supervision: Principles and Methods*. New York, Woman's Press (National Board of YWCA), 1950.

ACTIVITY LEADERSHIP METHODS AND NEEDS OF SPECIAL POPULATIONS

Ronald C. Adams: *Games, Sports and Exercise for the Physically Handicapped*. Philadelphia, Lea and Febiger, 1972.

Catherine Allen: *Fun for Parties and Programs*. Englewood Cliffs, New Jersey, Prentice-Hall, 1956.

American Red Cross: *Lifesaving, Rescue and Water Safety*. Garden City, New York, Doubleday, 1974.

David A. Armbruster, Robert H. Allen and Hubert S. Billingsley: *Swimming and Diving*. St. Louis, C. V. Mosby, 1973.

Elliott M. Avedon: *Therapeutic Recreation Service: An Applied Behavioral Science Approach*. Englewood Cliffs, New Jersey, Prentice-Hall, 1974.

Edith L. Ball: *Hosteling: The New Program in Community Recreation*. New York, American Youth Hostels, 1971.

John Batcheller and Sally Monsour: *Music in Recreation and Leisure*. Dubuque, Iowa, Wm. C. Brown, 1972.

Kenneth R. Benson and Carl E. Frankson: *Arts and Crafts for Home, School, and Community*. St. Louis, C. V. Mosby, 1975.

O. William Blake and Anne Volp: *Lead-up Games to Team Sports*. Englewood Cliffs, New Jersey, Prentice-Hall, 1964.

Charles E. Buell: *Physical Education and Recreation for the Visually Handicapped*. Washington, D.C., American Association for Health, Physical Education and Recreation, 1973.

Bernice W. Carlson and David R. Ginglend: *Recreation for Retarded Teen-Agers and Young Adults*. Nashville, Tennessee, Abingdon, 1968.

Donald R. Casaday: *Sports Activities for Men.* Riverside, New Jersey, Macmillan, 1974.

Maurice Case: *Recreation for Blind Adults.* Springfield, Illinois, Charles C Thomas, 1966.

Alan R. Caskey: *Playground Operation Manual.* Cranbury, New Jersey, A. S. Barnes, 1972.

David Currell: *The Complete Book of Puppetry.* Boston, Plays, Inc., 1975.

Frances C. Durland: *Creative Dramatics for Children.* Kent, Ohio, Kent State University Press, 1975.

Helen and Larry Eisenberg: *Omnibus of Fun.* New York, Association Press, 1956.

Gladys Andrews Fleming: *Creative Rhythmic Movement: Boys' and Girls' Dancing.* Englewood Cliffs, New Jersey, Prentice-Hall, 1976.

Andrew Fluegelman, ed.: *The New Games Book.* Garden City, New York, Doubleday, 1976.

Virginia Frye and Martha Peters: *Therapeutic Recreation: Its Theory, Philosophy, and Practices.* Harrisburg, Pennsylvania, Stackpole, 1972.

Dolores Geddes: *Physical Activities for Individuals With Handicapping Conditions.* St. Louis, C. V. Mosby, 1978.

Cecile Gilbert: *International Folk Dance at a Glance.* Minneapolis, Burgess, 1974.

Emily Gillies: *Creative Dramatics for All Children.* Washington, D.C., Association for Childhood Education, 1973.

Paula Gross Gray: *Dramatics for the Elderly: A Guide for Residential Care Settings and Senior Centers.* New York, Teachers College, Columbia University Press, 1974.

Scout Lee Gunn and Carol Ann Peterson: *Therapeutic Recreation Program Design.* Englewood Cliffs, New Jersey, Prentice-Hall, 1978.

Robert F. Hanson and Reynold E. Carlson: *Organizations for Children and Youth.* Englewood Cliffs, New Jersey, Prentice-Hall, 1972.

Jane Harris, Anne Pittman and Marlys Wallter: *Dance a While.* Minneapolis, Burgess, 1968.

Marie D. Hartwig and Bettye B. Meyers: *Camping Leadership: Counseling and Programming.* St. Louis, C. V. Mosby, 1976.

William Hillcourt: *New Field Book of Nature Activities and Hobbies.* New York, G. P. Putnam's Sons, 1971.

Darwin Hindman: *Handbook of Active Games.* Englewood Cliffs, New Jersey, Prentice-Hall, 1955.

Ronald W. Hyatt: *Intramural Sports Programs: Their Organization and Administration.* St. Louis, C. V. Mosby, 1975.

Sue Jennings: *Remedial Drama: A Handbook for Teachers and Therapists.* New York, Theater Arts Books, 1974.

Mary Bee Jensen and Clayne R. Jensen: *Folk Dancing.* Provo, Utah, Brigham Young University Press, 1973.

Mary Bee Jensen and Clayne R. Jensen: *Square Dancing.* Provo, Utah, Brighman Young University Press, 1973.

Max Kaplan: *Leisure: Lifestyle and Lifespan; Perspectives for Gerontology.* Philadelphia, W. B. Saunders, 1979.

Richard Kraus: *Square Dances of Today.* New York, John Wiley, 1950.

Richard Kraus: *Folk Dancing.* New York, Macmillan, 1962.

Richard Kraus: *Therapeutic Recreation Service: Principles and Practices.* Philadelphia, W. B. Saunders, 1978.

Susan H. Kubie and Gertrude Landau: *Group Work With the Aged.* New York, International Universities Press, 1969.

Marjorie Latchaw and Jean Pyatt: *A Pocket Guide of Dance Activities.* Englewood Cliffs, New Jersey, Prentice-Hall, 1958.

James Leisy: *The Good Times Songbook.* Nashville, Tennessee, Abingdon, 1974.

Mildred Lemen and Jo Washburn: *Outing Activities and Winter Sports Guide.* Washington, D.C., American Association for Health, Physical Education and Recreation, 1973.

Zaidee Lindsay: *Art and the Handicapped.* New York, Taplinger, 1972.

Betty Lowndes: *Movement and Creative Drama for Children.* Boston, Plays, Inc., 1971.

Bernard Mason and Elmer Mitchell: *Social Games for Recreation.* New York, Ronald Press, 1935.

William McNeice and Kenneth Benson: *Crafts for the Retarded.* Bloomington, Illinois, McKnight, 1964.

Toni Merrill: *Activities for the Aged and Infirm.* Springfield, Illinois, Charles C Thomas, 1967.

Donald Michel: *Music Therapy: An Introduction to Therapy and Special Education Through Music.* Springfield, Illinois, Charles C Thomas, 1977.

Alan Milberg: *Street Games.* New York, McGraw-Hill, 1976.

Joan Moran: *Leisure Activities for the Mature Adult.* Minneapolis, Burgess, 1979.

Anne C. Mosey: *Activities Therapy.* New York, Raven Press, 1973.

Pat Mueller: *Intramural-Recreational Sports: Programming and Administration.* New York, John Wiley, 1979.

Carole Mushier: *Team Sports for Girls and Women.* Dubuque, Iowa, Wm. C. Brown, 1973.

Larry L. Neal: *Recreation's Role in the Rehabilitation of the Mentally Retarded.* Eugene, Oregon, University of Oregon Press, 1970.

Glenn C. Nelson: *Ceramics: A Potter's Handbook.* New York, Holt, Rinehart and Winston, 1971.

John A. Nesbitt, Paul D. Brown and James F. Murphy: *Recreation and Leisure Service for the Disadvantaged.* Philadelphia, Lea and Febiger, 1970.

Gerald S. O'Morrow: *Therapeutic Recreation: A Helping Profession.* Reston, Virginia, Reston Publishing Co., 1976.

Terry Orlick: *The Cooperative Sports and Games Book: Challenge Without Competition.* New York, Pantheon, 1978.

Hally B. W. Poindexter and Carole Mushier: *Coaching Competitive Team Sports for Girls and Women.* Philadelphia, W. B. Saunders, 1973.

Janet Pomeroy: *Recreation for the Physically Handicapped.* New York, Macmillan, 1964.

Public Health Service: *Activity Supervisor's Guide: A Handbook for Activities Supervisors in Long-Term Nursing Care Facilities.* Washington, D.C., Public Health Service, U. S. Department of Health, Education and Welfare, 1969.

Claudine Sherrill: *Creative Arts for the Severely Handicapped.* Springfield, Illinois, Charles C Thomas, 1979.

Jay S. Shivers: *Camping: Administration, Counseling and Programming.* New York, Appleton-Century-Crofts, 1971.

Jay S. Shivers and Clarence R. Calder: *Recreational Crafts: Programming and Instructional Techniques.* New York: McGraw-Hill, 1974.

Jay S. Shivers and Hollis Fait: *Therapeutic and Adapted Recreation Services.* Philadelphia, Lea and Febiger, 1975.

John Squires: *Fun Crafts for Children.* Englewood Cliffs, New Jersey, Prentice-Hall, 1964.

Thomas Stein and H. Douglas Sessoms: *Recreation and Special Populations.* Boston, Holbrook Press, 1977.

Marianne Torbert: *Follow Me–A Handbook of Movement Activities for Children.* Englewood Cliffs, New Jersey, Prentice-Hall, 1980.

Graham Upton: *Physical and Creative Activities for the Mentally Handicapped.* New York, Cambridge University Press, 1979.

Maryhelen Vannier and Hally B. W. Poindexter: *Individual and Team Sports for Girls and Women.* Philadelphia, W. B. Saunders, 1968.

Adrian Waller: *Theatre on a Shoestring.* Totowa, New Jersey, Littlefield, Adams, 1975.

George S. Wells: *Guide to Family Camping.* Harrisburg, Pennsylvania, Stackpole Books, 1975.

Peter Werner: *A Movement Approach to Games for Children.* St. Louis, C. V. Mosby, 1979.

Audrey Wethered: *Movement and Drama in Therapy.* Boston, Plays, Inc., 1973.

Edwin Wilson: *The Theater Experience.* New York, McGraw-Hill, 1976.

Theodore Wilson, Virginia Gillespie and C. J. Roberts: *An Introduction to Industrial Recreation, Employee Activities and Services,* Dubuque, Iowa, Wm. C. Brown, 1979.

Shirley J. Winters: *Creative Rhythmic Movement for Children of Elementary School Age.* Dubuque, Iowa, Wm. C. Brown, 1975.

Jean Young: *Woodstock Craftsman's Manual.* New York, Praeger, 1972.

Appendix B—Guidelines for Course Development

As indicated in the Preface, this text is designed for use in two ways: (a) for courses in *leadership*, which would normally be found in undergraduate curricula; and (b) for courses in *supervision*, which would normally be offered on advanced undergraduate or graduate levels.

By emphasizing selected chapters for class reading and analysis, and through assignments that are appropriate to a given level, the instructor and students can make the fullest use of the material presented here. It should be recognized that many of the chapters are of value on both levels. However, it is also assumed that students in a leadership course have more limited experience and require a basic introduction to the topic, whereas those in a supervision course have broader backgrounds and are more concerned with improving their middle-management skills and understandings.

Design of Leadership Course

The focus of the course should be on developing face-to-face leadership skills, both in activity leadership as such and also in other areas of responsibility related to program planning, control and discipline of participants, public and community relations, accident prevention and first aid, care of supplies, equipment and facilities and similar concerns. Underlying all of these should be a sound understanding of the goals and principles of recreation leadership and of group dynamics.

Design of Supervision Course

The emphasis should be placed on more advanced responsibilities related to planning and carrying out programs on a broader scale, as well as a major concern for staff development. In addition, students should explore appropriate levels of involvement with budget planning and management, facilities planning and design, public and community relations, report preparation and similar tasks—supported by a sound contemporary philosophy of supervision and of human relations.

APPROACHES TO COURSE CONSTRUCTION

Traditionally, instructors have held the major responsibility for designing the courses they teach—and this is still the case in many academic curriculum areas. However, in some human-service fields, particularly those concerned with group processes, the favored approach in recent years has been to have students play a major role in designing course objectives, content and requirements.

The authors of this text take a middle ground. It is their view that instructors should have a fuller understanding of the appropriate goals and content, assignments and potential resources of a course in leadership or supervision than students could possibly have, and that it is the responsibility of instructors to play a major role in course-planning for this reason. At the same time, students should have the opportunity to present their own views of what the course should include and to work out in cooperation with the instructor the nature of course experiences and assignments. Throughout the course, students should have the opportunity to suggest needed changes in the course, and they should be involved in a meaningful evaluation of all elements of the course at appropriate points.

Beyond this, the authors suggest that the most meaningful learning takes place when students are actively involved in the process. Thus, students will not learn as much when the instructor *informs* them about leadership or group dynamics as they will when they take a direct responsibility for *leading activities themselves, evaluating the leadership of others, planning and carrying out special events, making other types of class presentations and sharing other group learning experiences and exercises.*

Recognizing that no single outline that might be presented in this book would be suitable for all class situations, the following sections provide (a) simple "bare-bones" outlines of suggested course units for courses in leadership and supervision; (b) a breakdown of how chapter readings and course assignments might be designed to fit either level of professional concern; and (c) an analysis of how three approaches to course construction (development of modules, competency-based design and contract-learning) might be used.

Defining Course Objectives

No matter what approach to developing a course outline is taken, it should begin by identifying the key purposes or objectives that the course is intended to accomplish. These should be clearly stated and unitary, in the sense that each purpose or objective should be presented independently.

Course objectives should also be behavioral and stated in terms of student growth in acquired skills and understandings. Ideally, they should be measurable in objective ways, so that the progress and effort of each student as well as the success of the course itself can be accurately evaluated. Finally, course objectives should be integrated or coordinated with the goals of other courses in the overall curriculum, so that each course has a unique set of purposes or functions that are essential to the curriculum and that do not overlap with those of other courses.

SUGGESTED COURSE OUTLINES

On the basis of these principles, the following simple outlines suggest possible breakdowns of courses into appropriate topics and units of class activity.

Recreation Leadership Course (15 weeks)

Unit 1: Overview of field: introduction to recreation leadership principles and professional roles; career development in recreation service.

Unit 2: Workshop in activity leadership. Instructor presents varied activities (games, songs, dances and so on) for class participation, placing emphasis on leadership methods. Then individual students lead activities for class participation, followed by constructive class critiques of their performance.

Unit 3: Principles of group dynamics and participation in group process exercises involving different leadership styles, values clarification and varied roles in group planning or problem-solving sessions.

Unit 4: Students form small groups to plan special events, which are then presented to the class or in other settings. Review and evaluation of process.

Unit 5: Examination of leadership functions in typical program settings (e.g., playground, community center) and in other special settings or with special populations. May involve reports on visitations to community programs, institutions and other recreation facilities.

Unit 6: Examination of problem-solving methods, and group analysis of case studies in recreation leadership.

Recreation Supervision Course (15 weeks)

Unit 1: Overview of field: introduction to recreation supervision principles and professional roles; career development in recreation service.

Unit 2: Analysis of contemporary philosophy of supervision, and detailed examination of supervision in selected settings (municipal, voluntary agency, hospital, industrial recreation and so on).

Unit 3: Guidelines for program development, facility management and other middle-management functions.

Unit 4: Supervisory approaches in staff development: recruitment and staff selection, orientation and in-service training, counseling, evaluation and so on. Includes examination of group dynamics principles and participation in group process exercises.

Unit 5: Approaches to community organization and development of advisory councils, and guidelines for working with volunteers.

Unit 6: Examination of problem-solving methods, and group analysis of case studies in recreation supervision.

In scheduling classes based on outlines of this type, each unit would not necessarily be given equal time. For example, in a recreation leadership course, four or five weeks might be given to activity leadership methods and only one or two devoted to examination of leadership functions in varied settings, according to the needs of class members and objectives that have been established for the course.

In terms of assigned readings, a recreation leadership course would obviously emphasize Chapters Three through Nine, which deal with principles of leadership, activity leadership methods, specialized functions in other settings and similar concerns. Similarly, a course in recreation supervision would make primary use of Chapters Ten through Fifteen, which cover supervisory theory and methods. In each case, other chapters might also be used as well.

A considerable number of individual or group assignments or projects are presented at the conclusion of each chapter in the text. These include such experiences as (a) direct leadership of activities; (b) observing and analyzing the leadership of others; (c) carrying out group dynamics exercises, values-clarification sessions or similar activities; (d) preparing manuals of leadership functions or scrapbooks or card-files of recreation activities; (e) visiting agencies and reporting on their programs or leadership functions; (f) examining or developing supervisory manuals or guidelines; (g) applying problem-solving methods to case studies in text or to others provided by members of class; or (h) preparing written research reports on leadership or supervisory methods, problems found in special settings or other relevant topics.

Ideally, assignments should include a blend of theoretical and practical tasks and should be carried out both individually and on a group basis. At a minimum, all students should have the opportunity to present activities or individual projects before the class, to be part of group-planning processes and to prepare an individual report, manual or other written project. The assignment may be variable, if the instructor uses the Performance Contract approach (see page 368).

At the end of the course, its evaluation by both students and the instructor should seek to measure the quality and value of each of the course experiences and assignments and the extent to which course objectives were achieved.

OTHER APPROACHES TO COURSE DEVELOPMENT

In addition to the general approach to course development that has just been described, instructors and students may wish to consider other, more specialized approaches, including (a) the competency-based approach to course or curriculum development, (b) the organization of courses on a module basis, and (c) the performance contract system. Each of these methods of course development seeks to organize learning experiences in an efficient and productive way, in which class activities and the performance of individual studies can be appropriately guided and evaluated.

Competency-Based Course Development

This approach became popular in the field of teacher education in the late 1960's. It also was widely utilized in other areas of personnel management, in which trainers or supervisors were urged to throw away general job descriptions and replace them with competency models. Essentially, the approach is based on the idea that the knowledges and skills needed to perform effectively within a given job field or situation can be clearly identified, and that the professional preparation or in-service education of practitioners in this field should be aimed very directly at helping them acquire the needed competencies.

The purpose of competency-based education is to make the learning experience more meaningful and effective and to correlate its effects (in terms of satisfactory levels of achievement) with improved and objectively measurable productivity or cost-reduction goals. Competence is generally regarded as the demonstrated ability to accomplish or perform an assignment, activity or project at a given level of proficiency. It involves the interplay of knowledge, skill and constructive work attitudes and values. Competency models are established by identifying correctly the critical competencies needed for effective performance within a given job situation or assignment. Measurement tools and levels are then determined to permit trainers or managers to measure the development of competence over a period or time.

Among the important elements of competency-based education are the following: (a) *accountability*, meaning that the learner knows that he or she must be able to demonstrate the specified competences at an acceptable level of performance and accepts the responsibility for this; (b) *individualization of learning*, which stresses that course objectives and experiences must be geared to meeting the personalized needs of individual class members; (c) *learning objectives* that are precise, explicit, behavioral in nature (indicating what the individual can *do*, rather than just *know*) and measurable in objective terms; and (d) *evaluative procedures* that provide concrete evidence of the success of failure of the overall experience and of each student's performance.

Although Ball and Cipriano have written a text on the use of competency-based education in the broad field of professional preparation in recreation and parks,[1] most of the specific interest in this approach has been in the area of therapeutic recreation service. Kelley, Robb, Park and others have prepared guidelines for a competency-based entry-level curriculum in therapeutic recreation,[2] and Jordan, Dayton and Brill have prepared a report on the theory and design of competency-based education in therapeutic recreation, based on a national symposium in this area.[3] A study at Temple University funded by the Bureau of Education for the Handicapped identified 30 important competencies that should be part of a master's degree curriculum in therapeutic recreation. These were the following:

1. Recruiting and hiring staff
2. Formulating a department philosophy
3. Developing policies and procedures
4. Preparing and presenting budgets
5. Preparing administrative reports
6. Participating in administrative meetings
7. Grantsmanship
8. Utilizing public relations
9. Promoting inter-agency coordination
10. Providing consultation services
11. Supervising paid staff
12. Supervising practicum students
13. Utilizing volunteers
14. Conducting in-service training
15. Evaluating in-service training
16. Developing a basic recreation program
17. Applying research to program development
18. Conducting program evaluation
19. Maintaining equipment and supplies
20. Functioning on a treatment team
21. Assessing functional levels of clients
22. Developing treatment plans
23. Analyzing therapeutic recreation activities

---

[1] Edith L. Ball and Robert E. Cipriano: *Leisure Services Preparation.* Englewood Cliffs, New Jersey, Prentice-Hall, 1978.

[2] Jerry D. Kelley, Gary M. Robb, Wook Park, Kathleen J. Halberg, and Nancy J. Edwards: *Therapeutic Recreation Education: Guidelines for a Competency-Based Entry-Level Curriculum.* Arlington, Virginia, National Recreation and Park Association, 1978.

[3] Jerry J. Jordan, William P. Dayton, and Kathryn H. Brill: *Theory and Design of Competency-Based Education Therapeutic Recreation.* Philadelphia, Pennsylvania, Temple University, 1978.

24. Conducting therapeutic recreation activities
25. Writing clinical reports
26. Providing leisure counseling
27. Maximizing community integration of clients
28. Conducting and reporting research
29. Handling legal liabilities
30. Monitoring legislation.[4]

In applying this approach to the design of a specific course in recreation leadership or supervision, it is necessary to identify the major competencies to be taught in the course and the specific levels of achievement that will be required of students. Following this, it is necessary to determine how the competencies can best be presented (through different types of class or field experiences) and to assemble them into modules of class instruction. Finally, provision must be made for appropriate and systematic means of assessing student performance and course outcomes.

It should be pointed out that competency-based education has both strengths and weaknesses. On the positive side, it helps to direct learning in a focused way and provides concrete, objective information about the extent to which students have gained needed skills. On the negative side, critics suggest that it may tend to limit or restrict learning in an arbitrary way and that many important competencies cannot really be taught, or measured, in a classroom situation. However, it clearly represents a useful approach to the design of courses in recreation leadership and supervision and is worthy of consideration by those who use this text.

Organization of Courses on a Module Basis

A similar, although somewhat simpler, approach is to design a course making use of major modules of instruction that incorporates the key areas of instruction or course objectives. This method provides a means of making course content uniform (if, for example, a given course were to be taught by several different instructors or in different institutions or agencies). It also provides flexibility, in that different modules may be offered as part of other courses or training experiences.

An excellent example of this approach may be found in the so-called 750-hour course designed by the National Therapeutic Recreation Society as a required training program that might be offered by different institutions or agencies around the United States to qualify individuals for NTRS registration under the category of Therapeutic Recreation Technician I. The curriculum content of this training program is organized into modules as follows:

---

[4]*B.E.H. Project Update in Therapeutic Recreation.* Study Report, Temple University, Philadelphia, Pennsylvania, February 1980.

Required Subject Matter[5]

(The specific Therapeutic Recreation subject matter listed below represents *a minimum* of 750 clock hours. The material is divided into content modules with the *required minimum* hours of instruction. In a college or university curriculum two or more modules may be combined into one course carrying a value of two or three units. Conversely, while module[s] [must have] minimum content and instructional time, a single module may be taught as part of a more comprehensive course requiring additional instructional hours. The 750 hours are to be allocated as outlined below.)

Modules	Course Content	Instructional Hours
I	Orientation to Therapeutic Recreation Services	16
II	Agencies, Institutions and Teamwork Involved in Delivery of TR Services to Special Populations	18
III	Introduction to Human Growth and Development Throughout the Life Cycle	36
IV	Basic Information on Disabling Conditions	36
V	Communication Techniques	18
VI	Dynamics of Group Leadership	36
VII	Recreational Activity Skills	180
VIII	Introduction to Activity Analysis	18
IX	Program Planning and Development	36
X	Administrative Practices	18
XI	Practicum	340

Within each module, the required qualifications of the instructor and the specific elements of the module (learning experiences and areas of skill or knowledge) are specified in the NTRS outline. For example, the learning objectives of Module IV, *Basic Information on Disabling Conditions*, are for the student to acquire

Knowledge about acute and chronic conditions that affect people's ability to engage in recreative activities.

Understanding of terminology used by practitioners in human service disciplines.

Understanding of the effect of relative states of health–illness upon ability to engage in recreative activities.

Each of the other modules has a similar set of learning objectives, with guidelines for sequencing of modules or linkage with other experiences, when appropriate. Although this represents a rather elaborate and ambitious structure, the basic approach may be of value to instructors who are designing

---

[5]*Outline of 750-Hour Recreation Technician Course.* Arlington, Virginia, National Therapeutic Recreation Society, 1978.

courses in recreation leadership and supervision for use with this text. To the degree possible, students should be drawn into the process of identifying objectives and appropriate class activities.

Performance Contracting in Course Development

A third approach to the design of courses in recreation leadership and supervision is the performance contracting system. As opposed to the traditional method of having uniform sets of course requirements, assignments, readings and reports, in which each student must carry out the same tasks and is rated according to the quality of his or her work, this method stresses individual choice on the part of students. In one typical application of the system, an instructor might designate three levels of assignments that students would "contract" to carry out. To illustrate:

All students would be required to carry out the following basic requirements, and to accomplish them satisfactorily, in order to receive a grade of C.

1. Attend class and participate in all class discussions and related activities.
2. Do required readings and take midterm and final examinations.
3. Present at least one recreational activity in class and be evaluated by other class members.
4. Write final report on approved topic.

In order to receive a grade of B, students would be required to meet all requirements for a C and, in addition, to do the following.

5. Take part in a group-planning assignment and present a special event in class.
6. Write three additional reaction papers on related articles or chapters of other textbooks.

In order to receive a grade of A, students would be required to carry out all the lower-level requirements and in addition, to do the following:

7. Observe and report on leadership performance or roles in two different community agencies.
8. Prepare a detailed recreation leadership manual, including policies and procedures, for a specified type of agency or department.

As in the other special approaches that have been described earlier, the performance contract method seeks to design meaningful course experiences for students and to make them responsible for their own learning goals and accomplishments. In practice it has certain weaknesses, in that it tends to require a considerable amount of bookkeeping and sometimes leads to excessive wrangling or "bargaining" between the instructor and students about both the nature of specific assignments and the acceptability of the work that has been done. Clearly, instructors should make use of the method that seems most appropriate and workable to them or that proves to be most effective over time with their students.

Appendix C—Group Process Guidelines and Exercises

This section includes a set of guidelines for effective process and two exercises that are useful in helping class members examine their attitudes and capabilities with respect to supervision and leadership in organizational settings. A number of other useful group dynamics exercises may be found in the text *Joining Together: Group Theory and Group Skills*, by David W. and Frank P. Johnson (see Bibliography).

GUIDELINES FOR EFFECTIVE GROUP PROCESS

When groups are formed in class to discuss issues or work on other specific tasks, it is helpful to have participants understand their roles and the ways in which they may function most effectively in the group situation. Typically, a *facilitator* might be assigned to help the group get under way, and to assist members in working together. In addition, the group should select a *task leader* and a *recorder* to carry out other important functions. The following guidelines outline their responsibilities.[6]

    1. *Designated Process Facilitator*
        a. Selects a task leader and recorder quickly, preferably by having individuals volunteer for these roles.
        b. Makes notes on the behaviors of group members that contribute

---

[6]Adapted from workshop materials used by Dr. Larry Krafft with Temple University College of Health, Physical Education, Recreation and Dance faculty, 1978.

to effective working together and on the behaviors that seem to hinder the group process.

 c. If the discussion or work process seems to be stymied or unproductive, he/she should try to help get things moving, especially by helping group members avoid "blocking" or other dysfunctional behavior.

 d. Tries to be aware of interpersonal processes that may inhibit certain members from contributing satisfactorily, and perhaps intervenes to facilitate more productive interaction.

 e. At a designated "processing" time, gives out questionnaires that have been prepared to help group members evaluate the positive and negative aspects of the session. Asks members to complete them *quickly*. Each person may then keep his/her questionnaire and take part in a discussion, as people are asked to share their perceptions and suggest what might be done differently next time to improve the process. The facilitator's written observations should help him/her focus on specific incidents, issues or behaviors during the group discussion.

2. *Designated Task Leader*

 a. Insures that everyone understands the task that has been set, the time schedule and the process that will be followed.

 b. Keeps the group's attention focused on the task or issue being discussed and keeps things moving so it is completed on time.

 c. Makes sure that no one person dominates the discussion and that all get an opportunity to share their views.

 d. If no one else does so, stops the group from time to time to make sure that the recorder has all important information.

3. *Designated Recorder*

 a. Keeps detailed notes on ideas expressed or other outcomes.

 b. Prepares summary for feedback to overall group or class when smaller groups report on their discussions.

 c. Prepares any formal reports needed for future use.

4. *Other Group Members*

While taking part in the discussion or task session, all other members should use the following general guidelines to maximize effective working together:

 a. View themselves as part of the group. Contribute, but do not repeat themselves or try to force their points; make no speeches or debating arguments. Make clear, direct statements or questions.

 b. Be flexible in their participation. If they see something that needs to be done, do it or support others who are doing it.

 c. Seat themselves in a face-to-face manner to facilitate interpersonal communication among all group members.

 d. Try to support and encourage all others to express their ideas. Listen. All members need to feel free to contribute themselves and should respect the contributions of others.

e. Maintain focus on the issue or task at hand and use the time available as fully as possible.

f. Strive for consensus if a decision is required, but move on if it is not possible to attain it in a short time. Make note of major differences if they exist.

g. Try to work well with others and enjoy the experience.

VALUES CLARIFICATION FORM— EMPLOYEE ATTITUDES[7]

This form is designed to measure your basic attitudes about people in relation to organizations, and what are the most effective means of maximizing their work output. Please circle the number on the scale that best indicates your reaction to each statement. When you have completed it, follow the directions at the end of the form in scoring it and in discussing the outcomes with other class members.

1. Most people need to be carefully directed and controlled in their work.

1 2 3 4	5 6 7 8	9 10 11 12	13 14 15 16
Strongly Disagree	Disagree	Agree	Strongly Agree

2. The average human being does not inherently dislike work.

1 2 3 4	5 6 7 8	9 10 11 12	13 14 15 16
Strongly Disagree	Disagree	Agree	Strongly Agree

3. A central function of management is to motivate workers to achieve organizational goals because they want to, rather than because they are forced to.

1 2 3 4	5 6 7 8	9 10 11 12	13 14 15 16
Strongly Disagree	Disagree	Agree	Strongly Agree

4. The expenditure of physical and mental effort in work is as natural to people as play or rest.

1 2 3 4	5 6 7 8	9 10 11 12	13 14 15 16
Strongly Disagree	Disagree	Agree	Strongly Agree

---

[7]Adapted from values clarification instrument used by Gary Harris in graduate course at Temple University, 1978.

5. Work may be a source of great satisfaction.

1 2 3 4	5 6 7 8	9 10 11 12	13 14 15 16
Strongly Disagree	Disagree	Agree	Strongly Agree

6. The average human being often wishes to avoid responsibility.

1 2 3 4	5 6 7 8	9 10 11 12	13 14 15 16
Strongly Disagree	Disagree	Agree	Strongly Agree

7. Most people have a high degree of creativity in the solution of organizational problems.

1 2 3 4	5 6 7 8	9 10 11 12	13 14 15 16
Strongly Disagree	Disagree	Agree	Strongly Agree

8. The threat of punishment is often the most effective means of bringing about employee effort toward achieving organizational goals.

1 2 3 4	5 6 7 8	9 10 11 12	13 14 15 16
Strongly Disagree	Disagree	Agree	Strongly Agree

9. The threat of punishment is often counterproductive as far as employee morale is concerned.

1 2 3 4	5 6 7 8	9 10 11 12	13 14 15 16
Strongly Disagree	Disagree	Agree	Strongly Agree

10. Most people fail to put forth adequate effort in their jobs unless they are carefully supervised.

1 2 3 4	5 6 7 8	9 10 11 12	13 14 15 16
Strongly Disagree	Disagree	Agree	Strongly Agree

11. Human beings by nature tend to be passive or resistant to organizational needs.

1 2 3 4	5 6 7 8	9 10 11 12	13 14 15 16
Strongly Disagree	Disagree	Agree	Strongly Agree

12. The average human being tends to seek responsibility.

1 2 3 4	5 6 7 8	9 10 11 12	13 14 15 16
Strongly Disagree	Disagree	Agree	Strongly Agree

13. The average human being tends to have relatively little ambition.

1 2 3 4	5 6 7 8	9 10 11 12	13 14 15 16
Strongly Disagree	Disagree	Agree	Strongly Agree

14. Most people tend to dislike work.

1 2 3 4	5 6 7 8	9 10 11 12	13 14 15 16
Strongly Disagree	Disagree	Agree	Strongly Agree

15. People will exercise self-direction and self-control in the service of objectives to which they are committed.

1 2 3 4	5 6 7 8	9 10 11 12	13 14 15 16
Strongly Disagree	Disagree	Agree	Strongly Agree

16. People basically work for monetary pay; other forms of satisfaction or personal reward are not really important to them.

1 2 3 4	5 6 7 8	9 10 11 12	13 14 15 16
Strongly Disagree	Disagree	Agree	Strongly Agree

Directions for Scoring

These questions have been designed to measure whether your personal philosophy of leadership and supervision is in agreement with McGregor's *Theory X* (human beings have a low level of intrinsic work motivation and must be carefully directed and supervised if they are to perform) or with his *Theory Y* (if they are given the opportunity to assume personal responsibility and work at creative tasks, people will be self-motivated to perform well).

Questions 1, 6, 8, 10, 11, 13, 14 and 16 are in agreement with Theory X. Questions 2, 3, 4, 5, 7, 9, 12 and 15 are in agreement with Theory Y.

Score yourself on each of these groups of questions separately, and then subtract the lower from the higher total score. The result will show you in which direction you lean and by how wide a margin.

Note: In a recreation leadership or supervision course, the instructor may have students fill out these forms individually and then compare notes to see what the general pattern is for the entire class, permitting students to see how their attitudes compare with those of their classmates. The exercise may also be used as the basis for class discussion of the issues presented in it, or it may be used as a way of measuring possible differences in class attitudes *before* and *after* class review and discussion of chapters on group dynamics, principles of supervision and staff development approaches.

CLASS ANALYSIS—LEADERSHIP/SUPERVISORY PERFORMANCE ANALYSIS

Throughout this text, you have been made aware of various leadership and supervisory abilities and skills necessary for successfully managing organizations and working effectively with other people. Each of us can build upon past successes experienced in various areas of life activity. This exercise will help you identify and assess your past leadership or supervisory successes and prepare you to meet new challenges.

How to Proceed:

1. Divide your life into three periods of time. For example, if you are 21 years old, the periods would be: 0–7, 8–14 and 15–21.
2. Identify four successful life events that you can recall experiencing during each of these three life periods. Then indicate the leadership or supervisory abilities and skills you demonstrated during each such successful life event. In this sense, "leadership" suggests working with other participants in some form of activity or task, while "supervision" implies having some degree of authority over other leaders or workers.
3. Considering all the successful life events you identified, select the one that you believe was the most meaningful in demonstrating your ability or skills as a leader or supervisor.
4. Next, identify one additional successful life event that you experienced during the last week. Indicate the leadership or supervisory ability or skill demonstrated by that event.
5. Identify two successful life events that you look forward to experiencing within the next few weeks.
6. Finally, complete the sentence at the bottom of the form.

Your responses should be shared with other classmates through small group discussions. Identify possible similarities or differences in the ways that successful life events have been recorded and used to indicate different abilities and skills for different classmates. Be candid and open in your discussion.

Note: This exercise may be used in conjunction with the chapters on career opportunities in recreation and parks, principles of leadership or supervision, or staff development approaches.

Leadership/Supervisory Ability and Skill Analysis Form

List Successful Life Events	*Indicate Ability or Skill Demonstrated*
1. 2. 3. 4.	
1. 2. 3. 4.	
1. 2. 3. 4.	
Most Successful Life Event:	
One Successful Event During Past Week:	
Two Anticipated Successful Life Events in the Next Few Weeks: 1. 2.	

A successful life event that indicates leadership or supervisory ability of skill for me involves:

_____

_____

_____

Index